A WORLD OF REGIONS

for Bruce and Meredith

in friendship

Pees

A volume in the series
CORNELL STUDIES IN POLITICAL ECONOMY

edited by Peter J. Katzenstein

A full list of titles in the series appears at the end of the book.

A WORLD OF REGIONS

Asia and Europe in the American Imperium

PETER J. KATZENSTEIN

CORNELL UNIVERSITY PRESS
Ithaca and London

Portions of this book have appeared in earlier versions in: Giovanni Arrighi, Takeshi Hamashita, and Mark Selden, eds., *The Resurgence of East Asia: 500, 150 and 50 Year Perspectives* (London: Routledge, 2003); Christopher Hemmer and Peter J. Katzenstein, "Why Is There No NATO in Asia? Collective Identity, Regionalism, and the Origins of Multilateralism," *International Organization* 56, no. 3 (Summer 2002): 575–608, © 2002 by the IO Foundation and the Massachusetts Institute of Technology; Peter J. Katzenstein, Natasha Hamilton-Hart, Kozo Kato, and Ming Yue, *Asian Regionalism*, Cornell East Asia Series no. 107 (Ithaca: Cornell University East Asia Program, 2000); Peter J. Katzenstein and Nobuo Okawara, "Japan, Asian-Pacific Security, and the Case for Analytical Eclecticism," *International Security* 26, no. 3 (Winter 2001/02): 153–85, © 2001 by the President and Fellows of Harvard College and the Massachusetts Institute of Technology; Thomas Risse-Kappen, ed., *Bringing Transnational Relations Back In* (Cambridge: Cambridge University Press, 1995); J. J. Suh, Peter J. Katzenstein, and Allen Carlson, eds., *Rethinking Security in East Asia: Identity, Power, and Efficiency* (Stanford: Stanford University Press, 2004), © 2004 by the Board of Trustees of the Leland Stanford Jr. University, all rights reserved; Kozo Yamamura, ed., *A Vision of a New Liberalism? Critical Essays on Murakami's Anticlassical Analysis* (Stanford: Stanford University Press, 1997), © 1997 by the Board of Trustees of the Leland Stanford Jr. University, all rights reserved.

First published 2005 by Cornell University Press

Printed in the United States of America

Library of Congress Cataloging-in-Publication Data

Katzenstein, Peter J.
  A world of regions : Asia and Europe in the American imperium / Peter J. Katzenstein.
      p. cm. — (Cornell studies in political economy)
  Includes bibliographical references and index.
  ISBN-13: 978-0-8014-4359-6 (cloth : alk. paper)
  ISBN-10: 0-8014-4359-8 (cloth : alk. paper)
  ISBN-13: 978-0-8014-7275-6 (pbk. : alk. paper)
  ISBN-10: 0-8014-7275-X (pbk. : alk. paper)
  1. United States—Foreign relations—1989– 2. United States—Foreign relations—1945–1989. 3. United States—Foreign relations—Asia. 4. Asia—Foreign relations—United States. 5. United States—Foreign relations—Europe. 6. Europe—Foreign relations—United States. 7. World politics—1989– 8. World politics—1945–1989. 9. Regionalism—Political aspects. 10. International relations. I. Title. II. Series.
  E840.K36 2005
  327.73′009—dc22

                                  2005008838

Cornell University Press strives to use environmentally responsible suppliers and materials to the fullest extent possible in the publishing of its books. Such materials include vegetable-based, low-VOC inks and acid-free papers that are recycled, totally chlorine-free, or partly composed of nonwood fibers. For further information, visit our website at www.cornellpress.cornell.edu.

Cloth printing   10 9 8 7 6 5 4 3 2 1
Paperback printing   10 9 8 7 6 5 4 3 2 1

For Mary, Tai, and Suzanne

CONTENTS

PREFACE

Years ago one of my Cornell students told me, "I am not interested in theories; I am interested in learning how the world works." My answer to "how the world works" is this: "Think of the world as regions organized by America's imperium." Although a growing number of scholars see merit in region-focused work, this is still not the way students are taught in the United States. The typical international relations textbook bypasses regional considerations in favor of extended discussions of analytical frameworks and abstract models.[1] Cross-regional comparisons are also very rare in the most widely used texts in comparative politics.[2] Regional comparison, linked to an analysis of the global power and processes that connect them, offers a promising way to understand "how the world works."

Nuance is an important trait that distinguishes a regional perspective from those who focus on states and empires, markets and globalization, civilizations and world culture. The insights of proponents of state power and the significance of empire for security issues are limited because they belittle new forces that undercut the power of their favored constructs. The analyses of advocates of market efficiency or the transformative power of globalization on socioeconomic issues are wanting because they neglect the relevance of traditional forms of domination. Analyses of civilizations and culture in world politics also often lack nuance. Many of them create reifications to which they attribute a false sense of geographic coherence and actorhood. Alternatively, others often reduce world culture to a script that is decoupled from purposeful human action. This book articulates a regional perspective that covers security, economic, and cultural domains, one that remains sensitive to how cross-cutting forces are experienced and deployed in different contexts.

1. E.g., Gordon et al. 2002.
2. Huber 2003.

In writing this book I have unavoidably become entangled with long-standing discussions about the role of area studies in the American social sciences.[3] The political and intellectual impetus for area studies came in the aftermath of World War II. A Social Science Research Council report advocated area studies as the most effective way for achieving three objectives: extending the relevance of the humanities in a rapidly changing world; linking the humanities to the social sciences; and safeguarding the U.S. national interest in what was rapidly becoming a global confrontation with communism.[4] After the end of the cold war, the salience of foreign-language training receded in an era of shrinking budgets, the spreading of English as a lingua franca in an era of globalization, and the growing appeal of mathematics and statistics as putatively better and cheaper avenues toward knowledge about the world. In the aftermath of the 9/11 attacks, glaring U.S. weaknesses in Arabic-language competence and knowledge of Islam and the Middle East, both in government and in the academy, have reshaped the debate about area studies once again.

Of particular relevance to this book is the emergence of an eclectic body of "area-based knowledge"[5] that draws on the insights of both the social sciences and the humanities. Advances in the theories and methods of the social sciences have proved to be extremely helpful for a deeper understanding of global affairs—as long as these advances are not severed from the insights of history and the humanities. When traditional academic disciplines focus exclusively on abstract concepts there is only a superficial or speculative connection to the variegated experiences of various parts of the world. Knowledge of history, language, and place remains indispensable for an analysis of world affairs. Exclusive specialization in a particular area, however, misses connections between developments in different parts of the world. Social scientific "literacy" thus is now necessary in a specific area of the world *and* in at least one specific social science discipline.

Because it is inherently multidisciplinary, area-based knowledge is criticized from two perspectives: disciplinary-based, "scientific" critics who value nomothetic approaches more than contextualization; and "cultural" critics who work from the perspective of the humanities. From a rationalist perspective Robert Bates insisted that the use of sophisticated research designs and the rigorous testing of alternative explanations of different outcomes would make area studies, at best, a handmaiden of social scientific approaches.[6] Critics pointed to Bates's ideological preconceptions and excessive ambition.[7] Yet in a more tempered restatement of his position and in implementing his research program, Bates and his collaborators illustrate the centrality of area-based knowledge.[8] Cultural crit-

3. The following is adapted from Katzenstein 2001, 2002a. See also Rudolph forthcoming; Szanton 2003; "Roundtable" 2002; Biddle 2002, 67–86; Hall and Tarrow 1998.
4. Hall 1948; Rafael 1994, 92–98.
5. Prewitt 1996a, 1996b, and 2002.
6. Bates 1996.
7. Johnson 1997; Elster 2000.
8. Bates 1997, 1998.

ics attack area studies from a cultural-humanistic, and at times a postmodern, stance.[9] In taking the contemporary nation-state as its unit of analysis, area studies naturalize and reify the identity of units that have been far from stable. Yet the charge is directed at the wrong target: area-based knowledge has been at the forefront of analyzing transnational relations, the global operation of nongovernmental organizations, and social movements spanning national borders.

Area-based knowledge offers to its scientific and cultural critics an opportunity to experiment with the unavoidable shortcomings that mark their favored approaches. In a welcome change from the scholarship of the 1960s, academic rationalists now are occasionally willing to concede the limits that a foundational assumption imposes on their insights: in playing the game of politics, participants share relevant (common) knowledge. Even though they are inflected by the cultural turn, area studies at times experiment with contingent generalizations that go beyond specific locales. Area-based knowledge is a verdant middle ground, drawing its water from different sources.

In writing this book I have come to appreciate the virtues of eclecticism. The promise of new insights is sustained by an intellectual tension between different approaches. In the 1960s, for example, a chasm divided proponents of traditional area studies from advocates of modern behavioralism. Disagreement typically centered on the advantages and disadvantages of different methods of analysis. Renewed debate in the 1990s focused instead on the proper calibration of social science and area studies approaches that creates the stock of area-based knowledge. Empirical anomalies give credence to the strategy of relying on complementary sources of insight. For example, between the 1960s and the 1990s East Asian states produced noteworthy successes in combining rapid economic growth with development, defying many of the expectations derived from the putatively universal model of neoclassical economics.[10] At the same time, the growth of East Asian welfare societies has been defined by demographic, economic, and political factors that are not simply area bound. Those who construct abstract theories dream of a future in which polities all over the world are alike; academics in the field of area studies dream of a past when each locale in the world was largely isolated.[11] Area-based knowledge is multidisciplinary, and those in the field readily accept both general and area-specific insights, as I do in this book.

This project started in the late 1980s with a set of memoranda eventually yielding the outline of a book that Bruce Cumings, Peter Evans, and I were planning to write under the auspices of the Committee on States and Social Structures of the Social Science Research Council. We were eager to learn more about types of states in different world regions. That project never materialized, as the end of the cold war sent us off in different directions. In the mid-

9. E.g., Rafael 1994.
10. Kang 2003–4, 166–68.
11. Kasza forthcoming.

1990s I organized two collaborative projects that looked at Germany in Europe as well as at Japan and Asia.[12] In the end, so many interesting questions were left unasked and unanswered that I decided to write my own book. My long-time editor and friend Roger Haydon insisted from the outset that the United States had to be a central part of that book. In principle, I agreed. But learning about Asia and Europe was for me of greater intellectual interest than searching for a simple American hook on which to hang my regional stories. Reflecting on the meaning of 9/11 made me think harder about the nature of American power and search out deeper connections linking the United States with different world regions.

In writing this book I have benefited greatly from fellowships at several institutions, supporting my research and offering that most precious commodity, uninterrupted time devoted to thinking and writing. An Abe Fellowship (1998–2000) permitted me to travel in Asia and Europe to collect data and interview officials. A fellowship at the Woodrow Wilson Center in Washington, D.C. (1997–98), permitted me to conceptualize cross- and interregional comparisons and to write early drafts of some of the empirical cases. A fellowship at the Russell Sage Foundation (2001–2) gave me a chance to develop my argument about the nature of the American imperium and its relation to world regions. I put the finishing touches on this book while a fellow at the Center for Advanced Study in the Behavioral Sciences at Stanford (2004–5). Apart from the generous financial support that I have received, I have benefited enormously from my many talks with an outstanding group of scholars. Having discussions with people doing cutting-edge scholarship in diverse fields was a source of unmitigated intellectual pleasure. They reminded me that learning more goes hand in hand with knowing less.

Between these oases I taught at Cornell University, a wonderful home for my entire academic career. Surrounded by challenging students and colleagues I was always kept on my toes and too often away from this manuscript.

I have incurred a large number of personal debts in accumulating, sifting through, and checking a massive amount of research material. For their wonderful research assistance with various parts of this project, extending in some cases over a period of years, I thank some very bright, hard-working, and energetic Cornell students: Brian Bow, Rachel Gerber, Richard Hedge, Reyko Huang, Angela Kim, Ulrich Krotz, Daniel Levin, Kevin Strompf, and, at the Russell Sage Foundation, Becky Verreau.

I have been invited to give so many lectures and seminars in the United States, Asia, and Europe on different parts of this project that there is no room to list them. Yet I do want to acknowledge how important the criticisms and suggestions of various audiences have been in shaping my thinking. Trying out inchoate ideas in front of different audiences, and in different formats, was indispensable in helping me develop clearer arguments. I thank all those who

12. Katzenstein 1997d. Katzenstein and Shiraishi 1997a.

invited me, and those who came to listen and argue, for giving me the opportunity to become less muddled.

I single out for special thanks groups of doctoral students and faculty members who took the time to discuss a full draft of the book manuscript at special meetings convened at the Wissenschaftszentrum Berlin (May 2003), the Cornell Government Department (September 2003), Dartmouth College (January 2004), the Munk Centre at the University of Toronto (February 2004), and the Australian National University (March 2004). Exploiting intellectual opportunities inside *and* outside the United States allowed me to become more self-conscious about the bias that comes from thinking about the world from an American vantage point. These discussions, which varied in length from half a day to two full days, confirmed my expectation that my arguments resonate differently in different parts of the world. Workshops held in Dartmouth and Ithaca, for example, had no problem with the opening sentence of a draft chapter claiming that the United States played *the* central role in world politics. By insisting that I should rephrase that sentence to read that the United States played *a* central role in world politics, my hosts in Berlin, Toronto, and Canberra suggested a small modification with large implications. This is a telling illustration of the very noticeable differences in intellectual sensibilities and political intuitions that distinguish the work of scholars in different parts of the world. Intensive discussions of my manuscript and the different reactions it provoked are a unique and unforgettable intellectual experience. Equally important, they helped me to nail down the final form of the book's core arguments.

I gained much from the criticisms and suggestions of experts who were kind enough to comment on individual chapters: Peter Andreas, Giovanni Arrighi, Brett de Bary, John Borneman, Dominic Boyer, Victor Cha, Peter Evans, Richard Friman, Gregory Fry, Oka Fukuroi, Albrecht Funk, James Goldgeier, Marie Gottschalk, Chris Hemmer, Leonard Hochberg, Stephanie Hofmann, Aida Hozic, Kathryn Ibata, Mizuko Ito, Alastair Johnston, Atul Kohli, Ulrich Krotz, David Leheny, Wolf Lepenies, David Levi-Faur, Andrei Markovits, John Matthews, Gil Merom, Andrew Moravcsik, Jacinta O'Hagan, John Ravenhill, Richard Samuels, Fred Schodt, Mark Selden, Saya Shiraishi, Tetsuya Tanami, Jun Wada, and Susumu Yamakage. Each of these scholars corrected mistakes and, based on their reading of one part, often shared with me shrewd insights about the whole.

Central to the work of any scholar is getting a full reading of one's work, tough and honest criticism, and suggestions on how to improve a flawed product. I acknowledge my debt here with gratitude. I benefited enormously from the unfailing generosity, acute insights, and trenchant criticisms of Rawi Abdelal, Allen Carlson, Tom Christensen, Matthew Evangelista, Peter Gourevitch, Derek Hall, Peter Hall, Wade Jacoby, Mary Katzenstein, Robert Keohane, Jonathan Kirshner, David Laitin, Henry Nau, Lou Pauly, T. J. Pempel, Janice Stein, Sidney Tarrow, Michael Zürn, and two anonymous readers for Cornell University Press.

My prose was much improved by Sarah Tarrow and, subsequently, by John Raymond. But my writing owes everything to Roger Haydon's incomparable mastery. Roger's editorial skills are legendary among scholars involved in academic publishing. I feel deeply grateful for the care with which he edited this book.

I dedicate this book to Mary, Tai, and Suzanne—a trinity that centers my life.

PETER J. KATZENSTEIN

Ithaca, New York

A WORLD OF REGIONS

CHAPTER ONE

American Power in World Politics

How should we think about world politics after the end of the cold war, after the breakup of the Soviet Union, after the September 11 attacks, with the onset of the war on terror? My answer is simple: ours is a world of regions, embedded deeply in an American imperium. A generation ago, Hedley Bull imagined a world without the cold war as a "more regionalized world system."[1] What was pure speculation then is now becoming a reality.

In support of this answer, and with specific attention to Asia and Europe, I develop a four-part argument. First, through actions that mix its territorial and nonterritorial powers, the American imperium has been having a profound effect on regions. Second, these regions differ in their institutional form, type of identity, and internal structure. Some regions, such as Asia and Europe, have core regional states, in these cases Japan and Germany, that over decades have acted as supporters of American power and purpose. Other regions, such as Latin America, South Asia, Africa, and the Middle East, lack such intermediaries connecting them with the United States. Third, spurred by U.S. policies that reflect its nonterritorial and territorial powers, complementary processes of globalization and internationalization are making this a world of *porous* regions. Its dynamics differ dramatically from those of the closed regions of the past. Finally, regional porousness is enhanced politically by vertical relations that link core regional states to America, regions to subregions, and America to regions. The American imperium is not only an actor that shapes the world. It is also a system that reshapes America.

This argument alters our understanding of the American imperium, Europe, Asia, and the connections among them. Imperium and region have been strong pillars for democracy and the welfare state in Europe, and for economic

1. Bull 1977, 261.

growth and democratization in Asia. They impose a desirable limitation on America's expansive dynamism, rooted in a comfortable coexistence of polities that the United States helped create rather than the risky confrontation with powerful adversaries that it seeks to contain or defeat. Recognition of the magnitude and character of American power, and of its limitations, is as necessary in the United States as it is in Europe and Asia. For the compatibility between imperium and region provides a modicum of political order and a loose sense of shared moral purpose that permits political struggles over well-being and justice to be settled in national and local politics.

America and Regions

Imperium is a concept I use for analytical rather than historical reasons. Its meaning has shifted historically. As Roland Axtmann notes, in ancient Rome, "imperium" referred to nonterritorial power. By the time of Augustus, imperium had come to be understood as power exercised over Rome's newly acquired lands.[2] This is how I use the concept here: the conjoining of power that has both territorial and nonterritorial dimensions.

Regions have both material and symbolic dimensions, and we can trace them in patterns of behavioral interdependence and political practice.[3] Regions reflect the power and purpose of states. They are made porous by two sets of factors: the fusion of global and international processes, and a variety of relations that link them to political entities operating outside and within regions. I think about globalization as resulting from processes that emanate from the world system in which regions are embedded. Global processes transform states and the relations between them. And I talk about internationalization as resulting from processes that are shaped by the system of states that make up different regions. International processes flow across existing state borders that are more or less open. Finally, regions are also made porous by links to the American imperium, to core regional states as well as to smaller state and nonstate actors in the regions, and to subnational areas.

American Imperium

Germany in Europe and Japan in Asia offer prime vantage points for exploring how regions operate in the American imperium. In the interest of containing the Soviet Union and preventing future wars through liberalizing the world economy, U.S. postwar policy anchored Germany and Japan securely in the American imperium. Other world regions mattered less. In both South Asia and Africa, for example, the United States failed to establish close partnerships

2. Axtmann 2003, 127. Morestein Kallet-Marx 1995, 337.
3. Deutsch 1981, 54.

with key regional states. In South Asia, containment of Soviet influence in Afghanistan drove U.S. policy to engage Pakistan, especially in the 1980s. The inevitable result was poor relations with India. In Africa, no core state emerged as a possible regional leader. Apartheid prevented South Africa from translating its economic and military strength into regional leadership. Nigeria remained hobbled by civil war, military rule, and economic failure.

In sharp contrast, Germany's and Japan's unconditional surrender and occupation by the United States created two client states that eventually rose to become core regional powers. Although it is of vital interest to the United States, the Middle East resembles South Asia and Africa in lacking regional core states that are both consistent supporters of the United States and central to regional politics. In the Middle East, Saudi oil and Israeli security have engaged vital U.S. interests. Yet no porous regionalism has emerged. The overwhelming importance of territory, claimed by three monotheistic religions, has voided the nonterritorial dimensions of American power. The political values of the Saudi regime are antithetical to America's; and Israel's central position in American domestic politics has stopped the United States, in the eyes of Arab states, from curtailing Israeli power. This is in sharp contrast to the political restraints that NATO, the U.S.-Japan security treaty, and international economic institutions imposed on Germany and Japan, thereby reassuring their nervous neighbors.

The United States has had vital interests in the Americas for much longer than in the Middle East. Yet here too no viable regional intermediary state or group of states has emerged. In its own backyard American power and influence has been too direct and too strong. Thus although the United States has had strong strategic interests in these four areas—the Americas and the Middle East, South Asia and Africa—none has developed stable regional intermediaries. Even though no one region defines the norm against which we can measure the performance of any other, we can already state two preliminary conclusions. Regional intermediaries are relatively rare; and so are porous regions.

In its decisive victories over fascism in World War II and over communism in the cold war, the United States has demonstrated the entwining of its political, military, economic, and ideological powers, the foundations of its preeminence in world politics.[4] The source of American strength is reflected in the character of the American imperium, which combines two different types of power. Territorial power was at the center of the old land and maritime empires that collapsed at the end of the three great wars of the twentieth century. The far-flung network of U.S. bases that encircled the Soviet Union during the cold war, and that has spread greatly after the attacks of September 11, points to the territorial dimension of the American imperium. According to statistics

---

4. At an abstract level, my thinking about America's imperium has been shaped by Michael Mann 1986, 1993, 2003, and Franz Schurmann 1974.

released by the Department of Defense, in September 2001 the United States deployed a quarter of a million military personnel in 153 countries. Adding the civilian employees and dependents doubles that figure to more than half a million. The United States had significant military bases in thirty-eight countries.[5] The nonterritorial dimension of American power is analyzed by Michael Hardt and Antonio Negri, who argue that "Empire is not a weak echo of modern imperialism but a fundamentally new form of rule."[6] In this view, there exist political logics in world politics that operate at levels other than that of the traditional nation-state. Nonterritorial politics is characterized by a fluid instability that manifests itself in hybrid identities, flexible hierarchies, multiple exchanges, and the production of new forms of authority and coercion across boundaries. Territorial "empire" and nonterritorial "Empire" are analytical opposites or ideal types.

In the twentieth century, powerful jolts have toppled territorial empires—the Habsburg and Ottoman empires at the end of World War I, the European empires after World War II, the Soviet empire at the end of the cold war. Over time, the social and political mobilization of opponents of territorial rule in the colonies simply outstripped advances in the technologies of coercion. Collapse came in part because these empires had been undermined gradually from within after they had lost control of vital sources of nonterritorial power. The dynastic and religious affiliations that the Habsburg and the Ottoman empires commanded at the beginning of the twentieth century constituted a small and dwindling stock of nonterritorial power. In the British, French, Dutch, Belgian, and Portuguese empires, the erosion of their nonterritorial power accelerated greatly during World War II, as nationalist independence movements became powerful political forces. And by 1989, the Soviet Union and affiliated Communist parties in Eastern Europe had used up all of the ideological capital they had gathered in 1945 as the result of a heroic and victorious war waged against German fascism.

Nonterritorial power was also central to the British Empire. Britain's influence stretched beyond the formal territorial control of colonies. Its "imperialism of free trade"[7] extended far beyond the territorial borders of British colonies, deep into the Egyptian part of the Ottoman empire and into vast stretches of China. The absence of "local lords" in Argentina did not stop Britain from implanting itself deeply in that rich country. A comparable tradition marks the American imperium. At the turn of the last century, free trade and informal rule over vital markets were both ideologically more agreeable, and economically more efficient, than the costly acquisition and maintenance of colonial regimes. "Open door" became the principle that drove U.S. expansion, and for U.S. policymakers the informal penetration of foreign societies and control over foreign markets were the most highly valued

5. Johnson 2004, 4, 154–60.
6. Hardt and Negri 2000, xii, 146.
7. Gallagher and Robinson 1953.

manifestation of the energizing impulse that America's liberal brand of capitalism was destined to bring to the world. After 1945, the growth of American multinational corporations supported both liberal arguments that national sovereignty was "at bay" and realist ones that a political "storm" was brewing over multinational corporations.[8] Informed by the experience of the last three decades, theories of globalization now point to the decline of classical notions of sovereignty and the rise of alternative forms of governance.

Reflecting the dual sources of its power, the American imperium shares important traits with both the British empire, which it supplanted in 1945–47, and the Soviet empire, with which it competed thereafter. Even more central than for Britain is the nonterritorial character of the American imperium; and as was true of the Soviet empire, the core of the American imperium resembled a territorial and ideological "bloc." But the differences are more noteworthy than the similarities.[9] Compared to these two empires, the American imperium has greater scope and greater depth. Despite direct or proxy expeditions to Cuba, the Horn of Africa, and Southeast Asia, the Soviet empire was largely limited to its border areas, whereas the American imperium stretches all over the world. Britain's empire had been a coalition of peripheries, for Britain's presence was weak on the European continent, the center of "great power" politics. In sharp contrast, after the conquest of the fascist powers in World War II, the American imperium has ruled from the center. Only two of the world's six power centers (Russia and China) lie outside the American imperium; four are fully integrated (the United States, Britain, Western Europe including Germany, and East Asia including Japan). In contrast to the British empire, which lasted for centuries, the American imperium has existed only since the end of the nineteenth century. There is not yet much evidence suggesting that the American imperium is beginning to weaken—unless the fearful triumphalism that has gripped the United States at the beginning of the twenty-first century and the fiscal recklessness of President George W. Bush's administration turn out to be early signs of U.S. decline.

In different political contexts, "imperium" designates both formal and informal systems of rule, and a mixture of hierarchical and egalitarian political relations. The American imperium is creating a world politics that is both enabling and constraining. The relative importance of its territorial and nonterritorial power has waxed and waned, shaped by domestic political struggles between conflicting coalitions. Victory and defeat in these domestic struggles have affected the reactions of U.S. foreign policy to porous regions in world politics.

Issues of terminology are confounding for any analysis of the U.S. role in twentieth-century world politics.[10] Some use the concept of empire as a value-neutral description of a hierarchical political relation. Others rely on the term

8. Vernon 1971, 1977.
9. Lundestad 1990, 47–48.
10. Lundestad 1998, 1–4.

to describe a particular period in history when a powerful country formally or informally controlled the internal and external affairs of another country, as in the "age of imperialism" in the late nineteenth century. Still others choose special visual markers, such as quotation marks placed around the concept "empire,"[11] or qualifying adjectives, as in "analog of empire" or "quasi-empire."[12] Or they take recourse to the concept of hegemony, often glossing over the difference between the material, territorial, actor-centric, and the symbolic, nonterritorial, and systemic dimensions of power. That hegemony, Bruce Cumings writes, "is least understood at its own point of origin"—what I call here the American imperium.[13]

Regions

What is a region?[14] Broadly speaking there exist three different approaches to defining regions: materialist, classical theories of geopolitics; ideational, critical theories of geography; and behavioral theories. I believe that materialist and ideational theories contain important, partial insights that I merge in a perspective of regional orders, defined by their distinctive institutional forms, which both alter and are altered by behavior or political practice.

In different national and political contexts, all of the *materialist theorists* of geopolitics believed that interstate war over territory was inevitable.[15] Some make a fundamental distinction between the strategic imperatives governing land and sea power. For Alfred Thayer Mahan, for example, naval power was the key to America's future rise to the status of a great power. Russia was accumulating enormous defensive power through its expansion into Asia during the nineteenth century.[16] The lack of access to warm-water ports demonstrated, at least in the eyes of maritime powers, a weakness of Russia's power. Yet this very lack of access may have concentrated Russian attention and resources on territorial expansion to the east. While naval powers like Britain or the United States could not conquer the inner core of the Russian empire, they could contain Russia along its periphery. Mahan's analysis foreshadowed Halford McKinder's notion of a pivot of history and of Nicholas Spykman's analysis of a Eurasian heartland and its maritime rimland. For Mahan a Russian pivot of history might lead to the domination of Europe, Asia, and Africa, a connected "World Island." For Spykman Russian control over the lands located at the margin of Eurasia—Western Europe and East Asia—might lead to global domination. Britain and the United States could either balance or fragment this control, most plausibly at the peripheries. In brief, space is intimately tied to strategy and the dynamics of power competition.

11. Lundestad 1990.
12. Maier 1989, 274, and 2002, 28.
13. Cumings 2000, 18.
14. Mansfield and Milner 1997, 3–4. Lake and Morgan 1997, 11–12.
15. Polelle 1999. Camilleri 2000, 1–14.
16. LeDonne 1997.

Other theorists of geopolitics focus exclusively on territoriality. Before World War II Karl Haushofer saw three rising powers—the United States, Germany, and Japan—challenging British world hegemony. Each was emerging as the dominant power in its sphere of influence, the United States in Latin America, Germany in Europe and by extension Africa and the Middle East, and Japan in the western Pacific. For Haushofer these emerging "pan-regions" were becoming the essential building blocs of world politics. After the end of World War II, with Germany and Japan defeated, progressive British theorists continued thinking in terms of a tripolar geopolitics.[17] Each of the three main victors of the war, the United States, Britain, and the Soviet Union, would dominate specific world regions. In his novel *1984*, George Orwell gave a chilling description of this world of regional blocs, marked by total mobilization and perpetual war between Oceania, Eurasia, and Eastasia.

Events turned out differently. Bipolarity prevailed over tripolarity, in line with the analysis of American geostrategists. Western Europe and East Asia, the rimlands of Eurasia, were strategic regions of overwhelming importance for the United States, as George Kennan famously argued in 1947.[18] Classical geopolitical analysis was revived—with a twist. In the implementation of America's new cold war strategy, the meaning of the term *containment* was no longer restricted to geography. Instead it became a label for protecting the religious and civilizational values of an entire way of life.

Because of its entanglement with the Nazi concept of *Lebensraum* or "living space," classical geopolitics was largely banished from the social and policy sciences after 1945. Yet starting in the late 1970s, and especially since the end of the cold war, it has regained credence in France, Germany, and other European countries.[19] In the 1980s, for example, a pitched battle among German historians focused on Germany's geographically central position (*Mittellage*). Conservatives saw it as a curse that had led Germany astray. Liberals rejected the reductionism of this geopolitical argument and insisted on the social and political causes of German exceptionalism. Despite the acrimony of the debate about the German past, both groups agreed that the cold war had given West Germany the opportunity to establish firm and durable Western ties. Historical hindsight suggests that Germany's territorial partition and NATO's security guarantee permitted West Germany to develop close and cordial ties with the dominant Atlantic powers—the United States, Britain, and France.

After the end of the cold war "geopolitics" once again came into its own as pundits and political scientists tried to make sense of an entirely new and different world. John Mearsheimer offers a contemporary application of geopolitical reasoning. In his way of thinking, the stopping power of water makes global hegemony a goal that is virtually impossible to achieve for any state, including the United States. "The principal impediment to world domination,"

17. Taylor 1990, 1992.
18. Kennan 1947, 1994.
19. Gray 1977.

Mearsheimer writes, "is the difficulty of projecting power across the world's oceans onto the territory of a rival great power."[20] In his view, insular states like the United States and Britain are no less ambitious or more prone to peace than others, but simply more constrained by geography. Playing the role of offshore balancer, they will intervene and then withdraw. Great powers can become regional hegemons at most, and while others have tried and failed, the United States in the Americas is the only regional hegemon in modern history.

Mearsheimer's argument is rigorously reductionist and highly implausible in its elegant parsimony. Water is certainly an impediment to the projection of land power. But not every empire has been a land empire. The Mediterranean, for example, was not an impediment to perhaps the most important and longest-lasting empire in the West. Rome found it relatively easy to project its power overseas. Once it had conquered the entire littoral, the Mediterranean became a Roman lake.[21] Furthermore, mountainous terrain can pose formidable obstacles to the geographic expansion of land power as Joshua Epstein showed with specific reference to a possible conflict between the Soviet Union and the United States in the Persian Gulf.[22] Imperial Japan's drive onto the Asian mainland in the 1930s and 1940s was not stopped by water, but rather was invited by the weakness of opposing states.[23] And what stopped the United States from conquering Canada and Mexico after 1850 was not water but something much more important in world politics: the forces of nationalism and social mobilization of the targets of imperial conquest.[24] Mearsheimer's application of classical geopolitical reasoning bypasses critical factors: relative capabilities, costs and benefits of the control over territory, alliances, nationalism, institutions, and domestic ideologies.

In a similar fashion Zbigniew Brzezinski has built geopolitical reasoning into his analysis of the relations between American hegemony and Eurasia as the world's geopolitically central continent.[25] While his analysis incorporates a liberal theory of America's power assets, including its soft, cultural power, its most important contribution lies in its revisionist geopolitical argument. After the end of the cold war Brzezinski called for a French-German-Polish-Ukrainian alliance to balance Russian power in Europe, thus advocating a dramatic reversal from a maritime to a continental orientation of the European rimland. His inclusion of geopolitics matches the renewed popularity of geopolitical theory in Russian political debates. Once believing that Russia's return to greatness was preordained by the laws of history, Russian nationalists, including such leading politicians as Vladimir Zhirinovsky and Gennady Ziuganov, now put

20. Mearsheimer 2001, 41.
21. I would like to thank Leonard Hochberg for pointing this out to me as well as for his critical comments and suggestions on earlier drafts of this section.
22. Epstein 1987, 44–97.
23. Mearsheimer 2001, 264–65.
24. Mearsheimer 2001, 488.
25. Brzezinski 1997.

their hope in geography—in space rather than in time. At the end of the Marx-ist or nationalist tunnel, it seems, there is always the promise of reassertion of Russian preeminence. "Eurasianism," writes Charles Clover, "has succeeded in reconciling the often contradictory philosophies of communism, religious or-thodoxy, and nationalist fundamentalism. Eurasianism . . . has become an um-brella philosophy, absorbing all that is radical in the bubbling cauldron of post-Soviet political thought."[26]

Such geographic "umbrella philosophies" illustrate the central point of *ideational, critical theories of geography:* regions are politically made.[27] This theory has different strands. Its political economy strand views regions as spatial man-ifestations of capitalist production processes that separate cores from periph-eries; its cultural strand focuses on regions as collective symbols chosen by groups to dominate specific places in the natural world.

In the modern state system, John Ruggie argues, "space is not given in na-ture. It is a social construct that people, somehow, invent."[28] From this perspec-tive, the unquestioned stopping power of water in Mearsheimer's argument becomes for Philip Steinberg the problematic object of analysis. Steinberg un-ravels the politics of different understandings of bodies of water: for example, "a non-territorial 'Indian Ocean' construction in which the sea is understood as an asocial space between societies; a highly territorial 'Micronesian' con-struction in which the sea is perceived and managed as an extension of land-space; and a complex 'Mediterranean' construction in which the sea is defined as non-possessible but nonetheless a legitimate arena for expressing and con-testing social power."[29] What is true for water is also true for land. Conflicts over sacred spaces illustrate a global phenomenon.[30] Land is not natural and undifferentiated; it means different things to different people. The more cen-tral and exclusive holy places are to different communities, the greater the chal-lenge facing a peaceful resolution of territorial conflicts. Thus the sacredness of place and the distances between land masses may differentiate land from sea into fundamentally different spheres for human cooperation and conflict.

Because it emphasizes the relative fluidity of spatial borders, the application of critical theories of geography to Europe and Asia yields insights in tension with classical geopolitical notions of "historical regions." What, for example, has "Europe" meant across the ages?[31] For the Greeks, the lands to their north and west were Europe, clearly separated from Asia to the east and Africa to the south. This classification was rethought with the Crusades and after 1500, as a Christian Europe subjugated the rest of the world. A conquering Christian Eu-rope was transformed once more when the Enlightenment discovered Europe

26. Clover 1999, 13.
27. Reuber and Wolkersdorfer 2001.
28. Ruggie 1999, 235.
29. Steinberg 2001, 207–8.
30. Hassner 2003. White 2000.
31. Pocock 1997. Taylor 1991.

to be modern and thus different from all other world regions. Europe became the embodiment of progress and, as the only center of the civilized world, its values were claimed to be universal. In this world, Europe was "not-Asia." The designation of "the Orient" presupposed Europe as an Occident that was governed responsibly not despotically, that was dynamic not stagnant, that was rational rather than prone to irrationality. After the end of World War II, renewed interest in European civilization, following its darkest decade, reflected the continent's division by two non-European powers. Gaullist anti-Americanism was matched by Eastern European insistence on the Soviet Union as an Asian, and hence alien, presence. The end of the cold war ended Atlantic Europe: Western, democratic, liberal, and above all anticommunist. The door was now open for rival conceptions—a neo-Gaullist Europe as a conventional great power in the making; a Europe of different small neighbors eschewing attempts at domination and cherishing national diversity in an evolving European polity; a "Europe for Europeans" as a menacing rallying cry against a rapidly growing number of immigrants.

East Asia, from the perspective of critical theories of geography, is not reducible to a collection of states undergoing more or less similar processes of economic and social change. The intersection of local specificity and transnational structures affects the ongoing processes of region formation.[32] Regions result from various forms of human interconnections. In Asia, these interconnections are hierarchical, crystallize around different urban nodes, and are based on different historical foundations—a Sinocentric tribute system in northeast Asia, a precolonial maritime system in Southeast Asia. As a concept, "Asia" lacks an obvious focal point or common tradition. And for some countries, especially the United States and Japan, Asia-Pacific and the Pacific Rim are concepts that denote an Asia that is inclusive. These new concepts are examples of an institutionalized language, what Bruce Cumings calls "rimspeak."[33] As a term, rimspeak may be annoying as a matter of plain English, but it undoubtedly matters politically. Such language captures and reflects political, economic, and cultural processes in Asia that are creating new relations between places and peoples. This variant of critical theory stresses discursive politics as the sole determinant in how a region is defined. Referring to an extensive body of scholarship that views regions primarily as symbolic constructs, Patrick Morgan asserts bluntly that "there is no way to identify regions, through geography, that enhances analysis in international politics."[34]

This is going too far. Regions have both material and ideational dimensions. The absence of full agreement on the boundaries of "Europe" and "Asia" has not stopped political actors from invoking and politically exploiting regional terminology. In the case of Asia, for example, the definition of the region that includes Southeast and northeast Asia—essentially the Association of South-

32. Bernard 1996. Nonini 1993, 162.
33. Cumings 1993.
34. Morgan 1997, 20.

east Asian Nations (ASEAN) plus China, North and South Korea, and Japan—and that excludes North America, Australia and New Zealand, and South Asia—that is, the lands of British colonial settlement and imperial control—has both been contested and proved durable in most political initiatives for bringing about Asian or East Asian regionalism. Furthermore, the concept of East Asia based on Chinese civilizational and cultural commonalities expressing natural international hierarchies has receded in favor of a Singaporean definition that focuses on East Asian regional interaction and nominal state equality.[35]

In the process of European enlargement, the meaning of Europe has also shifted. European governments have struggled with the question of whether Russia and Turkey are part of Europe. The boundaries of various subregions—specifically central Europe, central-eastern Europe, and eastern Europe—have shifted with amazing rapidity. The end of the cold war has moved world politics from centrally organized, rigidly bounded environments that are hysterically concerned with impenetrable boundaries, to ones in which territorial, ideological, and issue boundaries are attenuated, unclear, and confusing.[36] Yet conceptual imprecision does not undermine the fact that "Europe" and "Asia" are political reference points that are distinct from Germany, France, Japan, and China, and Berlin, Paris, Tokyo, and Beijing.

The third body of theory that concerns us is *behavioral theories of geography*. They focus on how regions are shaped and reshaped by political practice. Regions are material structures that have behavioral effects, and they also express concepts that both shape and reflect shifting political practices. Space has behavioral properties. Consider the maritime/territorial distinction. In the analysis of domestic politics, scholars have applied the same basic insight into the importance of water in subtle analyses of developments within rather than between states.[37] Once merchants began to exploit the economic opportunities of sea transport, the inhabitants of seaports and riverine ports cultivated outward-looking, commercial, river basins along the littorals. These regions differed starkly from inward-looking, mercantilist, and land-locked regions. The same logic holds also for the relations between countries. For example, in the 1940s Karl Deutsch analyzed the economic conditions that permitted the rise and eventual decline of an international civilization and medieval unity. The mode and cost of transportation permitted, but did not determine, the growth of highly commercial centers for the vast stretches of hinterland that remained cut off from long-distance trade and the specialization of production that commerce fostered.[38] The "Greater Caribbean" region, or plantation America, is another example.[39] This area, economically integrated by the slave trade,

35. Evans 2005, 197–98.
36. Jowitt 1992, 307.
37. Fox 1971. Hochberg 1986. Fairbank and Goldman 1998.
38. Deutsch 1944.
39. Taylor 1988, 262.

stretched from northeastern Brazil to Maryland. It was powerfully important between the seventeenth and nineteenth centuries, and today exists no longer. Regions are not simply physical constants or ideological constructs; they express changing human practices. Economic development, military expansion, and symbolic identification with particular places all can shift over time, and with them the boundaries and salient features of particular regions.

Numerous findings show that geography has direct and indirect behavioral consequences.[40] Geographical distance, for example, shapes the intensity of economic exchanges and the likelihood of war. Archeologists have shown that for the Roman Empire the cost of transportation by sea and river was much smaller than over land; the cost differential was greatest for commerce with the Germanic tribes beyond the Rhine frontier.[41] In statistical studies, economists have demonstrated the importance of geographical distance for the intensity of international trade flows.[42] A distance of 2,500 miles reduces trade by 82, equity flows by 69, and foreign direct investment (FDI) by 44 percent; the corresponding figures for 4,000 miles are 97, 83, and 58 percent.[43]

Choice holds consequences for subsequent behavior. In North America, individuals are ten to twenty times more likely to trade within the United States or Canada than across the U.S.-Canadian border. Railroad construction in both the United States and Canada proceeded along east-west lines, and economic behavior followed suit. Another illustration of the behavioral consequences of geography comes from Christopher Way. In a statistical analysis of war and trade Way finds much similarity across regions in Europe, Asia, and Africa: higher levels of trade are associated with lower levels of conflict. This relationship is much attenuated, however, in the Middle East, and Latin America does not follow this pattern at all.[44] Geographic distance thus appears to have different implications for conflict and cooperation in different regional settings. While statistical analysis establishes important behavioral consequences of geography, it does very little to help us understand what sets of processes are in play to produce these outcomes.

In sum, materialist, ideational, and behavioral theories of geography all contain helpful partial insights. I integrate them here in a perspective that stresses the importance of the distinctive institutional forms of different regional orders, which both shape and are reshaped by political practice.[45] Indeed, the conceptual boundaries of many other interesting political phenomena are also

40. Storper 1995, 1997.
41. Greene 1986, 40. I would like to thank Leonard Hochberg for alerting me to Greene's work and this passage in particular.
42. Frankel 1997, 37, 118. Isard 1956, 55–76.
43. Hirst and Thompson 2002, 258.
44. Way forthcoming. The exception is not due to the overwhelming influence of the United States. Eliminating all dyads from the statistical analysis that involves the United States changes the overall results very little. Way leaves the Latin American anomaly for future research.
45. This intellectual move replicates the resolution of an earlier debate between pluralists and Marxists that eventually yielded a very productive stream of research into the various institutional orders of democracy and capitalism.

blurred and changing. What Wittgenstein argues about "games" holds also for "geography": instead of a precisely delimited concept, we make do with family resemblance between different instances of a thing.[46] Geography has material and symbolic aspects, and creates among different groups of countries marked behavioral interdependencies over a wide range of different issues.

I argue in this book that regions are made porous by a variety of processes, vary greatly in their institutional forms, and differ in having (or not having) core states that support U.S. power and purpose. The consequences of these regional factors for world order are extremely important in an era of U.S. preeminence.

Globalization and Internationalization

One crucial feature of contemporary regionalism in world politics is its porousness. Journalists and politicians often use the concept of regional "blocs." In their view traditional international politics is replicated among a much smaller number of much larger and more powerful regions. Nothing could be further from the truth. Globalization and internationalization processes make regions porous, often in accordance with the power and purpose of the American imperium.

Since the end of the cold war, globalization and internationalization have dominated public discussion and scholarly writings. Although the terms are often used interchangeably, I see a vast difference.[47] I define *globalization* as a process that transcends space and compresses time. It has novel transformative effects on world politics. I define *internationalization* as a process that refers to territorially based exchanges across borders. It refers to basic continuities in the evolution of the international state system. Globalization highlights the emergence of new actors and novel relations in the world system, internationalization the continued relevance of existing actors and the intensifications of existing relations.[48] Territorially based international processes permit continued differences in national practices. Nonterritorial global processes push toward convergence of national differences and also toward a wide variety of local processes of specific adaptation to global changes. In a global economy, for example, transnational corporations undercut national public policies and tend to move corporate practices to one preferred global standard; but global corporate policies also give rise to a wide variety of supportive and oppositional local responses. In an international economy, by way of contrast, government policies continue to adapt the national economy to the operations of multinational corporations that are pursuing different strategies.

46. My thanks to Patrick Thaddeus Jackson for pointing this out to me.
47. Hirst and Thompson 1996, 185, and also 8–13.
48. Scholte 2000, 49.

Globalization

After the end of the cold war and the rise of the United States as the world's only superpower, globalization became for a while the preferred metaphor for journalists, businessmen, and politicians in describing world politics. In 1971, a large international database covering eight hundred publications on economic and business affairs did not contain a single entry with the words "global" or "globalization" in the title; in 1995 there were twelve hundred.[49] Articles containing the word "globalization" in the *New York Times* and *Washington Post* "took off in a near-vertical ascent in the late 1990s."[50] Op-ed pages and airwaves are filled with Panglossian or Cassandrian pieces about globalization. Yet it would be a big mistake to dismiss this change in conceptualization as simply an instance of "globaloney." This simultaneous, worldwide shift in public discourse may be as consequential as was the reported invention of the term "international" by Jeremy Bentham in the late eighteenth century.[51]

Technological change has unhinged social and geographic space. Globalization refers to the creation of new "transborder" spaces that are encroaching on traditional, territorial forms of social and political life. New, global spaces replace or coexist with old, territorial spaces. Contemporary life offers many ordinary and extraordinary examples. Missiles can devastate any spot on the globe within minutes. The Internet connects individuals all over the world in fractions of seconds. The marketing strategies of transnational corporations are global. Factories produce components that are shipped all over the world for final assembly. Global warming affects living conditions all over the world. And Hollywood movies are produced and marketed to appeal to a global audience.

Technology is creating a revolution in communication that compresses both space and time by vastly accelerating the flow of information, industrial products, and financial capital. Geographic distance is becoming of diminishing relevance for social interactions among a rapidly growing number of people. Advances in satellite, digital, and fiber-optic technologies have dramatically lowered communication and transportation costs, leading to increasing levels of "connectedness." A commission of academic experts, convened under the title the Group of Lisbon, expressed this idea in dramatic language: having erased familiar distinctions between the first, second, and third world, "the global world is the result of a profound reorganization. . . . The process of globalization is the beginning of the end of the national system as the apex of human-organized activities and strategies."[52]

Theorists of globalization marshal statistical data pointing to rapid change. By the early 1970s, levels of international interdependence had begun to ap-

49. Reinicke 1998, 234 n. 20.
50. Henwood 2003, 17.
51. Scholte 2000, 43–44. Taylor 1995, 1.
52. Group of Lisbon 1995, 19.

proach those last seen in the late nineteenth century. Measured in both absolute terms and in relation to changes in domestic flows, economic, military, technological, ecological, cultural, migratory, and political transactions have increased sharply since then. Emerging technologies are spreading at high rates. Annual increases in World Wide Web usage, for example, were in the high double digits throughout the 1990s. The globalization of production also illustrates profound change and has reached unprecedented levels in the 1990s. These macrolevel trends are driven by microlevel changes. Globalization, insists Charles Oman, is created "by the actions of individual actors—firms, banks, people—usually in the pursuit of profit and often spurred by the pressures of competition. Globalization is thus best understood as a micro-economic phenomenon."[53]

Globalization is creating complex cultural and social divisions not easily grasped by traditional, territorially rooted concepts of wealth and poverty. Traditional patterns between and within states and national economies are being transformed. Social marginalization is as visible in the core as are enormous concentrations of wealth in the periphery. Globalization is strengthening the emergence of a world civil society defined by processes of de-territorialization and the creation of new political actors. The growing power of corporate and nonstate actors on a global scale is a distinctive trait of this emerging world society.

Globalization leads to the convergence of different corporate and governmental standards of acceptable practice. Convergence can result not only from market pressures but also from political conflict and learning. Furthermore, in its economic and social dimensions, globalization is highly "uneven" in its effects on different parts of the world, pressing for convergence in some and locally diverse adaptation in others.

Theorists of globalization insist that state power recedes as it confronts both processes of global convergence and variegated local adaptations. Global networks of finance and technology are rendering more questionable the capacity of many states to collect taxes, provide social benefits, organize production and trade, control the media, police borders, and deal with unconventional security threats. In partial compensation for these changes, elites devise numerous inter- and quasi-governmental arrangements that connect emerging social and professional communities around the globe. World politics is thus moving from bargaining among governments toward a mixture of public and private systems of governance. The result is a partial erosion of legitimacy from "above" that is intensified by the rise of identity movements from "below." Governments now have less control over national affairs than they had in the past. Nonstate actors are gaining recognition and play an increasingly important role in the governance of world affairs. Transnational social movements; individuals empowered by new access to information; private or semipublic arrangements

53. Oman 1999, 38.

among corporations—these are some of the changes that are fundamentally altering the position of states. Sovereignty does not vanish, but it is located in institutional arenas that both constrain states and enable nonstate actors in novel ways.

New networks of transnational actors have spread rapidly in recent decades. According to one estimate, thirty-five thousand nongovernmental organizations (NGOs) are now operating in developing countries. Over fifteen hundred NGOs are now accredited with the UN's Economic and Social Council, delivering more development assistance than the entire United Nations system— and often providing local services that national governments should but do not.[54] The nonprofit Association for Progressive Communications gives these NGOs access to the Internet at the cost of a local telephone call, opening up new channels for influence. Social movements throughout the world can now create direct links to more established, better funded, and more media-savvy groups in Europe and the United States. The growth of transnational social movements has already altered traditional state diplomacy on issues as diverse as the environment, gender, and conventional arms control.[55]

Globalization is complex, but not necessarily peaceful. Efficient markets have corrosive effects on the networks of social ties and the political legitimacy of the institutions on which they rest. Economic globalization thus creates its own backlash. The character of collective violence changes. To be sure, many current manifestations of collective violence resemble the traditional wars, campaigns of ethnic cleansing, and mass murder that states and groups have practiced for centuries. Yet as wars between states are becoming less frequent, violence takes new forms, including high-tech warfare that the United States can wage with increasing impunity, and unconventional violence, which failing states or radical groups use in an attempt to level the military and political playing field. The absence of peace goes well beyond the realm of old and new military violence and national security. In a world where often uncontrollable risks are affecting at times even the basic necessities of life such as food, water, and air, the sense of security remains fragile and is easily punctuated.

Internationalization

In an international world, state sovereignty is not simply the marking of a territorial barrier separating inside from outside. It is also a bargaining chip in a set of complex political relations. Although internationalization does not necessarily diminish the power of states, it may reconstitute state power, especially around the nexus linking internal and external affairs. Internationalization is not simply the result of increasing flows of goods, services, capital, and people. Symmetric flows create conditions of interdependence and mutual vul-

54. Mathews 1997, 52–54.
55. Brock and Albert 1995, 268–70.

nerabilities; asymmetric flows produce dependence and one-sided vulnerabilities. Internationalization is thus an eminently political process in which different actors seek to exploit asymmetric power relations to their advantage. In addition, different polities have become more sensitive to one another's internal developments. In the area of finance, for example, small variations in national interest rates can create large speculative flows of capital. To cite a second example, on questions of human rights, national governments are increasingly held accountable to international standards.

Internationalization describes processes that reaffirm nation-states as the basic actors in the international system. It is thus grounded in what one might call methodological statism or nationalism. States defend their sovereignty, especially on issues of survival in an anarchic world. Nationalism is a central form of collective identity. Protected by states, national corporations trade goods and services across state borders. Increasing economic flows and social exchanges can lead to the realignment of domestic coalitions and some harmonization of divergent national policies and practices. They have not and cannot lead to the elimination of the nation-state as the basic actor in the international system, for governments remain the central actors for organizing the political context in which the internationalization of markets evolves; and varieties of capitalist regimes compete with one another in the international economy, working out distinctive solutions to similar external challenges.

Many statistical indicators record a gradual intensification of long-term trends in internationalization, trends that support the idea of growing openness in the world system. In the last three decades, world trade has grown twice as fast as world income, and trade in manufactures has grown three times faster.[56] These numbers may be understating recent development. Annual transactions in the illicit economy, made up mostly of illegal trade in narcotics, has expanded quickly, running at about half a trillion dollars in the 1990s.[57] The same is also true for the internationalization of capital markets. As Helen Milner and Robert Keohane conclude, "international transactions are of increasing importance in the world economy. No country can escape the dramatic effects of this change."[58]

This is not to argue, however, that recent years mark a radical departure from past developments. With specific reference to international finance, David Spiro, for example, argues that "money in the past has been much more global than most currencies today. . . . In today's world, I would argue, there is less internationalization of currencies than in the past few centuries, aside from the very notable exceptions of the dollar, the deutschmark, and the yen."[59] In all of the major industrial states except Germany, trade dependence, measured as a proportion of gross domestic product (GDP), was smaller in 1993

56. Milner and Keohane 1996, 10–14. Gilpin 2000, 21.
57. Friman and Andreas 1999, 2.
58. Milner and Keohane 1996, 14. See also Weiss 1999, 62–63.
59. Spiro 1997, 19.

than in 1913.[60] In 1920, about fifty foreign governments issued Moody-rated bonds on U.S. capital markets, a number that was surpassed only very recently.[61] The annual worldwide rate of increase in merchandise exports was 1.7 percent between 1870 and 1913, compared to 1.3 percent since the 1950s. Direct foreign investment as a proportion of global output amounted to 9 percent in 1913, compared to 4.4 percent in 1960 and 10.1 percent in the mid-1990s.[62] Multinational corporations operate in markets that have political foundations, and transnational organizations are giving states a growing number of issues with which to cope. These observations undercut the notion that recent increases in internationalization have diminished state power.[63]

More generally, the gradual increase in internationalization in recent decades does not necessarily weaken states. Steven Vogel, for example, argues that "even in the paradigmatic case of government withdrawal—the deregulation movement—I find little net loss of government control. And even in the most dynamic and the most global of industries—telecommunications and financial services—I find that governments are hardly overwhelmed by international market pressures."[64] The continued importance of state power and politics helps explain a persistent divergence in national policies. Distinct national models of welfare-state capitalism, for example, continue to show great resilience in the face of growing internationalization. Beyond a very small club of advanced economies, the statistical evidence does not support any general or secular trend toward economic convergence in the levels of productivity and standards of living.[65] Diverse forms of capitalism retain their distinctiveness while meeting the competitive pressures in world markets, despite the ever tighter restraints that the international economy imposes on government policy. The threat of "exit" by mobile capital has not vitiated the "voice" of citizens as the primary determinant of policy choice.

Similarly, national partisan politics continues to matter greatly in an era of internationalization.[66] The power of the Left and economic policies that ameliorate market inequalities has not been weakened, and may in fact be stronger now than in earlier decades. But perhaps what drives developments in national labor markets is not partisanship but another domestic cause: technologically induced structural transformation in national markets.[67] More generally, the effects of economic internationalization cannot be understood apart from the deeply rooted domestic institutions, ideas, and interests that shape the preferences of actors, thus bending considerations of international economic effi-

60. Arrighi 1997, 2.
61. Sassen 1996, 42–43.
62. Uchitelle 1998a.
63. Gilpin 1975. Krasner 1995.
64. Vogel 1996, 2–3.
65. Boyer 1996, 57–58. Wade 1996.
66. Garrett 1998, 1, 10, 24, 129.
67. Iversen and Cusack 2000.

ciency to distinctive national purposes.[68] Market pressures are indeterminate, as the signals they give to governments and firms are often opaque. National institutions shape the interpretation of these signals. Institutions tend to be sticky and overrule whatever pressures toward convergence may exist. And when convergence occurs, it operates not aside from, or around, but through national politics. National institutions matter greatly in an international world.

Interactions

Globalization and internationalization make today's regions porous. Their effects are transformative in the case of globalization, incremental in the case of internationalization. Interacting with each other they strengthen porous regions and undermine closed regions.

Theories of globalization and internationalization update earlier insights, specifically yesterday's writing about "international interdependence." Then as now, analytical concepts are deeply contested both analytically and normatively. In the 1970s, careful analyses of increasing levels of international interdependence, understood both as growing sensitivities and vulnerabilities of societies and states, pointed to their wide-ranging, powerful effects on world politics. Liberals saw an era in which traditional centers of authority would be challenged by new, nonstate actors. Marxists pointed to the inherent instabilities that growing international interdependence was creating for capitalism, both at home and abroad. And realists and students of domestic politics argued that even a sharp increase in levels of interdependence would not be strong enough to transform world politics.

Today's disagreements are similarly strong. They focus, for example, on the benefits of increasing efficiency and the costs of increasing inequality that come in the wake of globalization. Similarly, the spread of a global popular culture has energized many political countermovements that insist on the political primacy and moral superiority of nation-states or religious communities. Disagreement centers also on what many consider to be an outmoded organization of the international state system, with its inadequate response to challenges such as global warming and genocide. States are criticized for being too small for many of the big problems and too big for many of the small ones. In domestic politics, what is increasingly needed is not heavy-handed state intervention, but the light-footed tap dance of public-private partnerships.

Persistent political disagreements over interdependence, globalization, and internationalization do not mean that we have learned nothing new in the last three decades. In the early 1970s, the discussion of changing levels of international interdependence was framed narrowly. It focused on the international relations among rich states, disregarded the socialist camp, and was not closely

68. Keohane and Milner 1996.

linked to the discussion of dependency between rich and poor states. Most analysts subscribed to a rationalist epistemology and individualist ontology. Current debates are broader. They focus on processes that connect all parts of the
world, and they are open to interpretations based on a variety of epistemolog-
ical and ontological claims. This broadening in political and analytical perspective has been of little help, however, in resolving persistent debates about
the meaning of different statistical indicators.

Those focusing on processes of internationalization see a world populated
by a small and well-established cast of characters that plays an old game by
known rules: states bargaining within and about international regimes and resolving issues of peace and war; national champions and multinational corporations competing in national and international markets; and here and there
the odd nonstate actor seeking to shape the exercise of national power. Those
interested in tracking processes of globalization recognize, instead, a large cast
of new characters, many of whom are adhering to new rules: global governance
without and around government; transnational corporations spanning the
globe; and a multitude of nonstate actors bound together in transnational
alliances.

Such diverging interpretations are often shaped by different sociological
and economic styles of reasoning. Sociology focuses on relationships and
processes, economics on actors and attributes. Globalization points to possibly
transformative change. Sometimes it reduces political diversity by imposing
convergence. At other times, it creates an almost infinite variety of local modes
of selective appropriation and opposition. Internationalization underlines incremental change. It produces differences in the depth of connections and divergence in outcomes in different states. Globalization highlights processes
that reconstitute the spatial and social arrangements within and between states
and societies. Internationalization focuses on conditions that constrain states
and societies. Globalization affects the quality of processes, the degree of integration of dispersed activities, and change in inequality within and between
polities. Internationalization focuses attention on variations in openness, the
spread of activities across borders, and change in national autonomy. Globalization alerts us to governance without government and the changing character of states. Internationalization points to the changing balance between
deregulation and reregulation and the changing capacities of states. Disagreements about contemporary world politics are often rooted in such diverging
interpretations of globalization and internationalization.

These processes are not simple facts on the ground but are, instead, analytical categories that help us understand the world. The intertwining of reality
and concept is thus unavoidable. François Perroux noted long ago that around
internationalization as "a kernel of reality there develops a double process of
interpretation and of dramatization."[69] More recently, Michael Veseth illus-

---

69. Perroux 1950, 21.

trates the same point in the notion of the "selling of globalization."[70] Happily, my argument does not require me to sort out specific claims about internationalization and globalization, a fiendishly difficult task at best. I observe here only that both processes matter. Cumulatively and interactively, they fuse and thus create the conditions that make regions porous.

A regionalism made porous by globalization and internationalization remains available for processes that create ever larger regions, illustrated since the mid-1990s by the enlargements of NATO, the EU, and ASEAN. Regional enlargements go hand in hand with new forms of interregional engagement. Since 1996, for example, European and Asian leaders have met periodically in high-level talks. And the building of closer links between the European Union and Latin America's Mercosur is under active consideration. Often the result of American power and purpose, globalization creates changes in world politics that transform the capacities of territorial states and other actors. Internationalization is an incremental process of increasing national openness that does not touch the core competencies of territorially based states. Neither process shapes world politics to the exclusion of the other. While trade data lend support to the relative importance of internationalization, financial flows point to the pervasiveness of globalization.[71] As a devoted advocate of globalization and author of a best seller on the topic, Thomas Friedman combines the two dynamics in his characterization of world politics: "A new international system has now clearly replaced the Cold War: globalization."[72] Not quite. I argue in this book that globalization and internationalization coexist and complement one another. They make porous regions that are deeply embedded in America's imperium.

Porous Regional Orders

Regions are the creation of political power and purpose. Powerful states tend to extend their purposes beyond national borders through a combination of strategic action and sheer weight. They do so in the pursuit of what Arnold Wolfers has called "milieu goals," contexts that are familiar to them and suit their purposes.[73] The United States is a good example; so are Japan and Germany in Asia and Europe. After 1945, the United States had a large effect on the emerging political regimes of the two defeated Axis powers, infusing a substantial dose of Anglo-American liberalism into what had been illiberal political regimes. Subsequently, Japan and Germany, with their new commercial objectives and domesticated versions of political liberalism, have had a lasting effect on the regional politics of Asia and Europe.

70. Veseth 1998.
71. Stallings and Streeck 1995, 73–80.
72. Friedman 1999, 110.
73. Wolfers 1962, 67–80.

Regions are made porous by both global and international processes and also by a variety of vertical relations linking them to other political units. A world of regions is therefore not simply a territorially bounded system of geoeconomic blocs that extends national mercantilism onto a supranational plain. Nor is it a system that unbundles territorial sovereignty in an era of postnational politics. Porous regions offer both buffers against unwelcome constraints and platforms for exploiting new opportunities.

Finally, porous regions take different institutional forms. Power inheres not only in political actors but also in the social and institutional environments they inhabit. Regional orders are such an environment; they shape states like Germany and Japan as well as other actors, while also being shaped by them. What holds for the relation between regional orders and core states such as Germany and Japan holds in attenuated form also for the American imperium itself. It is an actor that has helped create that world. Simultaneously, it is part of a system that accords to Germany and Europe and Japan and Asia important positions to which the imperium must adapt.

Regions and U.S. Policy

State power and purpose have helped shape regionalism in the second half of the twentieth century. On questions of security, regional alliances such as the Rio Pact (1947), the North Atlantic Treaty Organization (NATO, 1949), the Southeast Asia Treaty Organization (SEATO, 1954), and the Warsaw Pact (1955) relied on Article 51 of the UN Charter and the right to collective self-defense. The world quickly divided into East and West, two rival blocs led by two superpowers. And in the "South," third world states eventually looked to regional organizations such as the Organization of American States (OAS), the Organization of African Unity (OAU), and the Arab League to defend their recently won national sovereignty. On economic issues, the political alliances that evolved during the cold war also reflected the power and purpose of states. As a matter of principle, the United States pushed for a lowering of tariff barriers and the establishment of freely convertible currencies. At the end of World War II, however, at least initially, national reconstruction in Europe posed obstacles to the liberalization of tariff and investment barriers among industrialized states. Moreover, the United States lacked the power to get that policy adopted by the Soviet Union, China, and the rest of the Communist bloc. India and other third world states favored policies of import substitution and high tariff walls. Subsequently, the formation of customs unions and free trade areas in Europe, Latin America, and East Africa pointed to a growing interest in regional integration. Other, noneconomic regional organizations also flourished in various parts of the world.

Since the mid-1980s, capitalist rivalry and socialist bankruptcy have reinvigorated regional politics. A change in U.S. policy has directly strengthened porous regionalism. Seeking to shore up its international position, under both

Republican and Democratic administrations, the United States developed regional initiatives to complement its traditional preference for worldwide liberalization.[74] This new policy move encouraged the formation of economic regions that remained open to the world economy, with the United States joining several of them.[75] Leveling the playing field in the name of "fair trade," the U.S. government sought to protect both its vulnerable and strategic industries, such as textiles and microelectronics, and to open up European and Asian markets through concerted political pressure and the creation of the North American Free Trade Agreement (NAFTA). By the early 1990s, the main driving force for porous regionalism was, in the opinion of Jagdish Bhagwati, the U.S. government's policy to accept and promote regional initiatives under Article 24 of the General Agreement on Tariffs and Trade (GATT).[76] A decade later, defenders of the World Trade Organization (WTO) argued that à la carte regionalism had become a systemic risk to the world trade system. This was not so in the eyes of the Bush administration, however, which remained committed to both the WTO's Doha round of trade negotiations and the U.S.-led plan to create a hemispheric free trade area for the Americas by 2005. In the view of James Mittelman and Richard Falk, regionalism has emerged "as a critical, yet still tentative, and even inconsistent feature of a neoliberal multilateral order—an adhesive often used to join the political and economic dimensions of global restructuring."[77]

U.S. policy has also strengthened porous regionalism indirectly, as U.S. politics in the 1990s tended to focus on domestic affairs. Freed from the pressures of the cold war and the scrutiny of the United States, countries now had an opportunity to improve their regional positions. In this new context, states are "racing to regionalize."[78] Governments find regionalism attractive for a number of reasons. Neighborhood effects, regional economies of scale, and savings in transportation costs encourage intensive trade, and investment relations can accelerate economic growth. Furthermore, efficiency and competitiveness are often strengthened through international forms of deregulation at the regional level. In the words of Sweden's former minister for foreign trade and European Union affairs, Mats Hellstrom, "One can foresee a future where the vast majority of world trade is governed by regional rules and preferences."[79]

In a world of increasingly permeable borders, large numbers of regional organizations are dealing with both economic and security affairs. The 1990s saw an explosion of regional initiatives, including the adoption of NAFTA; the creation of the European Economic Area, which liberalized trade between the Eu-

74. Helleiner 1994.
75. Fishlow and Haggard 1992, 7.
76. Bhagwati 1992, 540.
77. Mittelman and Falk 2000, 3.
78. Thomas and Tétrault 1999.
79. Richardson 1996, 17.

ropean Union (EU) and the European Free Trade Association (EFTA); the Miami Declaration of a Free Trade Area for the Americas; and the Declaration of Bogor of the Asia Pacific Economic Community (APEC). The thirty-three regional trade agreements signed between 1990 and 1994 constitute the largest number for any five-year period since the end of World War II.[80] A decade later, regional trade agreements continue to spread. In 2004, the United States signed an agreement with the states of Central America and Australia; seven South Asian states signed a free trade agreement; Mercosur was closing in on a free trade agreement with the European Union, while half-heartedly continuing negotiations with the United States over a free trade agreement for all of the Americas.

Since the end of the cold war, regionalism has also encompassed security issues. With the passage of the Goldwater-Nichols Act of 1986, for example, the U.S. armed forces have shifted a great deal of power away from civilians in Washington to five regional military commands. More generally, "efforts to cope with violent conflicts," David Lake and Patrick Morgan argue, "will primarily involve arrangements and actions devised and implemented at the regional level. . . . Regions are a substantially more important venue of conflict and cooperation than in the past."[81] In sum, U.S. policy has made regionalism a central feature of world politics.[82]

Porous Regions

Regionalism is made porous by international border-crossing exchanges and global transformations in interstate relations. Often such processes move and alter borders while stopping short of global scope.[83] International trade flows illustrate that it is a mistake to talk, as many do, about the emergence of inward-directed regional trading "blocs." The statistical work of economists and geographers contradicts the view that economic blocs are defining current world politics.[84] It is true that the United States and Germany have developed strong trade links with their neighbors, but these links were well-established before the mid-1970s and have been stable since. Japanese trade is much more globally oriented. The statistical evidence for the regional bloc hypothesis is, at best, weak and mixed. Albert Fishlow and Stephan Haggard conclude that interregional trade between the United States, Asia, and Europe is growing as rapidly as intraregional trade. And the small discriminatory effects that may accompany regional trade agreements are more than offset by the liberalizing effects of the free flow of foreign investment.[85] In the 1980s and 1990s,

80. Mansfield and Milner 1999, 601. Frankel 1997, 4.
81. Lake and Morgan 1997, 5, 7.
82. Gilpin 2001, 361.
83. Beisheim et al. 1999, 16.
84. O'Loughlin and Anselin 1996, 142, 144, 151, 153. Mansfield and Milner 1999, 598–602.
85. Fishlow and Haggard 1992, 8.

globalization and internationalization fused, and that fusion manifested itself in the growth of porous regions.

Regional trade arrangements have spread quickly since the 1980s. Between 1948 and 1994, GATT received 124 notifications of the creation of such arrangements, and between 1995 and 2000 the WTO received an additional 130, covering trade in goods and services. Of 214 agreements signed, 134 were in force in 2000, about a three-fold increase during the 1990s. Those numbers have increased further. At the end of 2002 over 170 regional arrangements had been notified and an additional seventy were estimated to be operational, although not yet notified.[86] In the early 1990s, about 90 percent of all GATT signatories were reported to be participating in regional trading arrangements.[87] Debates about the character of these arrangements encompass both Lester Thurow's analysis of a tripolar regional world and Jagdish Bhagwati's defense of a worldwide free trade regime.[88] Between these two positions, most analysts steer a middle course, arguing that regional trading arrangements tend to be open not closed, and that regionalization can be a source of both conflict and cooperation.

For decades regionalism and regionalization have been hitched to the wagon of multilateral negotiations on a global scale.[89] As a result, between two-thirds and four-fifths of total world trade and investment flows occur both within and between the economies of North America, Europe, and East Asia. In recent years, bilateral deals between states located in these three major regions and those in other, less important areas have begun to create systems of "minilateralisms" to complement existing multilateral ones. The launching of the multilateral Doha world trade round has initiated a rush to create new regional free trade agreements (FTAs) that liberalize trade, investment, and government regulations.

FTAs tend to be stepping stones, not stumbling blocks, for porous regions. Large corporations have given these developments a big push. Flexible and lean production methods are increasingly driving corporations to build up regional, rather than global or national, production and sourcing networks.[90] Outside the core of the world economy, regionalism is no longer driven so much by economic exchange and specialization in production as it is by innovation, induced by the creation of competitive advantages through networks that create economies of scale and scope in production, R & D, and marketing. This process often requires the cultivation of local resources.

Corporations grow most in the regions closest to their national home mar-

86. http://www.wto.org/english/tratop_e/region_e/rhttp://www.wto.org/english/tratop_e/region_e/regfac_e.htm. http://www.wto.org/english/tratop_e/region_e/summary_e.xls. (accessed December 4, 2004). Chase 2005.
87. Mansfield and Milner 1999, 600.
88. Thurow 1992. Bhagwati 1992.
89. Lawrence 1996, 3.
90. Oman 1994, 11–17, 33–36.

ket.[91] Microeconomic factors thus push corporations to organize their activities along regional lines. Throughout the third world, export processing zones have become favored sites for economic development. Two such zones existed before the mid-1960s, and there were twenty in ten countries in 1970; by 1986 those numbers had increased, respectively, to 175 zones and more than fifty countries; in 2002 there were about three thousand such zones. Thirty million of the thirty-seven million workers employed in these zones are Chinese.[92] Operating across national borders, large corporations create specific forms of dependence with suppliers, subcontractors, and customers. The tendency of foreign investment and operations to take place in adjacent regions, and the appearance of regional production complexes in Europe and Asia, illustrates how new spatial constellations both within and above the nation-state create regions that are open. Kerry Chase provides a compelling domestic politics argument that helps explain the trend toward porous regionalism: scale economies prompt interest groups, which stand to gain from regional integration, to lobby hard for the creation of regional trade arrangements.[93]

What is true of regionalism in general holds also for Asia and Europe specifically. Asia's regional political economy is institutionalized in social networks that operate in markets. It is deeply integrated with the rest of the world, and in particular with the U.S. economy. While liberalizing influences in many Asian polities have been clearly evident since the late 1980s, porous regionalism derives its political salience primarily from the asymmetry in the dyadic relations between various Asian states and the United States. Despite the sharp growth in intra-Asian trade, Asian economies depend greatly on U.S. markets. And dependence on the import of critical raw materials through sea-lanes protected by the U.S. Navy remains as large as ever. Military and economic dependence thus constrains any potential inclination to build an inward-looking Asia. In terms of trade, aid, investment, and technology, Japan and other Asian states have a more broadly diversified set of economic and political links to both the United States and poor countries than is true, for example, of Germany, which lives inside a European cocoon.[94] Asian states are very dependent on the United States, as is illustrated by the Internet. With the exception of Tokyo and Seoul, all Asian cities are connected indirectly to the Internet, as more than 99 percent of Asia's Internet traffic is routed through the United States.[95]

Confronted with failing efforts to further trade liberalization under WTO auspices, since 1999 Japan, Singapore, and Korea have been at the forefront of creating a "spiral" of bilateral FTAs that knit together northeast and Southeast Asia, as well as East Asia, Latin America, and Oceania; between 2000 and 2003, more than forty preferential trade agreements were proposed or imple-

91. Dörrenbächer 1999, 135–36, 152.
92. Yuan and Eden 1992, 1026. ILO 2002, 1.
93. Chase 2003.
94. Lincoln 1993, 135. Wan 1995, 98.
95. Ernst 2001.

mented.[96] Seeking to counter the growing competition with China for foreign investments, and interested in liberalizing trade further and faster than cumbersome multilateral negotiations would permit, Asian governments are rushing to conclude a large number of FTAs, capped by agreements for a China-ASEAN free trade area by 2010, a Japan-ASEAN comprehensive economic partnership, and various proposals for even more encompassing free trade areas in Asia. The dividing line between "trade liberalization" and "regional integration" is increasingly blurred, as encompassing multilateral arrangements and narrower minilateral ones break down national tariff and nontariff barriers.

Examples of porous regionalism exist also on questions of national security, understood here in narrow military as well as broad environmental terms. Asia's institutional order on questions of security is centered on states seeking to protect their security and sovereignty. In terms of war-fighting technologies, a number of Asian states (such as Pakistan, India, China, and North Korea) are investing heavily in long-range ballistic missiles and nuclear, chemical, and biological weapons of mass destruction that may fundamentally alter future asymmetrical conflicts between strong and weak states. As these military technologies spread, the need for creating international alliances against the United States may diminish. Indeed, U.S. military bases may become hostages as much as visible symbols of U.S. power.[97] Should terrorist networks expand in Central, South, and Southeast Asia, they will have a similar political effect. These changes open Asia on issues of security to developments in world politics. Conversely, conflicts between India and Pakistan, China and Taiwan, and the United States and North Korea have profound consequences not only for Asia but also for world politics. Going beyond traditional notions of military security, broad conceptions of security point in the same direction. Environmental security, for example, is directly affected by Asia's dynamic economic growth. By 2010, Asia is projected to produce more sulfur dioxide than Europe and the United States combined. By 2020 it will become the world's biggest source of greenhouse gases.[98] Japan's interest in regional environmental cooperation is driven in part by the need to achieve a mandated 6 percent cutback under the Kyoto Protocol through regional technological cooperation and financial aid. Thus both environmental and military security issues illustrate how the Asia-Pacific region is closely linked to developments in world politics.

Porous regionalism marks Europe as much as Asia. Its institutional form, however, is formal and political rather than informal and economic. The formation of the European Economic Community (EEC) in 1957 might well have encouraged a closed rather than an open regional political economy. Two factors militated against it. From the outset, an increasingly liberal world econ-

---

96. Munakata 2002. Ravenhill 2003.
97. Bracken 2000, 153.
98. Barkenbus 2001.

omy, made possible by strong U.S. leadership and the formidable presence of
U.S. corporations in Europe, provided strong links between Europe and the
world economy. Equally important, the rapid strengthening of liberal and democratic social forces in European societies made porous regionalism a natural
domestic choice. Today, the source of Europe's porous regionalism lies in what
Brigid Laffan calls its "betweenness."[99] Europe hovers between politics and
diplomacy, government and governance, Westphalia and post-Westphalia. The
density of ties and the depth of political institutions have made Europe a filter
for global and international processes. Porous regionalism in Europe is marked
by multiple locations of governance, multiple dimensions of integration, and
multiple modes of interaction. Multi-level governance occurs in, through, and
around European states.

This system is not restricted to the European Union. Located around the
multipurpose European Union with its many economic and social functions
are a variety of European organizations dealing with specific issues (such as
space, environmental protection, and civil aviation); specific geographical domains (for example, the Baltic, the Black Sea, and the Balkan regions); or specific norms, values, and practices (such as Europe's human rights regime and
the Organization for Security and Cooperation in Europe, OSCE). Europe's
porous regionalism also features distinct modes of interaction that shade over
into global and international arenas: supranational governance in the construction of common EU policies, European regulatory policies that affect
member and nonmember states alike, distributional policies of the European
Union that involve central and subnational levels of government, regulatory
agreements that transfer policy experiences among countries, and intensive
forms of transgovernmental cooperation and consultation and transnational
collaboration by social movement activists. It is often all but impossible to draw
clear boundaries between Europe's porous regionalism and global or international processes and institutional arrangements.

Europe's porousness is enhanced by EU enlargement. From the original six
members of the EEC in 1957, Europe has affected significantly a growing number of members. It has also left its impact on states hesitant to join such as Norway and Switzerland, as well as a large number of states bordering on Europe
and hoping to join as either full-fledged or associate members. The 2004 eastern enlargement of the European Union stretches from northeastern (Estonia,
Latvia, and Lithuania) to central-eastern (Poland, Czech Republic, Slovakia,
Slovenia, and Hungary) Europe, as well as the Mediterranean (Cyprus and
Malta). Other states in southeast Europe (Romania and Bulgaria), as well as
the successor states to the former Yugoslavia, may eventually follow. And there
is Turkey, which has waited since the 1960s. Within a decade, the European
Union may well have a population of slightly less than half a billion people,
more than the United States and Russia combined, and an economy of $9 tril-

99. Laffan 1998, 236–38.

lion—only slightly smaller than that of the United States. Short of formal membership, other states interact with the European Union, either through membership in an organization such as the European Economic Area (Norway, Iceland, Liechtenstein) or the European Free Trade Area (Norway, Iceland, Liechtenstein, and Switzerland), or through free trade arrangements (Switzerland). Other special arrangements may be made for states (Albania, Bosnia, Croatia, Serbia, and Macedonia) that cannot meet the triple conditionality that the European Union articulated in its Copenhagen summit in 1993: respect for democracy and human rights, a functioning market economy, and the capacity to adopt and implement past and future EU legislation.

EU association arrangements with former French and British colonies in Africa, the Caribbean and Pacific (the so-called ACP countries), and North Africa (Euro-Med relations) offer a second illustration of porous regionalism in action. It is true that the eastward shift in the European Union's attention has had deleterious effects on its relations with poor countries in Africa and Asia. The Barcelona Euro-Mediterranean conference of November 1995, the Palermo meeting of 1998, and the Stuttgart conference of April 1999 have, however, elevated the political significance of relations between the European Union and North Africa, with a primary focus on peace and stability, economic cooperation, market reforms, and cultural and scientific cooperation. Furthermore, after 9/11, the U.S. wars against Afghanistan and Iraq reinforce the importance of this political initiative. To date, the European Union has negotiated agreements with Morocco, Tunisia, Jordan, Israel, and the autonomous Palestinian government. Cyprus and Malta have joined the European Union, and negotiations with Turkey, Lebanon, and Algeria are proceeding. Generally speaking, however, these market-opening agreements are less far-reaching than those the European Union has negotiated in the process of its eastern enlargement. Yet EU institutions and strategy are the same: to stabilize adjacent regions by tying them politically more closely to Europe and by linking them more fully to global and international processes.

Porous regionalism in different institutional orders has effects that work themselves out differently in specific cases. Variable combinations of global-local and regional-national processes illustrate this point. Saskia Sassen, for example, argues that a digitalized global economy is grounded in global cities. Globalization "has entailed a partial denationalizing of national territories and a partial shift of some components of state sovereignty to other institutions, ranging from supranational institutions to the global capital market."[100] Some of the world's major cities are being transformed into the headquarters of various service, insurance, rating, and governance regimes operating in global financial markets. An archipelago of high-tech city-regions hosts transnational corporations that are central to the global economy. New local-global links are thus established through the movement of information, capital, and people.

100. Sassen 1996, xii.

The extension of control from a small number of urban hubs entails increasing inequality within world cities. Economic globalization and local social fragmentation thus occur together, with consequences for the sense of place that defines people's identities. Alternatively, nonlocal contexts and influences can also have profound local impacts through processes of integration, as in the combination of global and local, or "glocal," corporate networks of production. Global and local thus are thoroughly intertwined in ways that can strengthen simultaneously the forces of both integration and fragmentation.

Internationalization can also create different constellations operating within regions and across national borders. More than fifty years ago, François Perroux was criticizing the "illusions of localization" and writing about the "delocalization of economic activity."[101] The territorial unity and social homogeneity of national economies is undermined by a process that pulls simultaneously toward larger regional and smaller national loci of economic and political activity. The proliferation of regional trading arrangements that has occurred in the second half of the twentieth century is a good example. Scale economies and protectionist politics provide a powerful impetus. At the same time, internationalization and regionalization make it possible for small regions to find market niches that promise survival, even prosperity, in Europe and the Pacific as much as in other parts of the world. The interaction of regional and national effects is also evident in the competition among different national standards of best corporate and acceptable state practice. Competition in partially regulated markets can lead to interregional competition between different corporate and national models and eventual convergence in solutions that prove to be superior. The competitive standards that succeed do not result from the imposition of specific national solutions. They are hybrids that combine the elements of different national and regional approaches that are linked in border-spanning regional networks.[102]

Globalization and internationalization often reinforce each other. The ugly term "glocalization" captures the distinctive combinations that emerge from the interaction of global and local factors of economic production.[103] Cultural anthropologists write in a similar vein of the local appropriation of meanings of global systems of popular culture. And internationalization permits national processes to intersect with regional ones in different ways that can create either "deep" or "shallow" schemes of regional integration. In various constellations, such processes provide conditions favorable to regional orders that are porous.

Illustrating the Argument—Monetary Orders

The deep intermingling of global and international processes in Asia's and Europe's monetary orders provides an excellent example that illustrates the

101. Perroux 1950, 23, 24.
102. Storper 1995, 206. Bernard 1996, 653–58.
103. Ruigrok and Van Tulder 1995, 178–79.

two outstanding features of a world of regions: the powerful processes that push for regional porousness and the distinct institutional forms of different regional orders.

Benjamin Cohen suggests that "international relations are being dramatically reshaped by the increasing interpenetration of national monetary spaces."[104] Statistical data recording sharp increases in capital flows offer a powerful illustration of how globalization and internationalization interact to transform the world economy. In 1993–94, before the sharp run-up in global stock markets, the worldwide capitalization of stock and bond markets exceeded the $31 trillion mark, more than four times the U.S. gross domestic product.[105] Between 1980 and 1990, international lending (cross-border and domestic lending denominated in foreign currencies) increased from 4 to 44 percent of the combined GNP of Organization for Economic Co-operation and Development (OECD) members. The daily value of foreign exchange transactions totaled between $1.5 and $2.0 trillion at the end of 1998.[106] In 1983, foreign exchange transactions were ten times larger than world trade; a decade later they were sixty times larger.[107] In 2000, the stock of FDI was slightly under $6 trillion. In the same year, the global flow of FDI was about $1.1 trillion, compared to $401 billion in 1997, $217 billion in 1994, and a $123 billion average for the years 1986–88.[108] While direct foreign investment as a share of global economic output doubled from 5 to 10 percent, the proportion of capital raised in foreign markets, compared to world exports, quadrupled between 1980 and 1995, from 5 to 20 percent. Since 1980, the financial assets of rich countries have increased two and a half times faster than aggregate GDP, and the volume of trading in currencies, bonds, and equities has increased five times faster. Along with its magnitude, the mobility of capital has also increased greatly, spurred by liberalization and financial deregulation.[109]

In the absence of stable self-regulation, global financial markets remain crisis prone, making government intervention inevitable. Globalization and internationalization thus deeply condition each other. Currency crises illustrate this point. In Europe, national action occurs within the context of regional institutions, such as the European Monetary System (EMS) or the European Monetary Union (EMU), which have offered formal and informal mechanisms for collective coping. In Asia, national action occurs in the context of global markets and international financial institutions such as the International Monetary Fund (IMF), with its close links to the U.S. government. Confronting financial crises, Asian governments are thus more prone to national improvisation and bilateral deals than are European governments.

104. Cohen 1998, 3.
105. Prakash 1997, 577–78.
106. Broad 1999, 114.
107. Sassen 1996, 40.
108. *The Economist* 2001a. Howells and Wood 1993, 3–4, 153. UNCTAD 1998, 361.
109. Uchitelle 1998b, D6. See also Reinicke 1998, 44–48.

In Europe, several decades of evolution have yielded a regional monetary order. The initial steps toward monetary union date back to the early 1960s. German unification gave the negotiations that eventually led to the establishment of the European Monetary Union a sense of political urgency that they had lacked before. While the German government worked on Germany's monetary unification in the first half of 1990, the European governments decided in June 1990 to convene a second intergovernmental conference on political union, to complement the Economic Union conference held in December 1989. Both conferences were deliberate attempts, encouraged by Chancellor Helmut Kohl, to tie united Germany even more closely to Europe. In Maastricht, it was monetary, not political, union that was at the center of the 1991 treaty. The sharply increasing interest rate, which the Bundesbank instituted to respond to the inflationary pressures that had begun to build even before the government's postunification expansionary policies, illustrated the enormous costs that German domestic politics imposed on other countries.

The currency crisis of September–November 1992 and the summer of 1993 illustrated both the limitations and the strength of Europe's monetary order. During the summer of 1992, markets had concluded that, for reasons of prestige, Britain had entered the EMS with an overvalued currency. By September 10, Britain had negotiated an international support facility of 10 billion European Currency Units (about $14.4 billion at the time), a further signal to investors that the pound sterling was likely to be revalued inside the EMS. At the height of the crisis, on September 16, the Bank of England spent about half of its currency reserves, around fifteen billion pounds sterling, to ward off speculation in currency markets that were trading daily in excess of a trillion dollars. Heavy speculation against the British pound, as well as the Italian lira, compelled both to drop out of the exchange rate mechanism (ERM). Determined to stay in, the Swedish government briefly raised interest rates to the astronomical level of 500 percent. After a brief respite, a second speculative run on the krona in November forced Sweden to devalue. In terms of local currency, its unsuccessful crisis measures cost Sweden at least 25, and perhaps as much as 95, billion krona. By Christmas, Norway and Ireland had joined Sweden and the soft currency club of Spain and Portugal in devaluing their currencies inside the EMS.[110]

In all, the central banks of the major European countries spent more than $150 billion of their foreign exchange reserves to defend (unsuccessfully) the parity of the pound and the lira, as well as (successfully) the French franc against speculative attacks in international financial markets. In the month of September alone, Germany's Bundesbank supported weak currencies to the tune of $60 billion. In August 1993, after another bout of currency speculation, the central band for currency fluctuations inside the ERM was increased sixfold from +/−2.25 to +/−15.0 percent. The lesson drawn by most British

110. Stern and Sundelius 1997, 32, 36.

and American financial journalists at the time was that the EMS had failed. Governments had been forced to abandon an intra-European, quasi–fixed exchange rate system as global financial markets wreaked havoc on the EMS, a scheme of regional monetary integration that fell short of full monetary union.

This, however, was not the end of the story. The unifying constraints imposed by the formal ERM were less important than was assumed. While governments decided in August 1993 to broaden dramatically the band for currency fluctuations, in fact the value of currencies participating in the ERM continued to vary only at the margin. Widening the band was a cheap way of deflecting market pressures. Yet central banks continued to shadow the value of the deutschmark extremely closely.[111] Even in the absence of the constraints of the ERM, Europe's central bankers were willing to give up autonomy in their national monetary policy in anticipation of continued movement toward full monetary union. Especially for the countries at the core of the EMS, the difference between post- and precrisis parities was minuscule. Governments and markets thus were coupled. Increasing globalization in financial markets was tightly linked to an increasing internationalization of state policies.

During the last two decades, Asia-Pacific's financial markets have opened to global markets. Yet no regional lead currency, like the deutschmark or the euro, has emerged to rival the dollar. Nor has the region developed institutions comparable to the EMU, or even to the EMS. In contrast to Europe, Asian regionalism is organized not by formal political institutions but by informal, market-based arrangements. Both as a symbol, and as a reinforcement of the geostrategic importance of the United States in the Asia-Pacific region, the dollar has remained overwhelmingly important. The Asian financial crisis of 1997 offers a clear illustration of the high volatility in global markets and inadequate regulatory mechanisms of domestic financial institutions that have prompted government action.

As an export market, supplier, investor, creditor, and donor, Japan still looms very large in Asia, despite the ground China has covered in the 1990s. With the exception of South Korea and Vietnam, Japan is the largest source of imports for all Asian economies. It is also the single largest source of foreign investment, especially in Thailand, Indonesia, and Malaysia. Japanese banks are the region's leading creditors, accounting for 30 percent of all international loans in Asia. And the Japanese yen, not the Chinese yuan, trades freely in global currency markets. Because Japan has far surpassed the United States in regional aid, trade, investment, and bank lending in Asia, the dollar's continued primacy over the yen is far from natural. At the root of Asia's reliance on the dollar lies Japan's traditional unwillingness to internationalize its currency and to explicitly exercise monetary leadership, not only in Asia but worldwide. A greater role for the yen in Asia would arguably have been a stabilizing factor in 1997. Instead, national currencies, pegged either explicitly or implicitly to the

111. Abdelal 1998, 238–39, 249–57.

dollar, were left very vulnerable to shifts in the dollar-yen exchange rate and the full force of increasingly volatile global markets.

Japan's economic and financial weakness in the 1990s was a central ingredient of the 1997 crisis. Contributing to Japan's structural weakness were financial institutions abetting excessive investments in manufacturing sectors, flooding world markets with Japanese products in the 1980s. Furthermore, the policies through which Japan's government sought to stimulate the Japanese economy in the 1990s shaped capital flows and investment patterns in many Asian economies. The bursting of Japan's speculative bubble, severe asset deflation, flagging domestic demand, and yen revaluation prompted Japan's central bank to adopt a cheap money policy that drove interest rates down toward zero, while high private savings and large current account surpluses kept financial markets liquid. Hoping for an economic upswing, the government could finance record deficits, and commercial banks could roll over their bad loans estimated very approximately at $500 billion in 1999—as long as interest rates stayed close to zero.[112] Very low interest rates in Japan created a large flow of Japanese capital into Asia. In many Asian countries a loosening of capital controls made Asian firms hungry for this enormous pool of cheap capital. After 1995, external short-term debt grew rapidly, without Asian governments knowing its full extent: to $25 billion in the case of Indonesia, and $100 billion in the case of Korea. Japanese banks made a lot of money risk-free, borrowing at 1 percent in Japan and lending in Asia's emerging markets at 6 percent. They exported Japan's economic bubble to Asia.

Starting in the mid-1980s, a decade-long depreciation of the dollar against the yen also helped heat up Asia's economies. With their currencies tied to the dollar in a variety of ways, Asia's central bankers and governments suddenly faced a new situation once the dollar began appreciating against the yen in 1994–95. Now it was no longer possible to repay dollar-denominated loans in continuously depreciating dollars. The Asian financial crisis thus was due to the unhinging of a development strategy that was based on a tight link between the export competitiveness of Asian producers in U.S. markets and the regional needs that Japanese financial institutions had for recycling capital. The strong belief in the declining value of the dollar was tied to the widespread perception of Asia's rise and America's decline.

A contagion of speculative optimism thus preceded the contagion of speculative pessimism in the fall of 1997. A deterioration in the trade balances of Asian economies was covered by the influx of even more speculative short-term capital. The depreciation of the yen intensified the pressure on national currencies, which had already been destabilized after a sharp devaluation of the Chinese renminbi in 1994 had weakened the competitiveness of Southeast Asian producers in their traditional markets. Foreign investors, in a panic,

112. Godement 1999, 37.

eventually started pulling out their funds, thus creating the Asian financial crisis of 1997.

In response to the crisis, Japan's proposal for the creation of an Asian monetary fund was quashed quickly by the United States and the IMF. A year later, Japan's government developed a series of smaller initiatives designed to return East Asia to financial stability. By the end of 2000, Japan's total pledges in support of the region's economic recovery were only $20 billion shy of the $100 billion of its September 1997 Asian monetary fund proposal. Because not all of Japan's pledges were activated, this substantial commitment did not fully offset the rapid retreat of Japan's failing financial institutions from Asia.[113] The new approach sidesteps formal institutions in favor of informal arrangements, including the Miyazawa initiative of October 1998 for bilateral swap agreements with Malaysia and South Korea; the Asian Currency Crisis Support Facility set up within the Asian Development Bank in 1999; regional currency swap arrangements, eventually called the Chiang Mai initiative; the Manila Framework Group, which focuses on early warning mechanisms; regular meetings of the executives of East Asian and Pacific central banks; and attempts to create an Asian bond market.[114]

Yet regional monetary and financial cooperation in Asia remains extremely limited, at least by European standards. The spread of international prudential standards for banks is converging around global, not regional, standards. And as long as Asian governments weigh the dollar heavily in their exchange rate and foreign reserve policies, the freedom of action for Asian currency and macroeconomic cooperation remains limited. Greater reliance on the yen as a regional currency was undermined by the high transaction costs for yen-denominated assets before the 1998 liberalization of Japan's financial markets, and by the increasing fragility of Japan's financial institutions thereafter. A number of committees of central bankers and monetary authorities, organized under the auspices of ASEAN and neighboring East Asian and South Asian countries, facilitate an exchange of views. But they do not see it as their task to coordinate policy. Although financial cooperation in Asia is in the interest of a large number of states, very little has come of it.

In sum, these two episodes illustrate that globalization and internationalization are cumulative, interactive, and mutually reinforcing. Richard O'Brien expresses a widespread sentiment when he argues that financial integration is leading to "the end of geography." These illustrative cases suggest otherwise.[115] Financial crises in Europe and Asia in the 1990s illustrate how the combined effects of globalization and internationalization fuse and create porous regions. At the same time, these crises illustrate that Asia and Europe differ in-

113. Katada 2001, 188–89.
114. Evans 2005, 199–200.
115. O'Brien 1992. Payne and Gamble 1996, 2.

stitutionally in ways that are politically significant. Germany is so deeply embedded in Europe that multilateral action has become almost a habit in a state with a remarkably internationalized state identity. Japan's national identity is strong, and like most states in Asia, it tends to prefer bilateral over multilateral arrangements. The "Asian way" of flexible and informal political arrangements rests on specific institutional features that make European-style monetary integration politically unattractive. In Europe, clashing interests were harmonized in a political setting that, in the end, permitted the formation of the EMU. The currency crisis of 1992–93 showed the interaction between formal and informal financial institutions. The financial crisis of 1997 illustrated instead how closely Asia is linked to a U.S.- and IMF-centered, global rather than Asia-centered, Japanese-led approach to regional financial order. In brief, both financial crises show the fusion of globalization and internationalization in distinctly institutionalized porous regional orders.

Cases and Perspectives

"Given" by geography and "made" through politics, Asia and Europe offer promising terrain for exploring a world of porous regions. These two regions are arguably more important, measured along various dimensions of power, than are any others. And they are clearly central to the political foundation of the American imperium, as classical theorists of geopolitics have argued. Asia is understood here as encompassing East and Southeast Asia, Europe the entire continent except the former member states of the Soviet Union. Their sprawling character and political salience makes both regions appropriate for closer analysis. Europe illustrates with particular clarity the material, formal, and political aspects of regionalism; Asia, the imagined, informal, and economic ones. It is a serious mistake to assume that one of the two is "normal," the other "exceptional"—rather, both illustrate the political diversity fostered by a world of regions.

In this book I also focus on the role that Germany and Japan play in their respective regions. For the American imperium these are, of course, highly relevant states in Europe and Asia. Germany's destructive role in twentieth-century European history and its pivotal place in the cold war make it a readily intelligible choice. Given China's spectacular rise since the mid-1990s, however, my focus on Japan warrants a brief discussion. In terms of market prices Japan's GDP lead over China is about 4:1; on a per capita basis, about 40:1.[116] Between 2001 and 2005 Japanese banks wrote off about half of their total bad

116. GDP estimates vary widely between those calculated in market prices (as an approximate measure of relative power in the international economy) and those calculated in purchasing parity power (as a measure of comparative levels of total consumption). In terms of purchasing power parity China's GDP in 2000 exceeded Japan's by about one-third, whereas Japan's per capita income was six times larger than China's. See McNicoll 2005, 57–58.

debts; China barely began to grapple with its own debt crisis, which by all accounts is much more severe than Japan's. In high-tech weaponry and in its political proximity to the world's only superpower, Japan outstrips China by a wide margin. And while Japan's economic and political heart beat at a sluggish pace in the 1990s, various domestic crises suggest that Chinese hypertension is as likely as Japanese anemia to cause cardiac arrest. If I were to select different pairs of countries—China and France, for instance, or Singapore and Britain—I would have to adjust some of my argument to changed contexts. Still, I believe that my general approach and claims would hold.

Some might ask what the focus of this book adds to the study of liberal "trilateralism" during the cold war, or to realist "tripolarity" afterward. Moving beyond the dumbbell metaphor of a trans-Atlantic world that dominated the first two decades of the cold war, liberals supported trilateralism as a way to incorporate Japan and the Pacific in the 1970s. It was a skewed triangle at best, connecting the U.S. superpower with one large and dynamic Asian economy and one rich part of Europe. After the end of the cold war, building on the insights of classical theories of geopolitics, some realists modified that view to characterize the world after the collapse of the Soviet Union as tripolar. The underlying assumption of regions as actors, then and now, was shared by both liberals and realists. Washington, Brussels, and Tokyo were each thought to be in control of their respective hinterland. That form of trilateralism or tripolarity has little, if any, resemblance to the role Germany and Japan play in European and Asian regionalism today. Encompassing the majority of states and peoples in the world, Asia and Europe show enormous economic and political diversity. These two regions include both centers of great power and astounding wealth, and concentrations of dismal impotence and abject poverty. And they are not directed politically from any one center. Asia and Europe are not part of a rich trilateral club or a cohesive tripolar bloc. They are instead viewed more productively as porous regions in an American imperium.

How should we think about the selection of specific issues for more detailed analysis? In the interest of comprehensiveness this book covers economic and security issues in chapter 4 and cultural issues in chapter 5. Both chapters show how complementary international and global processes fuse in porous regions embodying distinctive institutional orders that typify Europe and Asia.

Technology and production are prime illustrations of global processes. They illustrate the shrinking of space and the compression of time as defining aspects of globalization. Geographic proximity, and the functional interdependencies and transborder externalities it creates, helps spur regional networks of technological innovation and production. These networks consist of spatially discontinuous processes, as regions embody different trajectories of production technologies that cluster in different parts of the world. The supply base of a national economy—the parts, components, subsystems, materials, and equipment technologies, as well as the interrelations among the firms that make all of these available to world markets—have in many ways been placed on distinctive regional bases.[117] Europe and Asia offer plenty of evidence to support this view.

Internal and external security policies illustrate the logic of states intent on defending their sovereignty. Internationalization creates increasingly dense connections among the different actors and sites of world politics without transforming underlying actor identities. On questions of security, porous regions matter, both before and after the end of the cold war. European and Asian regional security complexes are marked by distinctive processes. For example, after suffering disastrous defeats in World War II, both Germany and Japan have evolved security strategies that eschew violence. Germany adheres to an international strategy, Japan to a national one. Both have had a profound effect on the different security orders that have emerged in Europe and Asia. And both are shaped, in turn, by distinctive regional institutions and political practices. Europe differs from Asia in the greater density of institutions dealing with internal and external security issues. Since the end of the cold war, in contrast to the relative stability in Asian security institutions and practices, Europe's are going through a period of profound transformation. External and internal security issues reflect the existence of porous regional orders.

Finally, culture flows vertically and horizontally. Vertical flows belong to an international world in which states seek to control the content of culture. Through cultural diplomacy, for example, governments seek to present specific images to support or alter existing state identities. Through markets and other conduits, horizontal cultural flows between individuals are part of a global world. They lead to the creation and re-creation of popular cultures, with little direct government input. These two types of cultural processes thus reflect different international and global dynamics.

The case studies presented here offer an opportunity to examine closely the interrelations between the different processes that create porous regional orders. Do the cases that reflect global processes (technology/production and popular culture) show important commonalities that contrast with cases that typify international processes (internal/external security and cultural diplomacy)? Or is their regional placement in Asia and Europe more important? I shall argue that the fusion of globalization and internationalization and the differences between Asia's and Europe's characteristic institutions creates porous and recognizably different regional orders that do not vary across different policy arenas.

I focus, in the words of Charles Tilly, on "the interconnectedness of ostensibly separate experiences" without any prior assumption that there exists one overarching system, such as the global system of capitalism or the international state system, that encompasses all experiences.[118] I track these interconnections in chapter 6 with a particular focus on German-American and Japan-

117. Borrus and Zysman 1997.
118. Tilly 1984, 147.

American relations, the politics of subregionalism in Europe and Asia, and the two-way processes by which America influences the world, and the world America. Chapter 7, finally, restates the argument of how America links to Asia's and Europe's open regions and extends it to the Americas, South Asia, Africa, and the Middle East.

The approach I take in this book resembles recent inquiries of American historians who have begun to question the exceptionalism of American history by embedding national and local narratives in comparative and transnational contexts.[119] This is highly plausible for an outpost nation like the United States, which started as the imperial project of others and which is connected to, as well as shielded from, others by oceans. The significance of connections and the height of the shield has much to do with the depth of the belief that the United States, as Max Weber once wrote of the early Protestants, is "in but not of the world it commands; its destiny and experience are, by the very nature of things, exceptional."[120] Recent work in U.S. history questions this belief, not by doing away with national history but by situating it in broader contexts. Ian Tyrrell does so in his history of Australian and Californian environmentalism, Daniel T. Rodgers in his history of the transatlantic currents of the social politics in the Progressive Era.[121] These books provide useful pointers for how to engage in a substantive analysis of interrelated processes in different locations. A world of porous regions offers an ideal laboratory for such a task.[122]

Existing explanations of regionalism tend to highlight selective features of international politics: polarity, institutional efficiency, and culture (ethnic, religious, or civilizational ties and divisions). Rooted in realist, liberal, and sociological styles of analysis, each approach has considerable strengths in helping us to understand regional orders as the outcome of balances of power or threat, institutionally and organizationally coordinated policies, and contested identities. But each approach also confronts nagging difficulties. How many poles of power exist in contemporary world politics? How can institutional efficiency be measured? And how can the idea of clashing norms and identities be squared with the incontestable fact of pervasive hybridity?

Drawing on all three explanations, the theoretical perspective informing this book is eclectic.[123] I acknowledge the relevance of the material capabilities of the United States, Japan, and Germany, of institutional effects that highlight issues of efficiency, and of collective identities in European and Asian regional affairs. Rather than seek to test the relative explanatory power of each of these perspectives, I pull selectively from all three in the effort to establish the interconnections between various processes.

In doing so, I draw freely from contrasting approaches to the study of re-

119. Kammen 2003.
120. Rodgers 1998, 3.
121. Tyrrell 1999. Rodgers 1998.
122. McMichael 1990, 386, 395–96.
123. Katzenstein and Okawara 2001/02. Katzenstein and Sil 2004.

gionalism that scholars have developed over three generations of theorizing.[124]
I link regionalism—and not only on issues of security—to the system level, conceived here as the American imperium.[125] I acknowledge the relevance of collective identities that transcend the nation-state yet fall short of a global
consciousness.[126] My analysis of the different forms of regionalism in Asia and
Europe, going well beyond the issue of technology and regional production
networks, agrees with economists who have studied economic regions as intermediaries between world markets and national economies. I agree with those
political economists who link regionalism respectively to international and
global processes and structures,[127] and concur with others who see, respectively, the relevance of state institutions and market efficiencies as major driv-
ers in the formation of economic regionalism.[128] Finally, my argument in this
book incorporates the national level into its analysis of regional politics, without subscribing to a state-centric, realist insistence on the primacy of the political interests of state leaders over those of all other political actors in domestic
politics.[129]

    I also disagree substantially with important aspects of these approaches. I
avoid an ahistorical treatment of "the international system" as a "2 + 3 system"
during and a "1 + 4 system" after the end of the cold war.[130] My analysis of the
logic of the American imperium illustrates that without understanding the social purpose of the superpower, we cannot comprehend the dynamics of a
world of porous regions. I disagree with treatments of collective identities that
do not take full account of the cultural hybridization documented in chapter
5 with specific reference to popular culture.[131] My analysis avoids overempha-
sis on either internationalization or globalization in the shaping of contemporary regionalism.[132] Instead, I argue that porous regions fuse international and
global processes. I disagree with the deliberate downplaying of the many institutional differences that distinguish different regions.[133] I suggest that U.S.
policies do not uniformly strengthen the hands of internationalist coalitions,
and that globalization and internationalization create strong pressures for a
porous regionalism that tends to undermine policies of closure preferred by
statist-nationalist-confessional coalitions.[134] Finally, I disagree with the assumption of coalitional analysis that views firms as shaping policy directly, un-
mediated by institutions.[135] Instead, I track the institutional characteristics of

124. Värynen 2003. Breslin and Higgott 2002. Mansfield and Milner 1999. Taylor 1993, 1–46.
125. Buzan and Wæver 2003.
126. Huntington 1996.
127. Gilpin 2001, 341–61; 2000, 193–292. Payne and Gamble 1996.
128. Mattli 1999.
129. Solingen 1998, 2001, 2004. Chase 2003a, 2003b.
130. Buzan and Wæver 2003.
131. Huntington 1996.
132. Gilpin 2001. Payne and Gamble 1996.
133. Mattli 1999.
134. Solingen 1998, 2001, 2004.
135. Chase 2003a, 2003b.

Germany's welfare democracy and Japan's productivity democracy and the links they provide for embedding Germany and Japan in regional orders that differ greatly in their institutional form.

In the analysis of American elections, East, West, North, and South are common regional categories that conceal the specific constellations of variables shaping voting behavior. Although the problem of masking our ignorance behind deceptively simple labels exists also in the analysis of regions in world politics,[136] prior scholarship has made the problem less acute. The arguments that I develop in this book combine the emphasis of first- and second-generation scholars on the role of core regional states and the dynamics of the world system with the emphasis of third-generation scholars on regionalism as a spontaneous process. For the economic and security interests of the United States, the political salience of world regions varies greatly; so do regional institutional orders and the core states that inhabit them. The fusion of globalization and internationalization and the vertical links between regions, the American imperium, core regional states, and other actors resembles a swirly marble cake rather than a neat layer cake.

Existing scholarship suggests that regionalism and regionalization are too complex to be captured adequately by any one analytical tradition. What Robert Gilpin readily acknowledges for the power-oriented state-centric realism that he favors[137] holds also for alternative theoretical orientations that privilege institutional efficiency or collective identity: an understanding of the complexities of regionalism in world politics requires analytical eclecticism. I am not interested here in the development or restatement of rival analytical perspectives or the testing of specific hypotheses. Instead, my main concern is to characterize two very different institutional orders in Asia and Europe and to trace three processes that link the American imperium to a world of porous regions: globalization and internationalization, both of which keep regions porous, and regionalization, which reproduces and reshapes different regional orders.

We do not suffer from a lack of arresting images, slogans, and metaphors about the shape of world politics. In short supply, however, are analysis and assessment of the varied effects they imply. Sorting out such effects is tricky business. Kenichi Ohmae, for example, has articulated two contradictory regional visions in a series of books and articles published in the 1980s and 1990s. With the concept of "triad power," Ohmae sought to capture in the 1980s a world of regional blocs, poised for trade wars.[138] Although the tune of protectionism is sung in different languages, in this argument the core states in each of the three major economic regions—NAFTA and the United States, the European Union and Germany, and APEC and Japan—are building regional coalitions in order to defend themselves against unwelcome intrusions by global markets.

136. Lemke 2002, 126–28.
137. Gilpin 2001, 359.
138. Ohmae 1985.

Corporations wishing to succeed have no choice but to establish themselves in each triad. In this Orwellian view, we live in a world of "bloc regionalism."

A few years later, with comparable eloquence, Ohmae articulated an alternative vision. "The end of the nation state," the "rise of the region state" in a "borderless world," and the "invisible continent" were compelling phrases that he gave to the titles of his major books and articles in the 1990s.[139] They suggest a world that differs dramatically from "bloc regionalism." Economic activities do not follow the political boundaries of states or the cultural boundaries of civilizations. They follow instead what Ohmae calls the "dictates of the four *I*'s," the information-driven routes by which investment and industry seek to reach individual consumers. Economic nationalists everywhere are learning the painful lesson that the modern state is dysfunctional. In this view, states wither away as capitalism prevails in a new world in which all players can win. In sharp contrast to abnormal and inefficient political states, region states are "natural" economic zones that exist sometimes within states (northern Italy, Pusan, Silicon Valley, Osaka and the Kansai area, Malaysia's Penang Island), and sometimes between them (San Diego-Tijuana, Hong Kong-southern China, the growth triangle of Singapore, Johor Island, and Riau Island). History has moved to a new era of global regionalism that ignores national boundaries.

Both of these views are wrong. Because they overlook the centrality of the American imperium with its distinctive mix of territorial and nonterritorial power at the center of a world of porous regions, these visions are both too simple and too one-sided. The image of regional blocs is badly skewed, and so is the image of region states operating in a borderless world. A world split up into distinct regional blocs evokes a troubled past that the world has passed by. In neglecting America's nonterritorial power, this regional perspective is too "hard." A world lacking state borders projects a rosy future that may never come. In overlooking America's territorial power this view of regionalism is too "soft." Contemporary world politics is shaped instead by the multiple connections between the American imperium and porous regional orders.

During the second half of the twentieth century world politics was organized around two antagonistic superpowers. For decades they coexisted in sharp conflict and uneasy accommodation, separated by ideological clashes, an intense arms rivalry, and proxy wars fought in various parts of the world. Behind the cold war façade, a porous regionalism was gradually taking shape, especially in the U.S.-led Western alliance. With the end of the cold war, the collapse of the Soviet Union, and the onset of the war on terror, that regionalism has matured and is now in plain sight. World politics is now shaped by the interaction between porous regions and America's imperium.

139. Ohmae 1990, 1993, 1995, 1999.

CHAPTER TWO

Regional Orders

The United States plays the central role in a world of regions. Gone are the
clearly demarcated, rival blocs of East and West. Since the end of the cold war,
the collapse of socialism has made anachronistic the distinction between a first
and a second world. And even before the disintegration of the Soviet Union,
the third world had ceased to exist as a cohesive force in world politics. The distinction between an industrialized North and a nonindustrialized South became outdated with the rapid industrialization of numerous poor countries,
while the gap in income and wealth within and between North and South has
widened. The American imperium is now the hub in a wheel with many regional spokes. In short, world politics has undergone a huge shift from bloc
bipolarity to an American-centered regionalism.

Actions that the United States took in the late 1940s were crucial in bringing about the regional institutional orders that have characterized Asia and Europe for the last half century. Markets and law were the two key institutions
through which Asian and European regions organized. In Asia, regionalism has
been shaped by the powerful impact of ethnic capitalism in markets that are
typically organized through networks. In Europe, law and judicial institutions
are embedded in a variety of political institutions that link countries together
in a European polity. Drawing this sharp distinction is not to deny the existence
of important networks in Europe and of developmental states in Asia. But the
comparison of Europe and Asia highlights two important facts. European
networks are embedded in a legal context that profoundly shapes their operations; Asian states seek to ride markets that are evolving in broader networks.
The fact that similar institutions, in part emanating from U.S. influence, can
be found in both regions takes nothing away from the more important idea
that I develop here: the distinctive institutions that shape Europe and Asia differ greatly.

Regional Politics, Present at the Creation

Throughout the twentieth century, state power and purpose have shaped the ups and downs of regionalism. When the United States failed to back the League of Nations and the principle of universalism it stood for, Nazi Germany and the Japanese military developed different versions of closed regionalism, in the form of Europe's "New Order" and Asia's "Co-Prosperity Sphere." At the end of World War II, globalism and regionalism offered again two contrasting blueprints for world politics. U.S. Secretary of State Cordell Hull stood for universalism; British prime minister Winston Churchill championed regionalism. This split is preserved in the United Nations Charter: Article 24 charges the Security Council to preserve world peace and international security, whereas Article 52 emphasizes the importance of regional organizations. Soon after 1945, anti-Communist coalition politics came to define regional politics in both Europe and Asia. Reflecting a hierarchical view of the world that had strong civilizational and at times racial connotations, U.S. policy engaged Europe multilaterally and Asia bilaterally, with consequences that proved to be far reaching for the evolution of European and Asian regionalism.[1]

Anti-Communist Coalition Building in Europe and Asia

Dean Acheson claimed to have been "present at the creation" of America's preeminence, and so he was.[2] But babies signal their birth with a lusty cry, whereas the emergence of the American imperium was muffled by the lingering effects of the Great Depression. Did the ascendance of the American imperium start with the end of the world war in 1945? Or should we date its origin, less precisely, during the thirty years of war that engulfed the world starting in 1914?

In the conventional wisdom, the defeat of Nazi Germany and Japan in 1945 was a great victory for the two superpowers, the United States and the Soviet Union. The intense political and ideological competition between these two states made the international system bipolar. During the next four decades, the logic of bipolarity and nuclear weapons would prevent a cold war from turning hot. Linked intimately to this postwar settlement were two other developments. The first was decolonization. Scores of new states emerged from rapidly crumbling European empires. Nationalism and the prospect of national economic development were the most important issues on their political agendas. Frequently, however, these new states also became battlegrounds for the conflict between democratic capitalism and authoritarian socialism. The second development occurred among the industrial states of the West, which, in a telling twist of geographic terminology, came to include Japan. On which terms and

---

1. The following section draws on Hemmer and Katzenstein 2002.
2. Acheson 1969.

under which conditions were the defeated Axis powers to be integrated into the bipolar system?

An alternative view denies that new world orders spring to life overnight. Rather, they emerge gradually as the result of political struggles among domestic and international coalitions, institutions, and competing purposes. From this vantage point, the rise of American power dates back to choices the United States made during the Great Depression. Those choices deeply affected the reconstruction of the international system after 1945. In the 1930s, economic liberalism at home and political isolationism abroad were orthodoxies that no longer promised to solve pressing problems. Government intervention and internationalism did. The end of World War II was clearly a dramatic moment, but the American imperium took shape as the result of events that started in the early 1930s and ended with massive rearmament after the outbreak of the Korean War. The American imperium rested not on one coherent doctrine but on a set of contested ideas—more or less liberalism or intervention, more or less isolationism or internationalism, more or less bilateralism or multilateralism—that competing political coalitions brought into play and adjusted to the practicalities of politics at particular times.

We do not have to choose between these two historical interpretations. What matters is that by the mid-1950s the United States had succeeded in creating in Europe and Asia a strong anti-Communist, cross-regional coalition to balance against the Soviet Union and China. In an open international system, the United States enjoyed a preponderance of power in relations with its European and Asian allies. Germany in Europe, and Japan and Asia, were the two most important staging areas for the cold war. And porous regionalism made Europe and Asia the sites where the American imperium reached its fullest maturation.

Germany, seen as a potential cause of World War III, was at the core of the cold war. In 1945 neither Soviet nor U.S. decision makers recognized the existence of a clear bipolar system. Instead, they saw a variety of possible configurations of power. Europe figured prominently in their calculations, with the possibility that it might emerge as a third power containing a revived Germany and thus decisively affecting the geostrategic balance. Competition between the two superpowers occurred in a system that was latently tripolar. In this situation, the United States did not follow a unilateral, isolationist strategy, devoting all its resources to strengthening its own military power. Instead, it pursued in Europe a multilateral strategy that invested heavily in allies.[3]

In the early postwar years, U.S. decision makers saw Europe threatened primarily by its own weakness rather than by Soviet aggression. U.S. policy used European fears of abandonment to further a reconstruction of Europe that included Germany. U.S. policy was not premised on one grand design. It was instead based on an evolution of schemes that reflected the ups and downs of various coalitions in Washington at different times. In different ways, all aimed

3. Ikenberry 2001, 163–214. McAllister 2002, 15.

at a postwar European order that would deviate from the autarkic order that had caused depression and war in the 1930s and 1940s. The Atlantic Charter of 1941, and all the schemes that followed from it, were directed not only against the New Order of Nazi Germany and Japan's Co-Prosperity Sphere, but also against the British Commonwealth and the system of imperial preferences. American officials aimed to build a core of stable, open industrial democracies. In the end, American policy prevailed, but not without two important concessions to its European allies: a managed rather than a fully liberal economic order; and a binding security commitment with U.S. ground troops in Europe rather than the traditional maritime strategy of offshore balancing. Both concessions were essential to making the anti-Communist alliance in Europe endure.

To the consternation of a British government reluctant to fully embrace free trade, Secretary of State Hull never flagged in his insistence on fully liberalized international trade. The U.S. Congress proved to be stronger than Britain. Because the majority of U.S. senators believed that the new institution would wield excessive powers, the Congress eventually failed to ratify a treaty establishing the International Trade Organization. The GATT, successor to the ITO, was a stealth operation established by executive decree. There was more room for compromise between Britain and the United States over the postwar monetary order. Instead of relying on the free play of market forces, international monetary relations were to be managed by governments. In the negotiations leading up to the Bretton Woods agreement in July 1944, Britain's John Maynard Keynes and the American Harry Dexter White agreed on the need for negotiated, orderly changes in exchange rates, in a system that abolished exchange rate controls and restrictive financial practices.

On other key issues, including the provision of new international currencies and the obligations of countries that have a surplus to make credit available to bring the system back into balance, the eventual compromise tilted more in favor of White than Keynes. The Bretton Woods system avoided the reliance on domestic deflation and high unemployment that had characterized the nineteenth-century gold standard. The liberalism of the system was "embedded" in a political commitment to protect the domestic economy from external shocks.[4] "Even for the United States, where domestic stabilization measures remained the least comprehensive and the most contested," writes John Ruggie, "the international edifice of the open door had to accommodate the domestic interventionism of the New Deal."[5]

The second concession was on military issues. The United States resisted the idea of permanently stationing U.S. ground troops in Europe. Presidents Roosevelt, Truman, and Eisenhower all hoped that a revived Western Europe would be able to contain both the Soviet Union and Germany, permitting the

4. Ruggie 1982, 1991. Block 1977.
5. Ruggie 1996, 37.

United States to play the more comfortable role of offshore balancer. At the end of World War II, the Joint Chiefs of Staff did not even consider locating long-term bases in Europe.[6] Indeed, punitive policies aiming to contain Germany's future prosperity, as in the Morgenthau plan, and expansive support for various schemes of European integration were both rooted in the assumption that the long-term basing of U.S. troops in Europe was unthinkable. In his realist vision of a postwar order on the European continent, George Kennan hoped for a timely scaling back of what he viewed as the unnatural depth of U.S. engagement in European affairs that had resulted from World War II. On this point, Kennan and Dean Acheson agreed. European integration, they hoped, would solve the German problem.[7] In what Geir Lundestad calls an empire "by integration," the crucial motive for American policy was the need to integrate West Germany with its European partners in general and France in particular.[8]

Each of the major European states had its own reasons to resist U.S. policy.[9] Britain wanted to maintain its special relationship with the United States and on economic, political, and ideological grounds objected to the creation of a European third force. France was deeply worried about its capacity to contain Germany and the Soviet Union in an integrating Europe—it lacked the resources to defend its crumbling empire while at the same time building a new Europe. Long-term U.S. military engagement in Europe was thus an important objective of French policy. Acquiescence in German reconstruction became a bargaining chip for France and Britain to secure a long-term U.S. commitment to the defense of Western Europe. That commitment was eventually forthcoming in meetings culminating in the 1949 North Atlantic Treaty. But even then, the United States shied away from an unrestricted pledge: the Senate approved the treaty with the express provision that its power to declare war not be altered, despite the collective defense provision contained in the treaty's Article V. The Korean War and the Soviet bomb changed all that. German rearmament and U.S. long-term commitment became the political foundation for putting the "O" into the NAT.[10] The United States became a reluctant partner in a set of institutions that in subsequent decades would often enable and occasionally restrain the exercise of its anti-Communist policy.

In Asia, at about the same time, the U.S. government built an anti-Communist alliance under very different regional circumstances. Rebuilding and stabilizing Southeast Asia, the Truman administration hoped, would both contain China and restore Japan. Like Germany in Europe, Japan was the linchpin of an anti-Communist coalition. The victory of the Chinese Communists in 1949 consolidated the U.S. commitment to Japan. For Japan to prosper economi-

6. Larson 1985, 3.
7. McAllister 2002, 16–20.
8. Lundestad 1998, 22.
9. Trachtenberg 1999, 66–91.
10. Trachtenberg 1999, 95–145.

cally required U.S. involvement in Southeast Asia, an area historically of no more than marginal U.S. interest. Southeast Asia was important for two additional reasons. It was in the grip of a revolution in which nationalism and Communist insurgency were closely intertwined—and indeed the French war in Indochina was draining resources that France badly needed for the economic and political reconstruction of Europe. And Southeast Asia offered some hope, especially in the case of British Malaya, for reducing Britain's stifling dollar debt through a triangular trade involving the United States, Britain, and Malaya that would discriminate against U.S. producers.

U.S. aspirations in Asia were increasingly put to the question. U.S. policymakers wanted a united, non-Communist China accessible to trade and investment from the United States, Europe, and Japan. With Communist victory imminent, Truman and his advisors redoubled their efforts to maintain a strong presence through rebuilding Japan. At least since 1946, this had been an important policy objective, and the "loss" of China made it imperative. The Truman administration had aimed to reform Japan wholesale by punishing those top leaders, with the exception of the emperor, guilty of waging pre-emptive war. The U.S. occupation hoped to reform politics by replacing the country's top political leadership, dismembering military and economic conglomerates as the two institutions central to Japan's war machine, encouraging the unionization of workers, and making Japan part of a liberal international economy.

By late 1947, however, the reformist impetus of U.S. policy had taken a reverse course. Economic recovery now became more important than political reform, for Japan was to take China's place as the region's economic hub and the most important bulwark of anti-Communism. Of the 1,197 subsidiaries of Japan's conglomerates recommended for deconcentration in May 1947, two years later only nineteen had actually been reorganized. By May 1948, the political purge of more than two hundred thousand of Japan's leaders, implicated in Japan's policies in the 1930s, had been suspended. By 1952, only 8,700 individuals remained on the purge list; 139 formerly purged politicians had been elected to the Diet.[11] Japanese reparation payments ceased in 1949. U.S. economic aid was increased, in the hope that exports to Asia would kick-start Japan's economic revival and lessen its dependence on U.S. markets.

How to accomplish American objectives was far from clear.[12] Policymakers wavered between policy approaches with different implications for an area that stretched from Pakistan in the west to Japan in the east, as well as for the particularities of different countries in a highly diverse Southeast Asia. Furthermore, many in Southeast Asia remembered only too well Japan's military aggression and the brutality of its occupation. Finally, the intensification of economic ties between Japan and Southeast Asia would require bilateral, prefer-

---

11. Rotter 1987, 39, 41.
12. Rotter 1987, 46–48, 108–11.

ential trading arrangements that might turn out to have an uncanny resemblance to Japan's failed Co-Prosperity Sphere, which the United States had opposed strongly in the 1940s. Yet Communist victory in mainland China required action.

Nationalist liberation movements and Communist insurgency had created revolutionary conditions throughout the region, resulting in war in Vietnam, Indonesia, and Malaysia. The anticolonial sentiments voiced in the Atlantic Charter had led to U.S. withdrawal from the Philippines in 1946. Throughout the 1940s, that sentiment remained stridently opposed to the major imperialist powers in the region, specifically Britain, France, and the Netherlands. At the moment of Japanese surrender, and before the former imperialist powers could return, nationalist elites seized power throughout Southeast Asia. In the ensuing months and years, an uneasy truce quickly gave way to civil wars. The United States adhered for a while to an ambivalent policy that sought to avoid choosing between sticking by its principles to support various independence movements and backing the repressive and futile military campaigns of France in Indochina and the Netherlands in Indonesia. But to assemble a powerful anti-Communist coalition in the region, the Truman administration in the end chose to support colonialism over nationalism.

Although the combustible mixture of nationalism and communism varied from country to country, by late 1949 U.S. policymakers had articulated a rudimentary domino theory for East and Southeast Asia. The loss of China and fear of a French defeat in Indochina made it imperative to stem what U.S. officials increasingly viewed as successful Soviet expansion on a worldwide scale. Communist subversion in Southeast Asia and Japan was a particularly nefarious and threatening prospect that required a vigorous response. Between the middle of 1949 and the spring of 1950, several events occurred that galvanized the United States to action. The Soviet Union exploded its first nuclear bomb, ending the U.S. nuclear monopoly. In China, the U.S.-supported Kuomintang regime collapsed, and the Communists seized power, raising the specter of increased insurgency throughout Southeast Asia. And the economic recoveries in Europe and Japan were stalling. In the face of these developments, the United States chose to take a stand. When North Korean troops attacked South Korea on June 25, 1950, the Truman administration responded quickly and forcefully, in line with the anti-Communist policy that it had adopted over the previous years. American ground troops were sent into battle, and previously limited aid programs for the region were ramped up quickly. The economic stimulus of the Korean War proved to be decisive for the economic revitalization of Japan and Asia.

The war helped consolidate the sense that Europe's and Asia's fortunes were closely linked. Europe's economic stabilization in 1947–49 had pointed to the advantages of a triangular trade that might strengthen the sterling bloc's access to the U.S. market, thus bolstering Britain's sagging economic fortunes. The North Korean attack on South Korea was perceived to be even more serious

than Britain's economic problems, raising the prospect of all-out war in Asia
and Europe. In short, anticommunism reduced cross-regional political slack in
the U.S. imperium.

Multilateralism in Europe, Bilateralism in Asia

The anti-Communist alliance that the United States assembled in the late
1940s and early 1950s took different institutional forms in Europe and in
Asia.[13] Economic openness, political pluralism, and a broad range of legal institutions defined the imperium into which the United States attempted to
bind others, while committing itself with considerable caution. Yet the wide
range of views entertained in Washington makes it clear that the architects of
America's evolving imperium "were trying to build more than one type of
order."[14]

Different policy objectives, geopolitical realities, and material capabilities
made U.S. policy favor different institutional forms in Europe and Asia—forms
that were shaped also by policymakers' differing levels of identification with
these newly constructed regions. In dealing with its North Atlantic partners,
the United States preferred to operate on a multilateral basis, and with its
Southeast Asian partners, in bilateral settings. U.S. policymakers saw in their
European allies relatively equal members of a shared community. Potential
Asian allies, in contrast, were inferior and part of an alien community. Broadly
speaking, the United States was willing to create in Europe multilateral institutions that would restrain U.S. power in the short term only to enhance that
power in the long term. It was eager to build bilateral institutions in Asia, where
the concept of binding institutions did not seem as attractive as locking in the
advantages of the preponderant power of the United States through bilateral
relations.

The difference is blatant in the case of Japan, South Korea, and the Philippines, each of which was tied to the United States through a bilateral defense
treaty. A multilateral arrangement comparable to NATO, the Southeast Asia
Treaty Organization (SEATO) is also very revealing. Although signed by several states, SEATO was not multilateral in the same sense as NATO.[15] First, the
language of the treaty commitment was much weaker. Instead of the NATO
commitment to collective defense, which considers an attack on one as an attack on all, Article IV of the SEATO treaty merely classifies such an attack as a
threat to peace and safety. Furthermore, in SEATO the United States made it
clear that it retained its prerogative to act bilaterally or unilaterally. This was
formalized in the Rusk-Thanat joint statement of 1962, in which the United
States stressed that its commitment to Thailand "does not depend upon prior

13. Press-Barnathan 2003.
14. Ikenberry 2001, 184.
15. Ruggie 1997, 105.

agreement of all the other parties to the treaty, since the obligation is individual as well as collective."[16]

Organizationally, the differences were just as apparent. SEATO lacked a unified military command and specifically allocated national forces. Furthermore, any actions taken under SEATO auspices were handled individually by the member states and not by the institution as a whole.[17] U.S. policymakers had contemplated an Asian mutual security organization, which many prospective Asian members favored, but the United States remained adamantly opposed to using NATO as a model.[18] It even discouraged the use of the acronym SEATO, fearing unwanted comparisons. The lack of a Northeast Asia Treaty Organization (NEATO), Donald Emmerson argues, "cannot be explained by any dearth of perceived enemies in that part of the Pacific. The answer lies rather in the original distances and disparities—spatial, historical, economic, and cultural—between the United States and its anti-Communist Northeast Asian allies."[19]

An important reason for this difference in institutional form was prevailing perceptions of power and status in world politics. U.S. officials believed, quite correctly, that despite the reduction in capabilities inflicted by World War II, their European allies would soon regain their strength, whereas their Asian allies would remain permanently weak. Measured in relative terms, U.S. power after 1945 was much greater in Asia than in Europe. In 1950, the combined GNP of the four major European states equaled 39 percent of that of the United States; in 1965, the combined GNP of the seven major East and Southeast states was only 15.9 percent of U.S. GNP.[20] It was not in the interest of the United States to create institutions in Asia that would constrain Washington's ability to make independent decisions. Nor was it in the interest of subordinate states in Asia-Pacific to enter institutions in which they had minimal control, while foregoing opportunities for free riding and the reduction of dependence. Status also mattered. Europe was the home of the traditional great powers in world politics. Most Southeast Asian states in the late 1940s were only at the threshold of gaining full national sovereignty.

The military and civilian leaderships in the United States were in general agreement that Southeast Asia was less important and less threatened than Europe. In Asia, the primary issue for the United States was fighting Communist insurgencies. In Europe, NATO was designed to hold off a massive Soviet offensive. The variety of the internal subversive threats faced by different Southeast Asian states made a "one-size-fits-all" multilateral defense arrangement like

16. Rusk and Thanat 1962, 498–99.
17. Modelski 1962, 38–39. Webb 1962, 66.
18. Lundestad 1999, 208. Kim 1965, 65–66.
19. Emmerson 1993, 22.
20. It would increase, on the strength of Japan's economic ascendance, to 79.8 percent by 1989. Crone 1993, 503, and 510 n. 7.

NATO's inappropriate. In one of the few references to SEATO in his memoirs, President Eisenhower approvingly quotes Churchill's belief that "since sectors of the SEATO front were so varied in place and conditions, he [Churchill] felt it best to operate nationally where possible."[21]

Power, status, and threat perceptions were important, but the different forms of alliance politics in Asia and Europe were also rooted in the self-conception of the United States, which identified more with Europe, less with Asia. Once the North Atlantic was conceived of as a region, putting the United States in a grouping of roughly equal states with which it readily identified, the adoption of multilateral principles came quite naturally. As British foreign minister Ernest Bevin put it, bilateral relations imposed by the strongest power—as with the Soviets in Eastern Europe—were "not in keeping with the spirit of Western civilization, and if we are to have an organism in the West it must be a spiritual union . . . it must contain all the elements of freedom for which we all stand."[22] American policymakers agreed, believing that the Europeans deserved, and could be trusted with, the additional power conferred by a multilateral institution. The United States did not apply the same principles when it came to organizing the newly created Southeast Asian region. Southeast Asia was thought of by American policymakers as a region composed of alien and, in many ways, inferior actors; bilateralism followed naturally. U.S. policymakers did not believe that Southeast Asian states could be trusted with the increased influence a multilateral institution would offer; nor was there any sense that these states deserved the recognition such a structure would bring.

On what basis did the United States identify with Europe, and why did it not identify with Asia? U.S. officials typically referred to religion and democratic values as the bedrock of a North Atlantic community. They also mentioned a common race, though less often—perhaps because Nazi Germany's genocidal policies had thoroughly delegitimated racial concepts in European political discourse.[23] Perceived affinities reinforced the political trust rooted in democratic political institutions, the "we-feeling" and "mutual responsiveness" that Karl Deutsch and his associates have described as central ingredients for the emergence of a North Atlantic security community.[24] In the case of Asia, such affinities and trust were absent; religion and democratic values were shared with only a few countries; and race was invoked as a powerful force separating the United States from Asia. The American preferences for multilateral or bilateral security arrangements followed also from these different beliefs and sentiments.

The emergence of a North Atlantic region followed a dramatic change in the prevalent image of America's place in the world. Before the war, Alan Henrikson argues, maps were typically drawn with the United States in the center,

21. Eisenhower 1963, 368.
22. Jackson 2001, 428–29.
23. Horne 1999, 454–59. Hunt 1987, 161–62.
24. Deutsch et al. 1957.

surrounded by two oceans. However, the wartime efforts to resupply Great Britain and later to transport large numbers of troops to Europe caused a change in cartography. Maps appeared that put the Atlantic in the center, with the United States and Europe positioned on either side.[25] The shift to a "North" Atlantic focus was given a boost after 1945, when the Soviet Union pressured Norway to sign a defense pact. Had the Soviet Union established a zone of influence over Norway, it would have gained a large window on the Atlantic and thus exposed Europe's northern flank.[26]

The creation of the new geographic category of "North Atlantic" also served clear political ends, and was in some ways the product of political calculation. Martin Folly, for example, argues that "the idea of a North Atlantic system was a stroke of genius" on the part of Ernest Bevin.[27] In the early 1940s, the British government embarked on a political campaign aimed at preventing U.S. disengagement from Europe after the end of the war. Bevin recognized that the United States would hesitate to join a "European" alliance but would feel much more comfortable talking about sea-lanes, access to bases, and a "North Atlantic" alliance. A North Atlantic focus also meshed nicely with the U.S. military's concern with "stepping stones" across the Atlantic. Reliant on bases and stopping-off points for the transportation of men and equipment, the armed services' emphasis on the importance of Iceland, Greenland, and the Azores also put the Atlantic in the foreground.[28] In U.S. domestic politics, a North Atlantic community promised to be an easier sell than a European alliance to an electorate and a Congress wary of European entanglements.[29] Moreover, the concept of "community" established a basis for political identification that transcended narrow military-strategic considerations.

In 1948, official and public discourse regarding Europe shifted suddenly. Before March of that year, a possible transatlantic alliance was invariably discussed under the rubric of a European or a Western European alliance. Afterward, however, the focus of official discourse shifted radically, to an Atlantic or North Atlantic treaty system and community. Public discourse, as represented in the coverage of the *New York Times*, underwent a similar transformation in late 1948. In the editorial cartoons offered in the "Week in Review" section, for example, the geographical opponent of the Soviet Union changed from Europe, to Western Europe, to the West, and finally by December 1948 to the North Atlantic and NATO. The sudden emergence of this "North Atlantic" focus demonstrates that new regional identities can emerge quickly when political circumstances are ripe, bringing together political entrepreneurship, material power, and an idea that reverberates. Considering the rapidity of this shift, it is noteworthy that State Department officials insisted that signatories of

25. Henrikson 1975.
26. Henrikson 1980.
27. Folly 1988, 68.
28. Lundestad 1990, 251. Henrikson 1980, 19.
29. Kaplan 1984, 2–3, 7–8, 10, 31, 41–42, 52, 70, 78, 115–17.

the treaty did not invent the North Atlantic region. They maintained that the treaty merely codified a political community that had been in existence for centuries and that provided the basis for mutual identification. In the words of Dean Acheson, NATO was "the product of at least three hundred and fifty years of history, perhaps more."[30] Yet for all this stress on the long history of the region, prior to 1948, with the exception of a few references to the International Civil Aviation Organization, State Department officials had never talked about a North Atlantic region.

Regional labels were also problematic in Asia. Although the term "Southeast Asia" occurs occasionally in French and German geographic and ethnographic studies in the nineteenth century, the currency of the term increased dramatically only with the Pacific War. It designated the area south of China that fell to Japanese occupation.[31] The private correspondence between Roosevelt and Churchill during World War II reflects a gradual emergence of this regional designation. A first mention came in early 1941, when Roosevelt wrote about Japan's proposal to forego any armed advance into the "Southeastern Asiatic" area provided the United States made a similar pledge. Roosevelt further explained to Churchill that the U.S. response was to simply warn Japan against taking any military moves in "South-East Asia."[32]

The United States decided to concentrate first on the European theater, and discussion of Southeast Asia faded. When attention shifted back to the Asian theater, the question of what to call this region remained undecided. Churchill wrote in June 1943 that it was time for the allies to think more about "the South East Asia (or Japan) front," and he recommended the creation of a new command for that region. Later, Churchill reiterated this call, but now denoted it as "a new command for East Asia." Here, practical political calculations heavily influenced the naming process, as Roosevelt rejected Churchill's call for a unified East Asian command as likely alienating Chiang Kai-shek, who controlled the China theater. To avoid such offense, Roosevelt moved the focus back to "South-East Asia." Churchill accepted Roosevelt's worries and agreed that "perhaps it would be desirable to give the new command the title of 'South-East Asia' instead of 'East Asia.'"[33] At the Quebec conference in August 1943, the United States and Great Britain agreed to create the Southeast Asian Command. SEAC's area of responsibility corresponded roughly to what today is conventionally called Southeast Asia.

After the Communist victory in China, the hands-off policy that the United States had adopted after the Pacific War shifted quickly. In Andrew Rotter's words, the Truman administration "'discovered' Southeast Asia at the intersection of its policy toward China, Japan, Britain, and France."[34] Bolstering pro-

30. Acheson 1949, 385.
31. Williams 1976, 3. Warshaw 1975, 1.
32. Kimball 1984, vol. 1, 275–76.
33. Kimball 1984, vol. 2, 248, 263, 275–77, 282.
34. Rotter 1987, 5.

Western forces in what they now conceived of as a region, U.S. policymakers hoped, would help contain China, restore Japan, strengthen Britain, and halt the bleeding of France. "American policy makers," writes Rotter, "no longer regarded Southeast Asia as a disparate jumble of unrelated states, but as a region that had to be tied to the most important independent nations of the Far East and Western Europe."[35] Established in September of 1954, SEATO extends this perception of a region and the political attempt to tie the region to the rest of the world. Only two of SEATO's members, Thailand and the Philippines, were geographically part of Southeast Asia. The other six members (Australia, France, Great Britain, New Zealand, Pakistan, and the United States) were outside the region as conventionally understood.

Such tensions between geography and identity existed also in Europe. One of the most striking aspects of discussions of the formation of NATO was the pervasive identification of the United States with Europe, exemplified by the strident assertion that the North Atlantic already existed as a political community: the treaty merely formalized this preexisting community of shared ideals and interest.[36] As W. Averell Harriman put it, "There is a spiritual emotion about that . . . freemen are standing shoulder to shoulder."[37] Even while criticizing the Truman administration's overall policies, the columnist Walter Lippmann argued that the members of the "Atlantic Community" are "natural allies of the United States." The nucleus of this community, according to Lippmann, is "distinct and unmistakable," based on geography, religion, and history.[38] The rhetoric of America's European allies similarly referred to a "spiritual federation of the West," protecting "Western bastion[s]," "the virtues and values of our own civilization," and how the "community of Atlantic nations is based upon a common heritage of moral and cultural values."[39] This sentiment found ultimate expression in the preamble to the NATO treaty, which affirmed the determination of members "to safeguard the freedom, common heritage and civilization of their peoples."

Mutual identification had at times undeniably racial components. Assistant Secretary of State Will Clayton hoped that NATO could be the first step in the formation of an Atlantic federal union. In testimony, Clayton explicitly linked his support of closer relations to racial as well as cultural factors: "My idea would be that in the beginning the union would be composed of all countries that have our ideas and ideals of freedom, and that are composed of the white race."[40] The U.S. reaction to the formation of SEATO was starkly different. Indeed, it is the differences, not the commonalties, in civilization, race, ethnicity, religion, and historical memories that led to strong doubts about the

35. Rotter 1987, 165.
36. Hampton 1995.
37. U.S. Senate 1949, 206.
38. Jackson 2001, 320–21.
39. Jackson 2001, 427–28. Gheciu forthcoming, chaps. 2 and 7.
40. U.S. Senate 1949, 380.

contributions these states could make to an Asian alliance. Even as colonialism was ending, the colonial mind-set remained strong. There is a strong note of condescension in many of the U.S. discussions of SEATO, one that did not exist with regard to NATO. Many U.S. policymakers did not see Asians as ready to enjoy the trust and the power that the United States had offered to European states.

This downplaying of the importance of Asia and the skill of Asians reached the highest levels in the State Department. While Dean Acheson was secretary of state, he visited Europe at least eleven times, but he claimed to be too busy to make even a single trip to East Asia. With the outbreak of war on the Korean Peninsula in June 1950, Acheson decided to actively support U.S. involvement in the war, primarily to demonstrate U.S. credibility to its new European allies. Walt Rostow attributed Acheson's eventual opposition to U.S. involvement in Vietnam to the former secretary of state's Eurocentric worldview.[41]

This outlook stemmed in large part from the personal backgrounds of the men who dominated U.S. foreign policy after World War II. They were drawn from elite New England prep schools, Ivy League universities, and Wall Street businesses and law firms, the so-called Eastern establishment, which was then in its heyday. These men, alternating between their private and public sector careers, switching positions "like lines in a hockey game changing on the fly," ventured into the post-1945 world with a Western European bias.[42] Having "grown up and succeeded in a world marked by European power, Third World weakness, and nearly ubiquitous racial segregation," these men accepted such distinctions between Europeans and others without question.[43] Indeed, when they attempted to explain what they saw as the alien behavior of the Soviet Union, they invariably stressed the "Asiatic" or "Oriental" nature of Stalin's regime.[44] As Senator James Eastland of Mississippi viewed the nascent cold war, it was a struggle between "eastern and western civilization," a battle between "the Oriental hordes and a western civilization 2,000 years old."[45]

There existed, of course, some segments in American society more heavily involved in Asia than in Europe. Represented mostly by the midwestern and Pacific wings of the Republican Party, these individuals had called for an "Asia-first" strategy after Pearl Harbor and continued to criticize U.S. foreign policy for paying too little attention to Asia. Some of the attention they gave to Asia was driven by a desire to criticize the Europe-focused Eastern establishment that dominated the Democratic Party, the presidency, and the foreign policy apparatus of the U.S. government. A large part, however, was driven by the commercial links that western businesses had forged across the Pacific and the

41. Isaacson and Thomas 1986, 698.
42. Isaacson and Thomas 1986, 428, 19–31.
43. Borstelmann 1999, 552.
44. Borstelmann 1999, 552–53. Isaacson and Thomas 1986, 306, 320.
45. Jackson 2001, 293.

large number of American missionaries that had gone to Asia.[46] Unlike the
Eastern establishment, these counterelites did not control the levers of power
within the American imperium, and Eisenhower's victory over Taft in the 1952
Republican presidential primaries solidified the triumph of the Europeanist
wing within the Republican Party. But even if they had won, the Asia-firsters
were not willing to pursue a multilateral path in the region. Their interactions
with Asians, especially as part of Christian missionary work, did not lead to the
development of an identity with Asian peoples that could serve as a basis for a
multilateral institution. Asians were "barbarian but obedient," and Asia was "a
region of vast resources and opportunities, populated by dutiful and cringing
peoples who followed white leadership."[47] The goal was not cooperation
among equals but unilateral U.S. dominance.

This is not to argue that the difference was one of day and night, or of white
and nonwhite, for that matter. After signing a bilateral treaty with Japan, John
Foster Dulles explained that there could be no Asian equivalent of NATO, but
he included Japan and the Philippines on a list of nations with which the
United States shared a common destiny.[48] The discrepancy indicates the varying strengths of America's post–World War II identifications. Although Japan
and the Philippines were outside what Dulles saw as a Western "community of
race, religion and political institutions," shared historical experiences (the war
and subsequent occupation of Japan, the colonization of the Philippines) were
important. Identification is a matter of degree, not an all-or-nothing proposi-
tion. If race, religion, and shared political institutions helped to put America's
European allies in a class ahead of its Asian allies, shared history helped put
some Asian allies ahead of others.

It is important to note that these differences in identification and in the policies the United States followed in Asia and Europe after World War II were not
an aberration. In many ways, they continued American wartime attitudes that
had led to a "Europe- first" strategy; the internment of Japanese-Americans; a
greater degree of hatred toward America's Asian enemies than toward its European opponents; greater attention in the popular press to Japanese atrocities in China than to German atrocities in Eastern Europe and the Soviet
Union; and the basic decision, taken even before the war in Europe was over,
to use the atomic bomb first in Japan, not against Germany. Indeed, there is a
long tradition in American foreign policy thinking of dividing the world into a
racial hierarchy, as Michael Hunt and Paul Kramer have argued, with Americans and British at the top, followed by other European peoples, and with
Asians, Latin Americans, and Africans further down the list.[49] The men in
charge of handling U.S. post–World War II foreign policy fit that mold.

46. Westerfield 1955, 240–68. Purifoy 1976, 49–73.
47. Cumings 1990, 96, 93, 79–97.
48. Dulles 1952, 183–84.
49. Hunt 1987, 46–91. Kramer 2002.

Franklin Roosevelt likened "the brown people of the East" to "minor children . . . who need trustees." Similarly, Harry Truman's private writings often lavished great praise on the British, while speaking dismissively of "Chinamen" and "Japs." President Eisenhower placed "the English-speaking peoples of the world" above all others; and as one of his advisers put it, "The Western world has somewhat more experience with the operations of war, peace, and parliamentary procedure than the swirling mess of emotionally super-charged Africans and Asiatics and Arabs that outnumber us."[50] With the passing of time, these overtly racial categories have become less prominent, replaced in recent years by allusions to cultural and civilizational values. Still, a hierarchical view of the world is at times still recognizable in current public debates.

Regional Consequences

The U.S. preference for a multilateral approach in Europe and a bilateral approach in Asia is due to a complex mix of political, material, institutional, and identity factors. Undeniable is the central fact that the different policies the United States adopted in the late 1940s had important institutional consequences for the evolution of European and Asian regionalism.

NATO and SEATO were both offspring of the cold war strategy of the United States. NATO succeeded in transforming the security relations of its members. Only the dramatic turn toward unilateralism in U.S. foreign policy after September 11, 2001, has called into question the transatlantic security community organized by NATO. In sharp contrast, SEATO remained a paper tiger that passed from the scene in 1977 "with little fanfare and no sense of loss."[51] Indeed, since the end of the cold war, the absence of historically rooted, multilateral arrangements has made adaptation to political change more difficult in Asia than in Europe. Today, China and Japan remain cautious about formal institutions. China fears being trapped in institutions not of its own making, and Japan no longer needs formal institutions, as it did in the 1960s, to overcome its diplomatic isolation.

In Europe, by contrast, the U.S. government was firmly committed to the principle of multilateralism. For different reasons, the European states were themselves very interested in committing a reluctant United States to long-term military and political engagement in Europe. NATO became a historically unique institution that evolved from an alliance to a security community with a far-reaching integration of military forces in times of peace. The process of German unification was bargained over by a small number of governments, most of which had operated for decades within the context of well-established multilateral arrangements inside NATO and the European Union. Without that institutional context, the process would have been more difficult. John

50. Hunt 1987, 162–64. See also Lauren 1988.
51. Kaplan 1981, 15.

Ruggie concluded in the early 1990s that "whereas today the potential to move beyond balance-of-power politics in its traditional form exists in Europe, a reasonably stable balance is the best that one can hope to achieve in the Asia-Pacific region."[52]

Yet in the 1990s, an incipient multilateralism began to appear in Asian-Pacific security arrangements. On questions of both internal and external security, that incipient multilateralism and an entrenched bilateralism do not contradict each other.[53] Personal relations provide a link between the two sorts of arrangements.[54] In institutional terms, Amitav Acharya speaks of an interlocking "spiderweb" of bilateralism that compensates in part for the absence of multilateral security cooperation in the Asia-Pacific.[55] In the 1960s and 1970s, for example, anticommunism provided a political base that allowed for joint police operations and the right to cross borders in "hot pursuit" of Communist guerillas, for example, between Malaysia and Indonesia as well as Malaysia and Thailand.

What was true of internal security in the 1960s and 1970s was true of external security in the 1990s. Two crises involving North Korea's nuclear weapons program illustrate, as Michael Stankiewicz observes, "the increasing complementarity between bilateral and multilateral diplomatic efforts in Northeast Asia."[56] Improvement in various bilateral relations in Asia-Pacific is fostering a gradual strengthening of multilateral security arrangements. In April 1999, for example, Japan, South Korea, and the United States created the Trilateral Coordination and Oversight Group to orchestrate policy toward North Korea. And the negotiations between the United States and North Korea in 2003 also occurred in a multilateral setting provided by the Chinese hosts. U.S. policy has also changed, as it is the U.S. military that seeks to encourage multilateral meetings among professional military officers. Moreover, some Asian governments seek to support multilateralism for their own specific reasons. Through the renegotiation of military base arrangements, Singapore, for example, has sought to ensure that the U.S. Navy remain engaged in the maritime Asia-Pacific—since the late 1980s a political hedge for Singapore against China's and Japan's political aspirations and economic weight. Historical foundations inimical to Asian multilateralism do not constrain political possibilities for all times. They do, however, shape what is considered feasible and desirable.

European regionalism evolved along multilateral lines to support collective decisions. By the late 1950s, a small number of European governments had agreed to submit core economic sectors, including iron and steel, atomic energy, and agriculture, to collective decisions. In subsequent decades in the area

52. Ruggie 1993, 4.
53. Capie, Evans, and Fukushima 1998, 7–8, 16–17, 60–62, IV/3–4, 7. Evans 2004.
54. Bredow 1996, 109–10.
55. Acharya 1990, 1–12.
56. Stankiewicz 1998, 2.

of foreign trade, Western Europe's ability to submit to collective decisions
made it a powerful voice in what often turned into de facto bilateral negotiation sessions with the United States under the auspices of GATT and later the
WTO. Asian regionalism, by contrast, typically centered on a convergence of
interests in bilateral deals for the provision of some collective goods. Political
initiatives to create regional trade organizations in Asia, for example, typically
were bargaining chips, motivated more by international trade negotiations or
developments in other world regions than in the intrinsic interest of creating
trade institutions for the Asia-Pacific region. Bargaining interests were constrained by multilateral GATT norms, however, and these norms had a significant effect.[57] The foreign policy choices the United States made in the late
1940s had long-term consequences for the institutions that have shaped Europe's and Asia's regional orders.

The multilateral and bilateral mechanisms through which anti-Communist
coalitions in Europe and Asia were linked to the center of the American imperium also had a strong effect on Germany and Japan after 1945—both domestically and in their interactions with their regional partners. U.S.
occupation after 1945 brought about a political process of "creative destruction" in both countries.[58] In eliminating discredited elites and redirecting outmoded institutional practices, the U.S. government prepared the ground for
new political and economic institutions, in Germany more so than in Japan.
U.S. policies also set in motion processes that affected profoundly how German
and Japanese elites exercised power, domestically, in Europe and Asia, and in
the world at large.[59] What emerged from these policies, both imposed from
without and set free from within, were German and Japanese polities that were
fundamentally altered in some ways, moderately changed in others, and unre-
constructed in still others.

Ethnic Capitalism in Asian Market Networks

China and Japan are important centers of the new Asian regionalism, but in
ways that differ from the regionalism of Japan's Co-Prosperity Sphere of the
1930s and 1940s. The old regionalism emphasized autarky, the new one relies
on open networks. East Asia's regional networks are linked tightly to the world
at large. The region's leading dozen metropolitan areas account for about 80
to 90 percent of its international activities.[60] Currently, Asian regionalism takes
two different forms. Japanese capitalism is the result of indigenous economic
developments and a conscious political strategy, orchestrated jointly by government and business elites. At the regional level, by contrast, Chinese capi-

57. Aggarwal 1993, 1035–40. Crone 1993, 519–25.
58. Herrigel 2000, 341.
59. Herz 1983. Montgomery 1957. Moulton 1944.
60. Rohlen 2002, 8–9.

talism lacks both an integrated, indigenous political economy and a coherent political strategy. It is almost unlimited in its flexibility.[61]

Japan

Japan's economic insularity is partly a function of the relatively small number of Japanese living in Asia. More than one million overseas Chinese lived in Southeast Asia in the first half of the nineteenth century, a population that doubled between 1900 and the early 1930s.[62] There were about eight to ten million ethnic Chinese in Southeast Asia in 1945, about 5–6 percent of the total population.[63] Because of the long tradition of isolationism under the Tokugawa shogunate (1603–1868), corresponding figures for Japanese nationals were much smaller. The spontaneous movement to Southeast Asia of marginal groups in Japanese society, "prostitutes, pimps, and subsequently, shop owners, clerks, and plantations workers," increased in the early decades of the twentieth century from only 2,800 in 1907 to 36,600 in 1936.[64] Local consulates, local bosses, local Japanese associations, and eventually the spread of Japan's uniform education system beyond national borders, all served to "re-Nipponize" Japanese colonial communities throughout Southeast Asia. At the same time, overseas Japanese relied on Chinese business networks to become competitive, especially in retail trade.[65] In 1945, the Japanese population in Southeast Asia dropped to the vanishing point. Japan's postwar relations with Asia were built on these historical connections and the many legacies of its military occupation, especially of Southeast Asia.

In recent decades, Japan's approach to Asia has been shaped by Kaname Akamatsu's flying geese theory of industrial growth and senescence.[66] Akamatsu's work on industrial change was based on a conception of Asian markets in which governments were directly involved in the flow of trade, investment, and aid. Saburo Okita, deeply influenced by Akamatsu, became head of the research division of Japan's Economic Planning Agency in 1955. Following Akamatsu's basic insight, Okita's plan for expanding Japanese exports focused on the unavoidable and hoped-for economic development of Asian economies. If Japan assisted that development, it would dispel historical animosities, divert attention from dangerous and wasteful political quarrels in Asia, enhance regional growth prospects, and create a more stable international environment that would be especially profitable for Japan's highly competitive capital goods sector.

This understanding of development provided a strong intellectual founda-

---

61. This section is adapted from Katzenstein 2000.
62. Hui 1995, 41, 143.
63. Hui 1995, 143–44.
64. Shiraishi and Shiraishi 1993, 7.
65. Hui 1995, 175–76.
66. Akamatsu 1961.

tion for Japan's Asia policy. Kiyoshi Kojima, Akamatsu's most distinguished and influential student, pursued in the 1960s the idea of creating a regional system in the Pacific area, one that would support regional economic integration through which Japan and its Asian neighbors would be indelibly linked. The "Pacific free trade area" that Kojima proposed in 1965 included the United States, Canada, Australia, and New Zealand. It was to be linked to an integrated region encompassing the Southeast Asian economies. Thus Japan would be connected to the advanced U.S. economy, on whose markets its exports depended, as well as to backward Southeast Asia, destined to absorb Japan's sunset industries.

Throughout the 1960s, the Japanese government proposed different schemes for the regional integration of Asia.[67] Informed by the same broad conception of Asia-Pacific as a region at the center of Japan's diplomacy in the 1980s and 1990s, these schemes were stymied by the other Asian states' deep suspicions regarding Japan. In reaction to the failures of the 1960s, Japan favored subsequently an informal and soft form of economic regionalism in Asia.[68] The Japanese government supported looser, nongovernmental institutions that either diffused Japanese influence through broad memberships or operated without Japanese participation.

The Pacific Basin Economic Council was the first such grouping. Created in 1968, it initially included businessmen from the five Pacific Rim countries and subsequently opened to many other Asian states. The "second-track" meetings that started in 1969 became a powerful lobby for integrating business in a broad Pacific area. A decade later, Foreign Minister Okita and Prime Minister Masayoshi Ohira, together with Australian prime minister Malcolm Fraser, convened a meeting that led to a nongovernmental international seminar (the Pacific Economic Cooperation Conference). It furthered a broad, market-based approach to Asia-Pacific. PECC embodied a regional idea requiring economic rather than political language. It reinforced rather than undermined national sovereignty. And it put economic development and the future ahead of political atonement for past transgressions. In contrast to the failed initiatives of the 1960s, these nongovernmental institutions emphasized personal networking and the exchange of information over political negotiations and binding decisions.

The sharp appreciation of the yen in 1985 started a surge of Japanese direct foreign investment and aid, setting the stage for a dramatic regional extension of Japanese firms and the emergence of vertical networks of subcontractors and affiliated firms. These groups moved quickly to recreate their accustomed supplier chains abroad, first in textiles and electronics, later in automobiles. Multinational corporations now control an unprecedented share of foreign trade in Asia. These chains link myriad hierarchically organized subcontractors and pro-

67. Katzenstein 1997a, 16–18.
68. Lincoln 1992, 13.

ducers of components in complex, multitiered arrangements that are either producer- or buyer-driven. Japanese foreign investment creates production chains and methods of technology transfer that have a deep impact on the trajectory of economic sectors, individual countries, and the entire Asian region.

Japan's growing economic enmeshment in northeast and Southeast Asia helped create an integrated Asian regional economy. It also reinforced a triangular trade structure in which Japanese exports and investments resulted in a rapid expansion of exports to Western markets, primarily the United States. Backed by a surge in foreign investment, trade, and the largest aid disbursements in the region, the Japanese government also sought to influence business and government abroad by exporting, with minor modifications and more or less successfully, its prized system of administrative guidance.[69] In the fall of 1990, Japan's Ministry of International Trade and Industry (MITI) set up organizations in various Asian countries to facilitate periodic meetings between local businessmen, Japanese investors, government officials, and MITI bureaucrats. These offices, it was hoped, would offer "local guidance."[70] Japanese aid programs also exported the Japanese practice of bid rigging (*dango*), common in Japan's domestic public work programs. In the words of David Arase, Japan's request-based approach to foreign aid allows "for graft and corruption while giving the Japanese government deniability."[71]

This regionwide Japanese system of political and economic power is especially adept at maximizing technological efficiencies, thus fortifying its economic and political leadership over an Asia that is developing in Japan's embrace. In Walter Hatch and Kozo Yamamura's view, increasing technological disparities translated in the 1980s and early 1990s into economic and political domination.[72] Asian regionalism is in this view little more than an international extension of Japan's approach to economic development. That approach has become institutionalized since the mid-1980s in far-flung regional production networks, supported by a broad array of trade, aid, and investment policies. This regional extension of Japanese practices is remarkably coherent across different domains of policy. It is, however, guided by no secret master plan. Rather, Japan's regionalization extends the useful life of domestic arrangements and practices that in the 1990s proved to be increasingly unworkable at home.[73]

Overseas Chinese

Chinese business in Asia-Pacific has witnessed vast changes since 1945, in particular the rise of developmental states and the growing importance of foreign

69. Hatch 2002, 187–94.
70. Lincoln 1993, 125, 127–28, 145–46, 178, 192.
71. Arase 1995, 161.
72. Hatch and Yamamura 1996, 97–129.
73. Hatch 2000.

multinationals. Chinese networks became important intermediaries connecting bureaucrats, the military, and politicians, on the one hand, and foreign
firms, on the other—both in the phase of import-substitution during the 1950s
and 1960s, and in the phase of export-led industrialization since then. The
core of Chinese business has remained family-controlled, but surrounding lay-
ers of equity-holding and political control were taken over by members of the
indigenous elite. In the late 1980s, the overseas Chinese economy in Southeast
Asia, Taiwan, and Hong Kong reportedly ranked fourth in the world in terms
of its "economic size."[74]

"Overseas Chinese" are people of ethnic Chinese descent living outside mainland China. Before the twentieth century, overseas Chinese lacked a homoge-
neous identity: hometowns, dialects, blood relationships, and guild associations
were far stronger than the sense of being Chinese. Eventually, a diaspora identity began to spread as a result of the revolutionary upheavals on the mainland.
As a social category, however, "overseas Chinese" unduly minimizes the wide diversity of the Chinese experience in different parts of Southeast Asia.

It is thus not surprising that the cultural characteristic typifying the Chinese
business diaspora is its enormous flexibility.[75] As the Chinese state crumbled
in the nineteenth and early twentieth centuries, Chinese capitalism spread
throughout Southeast Asia, creating networks that overcame political divisions
and state boundaries. As the Chinese political order declined and collapsed,
the main network nodes were safe havens on the Chinese coast, such as Shanghai, Canton, and other treaty ports, as well as overseas in Southeast Asia,
Hawaii, and the American West Coast.[76] Chinese regional networks covered finance, trade, and production.

The entrepreneur Gordon Wu suggests that the business organization of the
overseas Chinese is like a tray of sand. The grains are families, not individuals,
and they are held together by blood, trust, and obligation, not law, government,
or national solidarity.[77] Enterprise groups are family-centered, and the carriers
of Chinese capitalism typically are heads of households. In Taiwan, for example,
irrespective of their size and independence, family firms predominate over large
conglomerates.[78] In these firms "there is very little delegation of responsibility,
even to the sons . . . if the old man says go right, you go right."[79] Social ties are
not simply a matter of blood and marriage but rely on social norms that govern
specific relationships marked by submission, trust, loyalty, and predictability. Interpreted by the participants in both personal and instrumental terms, these social norms permeate the economic institutions of Chinese society, embed
economic activity, and produce distinctive forms of allocative efficiency.

74. Kao 1993, 24. Hui 1995, 16–17.
75. Hui 1995, 25; see also 287–88.
76. Hamilton 1996, 336.
77. Brick 1992, 5.
78. Hamilton and Kao 1990, 142, 147–48.
79. Quoted in Ridding and Kynge 1997, 13.

A survey of more than 150 overseas Chinese entrepreneurs in the early 1990s confirmed that, to their way of thinking, only family members can really be trusted.[80] Keeping strict control within the family typically constrains size and growth, especially of high-tech firms. Because of the strength of kinship, wealthy businessmen often invest in extensive networks of small firms covering numerous economic sectors or sector segments. Hence, economies of scale are achieved not from the acquisition of individual firms but from networks that connect small firms.[81] Statistically speaking, in terms of employment, Taiwanese business groups, not firms, are five to six times smaller than Japanese business groups, and they hold a less central position in the national economy.[82] Yet Chinese not Japanese tycoons dominate most of the economic life of Southeast Asia and Hong Kong. Chinese capitalism, Gary Hamilton argues, "is a nonpolitically based form of capitalism that is very flexible and readily adaptable to external economic opportunities."[83]

Chinese networks do not simply serve economic purposes. They are also social systems.[84] Formal overseas Chinese mutual aid associations are based on clan, province, or dialect (including Cantonese, Hakka, Hokkien, Chiu Chow). "These associations act like banks through which members can borrow money, trade information, recruit workers, and receive business introductions." And in the many situations where markets are underdeveloped and law is unpredictable, these networks are the preferred vehicle for complex business transactions that enforce the handshake deals on which much Chinese business is based.[85] Local, regional, and occupational groups and relational kinship systems, not the state, promoted the standardization and predictability that are necessary for the growth of economic transactions.

The existence of powerful overseas Chinese business networks left the government of the People's Republic of China with a difficult issue. The 1953 census listed the overseas Chinese as part of China's population, and the 1954 Constitution of the People's Republic of China provided for representation of all overseas Chinese in the National People's Congress. Soon thereafter, however, the PRC government abandoned the doctrine of *ius sanguinis* and left the choice of national citizenship to individual overseas Chinese. A bitter conflict with Indonesia over the discriminatory regulations with which Jakarta had targeted ethnic Chinese eventually pushed the government of the PRC to adopt a pragmatic policy in the late 1950s, altered only during the early years of the Cultural Revolution. That policy sacrificed the security interests of overseas Chinese to the foreign policy interests of the PRC.

Growing affluence and national policies of economic discrimination have

80. Kao 1993.
81. Hamilton 1996, 334–35.
82. Hamilton and Kao 1990, 140, 142.
83. Hamilton 1996, 335.
84. Esman 1986, 149.
85. Weidenbaum and Hughes 1996, 51–52.

caused the overwhelming majority of overseas Chinese to accept citizenship in their new homelands, claim equal rights there, and hope for nondiscriminatory policies. Within the first three decades after the Communist takeover of China, more than 80 percent of overseas Chinese had adopted the nationality of their Southeast Asian countries of residence.[86] The connotations of the term "Chinese" became more cultural than political, and "overseas Chinese" now denotes ethnic Chinese of Southeast Asian birth and nationality.[87] Today, more than 95 percent of overseas Chinese in Southeast Asia were born there.[88] Virtually all are firmly settled, if not fully assimilated, in Southeast Asian polities. Their control over economic resources in each of the major Southeast Asian countries is impressively large. Although estimates vary, ethnic Chinese are reported to control up to 80 percent of the corporate sector in Malaysia, Indonesia, and Thailand, and about 40 percent in the Philippines.[89]

Since the 1980s the Chinese government has been very interested in strengthening economic relations with the overseas Chinese through active encouragement of foreign investments, remittances, and tourism. Government policy is now fully supportive of what Barry Naughton calls the "China Circle" that connects Hong Kong, Taiwan, and overseas Chinese throughout Southeast Asia with the Chinese mainland.[90] Since the mid-1980s, about four-fifths of contracted and two-thirds of realized foreign investment in the PRC is estimated to have come from business networks in this China Circle.[91] After Asia's 1997 financial crisis, closer tie-ups between overseas and mainland Chinese are constituting the next phase in the spread of Asian business networks. The importance of these networks for the political economy of Asia-Pacific is by all accounts far greater than that of formal institutions such as APEC. Equally important, the evolution of Chinese capitalism cannot be understood as a domestic phenomenon. It is inherently international and linked closely to the dynamics of the global economy.[92]

A web of entrepreneurial relationships thus has reintegrated "Greater China" since the late 1980s. Ethnic and familial ties help establish regional business networks that are "informal though pervasive, with local variations but essentially stateless, stitched together by capital flows, joint ventures, marriages, political expediency and common culture and business ethic."[93] What is distinctive about Chinese business networks, compared to those in Europe or the United States, is the vast distances they cover, the large amount of interpersonal trust they embody, and the lack of formal institutionalization they exhibit. Through mutual shareholding and other mechanisms, overseas Chinese firms

86. Hui 1995, 191. Gambe 1997, 19–22.
87. Hui 1995, 172, 191, 194.
88. Hicks and Mackie 1994, 48.
89. Hui 1995, 254–58.
90. Naughton 1997.
91. Berger and Lester 1997, 5. Esman 1986, 150–53. Hui 1995, 259–68.
92. Hamilton 1996, 331. Hui 1995, 13–14, 219.
93. Sender 1991, 29.

have cooperated and thus strengthened one another. These firms have been linked to small- and medium-sized enterprises in retail and wholesale that have acted as intermediary agencies. In the 1990s, large Chinese family firms began to engage financial markets on a worldwide scale and to diversify, moving away from their dependence on Chinese banks.[94]

Japanese and Chinese Networks

Asian regionalism is institutionalized in different business networks, with national Japanese and ethnic Chinese identities playing an important role. The benefits of cultural affinities and old familial and business ties in overcoming problems of trust and reliability offer some advantages to a Chinese mode of organizing that contrasts with the dynamic technological efficiencies created in more hierarchical Japanese networks. While Chinese networks are excellent for rent-seeking behavior and quick returns on capital, Japan controls the flow of aid and technologies and provides producers in other countries with capital and intermediate inputs.[95] South Korea and Taiwan, though closing the development gap quickly, specialize in somewhat less sophisticated goods and remain dependent on Japanese imports for key technologies and intermediate products. Thus, they have taken their place between Japan and Southeast Asia, which currently provides raw materials and markets and is upgrading industrial platforms for assembly and increasingly indigenous production.

The overlay of Japanese and Chinese business networks is evident in the case of Thailand. On the basis of his field research, Mitchell Sedgwick concluded:

> Japanese multinationals in Thailand have reproduced an atomization of labor and strong centralization of decision-making authority. . . . Beyond internal plant dynamics, however, the strict centralization is also reflected in the position of subsidiaries vis-à-vis headquarters. Subsidiaries in Thailand are part of a tightly controlled and rigorously hierarchical organizational structure extending down from Japan.[96]

Thailand's Chinese-dominated business community, in contrast, has taken different forms over time; but in the last three decades, younger Chinese entrepreneurs have responded to the internationalization of the Thai economy by running their businesses along traditional Chinese lines and maintaining close contacts with the Chinese business communities in Hong Kong, Singapore, Taiwan, and China. Thailand illustrates that rapid corporate growth can result from the horizontal and open networks of the overseas Chinese as much as the vertical and closed ones typical of Japan.[97]

94. Yeung 2003.
95. Hatch and Yamamura 1996, 96.
96. Sedgwick 1994, 8.
97. Hamilton and Walters 1995, 94, 99–100.

These Japanese and Chinese variants of Asian regionalism take the form of ethnonationalist business networks and subregional zones, but their historical sources differ greatly. Japanese capitalism flowered between 1870 and 1930 in an era of state- and empire-building; Chinese capitalism, developing at the same time, bears the marks of imperial and state collapse.[98] Since the mid-nineteenth century, the population of overseas Japanese has been dwarfed by the Chinese diaspora; and Chinese business networks are more extensive and have deeper historical roots than do their Japanese counterparts. Japanese officials have built up Japanese networks in full awareness of the severe limitations that Japanese firms face in Asia. Different historical origins thus have shaped the character of China's and Japan's economic extensions into Asia.

This general pattern is evident in specific industrial sectors. Japanese networks of firms rely substantially on known Japanese suppliers with comparable technical capacities. Overseas Chinese firms work through networks that draw on the increasing technical specialization of small- and medium-sized firms scattered throughout Asia. Japanese networks are closed, vertical, Japan-centered, and long term. Chinese networks are open, horizontal, flexible, and ephemeral.[99] In vertical organizations, groups are controlled by shareholding ownership, whereas horizontal networks favor family ownership and partnerships. Within a group, vertical networks control through cross-shareholding and mutual domination; horizontal ones manage through multiple positions held by core personnel. Vertical systems organize between group networks with cross-shareholding; horizontal ones favor loans and joint ventures by individuals and firms. In the former, subcontract relations are structured or semiformal; in the latter, they are informal and highly flexible. Growth patterns are differentiated by bank financing in vertical systems, and informal financing and reinvestment in horizontal ones.[100]

Japanese and Chinese patterns of organization are both distinct and complementary. The new crop of Chinese tycoons in Southeast Asia often cooperates with Japanese business, for example, in the Siam Motor Group in Thailand, the Astra Company and Rodamas Group in Indonesia, the Yuchenco Group in the Philippines, and the Kuok Brothers in Malaysia.[101] Of 138 joint ventures between Japanese and Indonesian firms in 1974, 70 percent of the Indonesian partners were local Chinese.[102] Frequently, Japanese firms find it very difficult to work without Chinese middlemen. Furthermore, foreign trade between China and Japan is expanding very rapidly. In 2003 the weekly air traffic of about ten thousand people between Japan and China exceeded the total number for all of 1992. When Hawaii is excluded, Japanese buy more package tours to China than to the United States. And as Japanese business is now convinced

98. Hamilton 1996, 332–33, 336.
99. Hamilton, Orrù, and Biggart 1987, 100. Hamilton and Feenstra 1997, 67–73.
100. Orrù, Biggart, and Hamilton 1997.
101. Hui 1995, 189.
102. Hui 1995, 189. Brick 1992, 3–4.

that China is the most important market to pull the Japanese economy out of its long stagnation, foreign investment is booming. There are forty-six hundred joint ventures in the Shanghai region alone; in 2003, two or three new Japanese businesses opened in and around the city every day.[103]

In sum, Asian markets do not consist of a series of unconnected and atomized individual transactions. "Interlinked commodity chains," writes Gary Hamilton, "simultaneously are embedded in the social and political institutions of locales and are extremely sensitive to such global conditions as price and currency fluctuations."[104] At the regional level, these social and market links typically follow ethnic Chinese or national Japanese lines. Both types of business network avoid formal institutionalization, as Japanese conglomerates structures and Chinese family firms bring about economic integration without formal political institutions. In the 1990s, regionalism and regionalization in Asia was porous to developments in the world economy; its economic form was networklike; and its political shape was multicephalic.

Law and Politics in a European Polity

"Return to Europe" is the political metaphor that dominates the study of regional integration and enlargement in Europe since the end of World War II, and especially since the end of the cold war. Examples are legion: Germany after 1945; Spain, Portugal, and Greece in the 1980s; the central and eastern European states since 1990. What is the "Europe" to which these states wish to return? Postwar European regionalism rested on a liberal view that was both antifascist and anticommunist. The onset of the cold war quickly began to narrow the Pan-European vision to a West European one. With the end of the cold war, and in the interest of strengthening and broadening this liberal community, the European Union reaffirmed its commitment to overcoming Europe's division between East and West at its Strasbourg summit in December 1989.

European regionalism differs greatly in its institutional form from Asia's. This is mostly due to the European Union. The values of liberal democracy define the membership rules. The rule of law, private property in a market economy, the rights of democratic participation, and respect for minority rights and social pluralism all are part of the liberal human rights that are central to the European Union. They are embedded in a system of multilateral arrangements of states committed to a peaceful resolution of all conflicts. Since 1957, these values have been cast in legal language and are specified in various treaties that European governments have signed and ratified. They were restated succinctly by the European Council in its 1993 Copenhagen meeting.

With the passing of time, regional integration in Europe has changed from

---

103. Pilling and McGregor 2004.
104. Hamilton 1999, 52.

a system of bargaining between governments to a polity in which, among others, governments and other institutions also bargain. Governance in Europe is
driven by functional needs, has a large bureaucratic component, and occurs at
multiple levels that link subnational, national, and European institutions.
Groups, parties, and government bureaucracies are drawn into a polity that is
acquiring legitimacy while remaining contested. This process is leading neither
to unification through the creation of a European superstate nor to fragmentation into a plethora of nationalistic states.

The European polity suffers from persistent decisional inefficiencies that
come from this in-between status. They are rooted in a growing gap between
"positive" and "negative" integration, between far-reaching, legally mandated
eliminations of economic and social borders on the one hand and, at best, cautious and uneven advances in regulating merging European markets on the
other. Central in that enterprise are formal institutions—the Council of the
European Union, formerly the Council of Ministers; the European Commission; the European Parliament; the European Court of Justice—that share
powers with national governments and with one another.[105]

The European Union has evolved into a distinctive polity that fuses executive and legislative powers in different institutions operating at the European
level, as well as between the European and the national levels. The Council of
Ministers and twenty-two different functional councils of ministers deal, respectively, with foreign policy and a broad array of specialized issues. Although
these councils have many executive prerogatives and are sites for the creation
of transgovernmental coalitions, they are also the most important legislative
bodies of the European Union. In the execution of policy, furthermore, they
are linked closely to national bureaucracies. Addressing often highly technical
issues, these councils interact with committees of the European Parliament and
interest groups operating at national and, increasingly, European levels. As the
councils work mostly by consensus, their operations are typically shrouded in
secrecy. They illustrate how power in the European Union is spread among different centers of power and across different levels of governance.

With its twenty members meeting as a cabinet, the Commission acts in concert with the Council of Ministers. It supervises the roughly thirteen thousand
civil servants who work in Brussels. It also initiates most of the European
Union's important legislation. Issued largely by the Commission in the form of
regulations and decisions, the total legislative output of the European Union
since 1957 reportedly approaches one hundred thousand pages. About half of
the new laws adopted in EU member states are drafted in Brussels, especially
those dealing with issues of the environment, public health, consumer protection, and internal security; pensions, welfare benefits, and education are still
primarily subject to national legislation. Furthermore, although it lacks enforcement powers, the Commission supervises the implementation of EU laws

105. The following paragraphs draw on Katzenstein 1997b, 33–36.

by member states. It often relies on the expertise of national bureaucracies, both in the development of new policies and in the implementation of existing ones. Because it seeks to lessen its dependence on national governments, the Commission is a voracious consumer of the information provided by nongovernmental sources. In its operation, the Commission thus merges both legislative and executive as well as supranational and national powers.

Elected directly since 1979, the members of the European Parliament caucus along ideological rather than national lines. But despite the provision for limited co-decision, the European Parliament's power has remained largely advisory. It can delay actions, and it has the right to impeach members of the Commission. But its veto power is restricted to less than half of the EU budget. For example, the European Parliament has no significant budgetary control over agricultural spending, the largest single budget item. Because of the absence of a European public, elections to the European Parliament are often plebiscites on unrelated national issues rather than focused on the substance of the European polity. Institutional changes introduced in the mid-1980s have, however, enhanced the European Parliament's power. The result has been an intensification of bargaining prior to the introduction of Council or Commission proposals. In the eyes of the German, but not of the French or British, governments, these reforms fall far short of remedying the European Union's democratic deficit. In the future, that deficit is likely to narrow due to the forging of stronger links between the European Parliament and national legislatures. Parliamentary practice thus bridges different arenas of power and levels of government.

The emergence of a wide range of institutions at the European level is noteworthy, but the feature that most clearly distinguishes Europe from Asia is its far-reaching process of *legal* integration. The European Court is known for its activism, as its judicial identity shields it from political interference. At the national level, in contrast, courts and executives explicitly contest the institutional prerogative of who defines the balance of power among government institutions, as well as the pace, scope, and manner of an integrating European polity. The Commission's right to sue member states (Article 169), the right of member states to sue one another (Article 170), and the Court's right to review the legality of all actions taken by the EU Council and the Commission (Article 173) aim at securing compliance with the obligations of the Treaty of Rome, which established the EEC in 1957. But the prime task of the Court is to enforce a uniform interpretation and application of European law (Article 177). Furthermore, as part of its evolving practices, the Court monitors national laws for possible incompatibilities with the treaty. In this role, the Court rules on cases in which individual citizens sue national legislatures and executives. Finally, as specified in Article 177, the Court rules on general issues involving the validity of European Union law. That the Court does not decide these issues directly is an indication of the strong link between the supranational and national levels of governments. Rather, the Court issues "preliminary rulings" and thus seeks to guide lower courts in their judgments. There are reasonable grounds for disagreement on whether the Court's decentralized method of enforcement is a source of weakness, or strength, or both. But it is evident that the Court's activism occurs in the context of the actions taken by national courts.

The evolution of European law has been marked by the constitutionalization of the EC treaties by the European Court of Justice and national courts. This process combined institution building with legal interpretation. The term "constitutionalization" describes the process by which a set of treaties evolved "from a set of legal arrangements binding upon sovereign states, into a vertically-integrated legal regime conferring judicially enforceable rights and obligation on all legal persons and entities, public and private, within EC territory."[106] Constitutionalization results both from the European Court's judicial activism and from an incessant judicial dialogue between the Court and national courts.

The process of constitutionalization occurred in two waves.[107] In the first period (1962–79), the European Court of Justice succeeded in securing both the principle of the supremacy of European over national law and its direct effect on all legal subjects in the European Community. In the second period (1983–90), the process of legal integration gave national judges enhanced means for guaranteeing the effective application of EC law. In 1983, for example, the Court established the principle of indirect effect, which compels national judges to interpret existing national law to conform to EC law. It extended the principle of indirect effect in a 1992 ruling: in situations where directives have not been adopted, or have been adopted incorrectly, national judges must interpret and apply national law in conformity with European law: "The doctrine empowers national judges to rewrite national legislation—an exercise called 'principled construction'—in order to render EC law applicable in the absence of implementing measures."[108] In 1990, a high point in Europe's legal integration, the Court established the doctrine of government liability. Under this doctrine, a national court can hold a member state liable for the damage it may have caused by not having properly implemented or applied an EU directive.

Over time, the European Court of Justice has pushed legal integration much further than member states initially had contemplated, and also beyond economic or political integration.[109] Legal integration results from the institutionally linked decision streams of a variety of actors, including litigants, lawyers, and judges. The process by which national courts have accepted the supremacy and the direct effect of European law is highly variable and path-dependent. Rather than looking at legal developments at different levels, Thijmen Koopmans, a judge on the Court of Justice during the 1980s, argues that

106. Stone Sweet 1998, 306.
107. Stone Sweet 1998, 306–8.
108. Stone Sweet 1998, 307.
109. Stone Sweet and Brunell 1998, 67–68. Mattli and Slaughter 1998, 254.

it is "more rewarding, intellectually, and also more interesting, to look at it as one global process: that of the progressive construction of one many-sided legal edifice."[110]

The competition among national courts, and between courts and other political actors, normally promotes, though at times retards, Europe's legal integration. Between the mid-1980s and mid-1990s, in particular, the European Court of Justice attempted to strengthen a decentralized system of enforcing European law. This development created conditions in which lower and higher national courts compete in the use they make of European law. "It is the difference in lower and higher court interests which provides a motor for legal integration to proceed," writes Karen Alter.[111] Lower courts tend to use European law to achieve desired legal outcomes. Higher courts tend, instead, to restrain the expansion of European legal orders into national ones. Generally speaking, lower courts have moved higher courts to a position where the latter must accept the supremacy and direct effects of European law.[112]

Legal integration, however, is not a one-way street. The judicial process in different states can also lead to a retardation of legal integration. In famous decisions in 1974 (Solange I) and 1993 (Maastricht), the German Constitutional Court significantly constrained the process of European legal integration.[113] And short of outright legal obstruction, the ambiguities of national compliance with new European law are unavoidable. They derive from the application of new legal rules in national settings with deep-rooted legal traditions and often very different interpretations of the social meaning of legal rules. Lack of state capacity or clarity about priorities and obfuscation of responsibilities and opportunities creates "contained compliance" as a distinctive trait of the European Union's legal order.[114]

Legal integration occurs also through dialogue. That dialogue has two parts: the creation of new doctrine, such as the primacy and direct effects of EU law; and the acceptance of this new jurisprudence by national courts and national politicians. The European Court of Justice has typically created this jurisprudence in cases brought by national courts. Although all national judiciaries insist on a national constitutional basis for the supremacy of European law, national courts now apply the decisions of the Court even when national politicians and administrators object.[115] The constitutionalization of the EC treaties and the process of legal integration thus rest crucially on how national courts interpret, apply, and challenge European law, and how the national reception of that law influences subsequent decisions of the European Court of Justice. At the intersection of law and politics, Europe's legal integration is a process

110. Koopmans 1991, 506.
111. Alter 1998a, 242.
112. Alter 1998a, 243, 249–50; 1996. Stone Sweet 2000, 153–93; 1998, 324–25.
113. Alter 1998b. Mattli and Slaughter 1998, 270–71, 274–75.
114. Conant 2002, 52.
115. Alter 1998a, 227–28, 231. Witte 1998, 292–93. Stone Sweet 1998, 312–23.

in which judges and other political actors navigate within the institutional order of a European polity.

These EU developments suggest an image of politics under law rather than of law contingent on politics.[116] In a prescient summary, an early student of European law, Stuart Scheingold, concluded in 1971 that "a rather flexible process of litigation is taking shape within a consensual framework of modified national choice."[117] Instead of focusing attention on the advantages or disadvantages of intergovernmentalism or supranationalism, the Europeanization of law underlines instead the dynamics of legal integration in a multitiered European polity—one that combines traditional, hierarchical, and centralized elements of state power with nontraditional, nonhierarchical, and plural systems of governance.

These legal and political aspects of European unification are hardly the only dimensions of Europeanization. Other dimensions also help define Europe as an evolving, multitiered polity.[118] Two are especially noteworthy here. First, Europe seeks to export its own political models, distinctive institutions and practices, which it hopes will affect the conduct of world politics. "Europeanization" refers to a different calibration of the requirements of economic efficiency with social justice, resistance to treating culture as a commodity, stronger opposition to the death penalty, more self-conscious commitment to environmental causes, and insistence on the primacy of international law and multilateral international organizations in world affairs. Second, through the process of enlargement, Europeanization has an even stronger effect on the domestic institutions and practices of member states and, especially, the accession countries in southern and eastern Europe. Europeanization processes are quite marked on the economic and social issues that are at the center of capitalist welfare states. But European regulations also cover moral and cultural issues that stretch well into the sphere of social morality.[119] In the competition for legitimacy in world affairs, Europeanization often takes precedence over the exercise of coercive military power in the pursuit of narrow national security interests.

Institutionalization in Europe is a pervasive phenomenon affecting many dimensions of social and political life. Yet, compared to Asia, it is the constitutionalization of the European treaty system, more than the adoption of a European constitution, that is the distinctive trait of the evolving European polity. Consensus decision making occurs in a multitiered political system that fuses and separates power and is always open to serious conflicts of interest, pitting national governments against one another. Joseph Weiler draws our attention to the principle of constitutional *tolerance*. Very different European states are committed to coming together in an ever closer union. They are con-

116. Armstrong 1998, 163.
117. Scheingold 1971, 14.
118. Olsen 2002.
119. Kurzer 2001.

nected through a growing number of ties that invite, more than oblige, the submission of national power to the decisions of a political community—one in which other states, not a democratic public, exercise authority. "European federalism," concludes Weiler, "is constructed with a top-to-bottom hierarchy of norms, but with a bottom-to-top hierarchy of authority and real power."[120] These intersecting political processes direct our attention to Europe as a problem-solving, deliberative polity that complements the alternative political logics of state sovereignty and societal associability.[121]

U.S. policy has had a lot to do with the core differences in Europe's and Asia's regional orders. After 1945 multilateralism was an institutional innovation that U.S. policymakers pursued vigorously in Europe but not in Asia. Washington helped set the two regions on different institutional trajectories, leading to ethnic capitalism in Asian markets and law embedded in various European political arrangements. These differences are consequential both for the American imperium, which seeks to manage a world of regions, and for Germany and Japan, which play leading roles in two of the world's most important regions.

120. Weiler 2000, 244, 240.
121. Cohen and Sabel 2003.

CHAPTER THREE

Regional Identities

Asia's and Europe's regional orders have distinct identities that are part and parcel of their different institutional forms. These identities, I believe, complement rather than replace typically stronger national, subnational, and local identities. In Asia the cultural and civilizational content of regional identities is less important than a combination of universal and local referents that are largely deployed by political elites for clear political purposes. In contrast, Europe's regional identity is grounded in deeply contested cultural and civilizational notions; rooted in social processes, it remains extremely variable across different locales and social strata.

There are deep historical roots for this basic difference, predating by centuries the different institutional orders that the United States imposed on Asia and Europe after 1945. Recent evidence from the fields of cultural psychology and economic sociology undercut, however, the notion that Orient and Occident are separated by irreconcilable cognitive processes and incommensurable intellectual traditions. Because the geographic focus of Europe and Asia that is the object of collective identities has fluctuated widely over the centuries, it is no surprise that the internal variability of West and East is enormous. A discussion of civilizational thought processes and intellectual traditions suggests that people and polities are what they are, and that they can become different. We can recognize porous regions in the American imperium only by sidestepping the temptations that reductionism and reification offer for an analysis of world politics. The point is driven home by a comparison of postwar Germany and Japan. Their successful political maturation and economic reconstruction have resulted in core regional states that have helped shape and be shaped by Asia and Europe, while at the same time remaining supportive of American purpose and power.

Regional Identities in Asia and Europe

Significant differences in the character of regional institutions and practices in Asia and Europe are reflected in the character of regional identities. State identities are primarily external and are shaped by processes in the international society of states. National identities are primarily internal and describe the processes by which mass publics and elites acquire, modify, and shed collective identities. Regional identities complement, rather than replace, evolving state and national identities. In Asia, regional identities evolve in relation to both universal and local referents, yet eschew more specific cultural and civilizational aspects. In Europe, a regional identity is gradually emerging, to different degrees in different countries, among different social strata, and in different parts of Europe. Eurasia is one landmass, but it refers to two continents and at least two civilizations and economic zones.[1] Only in Russia does the ideology of Eurasianism provide a potentially unifying symbol.[2] In contrast, regional identities in both Europe and Asia are most clearly marked when defined in opposition to an external "other." This explains the powerful traditions of Orientalism in Europe, and of Occidentalism in Asia.

Even though "England did not move a geographical inch," the year 1066 marked a decisive change in what Kenneth Jowitt calls "the conceptual geography" of Europe.[3] After innumerable political upheavals, the tectonic plates of European politics shifted once again in 1989. Acutely aware of the political importance of physical proximity, one German foreign office official argues, "You know, 50 percent of politics in Europe is geography and you cannot simply move away."[4] This leaves the other 50 percent. Georg Simmel is probably right when he argues that a border is not only a geographic fact with sociological consequences but also a social fact that takes geographic form.[5] Although the author of a theory of civilizational clashes would probably not settle for a 50/50 split, even Samuel Huntington concurs that geography and culture do not coincide neatly.[6] With specific reference to the geography of money, Benjamin Cohen writes that there exists "a growing gap between image and fact."[7] Geographic borders create discontinuities in perceptions and behavior. They may appear unalterable in particular historical eras, but regional borders always remain subject to political reconstruction. Specific instances provide a useful reminder of how things that are taken for granted at one point in history can become deeply problematic at another. They illustrate also that ideas cycle between, for example, different forms of nationalism and international-

1. Evers and Kaiser 2001, 65.
2. Brzezinski 1997, 109–13.
3. Jowitt 1992, 307.
4. Wallander 1999, 53.
5. Gienow-Hecht 2000, 488.
6. Huntington 1999, 49.
7. Cohen 1998, 4.

ism. Regional trajectories are rarely synchronized across such cycles. For example, after 1945 postcolonial nationalism in East Asia differed enormously from the region-wide spread of the idea of Europe. In the 1990s, however, nationalism in Europe was on the rise, spurred by widespread fears of immigration, while in East Asia the idea of Asian values gained greater credence.

Asia

Australia is a promising place to start our analysis of the evolution of Asian identities.[8] Cultural and political similarities in relations between the United States and Australia, as well as the United States and Canada, permit us to isolate differences in the effects of geographical distance. In the 1970s, in the words of Brian Beedham, Australia's problem was self-evident: "Think of a Canada that had been towed away from where it is, and moored off Africa, and the problem of Australia's physical location becomes clear."[9] Looking for Australia three decades later, salvage crews exploring off the coast of Africa are likely to come up empty-handed. Responding to dynamic economic growth in Asia, opposition leader John Howard appealed to the laws of geography when he stated that "there is no doubt that we are incredibly fortunate that our geography has cast us next to the fastest growing region in the world."[10] Howard's view that Australia's fortunate geography is its destiny contradicts Beedham's pessimistic assessment from only a couple of decades earlier.

More important, it overlooks the intense domestic clashes over Australia's collective identity, intensified by the policies of the later Howard government. Over the last two decades, debates highlight the political processes by which Australians are taking their turn toward and away from a multiracial and multicultural polity. The symbols of Australia's constitutional and national identities, flag and anthem, are subjects of serious controversy. Australia is in the process of becoming more Asian, but in a very specific manner. "Without actually becoming Asian," writes Gavan McCormack, "Australia is struggling to articulate a regional universalism and to become simultaneously post-European and post-Asian, transcending both its own European racial and cultural heritage and any racially or culturally specific Asia."[11]

In Singapore, by contrast, identity entrepreneurs have developed Asian values rather than regional universalism as their central message. Singapore's geographical placement in Asia is uncontested. But Asia is also an "imposed identity: a fantastic ideological construct without racial or cultural meaning."[12] Singapore's forceful articulation of a regional ideology of Asian values occurred in government-funded organizations charged with developing a legiti-

8. The following pages are adapted from Katzenstein 2002b.
9. Quoted in Keohane and Nye 2001, 146.
10. Quoted in Hudson and Stokes 1997, 146.
11. McCormack 1996, 178.
12. McCormack 1996, 161.

mate ideology to support state-building in a multiethnic society. In the words of Diane Stone, "Think tanks, as discourse managers, are a means to project Asian identities outwards to the West. They articulate concepts about an 'Asian Way' and provide intellectual justification for this discourse."[13] Subsequently, that discourse would prove useful for a different political purpose.

Which Asian values are to be invoked is a matter of serious disagreement, as is the degree of incompatibility between Asian and Western values. Singapore's stunning success in engineering an ambitious modernization has given special urgency to policies that insist on the country's uniqueness. Modernization without Westernization offers a way to build a distinctive culture in a multiethnic society. During the last thirty years, the government has attempted to establish an ideological consensus around the articulation of a newly invented tradition, which gives it a legitimate claim to political and moral leadership. The translating of traditional Asian values into modern life is a central preoccupation and a source of governmental power.

The classification of Singapore's population into four main groups (Chinese, Malay, Indian, and Caucasian), for example, disregards numerous subgroups within these ethnic communities. Eschewing a bottom-up "melting pot," Singapore has adopted instead a top-down "salad bowl" approach to managing its ethnic pluralism. "Asian values" sidestep both the potentially disintegrative pulls of Chinese, Malay, and Indian cultures, and the potentially absorptive reach of Western influences. Geographically undefined Asian values, then, are not a temporary expression of the cultural arrogance of one of Asia's miracle economies. Rather, they offer Singapore's political elites a politically useful ideology for building a new state. Singapore's championing of Asian values has some parallels in Malaysia's blunt criticism of the dangers of Western human rights policies, as well as its outspoken support for a cohesive East Asian community without U.S. or Australian participation. Such Asian values subordinate individual rights to community obligations. For Malaysia, the idea of an Asian political community is tied directly to the legitimacy of a soft-authoritarian government dedicated to high economic growth and opposed to some core Western values.

Australia's universal regionalism, and Singapore's and Malaysia's insistence on the specificities of an Asia that suits their domestic and international needs, are part of the emergence of a more encompassing Asian-Pacific region. Yet the articulation of a regional ideology is not simply a ploy of governments seeking to eschew the pressures of democratization and liberalization. Regional ideologies that entail specific collective identities are as important for Japan and the United States as they are for Singapore and Malaysia. The Pacific Rim and Asia-Pacific offer good illustrations. They have only a vague geographic referent.[14] The United States has a strong commitment to Asia-Pacific, an indica-

13. Stone 1997, 12.
14. Dirlik 1993a.

tion of its interest in a continued involvement in Asian affairs. The U.S. government strongly supported the creation of the Asia Pacific Economic Cooperation Ministerial Conference, which led to the Asia Pacific Economic Community (APEC). It was inaugurated in Canberra in November 1989 and held its first summit in Seattle in November 1993. With a broad membership, APEC supports the policies of economic liberalism that the United States championed throughout the 1980s and 1990s. In the early 1990s, intense conflicts between the United States and the European Union, and growing trade friction between the United States and Japan, made APEC an attractive counter to a rising tide of protectionism. Business and government leaders and their economic advisers saw in Asia's market-based and open regionalism a stepping stone to a liberal, global economic order.

Such a view of Asia-Pacific or the Pacific Rim is at odds with that of many Asian governments. APEC's 1994 commitment to reach full trade liberalization by the year 2020 was, at best, no more than a reluctant acquiescence to pressures from the United States and Australia. In the aftermath of the Asian financial crisis, lukewarm attitudes cooled further, to the point where the policy objective and target date may well become, as for Malaysia, merely indicative and nonbinding. Many governments in Asia-Pacific see market-based integration as a way to retain government involvement in markets rather than as a way to weaken state institutions in the face of a liberalizing world economy.

Although the United States was becoming part of an emerging Asia-Pacific region in the 1990s, this trend was not accompanied by a politically significant strengthening of an Asian American identity among U.S. citizens. In a Eurocentric, Anglo-American culture, Asian Americans have been viewed as more Asian than American. Trans-Pacific ties did not further the recognition of Asian elements in the collective identity of the United States; in fact, they often denied Asians membership in the American polity. For the United States to embrace Asia-Pacific as a deeply held and meaningful aspect of its collective identity, the domestic politics of multiculturalism would have to politicize fully a strain of Asian American identity that, to date, remains largely submerged.[15]

Despite these limitations in U.S. domestic politics, the very newness of the category Asia-Pacific illustrates the pull of new developments and the American need to remain engaged in Asian affairs. Standing before the Japanese Diet in February 2002, President Bush argued that "America, like Japan, is a Pacific nation, drawn by trade and values and history to be part of Asia's future."[16] The contrast with Britain is instructive here. Concepts such as Asia-Pacific or the Pacific Rim designate a region that Britain has referred to as "Asia" or the "Far East." The Far Eastern and Pacific Department of the British Foreign Office continues today to cover, as it has for the last century, both China, Japan, Korea, and Mongolia (the "Far East") and Australia, New Zealand, and a large

15. Dirlik 1993b, 305.
16. Bumiller 2002.

number of small islands (the "Pacific").[17] Britain's unchanging designations contrast with the changing political needs of the United States.

Europe

In the most important article on comparative regionalism published in the early 1960s, Ernst Haas argued that the frequently invoked "immanent myth" of European unity should not be used to support the assumption that an earlier historical experience of unity will lead to the "natural and inevitable re-emergence of this happy state of affairs."[18] It is not the historical experience as much as the social processes and changing political interpretations of that history that matter. In the 1990s, Europe offered plenty of confirmation in three different areas: the different and changing configuration of national and European identities in Britain, Germany, and France; the reconfiguration of collective identities in various parts of Europe including Scandinavia, the Baltic states, and central Europe; and the relations between Europe and areas considered to be inherently non-European, specifically Russia, as well as Turkey. These evolving identities have created a permissive consensus for European integration, one that is reflected in the gradual emergence of institutionalized symbols of an ambiguous collective European identity.

Collective identities are layered. Old local identities are not eviscerated by national ones, and national identities can coexist comfortably with new regional ones. In 1999, the European Union reported the number of those identifying themselves only by their country to be as large as those identifying themselves first by their country and second as European; both figures dwarfed those who identified themselves only as European or first as European and then by country.[19] At the elite level, concludes Jeffrey Checkel, the socializing effects of numerous meetings over long periods in European institutions "are uneven and often surprisingly weak, and in no sense can be construed as shaping a radically new, post-national identity."[20] It is therefore not so surprising that EU cultural policy, as I argue in chapter 5, seeks to enhance legitimacy by stressing "unity in diversity."

Identification with Europe does not supplant national identities and create a unified European identity. For one thing, mass publics are remarkably uninformed about Europe, relying on their views about national politics as proxies for their European attitudes. Furthermore, public support of Europe varies a great deal. Policy sectors that touch on issues of national identity, such as culture and education, are the most resistant to Europeanization.[21]

Public identification with Europe changes over time. After a decade of "Eu-

17. William Wallace, personal communication, 1999.
18. Haas 1966, 94–95.
19. European Commission 2000b, 11.
20. Checkel forthcoming.
21. Dalton and Eichenberg 1998, 257–62.

ropeanization" in the 1980s, the 1990s revealed the opposite trend, toward "renationalization," measured in the net decline of EU support. This decrease occurred at the very time that the treaties of Maastricht (1991) and Amsterdam
(1997) were shifting important powers to Brussels. Public support for Europe
varies not only by decade but also by year. Between 2000 and 2003 the proportion of Europeans who felt "fairly" attached to Europe first declined, and
then in the run-up to the Iraq war rose by about 15 percent.[22] Such changing
contours in public support are, however, quite distinct from the growing legitimacy that the European Union has enjoyed in the eyes of European elites.
Among top decision makers sampled in 1996, national support for the European Union varied by only 12 percent, between a high of 98 percent in Germany and a low of 84 percent in Sweden. These figures compare to a 48 percent
spread in the mass public, with a high of 75 percent in Ireland, Italy, and the
Netherlands, and a low of 27 and 29 percent in Austria and Sweden.[23]

The Europeanization of collective identities is also uneven across different
societies, as the experience of the three major West European states illustrates.
It is stronger in Germany than in Britain, with France holding the middle
ground. Of all the major European states, Germany has the most Europeanized
collective identity. This finding has more to do with the failures of German hy-
pernationalism than with the inherent attraction of a European identity. The
political elites of the Federal Republic of Germany turned to Europe as the only
alternative to a German identity discredited by the policies of Nazi Germany,
national devastation, defeat, and division. Europe was an option for both the
German past and the German present, with Communism occupying one part
of Germany. In the words of Thomas Risse, "German nationalism came to be
viewed as authoritarianism, militarism, and anti-Semitism. Germany's nationalist and militarist past constituted the 'other' in the process of 'post-national'
identity formation whereby Europeanness replaces traditional notions of nation-state identity."[24] Christianity, democracy, Western values, and the social
market economy all facilitated Germany's turn toward Europe. Both pragmatic
and idealistic motivations came into play. But with the passing of time, this turn
has been accepted as quite natural, not least because of the stable and prosperous international environment that an integrating Europe provided for
Germany.

Britain offers a striking contrast. For reasons of history and politics, British
elites have regarded Europe with a distance that simply does not exist in Germany. For Europe, Britain remains an awkward partner.[25] As important as the
fervent anti-Europeanism of the Conservative Party's right wing and the
Labour Party's left wing is the quasi-Gaullist vision of the Europeanist main-
streams of both parties, which champions a shallow integration in a Europe of

22. Eurobarometer 60 (Autumn 2003).
23. European Commission 1996, 4.
24. Risse 2001, 209.
25. George 1994.

nation-states. Only the Liberal Democratic Party, which is on the margins of political power, articulates a federalist position.

The gap between "them" on the Continent and "us" in the British Isles is particularly strong in England. The Crown symbolizes external sovereignty, and Parliament, internal sovereignty. Together they offer an institutionalized view of independence sanctioned by almost a thousand years of history. The English are loath to sacrifice such institutions for rule by unelected bureaucrats in Brussels. With the disastrous loss of Conservative support in Scotland and Wales and the creation of regional assemblies, it is not inconceivable that the Conservative Party will become totally isolated as the party of English reaction around the European issue, as is the Labour Party's hope.

The rate of Europeanization of French identity in the last two decades has perhaps been greater than either Germany's or Britain's. After 1945, French leaders stumbled into a policy that eventually bound Germany tightly to an integrated European polity, only to see internal divisions in France lead to the defeat of the European Defense Community in 1954.[26] President Charles de Gaulle extricated France from Algeria and articulated a political vision for France in a Europe of nation-states. As a natural leader of that Europe, France naturally held pride of place—a France that was both universal in the values it championed and unique in its civilizational mission. The Gaullist vision lingered for another decade, eventually giving way to the Left in the 1980s and to the Right in the 1990s. For the Left, the critical experience was the collapse of the Socialist Party's economic policy in an interdependent Europe in 1983; for the Right, it was the end of the cold war and German unification without significant French participation. For both Left and Right, the acceleration of European integration, the Single European Act, and the Treaty of Maastricht became the most promising avenues for reclaiming at the supranational level some of the sovereignty that France had been compelled to sacrifice at the national level. In essence, specific aspects of French identity were projected onto the European level, a view that remains controversial among traditional Gaullists, and one of several reasons for the persistent divisions of the French Right.

A Europeanization of collective identities is observable not only within Europe's major states but also in the Nordic Council (or Norden).[27] During the cold war, Scandinavia, including Finland, succeeded in making this region less tension-filled than the divided larger Europe. Furthermore, Scandinavian welfare states pointed toward a possible third way between capitalism and socialism. The economic changes of the 1980s and 1990s and the end of the cold war robbed Norden of some of its distinctiveness. The architecture of the new Scandinavian embassy complex in Berlin expresses this sense of a common yet separate identity: screened by movable components, on the outside the com-

26. Parsons 2003.
27. Neumann 1999, 113–41.

plex gives the appearance of a common facade; inside there are distinct and very different buildings, which share some infrastructure for an efficiently run group of embassies.

Increasing Baltic cooperation is linked to changes in Scandinavia and offers another illustration of the Europeanization of collective identity. The answer of one Lithuanian to the question "What is Europe?" is tellingly simple: "Europe is . . . not Russia."[28] In their pro-European and anti-Russian orientation, the Baltic states stand in striking contrast to Belarus and some other post-Soviet states. In this regard, there is an important similarity between the Baltic states and those of central-eastern Europe. Before 1989, Polish and Czechoslovak dissidents actively nourished a central European identity as a plausible counter to Soviet-style Communism. After the Velvet Revolution, many of those former dissidents, some now in leading political positions, initially supported a variety of central-eastern European schemes of cooperation. But within a few years, they learned that subregional groupings might be no more than waiting rooms for delayed accession to the European Union.

In the Baltics and central-eastern Europe, one of the core elements in the formation of collective identity was Europe as the "self," in contrast to the Soviet Union or Russia as the dreaded "other." This strong dichotomy more generally marks identity formation in Europe. Exclusive demarcation, not inclusive affirmation, is key to the emergence of a European sense of identity. European principles of social pluralism, political democracy, capitalist efficiency, and international openness are perceived to run counter to the painful experiences of the Soviet past and the feared possibilities of Russia's future.

Anti-Russian elements are replicated in different form along some of Europe's other real or imagined borders, with the Balkans in the east and with North Africa in the south. German political discourse, for example, often refers at least obliquely to a civilizational divide between the Catholic Church in the West and the Orthodox churches in the East. Germans in particular now see ethnic cleansing as a fundamental challenge of Balkan political pathologies to the European human rights regime that Germany supports fully—only two generations after Germans had conducted their own campaigns of ethnic cleansing in the name of Nazi Germany's New Order. And in the 1990s, the xenophobic nationalism of France's right-wing parties was directed against, among others, those seeking to flee a bloody civil war in Algeria.

Associate EU membership that dates back to the 1960s has not helped Turkey's attempts to become a full-fledged member. As the Islamic movement in Turkey gained strength and the war with the Kurds intensified so have old images of Turkey set off from Europe by a deep religious and cultural divide. The 9/11 attacks and the war on terror have both reinforced such developments and intensified political pressures to open negotiations concerning Turkey's eventual EU membership. The Europeanization of collective identi-

28. Ash 1994, 18.

ties thus generates counterpressures. Efforts to draw a clear distinction between "us" and "them" may strengthen European collective identity in relation to those perceived to be outside Europe, whatever its imagined shape. But they can also weaken a collective European identity, as allegiance to local place and people increases and spills over into the revival of an aggressive and at times racist neonationalism directed against immigrants and refugees. Such sharp breaks demarcating self from other are hard to find in Asia's more fluid and ephemeral sense of collective identity.

European identity has many sources. The theme of a Europe marked by "unity in diversity" is an important constitutive element of European identity. So is the cultural legacy of European Enlightenment invoked by education exchange programs such as ERASMUS, which contradicts an alternative history of European colonialism, racism, and militarism.[29] European identity is also rooted in a heroic birth myth, in the acts of three visionary founding fathers: Jean Monnet, Konrad Adenauer, and Alcide De Gasperi.

The European Union has all the symbolic trappings of a national state: an anthem (Beethoven's "Ode to Joy"), an almost common currency (the euro), a newspaper (the *European*), European television stations (such as English SKY and French-German ARTE), a university (the EUI in Florence), a soccer champions league, film and song festivals, a parliament, a bureaucracy, a court, a common passport, a common flag, and a rotating "cultural capital."[30] Most of these symbols and practices are of relatively recent origin, reactions to war (both hot and cold) and subsequent policies favoring European integration. In Europe's external relations, Europeanization feeds off economic competition with advanced industrial states such as the United States and Japan, as well as fears about immigration from poorer countries. Moreover, Europeanization is altering internally both the forms of, and the degree of identification with, peoples and territories, without replacing existing state and national forms of identification. European symbols of collective identity thus are distinguished by being deliberately incomplete. The flag is not a flag but a "logo" or "emblem"; the anthem is a melody without words; currency and passport mix national and European visual elements.[31]

In terms of language, Europeanization offers partial convergence around English, not Esperanto, as the standard European language. Language integration is not duplicating the rationalization of multiple regional languages into the creation of national languages that occurred in various European states in the sixteenth to nineteenth centuries. That rationalization was in any case limited in Europe generally and in France in particular (the case often regarded as typical). Sixty-seven distinct languages (let alone dialects) are currently spoken in Europe. In France alone, linguists count at least twenty-five

29. Shore 1996, 483–86.
30. Borneman and Fowler 1997, 487–88.
31. Theiler 1999, 1. Katzenstein 1997b, 20–24. Shore 1996, 481–82. Pantel 1999, 53–54.

different language communities.[32] Europe is evolving into what David Laitin has called a 2+/−1 language regime, resembling twentieth-century, postcolonial India.[33] In some countries and regions, such as southern England, people will be able to get by with only one (2−1) language (English). In other places, such as Catalonia, they will operate in three (2+1) languages: Spanish, Catalan, and English. And in most countries they will function in two languages: the national language and English. In a recent EU poll, and excluding those living in the United Kingdom, over 40 percent of the respondents claimed "to know English."[34] English is growing in importance without displacing national languages. Regional languages in Europe are on the rise, as are local dialects. As with other cultural symbols, so with language: Europe is evolving along multiple dimensions that create a multilingual space.

Collective Memories and Anti-Americanism

Regions are not only geographically given but also politically made. Our discussion of Asian and European identities underlines their highly malleable and elite-centered character, especially in Asia. Identities are wrapped in collective memories, primarily intensely experienced national memories, that link the present to the past; and they are embedded in an American imperium that provides both a common regional foil of anti-Americanism and a common experience of Americanization.

Globalization and internationalization reinforce the vitality of historical memory and identity politics. In both Germany and Japan, political elites and institutions remember the past as a morality play about the perils of chauvinist racism and nationalist militarism. The Germany and Japan of the 1930s and 1940s have become the "other" against which the modern, liberal, internationally engaged German and Japanese "self" defines itself. The break with the national past, on the nationalist Right, may be less sharp, but for the German and Japanese polity at large the rupture in history that is 1945 has been reinforced by two generations of policymaking aimed at sovereignty pooling in Europe and market competition in Asia-Pacific.

The differences between Germany's and Japan's collective memories are, however, as notable as the similarities.[35] In sharp contrast to Japan, Germany's memory, in the words of Ian Buruma, is "like a massive tongue seeking out, over and over, a sore tooth."[36] This difference between Germany in Europe and Japan and Asia is due primarily to politics rather than inherent cultural difference. After 1945, the political class in Germany was recruited from the democratic parties of the Weimar Republic. Members of the new class had been in

32. Borneman and Fowler 1997, 487, 499–500.
33. Laitin 1997.
34. European Commission 2001.
35. Hein and Selden 2000.
36. Buruma 1994, 8.

prisons or concentration camps, or they were emigrants or politically not implicated in the Nazi regime while in "internal emigration." Most were committed to the creation of a new collective memory. Furthermore, West German educational policy was made not by the federal government but by the individual states. Government bureaucracies, especially in states dominated by Social Democrats, were much more willing to engage Germany's problematic past. They tended to delegate power over the writing of historical textbooks to professional historians, who typically worked up standard narratives in cooperation with historians from other European countries. Such internationalized histories became part of the school curriculum in Germany as well as other European states.

In sharp contrast, except for the very top leadership, Japan's political class remained relatively unchanged after 1945. That class operated within established institutions, most importantly the emperor system and a conservative state bureaucracy. Once it had won the battle over the centralization of education policy in the late 1950s, the conservative bureaucracy of the Ministry of Education gradually came to prevail over the left-wing Japan Teachers' Union. The government bureaucracy has favored textbooks that express a strong, nationalist historiography, in sharp contradiction to the Marxist interpretation that for decades has dominated Japanese academic writing.

This difference in collective memory has been consequential. German diplomacy in Europe has been helped immensely by the willingness of German elites to acknowledge and to apologize for the heinous crimes that Nazi Germany committed. In Japan, the memory of Japanese atrocities in Asia is largely silenced or subject to incessant controversy. The unwillingness of Japanese leaders to apologize publicly has undermined greatly the trust Japan enjoys in Asia and hampered the emergence of a regional collective identity in Asia.

Collective identities are also embedded in the American imperium in the language of anti-Americanism. Anti-Americanism is not a coherent phenomenon. It is not simply the expression, for example, of views toward the United States and its policies on the one hand, and American society and its values on the other. It is, instead, rooted in perceived differences in identity, and assessments of the impingement of the United States on cherished values. These perceptions generate a diverse set of political practices by which political elites contest for power and legitimacy. By most accounts, anti-Americanism in Europe and Asia is a mixture of admiration and resentment. The result is ambivalence.

In Asia, anti-Americanism reflects a desire for respect and disappointed hopes for a benign American predominance. At times it may also express sentiments of getting even or doing harm. In contrast to Europe, the intensity of anti-Americanism is modified by painful memories, unanswered questions, and missing apologies that lurk under the surface of increasing regional prosperity. In Europe, especially among the elite, anti-Americanism is one among several ingredients of an embryonic collective identity. An editorial of London's centrist *Independent* provides a convenient listing of most of the cultural stereo-types that, from time to time, foster surges of anti-Americanism:

> The dumb certitude; the contempt for the poor; the facile amiability; the ostentatious religiosity; the callous laws; the love of guns; the Holly-wood sensibility; the all-consuming fetish for material success; the showy insubstantiality of its politics; the celebrity of junk; the infantile literal-mindedness; and the faith, withal, in America's planetary moral superiority.[37]

Europe's anti-Americanism is marked by numerous contradictions. Its po-litical version takes the form of sharp criticism from the Left that focuses on the United States as an imperialist power. From the Right, especially during the cold war, it is a sharp rebuke of the permissive, multiracial, and ultimately un-reliable character of the United States as leader of the Free World. In its cul-tural version, anti-Americanism is favored by both conservative intellectuals and progressive nationalists. Both see in America the leveling effects of a cap-italist economy that specializes in the commercialized vulgarity of mass culture. Anti-Americanism is part of the cultural repertoire that contributes to Euro-pean and Asian collective identities.

The success of Japan's manufacturing system and popular culture indus-tries, as I shall discuss in chapters 4 and 5, rests in part on indigenizing aspects of America and re-exporting them in a form that makes them available for lo-calization throughout Asia. Contemporary Asian urban consumerism is rooted in such intersecting processes. This is also true of Europe. As politics, law, and markets push European nations closer together, culture keeps them apart. Eu-ropeans travel more than ever. Yet in the visual arts, theater, literature, con-temporary classical music, movies, and pop music, national preoccupations have not lost their grip. Harry Potter is the proverbial exception that proves the rule: the most common cultural link across widely different national cul-tures is a collective European devotion to many aspects of American popular culture.[38] The plasticity of Asian and European collective identity absorbs and selectively appropriates elements of America and combines them into dis-cernibly different regional identities.

Embedded both in deep historical memories and in opposition to the Amer-ican imperium, Europe and Asia reflect their porousness in their malleable col-lective identities. Germany in Europe and Japan in Asia differ starkly in how they have come to terms with the memory of their own chauvinist racism and nationalist militarism. They are quite similar in how they engage the politics of anti-Americanism and experience different processes of Americanization. Ger-many and Japan differ sharply both from what they once were and from Amer-

37. Cumings 2000, 16.
38. Riding 2004.

ica. What is true for these two countries holds more generally for Asia and Europe: collective identities are articulated in political processes that link both regions to their pasts and to America.

East and West

The internal political dynamics of regional orders and their connections to the American imperium have an important consequence. Porous regions are not converging around common patterns of industrialization, democratization, and secularization. The depth of their different historical roots reinforces that conclusion. Yet it would be wrong to insist that because regions have differed in the past, so they are destined to differ in the future. Recent contributions in cultural psychology and economic sociology help us to recognize the important role that learning and empathy play as sources of political innovation that are both systemic and unplanned.

The different institutional logics of Europe and Asia stretch back as far as the Holy Roman Empire and the Sinocentric world. Before the end of the nineteenth century, argue Charles Bright and Michael Geyer, "global development rested on a series of overlapping, interacting, yet essentially autonomous regions, each engaged in distinct processes of self-organization. . . . Any interpretation of world history in the twentieth century ought to begin with a decisive emphasis on regionalism in global politics."[39] From the perspective of economic history, other scholars agree.[40] Economic activity is plausibly viewed as regional rather than national or global. For Eric Jones, Asia's imperial and Europe's state system provide the relevant political contexts for a cross-regional comparison. And for a variety of reasons deeply imbedded in the two regions, similar processes of international competition led to diametrically opposed outcomes: universal domination in ancient China and balance of power in early modern Europe.[41] Regions thus are modern in multiple ways.[42] The rationalism and secularism that created Europe's modernity are adapted and transformed in other regional contexts. Historical contingency and indeterminacy offer ample ground for such processes of selective appropriation. The differences between Germany, located in the sphere of one of the world's great religions, and Japan, which is not, confirms the institutional plurality of modern regions.

The central role of law and a complex institutional machinery in contemporary Europe reenacts a more distant past. The seventeenth-century Holy Roman Empire, at the center of Germany and Europe, was a fully institutionalized legal regime.[43] The Peace of Westphalia perfected a system of interdepen-

39. Bright and Geyer 1987, 71–72.
40. Jones 1987, xv–xvi.
41. Hui 2004, 176, 185.
42. Eisenstadt 2000a, 2. See also 2000b.
43. Osiander 2001, 270–81. See also 1994.

dence among autonomous political units that had little to do with conventional notions of sovereignty. Before 1618, the empire was not a unified state, for the constitution limited the power of the emperor; and after 1648, the emperor's position remained stronger than conventionally depicted. The constituent parts of the empire were not sovereign territories, alike in their basic legal attributes. Far from it. Strong powers of the emperor were balanced by the exclusive territorial jurisdiction (*Landeshoheit*) of the princes and the free cities. This jurisdiction was limited externally by the laws of the empire and internally by various constitutional arrangements. Changes in these limitations required the consent either of the majority of two of the three imperial councils and that of the emperor, or of the various representative bodies in the territories concerned.

The empire had two supreme courts deciding complaints: for violations of imperial laws, the Imperial Cameral Tribunal; for violations of the laws of its constituent units, the Imperial Aulic Council. Both acted as courts of appeals in civil proceedings, and judges had to have high legal qualifications. Access to these courts was limited except where litigants could establish to the satisfaction of the court that they had been denied due process. Anyone in the empire could take his ruler to court—the sole exception was the emperor, who enjoyed immunity from all court proceedings. In general, the courts appear to have been sympathetic to complaints brought by subjects, including lower-class individuals, against their rulers. In the eighteenth century, the Cameral Tribunal received between 200 and 250 new cases annually, and it produced about one hundred decisions annually in the 1790s. The Aulic Council handled 2,088 cases in 1767, compared to 3,338 in 1779; it averaged about 2,800 in each of the following five years.[44] Prolonged conflicts between the estates and local dynasties played out, sometimes over decades, in the imperial courts and occasionally led to the deposition of regents by the emperor. The Aulic Council also watched over the finances of individual states and in unusual situations could take over government finances in a manner more intrusive than today's International Monetary Fund.

This is not to suggest that political relations in the empire were peaceful or supported by strong interdependence norms. They were not. The ratio of battlefield deaths to total population was about seven times greater in the eighteenth than in the nineteenth century. Only in the nineteenth century did states aim to preserve the continued independence of weak states rather than subject them to partition. These changes illustrate a taming of power politics, writes Paul Schroeder, "a dramatic shift in the purposes and goals of international politics."[45] Yet throughout the eighteenth century, the empire's complex legal machinery and the protection it granted to corporate bodies and individual citizens alike accorded it a welcome measure of legitimacy. Like the nine-

44. Osiander 2001, 275–76.
45. Schroeder 1994, vii–viii.

teenth-century Philadelphia system in North America[46] and the contemporary European Union, the Holy Roman Empire illustrates that in a regional context "empire" and "sovereignty" did not create mutually contradictory norms for state behavior. Compared to the much looser European state system, the empire was a fully institutionalized, legal regime. Matters of common concern were governed collectively; internal governance was reserved, within well-specified limits, to each of the constituent states. The empire's collective purpose and legitimacy both empowered and restrained its constituent parts. The decisive break with the past, on this account, occurs not in 1648 but in the nineteenth century. After the transition of an exceptional long century and a half, Europe since 1945 has returned to its seventeenth- and eighteenth-century legal roots, this time in a peaceful mode. "The closest contemporary parallel to the early modern Holy Roman Empire," Andreas Osiander concludes, "is the European Union."[47]

The nineteenth and twentieth centuries left the welfare state as a second legacy shaping contemporary European regionalism. The growth of the European welfare state would have been impossible without a series of prior, distinctive historical transformations including the separation of church and state, the growth of secularization and modern science, rationalized state administration, and the emergence of human rights. Besides these distinctive aspects of European social structures, Hartmut Kaelble identifies processes that generate convergent pressures in the areas of industrial production and employment, education, urbanization, and the development of the welfare state. The result has left Europe with a degree of internal variation roughly comparable to that of countries of continental size, such as the United States and Russia. Kaelble concludes that "European integration has been accelerated by the growing similarity between European societies and their increasing interaction. . . . There has been an increasing exchange of social models, ideas, lifestyles and consumer trends between European countries . . . the long-term view thus confirms that a truly European society is emerging to a far greater extent than has previously been demonstrated or recorded."[48]

Asia's regionalism has even deeper historical roots than Europe's. Historically, Asia has been at peace when China was strong. Hierarchy and stability went hand in hand. China's military and economic predominance and intense cultural exchanges across borders allowed for a combination of formal hierarchy and informal equality. Suzerainty, not sovereignty, defined a regional system in which China encompassed other units while leaving them considerable room for maneuver. In the Sinocentric world, at the symbolic level, states acknowledged the superiority of the Qing emperor, paying periodic obeisance through elaborate rituals. In practice, as in the institution of tributary trade, these exchanges were profitable for the weaker party, and in some instances

46. Deudney 1995.
47. Osiander 2001, 283.
48. Kaelble 1990, 1–2, 160.

they occurred on the basis of equality. The emperor allowed aliens lacking sufficient virtue and cultural attainment—for example, Westerners living in treaty ports—to govern themselves. The authority of the emperor rested on his moral and cultural superiority, and virtue enabled him to bring order and prosperity to the realm. The authority of the emperor was not clearly bounded. He had the right and obligation, in the interest of peace and harmony, to get involved in the affairs of political units beyond his own domain. Despite this ambiguity, many rulers in the Chinese periphery emulated the Chinese system of rule. Even today Asian states appear to favor bandwagoning with, rather than balancing against, a rising China.[49] Even a country as powerful as Japan has behaved in ways that for decades have stumped the predictions of realist theorists. It is balancing against neither China nor the United States.

In this regional order, political and military domination and resistance did not fall into distinct spheres of international and domestic politics.[50] Law was not a fundamental institution. The empire's influence was less constraining than the stylized descriptions through which intellectuals sought to depict the court's power and glory. State officials were, for example, often less supportive of than parasitic on business networks. For a thousand years, petty capitalism was one of China's main motors. It both drove and undermined a state-managed tributary mode of economic production and exchange. Exploiting economic niches, petty capitalists acted "with clever dishonesty. Their practices have been subversive, contorted, dangerous and liberating."[51] Meanwhile, it was the strength of different political coalitions fighting over changing definitions of Chinese state identity that shaped the policy interests of the Ming dynasty. When China's power and legitimacy went unquestioned, there was little need for interstate wars. The absence of a Western concept of sovereignty made ambiguous settlements possible. This possibility is now precluded since Western notions of sovereignty have penetrated East Asia more fully.[52]

The historical genealogy of Asian states differs from those in Europe. "Asian history," writes Wang Gungwu, "can be deciphered as a succession of greater or lesser empires bordered and interspersed by polities, fragments of polities, with or without kings, princes, and tribal chiefs of one kind or another."[53] Contemporary Asian states are shaped by the legacy of universal empires, regional kingdoms, and subcontinental empires—a history that predates modern European states by many centuries. These empires and kingdoms, Suzanne Rudolph argues, rose and fell by cyclical conceptions of dynastic time, not by unilinear and teleological conceptions of progress in history characteristic of the European intellectual tradition.[54] The notions of unified sovereignty and

49. Kang 2003a, 2003b, 169–74.
50. The following is adapted from Katzenstein 1997a, 23–31.
51. Gates 1996, 43.
52. Oksenberg 2001, 87, 91.
53. Gungwu 1994, 237.
54. Rudolph 1987.

of the monopoly of force do not capture Asian political realities. In Southeast
Asia, for example, overlapping "circles of kings," or *mandalas,* represented "a
particular and often unstable political situation in a vaguely definable geographical area without fixed boundaries . . . where smaller centres tended to
look in all directions for security."[55] The Chinese and Vietnamese states, on the
other hand, presupposed that "any state should be associated with rules of dynastic succession and be described by fixed boundaries." But even in northeast
Asia, the political center, or king of kings, presided over a self-regulating civil
society.

To be sure, the center ruled by force at times, and it tried to extract resources
from civil society. But these activities did not define the character of Asian empires and kingdoms. The relation of the political center to civil society was cus-
todial and ritualized,[56] and civil society was divided into regions, castes, classes,
guilds, religious communities, and subkingdoms. Asia was a patchwork of galac-
tic polities, not absolutist monarchies. In these polities, a system of repulsion
and attraction kept all units circling in one orbit. At the center of the political
universe was not a "sun king," as in France or Spain, but an all-encompassing
sense of order. Rather than claims to effective sovereignty, ritual sovereignty
prevailed. Clifford Geertz's description of Negara, the theater state in Bali,
points to the ceremonial and aesthetic aspects of sovereignty and the importance of encompassing processes of cultural assimilation rather than restrictive
practices grounded in formal institutions.[57] These aspects of statehood helped
create a common form of life and express an encompassing cosmology. Military penetration and conquest played an important role. But so did social repli-
cation, through processes of diffusion and emulation. They helped create
common social and cultural domains tenuously related to the formal control
of a political center.[58]

Differences in Europe's and Asia's historical evolution are so deep as to suggest to some cultural psychologists and economic sociologists that cognitive
processes and intellectual traditions differ fundamentally. In taking stock of the
research in the field of cultural psychology, Richard Nisbett has charted the geography of thought in East and West. Aware of the risks of essentializing diverse
cognitive styles, and supported by experimental evidence, Nisbett finds the
modal differences in the responses of East Asian and U.S. subjects to be sufficiently great to warrant detailed attention:

> My research has led me to the conviction that two utterly different ap-
> proaches to the world have maintained themselves for thousands of
> years . . . there are very dramatic social-psychological differences be-
> tween East Asians as a group and people of European culture as a group.

55. Wolters 1982, 17, 13.
56. Rudolph 1987.
57. Geertz 1980.
58. Iriye 1992, 9.

East Asians live in an interdependent world in which the self is part of a larger whole; Westerners live in a world in which the self is a unitary free agent. . . . Westerners' preferred simplicity and Easterners' assumed complexity encompass more than their approaches to causality. Their preferences extend to the ways that knowledge is organized more generally. . . . My claim is not that the cognitive differences we find in the laboratory cause the differences in attitudes, values and behaviors, but that the cognitive differences are inseparable from the social and motivational ones. People hold the beliefs they do because of the way they think and they think the way they do because of the nature of the societies they live in.[59]

It is wrong to argue, in the tradition of Orientalism or Occidentalism, that people are what they are and cannot be different. The experiments of cultural psychologists offer considerable evidence of the internal variability of "the West."[60] A comparable gradient separates different groups in the United States, with Catholics and Jews closer to the Asian ideal type and Protestants tending toward the "extreme West" position. In East Asia, notable differences exist between Japanese and Chinese.[61] Furthermore, Westerners living in Asia learn the cues of their new environments, as do Asians living in Western societies. When a Canadian who had lived for several years in Japan applied for university positions in North America, his letter of introduction began with an apology for his unworthiness. And Japanese who have lived in the West for a while report a notable increase in self-esteem.[62] People living in Hong Kong and Asian Americans think either in Asian or in Western ways.[63] Experiments conducted in English or Chinese, whether in the United States, China, or Taiwan, suggest that language makes a substantial difference for those learning the second language relatively late. But for subjects in Hong Kong and Singapore who had learned the second language early in life, the results were strikingly different. The language in which the test was conducted made no difference, and the preferences were less marked for grouping words by categories, as in the typical Western style of cognition, rather than relationships, as is typical of Eastern cognition. "There is an effect of culture on thought," concludes Nisbett, "independent of language."[64] The movement of people and language acquisition thus probably have an effect on cognition. Nisbett concludes by pointing to the possibility that social change may be conducive to a blending of Western and Eastern cognitive forms and social systems and values.[65] While one-third of the Korean population is now Christian, resorts in the Catskills that formerly

59. Nisbett 2003, xx, 76, 135, 201.
60. Nisbett 2003, 69, 84–85.
61. Nisbett 2003, 71–72.
62. Nisbett 2003, 68.
63. Nisbett 2003, 118–19, 226–27.
64. Nisbett 2003,161.
65. Nisbett 2003,224–29.

catered to a middle-class Jewish clientele are now transforming themselves to become centers for the study of Buddhism. According to Nisbett, "There is in fact evidence that changes in social practices, and even changes in temporary states of social orientation, can change the way people perceive and think."[66] Such hybridity is likely to become more important in a world of porous regions.

Nisbett's argument agrees with that of Yasusuke Murakami, a sociologically inclined economist who also draws a sharp distinction between Eastern and Western intellectual traditions and styles of thought.[67] The West is characterized by metaprogressive, justice-oriented, transcendental-religious, and scientific thought based on the assumption of objective laws, the split between subject and object, and a self-contained self. The East is characterized by metaconservative, hermeneutic, rule-oriented, historical thought based on the assumption of an epistemologically split self that is self-reflective and must be construed primarily in terms of social relationships that create overlapping images of reality. Like Nisbett, Murakami argues that Eastern and Western "modes of thought should be mutually complementary and should support each other. This, I believe, is what occurs in human lives and history."[68] A recalibration of Western and Asian thought could provide a common ground in the resolution of bitter conflicts, for example between different nations in the international state system, between different forms of capitalism in the international economy, and between different civilizations in the global culture. The case Murakami builds for a polymorphic liberalism rests on a willingness to run intellectual risks in the search for a perspective that encompasses and integrates elements drawn from both East and West.

Although his is a book of political economy, Murakami starts and ends with culture. "Our touchstone," he writes, "for the twenty-first century is surely understanding between different cultures."[69] The future, he argues, will be marked not by homogenization but by diversity. The question of international understanding will require not a "communization" of cultures around standards set by modern science and the West. Instead, it requires a growing "commensurability" of cultures based on the power of individual imagination and empathy as the basis for a rule- rather than a justice-based interpretive framework and approach to life. The acknowledged individuality of different nations, civilizations, and regions lays the foundation for Murakami's approach: "Our task must be to accept the shift to borderlessness in the visible dimensions, and to build a world in which much cultural individuality can exist."[70]

The analysis of porous regions and the processes of regionalization offers more concrete and specific insights into the pathways toward different world orders. We do not have to view cultural processes as operating philosophically

66. Nisbett 2003, 226 and 227–29.
67. Murakami 1996 and 1990. I draw in the following two paragraphs on Katzenstein 1997c.
68. Murakami 1996, 21.
69. Murakami 1996, 389.
70. Murakami 1996, 65.

and psychologically at the individual level. The kind of regional arrangements that are likely to become politically important in the future, on questions of culture as much as on questions of economy and security, are collective not individual and institutional not psychological.

Germany and Japan

Asian and European regionalism are organized along different lines.[71] Asian regionalism is distinguished by the competition of national economies and ethnic groups in growing markets, European regionalism by law in an emerging polity. Both regions have distinctive though diluted regional identities. Germany and Japan are core regional states that both shape and are shaped by their regional context. Total military defeat and occupation created the space for substantial political reforms that remade both countries and thus, indirectly, their regions.

Germany and Japan were both relative latecomers to the Industrial Revolution and the game of international power politics. Germany's belated unification and Japan's Meiji Restoration set the stage for delayed, rapid industrialization and the growth of militant nationalism. Each country found distinctive responses to two historical challenges, the domestic incorporation of the working class and international competition in an imperialist era. In the late nineteenth century, Prussia and later Germany served as an institutional model for Japan. The military alliance that linked Germany and Japan during World War II thus reflected common historical trajectories. Authoritarianism prevailed over democracy at home. Power politics dominated over commercial expansion abroad. Surprise attack was the military strategy with which both countries hoped to reach their political objectives. In the thirty-years war that defined world politics between 1914 and 1945, Japan and Germany were revisionist powers. Their military and fascist regimes adopted autarchic policies, prepared for and waged imperialist wars, and conducted brutally violent campaigns of ethnic cleansing in the territories they conquered, which, in the case of Germany, escalated into a genocidal holocaust.

The transformation of Japan and Germany from challengers to clients and later to supporters of the United States had a major influence on European and Asian regionalism, one that helped stabilize world politics in the second half of the twentieth century.[72] This historical evolution prevented them from turning, as some feared at the end of the cold war, into "new superpowers,"[73] ready, at best, for a "cold peace."[74] The outcome of World War II and the history of postwar growth left both Japan and Germany with a substantial dis-

71. I draw here on Katzenstein 2003a.
72. Schmidt and Doran 1996. Katada, Maull, and Inoguchi 2004.
73. Bergner 1991.
74. Garten 1992.

crepancy between their socioeconomic and military power. Although on military issues they were content with playing a secondary role, on economic issues they are central players, and on issues of environmental and aid policy they have become world leaders.[75] Both states project their power onto other societies through economic, social, and cultural means, at times refusing to acknowledge the new sources of power they have created. Journalists described Germany in the 1970s and Japan in the 1980s as economic giants and political dwarfs. Since the mid-1970s, events have pushed both, Germany a bit earlier than Japan, toward a more active definition of their roles in world politics. The Japanese state tends to rely on national means to achieve its political goals, the German state on international ones. Neither state is likely to exchange technological, economic, social, and cultural power for military power, thereby transforming itself from a trading back to a warfare state.

This postwar transformation gave Japan and Germany some strikingly similar domestic features. Broadly speaking, the convergence of political conservatism with a moderate economic liberalism has taken hold in both countries.[76] Both countries have come to embrace some of the American objectives and values that were imposed on them after 1945. Both, for example, cherish, together with the United States, what Charles Maier has called the "politics of productivity."[77] As exemplars of "coordinated market economies"[78] and different brands of welfare capitalism, both have tried to resist the rise of what Ronald Dore calls "financialization" as the sole determinant of economic performance.[79] By the end of the 1990s, their evident problems of adjusting to new conditions in labor and capital markets was raising the question of "the end of diversity"—a bit more urgently perhaps before than after the 2001 collapse of the U.S. financial and telecom bubble.[80] Finally, in both countries, state and society have been realigned to conceal or transform state power. Japan relates state strength to market competition; Germany combines state power with semicorporatist arrangements.

It would be a mistake, however, to overemphasize their similarities. Japan's and Germany's welfare states differ along numerous dimensions. The sources of their economic difficulties in the 1990s differed also: for Germany, supply-side shocks in the wake of unification; for Japan, demand-side deflation in the wake of the collapse of an economy geared too heavily toward exports and prone to financial speculation. The collective purposes of each country's economic activities and social practices differ sufficiently to warrant their analysis as exemplars of *different* varieties of capitalism. Power is distributed differently in the two states. In Germany labor is stronger in its relations with business than

75. Katzenstein 1996, 153–90. Schreurs 2002. Kato 2002.
76. Streeck and Yamamura 2001.
77. Maier 1978.
78. Hall and Soskice 2001.
79. Dore 2000, 2.
80. Yamamura and Streeck 2003.

in Japan, while in Japan the state plays a stronger role in microeconomic planning and technology development.[81] The institutional mechanisms of coordination also differ significantly. Qualitative differences distinguish Germany's and Japan's systems of industrial relations, education and training, finance, and company-to-company relations.[82] And there exist important differences between Germany's industry-coordinated and Japan's group-coordinated market economies.

Different types of democratic capitalism follow different political logics. Whatever label one chooses, the evolving relations that link state and society in Germany and Japan are complex. In Japan's developmental state, business plays the central role in a system of "creative conservatism."[83] Business, especially big business, is at the center of the political coalition that sustained the Liberal Democratic Party in power for four decades before it was briefly toppled in 1993–94 by the excesses of money politics. Political change in the 1990s led to a dramatic weakening of leftist parties and left the LDP in a leading position. After a brief period of explosive growth in the immediate postwar years, Japan's labor movement found itself trapped in relative political isolation. Reorganization of the labor movement over the last two decades has given it a stronger voice in influencing some policy issues, but compared to what has happened in Germany its influence has remained weak.[84]

Government and bureaucracy have been the central actors in the evolution of Japan's postwar society and economy. The network linking the different actors in Japan's political economy is relatively tight. Traditionally, Japan's financial system was based not on autonomous capital markets but on a system of administered credit, which accorded the state bureaucracy a prominent role in influencing investment flows. Chummy relations between government and the financial sector are at the root of the mountain of bad debt that in recent years has become a serious drag on the economy and a constant invitation for ineffective policy tinkering and substantial social changes, such as the erosion and the weakening of a public education system based largely on meritocratic principles.

Distinctive of German politics is equality in the distribution of power among different actors. No great disparities exist, by the standards of Japanese politics, between business and labor or between the two major parties. In Germany, business and labor are politically so well entrenched that they can accommodate themselves with relative ease to changes in government control by center-right or center-left coalitions. The organizational strength and institutional presence of both business and labor is variable, though always impressive by Japanese standards. As in Japan, both are closely linked in the political econ-

81. Tilton and Boling 2000, 1.
82. Soskice 1994.
83. Pempel 1982.
84. Kume 1998.

omy, though at a larger number of nodes. The relation between industry and banks continues to be close, based on a system of competitive bargaining rather than one of private capital markets or credits administered by the state. Tight links among interest groups, political parties, and state bureaucracies create an inclusionary politics. The Constitutional Court and the Bundesbank, and its offspring the European Central Bank (ECB), act as watchdogs and institutional restraints. Political issues that appear too hot for party politicians to handle are left to judges and bankers.

German unification was an important break, but what is surprising is not how much but how little Germany changed after 1990. The core institutions of West Germany became German. Opportunities for basic change, where they existed, were quickly discarded. Attention focused instead on a rapid diffusion of West German institutions to the east and on a vast mobilization of resources to modernize East German society and economy. The results of that policy have yielded both impressive results in the pace of physical reconstruction and glaring failures in the regional concentration of unemployment. With the German economy sputtering through much of the 1990s, some basic political institutions, such as federal revenue sharing and the governance of labor markets, came under attack. In its cautious treatment of the symptoms of crisis, the new Germany has resembled the old.

In Japan, policy revolves around the interaction between party politicians and the state bureaucracy. Government policy relies on information, moral suasion, financial incentives, and political muscle, rather than on legal instruments. This tendency generates a symbiotic relation between business and government that puts little store in transparency. Informal connections rather than formal institutional rules define Japanese politics. In Germany, policy centers on the relations among party politicians, powerful interest groups, the federal and state bureaucracy, and a variety of parapublic institutions. A consensual style of politics prevails, often built on legal foundations. In times of rapid political and economic change, the legalization of politics creates rigidities not easily shed by Germany's way of conducting political business.

These thumbnail descriptions of "productivity democracy" in Japan and "industrial democracy" in Germany suggest that it is important not to mistake the liberal Anglo-American tree for the capitalist forest. In Germany, a wide variety of parastatal organizations open the state to group influences, at the same time providing state officials with channels that reach deep into society. Law offers the normative context for the formulation and implementation of public policies. By contrast, in the Japanese polity, normative context is defined by informal ties. A large number of formal and informal consultative mechanisms make Japan, even more than Germany, a structure geared to the creation and re-creation of social consensus.

Germany and Japan also differ in how they are "placed" in their regions. T. V. Paul explains Germany's and Japan's nonnuclear security policies as the result of "the regional dynamics arising out of security interdependence that these states entered into in the aftermath of World War II."[85] The acquisition of offensive weapons would have destabilized the security of neighboring states. In the case of Germany, regional dynamics led to participation in NATO and, subsequently, in other European security institutions. In the case of Japan, they meant a close alliance with the United States.

On other issues, too, the regional placement of Germany and Japan differs. In Asia, Japan's smaller neighbors seek to cope with dependence on Japan in two different ways. Until recently they often chose to imitate Japan's institutional model of a developmental state, adapting it to local conditions. They also seek to enhance their margin of choice in the various production networks that Japanese, overseas Chinese, Americans, and others have built up over the last three decades. These networks differ in their degree of openness, flexibility, and reaction time. Seeking to cope with Japan's size and power, the smaller Asian states navigate as best they can within and between different networks.

The experience of the smaller European states in dealing with Germany in numerous multilateral European institutions has created a different situation.[86] In political terms, it has neutralized their economic dependence. The institutionalization of interstate relations has fostered the gradual emergence of a European polity that Germany has consistently supported. Multilateral institutions are the arena within which bilateral relations between European states are conducted. This situation helps the smaller European states compensate for existing economic asymmetries. Specific domestic institutions, such as democratic corporatism, also help in coping with international economic dependence. Both international and domestic political arrangements have thus counteracted economic and political dependence and helped neutralize the fear of German hegemony.

The extension of legal rules into Europe and of informal political arrangements into Asia reflect ways of conducting political business that Germany and its European partners and Japan and its Asian partners consider quite normal. Germany and Japan are anomalies, militarily incomplete states with formidable economic strengths and politically soft shells, and their anomalous character has shaped European and Asian regionalism. For Germany, building the European Union became a natural response to both the terrible memories of its unilateral pursuit of power and the challenges that global and international changes are creating for all European states. In sharp contrast, Japan seeks to meet current challenges primarily through informal initiatives and arrangements that are typically linked to economic transactions in regional and global markets. Differences in contemporary approaches play out against different ways of dealing with the past. Diffusing the fear of Germany's or Japan's reemerging hegemony is a very important political fact in both Europe and

85. Paul 1996, 2.
86. Katzenstein 1985, 2003d.

Asia. Japan has shown extreme reticence about acknowledging the acts of military aggression and human atrocities it committed in the 1930s and 1940s; German public discourse has been more forthcoming. As a result, political anxiety over the prospect of a regional hegemon is greater in Asia than in Europe.

Germany and Japan differ starkly in the strength of the international and national convictions of their leaders. Their experiences of defeat and occupation had a bearing on this difference. Gerhard Lehmbruch insists that the different trajectories of the two polities after 1945 depended on the reconstitution of different coalitions during the period of occupation. Germany ceased to exist and was partitioned.[87] The power of the central state bureaucracy was ruptured totally, while the country's managerial capitalism continued. In sharp contrast, Japan and the Imperial Household continued to exist without interruption. The power of the central bureaucracy was altered, not transformed, whereas a rupture in Japan's system of family capitalism created a "managerial revolution from above."[88]

Japan's and Germany's national and international identities were also shaped by the institutions that the United States put in place in Europe and Asia after 1945. As a result, Japan and Germany have taken different stances toward the world, which I have elsewhere dubbed "Hobbesian" in the case of Japan and "Grotian" in the case of Germany.[89] For Japan, the world is a hostile place, and Japanese actors must cope on their own. For Germany, the world is a community—European, Atlantic, global—to which Germany belongs. Japanese politicians act with a mixture of guile and goodwill in developing long-term, interest-based relations. Political and economic asymmetries are, from the Japanese perspective, sources of both power and community. But a clearly defined national sense of self is never in doubt. In the case of Germany, collective identity has a more international cast. Germany is part of an international community of states whose conduct is defined by legal rules. And it is that community that helps define the interests that Germany pursues. As a prominent Krupp executive told Isaac Deutscher in 1946, "Now . . . everything depends on whether we are in a position to find the right, great solutions on a European scale. Only a European scale, gentlemen, isn't that so?"[90]

This difference in purposes between the Japanese and German states is central to the characteristically different approaches they take to many problems. These include their commitment to multilateral or bilateral principles; the depth of their involvement in international organizations; and the degree of their activism or passivity in international affairs, as illustrated by their willingness to lead in international initiatives and participate in collective problem solving. Also important is their willingness to identify as part of the core of a Western international society of states and the international alliance that sur-

87. Lehmbruch 2001.
88. Aoki 1988, 185.
89. Katzenstein 1996, 153–54.
90. Quoted in Kramer 1991, 158.

rounds the United States.[91] Germany and Japan vary consistently along all of
these dimensions, with Germany tending more toward the international, and
Japan more toward the national pole.

For Japan, national and international orientations are closely linked. Defeat
in the Pacific War and U.S. occupation offered new opportunities. Prime Minister Shigeru Yoshida seized the moment to construct an alternative vision of
Japan: a peaceful state bent only on commercial expansion. This identity was
deeply contested in the 1950s but eventually prevailed, in part because of the
strong opposition of a Left fully mobilized against attempts to refurbish police
and armed forces in the image of the 1930s. Japan's gradual internationalization since the early 1970s is a widely debated process that aligns changes in international conditions to Japan's national purposes. Pressures from the
external world point to contradictions between a symbolic emperor and a sovereign people. They spur intense debates at times but no mass political mobilization. Identity fluctuation by stealth, rather than transformation by identity
entrepreneurs, has been the result. Japan seeks to meet the requirements of internationalism within an evolving nationalist frame.

The international orientation of Germany is intimately linked to a Europe
that serves many of Germany's most cherished national goals. In contemporary
Germany, it is rarely productive, and frequently impossible, to sort out clearly
Germany's "national" from its "European" interest. Half a century of experience with European integration and NATO are one important reason. Nationalism led to catastrophic defeat, economic collapse, and national division;
internationalism, to prosperity in peace and eventual unification.

German internationalism is nurtured by German and European institutions
that are quite similar. Germany's "cooperative" federalism and parapublic institutions share important traits with Europe's system of multilevel governance.
And so, for reasons that have a lot to do with German power and influence, do
the positions that the central bank and the court occupy in both Germany and
Europe. In contrast to Britain, which favors NATO over the European Union,
and France, which prefers the European Union to NATO, Germany is strongly
committed to both. Germany has always supported the cause of enlargement
of both institutions, because of its strong preference for relating to other states
multilaterally. Put differently, Germany does not shy away from far-reaching
moves toward integration based on a broad definition of Europe. The internationalization of Germany's state identity is subject to intense domestic debates, especially on issues of citizenship, yet elite consensus on the benefits of
an international identity, as measured by support for European integration, is
stronger in Germany than in any other European state.[92]

Thus, in contrast to Japan, Germany has been more receptive to international liberalization in recent decades. A strong commitment to multilateral-

91. Gurowitz 1999.
92. European Commission 1996, 4.

ism rather than bilateralism in Europe's regional affairs has much to do with that difference. The U.S.-led drive for international liberalization after 1945 made provisions for customs unions operating under the auspices of the General Agreement on Tariffs and Trade. In 1957, six West European states, Germany among them, formed such a union with strong U.S. support. No such union emerged in Asia. The U.S. market looms large for Japan, the European market for Germany. This difference in regional market integration has left Germany and Japan with different types of "soft-shell" political systems, open, as I shall argue in chapter 6, to different forms of external political influence.

An institutionalized process of integration has embedded Germany deeply *in* Europe. Multilateral institutions such as the European Union have had a profound effect on the internationalization of Germany's state identity. Furthermore, the European welfare state has generated a nationalism of individual entitlement that has undercut the internationalization of state identity much less than a more traditional nationalism of collective assertion might have done. Japan *and* Asia are less deeply entangled with each other. The multilateral institutions that are beginning to spring up in Asia serve the purpose of enhancing transparency and reducing uncertainty. They are too weak, at least to date, to undermine significantly the grip of other collective identities that operate in various network structures. And a traditional nationalism continues to have a powerful hold on the collective imagination of various societies. These differences between Germany and Japan thus are congruent with the differences in regional identities that separate Europe from Asia.

CHAPTER FOUR

Regional Orders in Economy and Security

In combining global and international processes with different institutional orders, regions shape very different policy domains. To support this claim, I draw evidence from technology and production networks on the one hand, and external and internal security on the other. Global and international elements are deeply intermingled in both cases. Yet it turns out that technology and production illustrate global processes with particular clarity, whereas internal and external security do the same for international processes.

Technology pulverizes groups, nations, and cultures and, in the words of Langdon Winner, "now governs its own course, speed, and destination."[1] During the twentieth century, technology was increasingly regarded as a means toward broad social development goals, serving the dual objectives of efficiency and equity. It is now by its very nature an activity that is largely public and accessible on a global scale. Government attempts to nationalize science have been largely unsuccessful, and this is increasingly true of technology as well. "The entire concept of a country's technology," writes Ernst-Jürgen Horn, has "inherent limits in the presence of an open international trade and investment system. A particular technology is first produced in an individual country, but it can then be licensed or sold abroad or applied through foreign affiliates. The know-how involved will become internationally diffused sooner or later."[2] The result of this process is the worldwide availability of technologies of best practice.

How can we measure the extent to which technology has spread globally? The growth of direct foreign investment is often used as an imperfect proxy. Among the rich industrial states, direct foreign investment grew at twice the

1. Winner 1977, 16.
2. Horn 1990, 67–68.

rate of GNP in the 1960s and four times the rate in the 1980s. It has most likely accelerated since then.[3]

Questions of state security illustrate processes of internationalization extremely well. Realists argue that the national security interests of major states provide the foundations for international order. For brief moments, to be sure, social and ideological changes may conceal the harshness of international competition, and the years following the end of the cold war may have been such an exceptional period. Yet the Gulf War, the wars in the Balkans, the 9/11 attacks, and the wars the United States fought against Afghanistan and Iraq are reminders of the enduring realities of international life. At best, anarchy can be ameliorated by international institutions. For the last four centuries, and for the foreseeable future, states will remain the main guarantors of national security and the basic building blocks of international order.

The nuclear revolution after 1945 illustrates this point. At first glance, it appeared to herald the decline of the nation-state. For the first time in history, state borders were made permeable by weapons so powerful that they could end life on earth. The very existence of any state, even the two superpowers, was put at risk. With the advent of the nuclear revolution, global security needs appeared to have outstripped the security logic of the international state system. But instead of changes in warfare revolutionizing international politics, governments developed a system of deterrence that reinforced the power of states and created a stable cold war balance of power. Military technology was bent to the security needs of states. Realists insist that the new war-fighting technologies now on the horizon will similarly be shaped by the logic of the international system and the imperatives it creates for the provision of state security.

For good or ill, states remain the ultimate repository of power. Within a couple of months after 9/11, war between the United States and Afghanistan's Taliban government had eliminated the territorial bases from which al Qaeda had operated, and severely cramped, though it did not eliminate, its ability to plan large-scale attacks. Furthermore, 9/11 convinced the Bush administration that the preventive elimination of "evil states" with weapons of mass destruction had become a strategic imperative. The U.S. attack on Iraq in the spring of 2003 illustrated this dramatic shift in U.S. policy and raised the specter of similar wars in the future. States thus remain central actors seeking to guard their prerogatives in international politics and national affairs. Both orderly states like Taiwan, and messy ones like Afghanistan, provide the institutional base from which crime organizes itself on an international scale.[4] Indeed, the very existence of states imposes the definition of criminality in the first place.

Striking regional commonalities across these very different policy sectors set

---

3. Between 1986 and 1988, the average annual flow of DFI was $123.4 billion; by the year 2000, close to the peak of a global investment boom, it had reached $1.5 trillion before declining to $735 billion in 2001 and $534 billion in 2002. Howells and Wood 1993, 3–4, 153. *The Economist* 2001a. Williams 2002.

4. Myers 1995.

Europe apart from Asia. For example, German technology policy in Europe is driven by economic and political considerations. German producers seek to minimize cost. They have relied on eastern Europe since the end of the cold war—as they did on southern Europe in the 1970s and 1980s—as extended workbenches for German industry, while paying minimal attention to issues of technology transfer. For the government, technology transfer is an important political issue only in its broader European rather than its narrower business context. Germany's internal and external security policies betray a similar orientation. Its security institutions are more internationalized than perhaps those of any large state. Its preference for peace is strong but tempered by the requirement of working with its European partners and the United States in a host of international security organizations. This context does not preclude occasional deviations due to intense domestic pressures, as in the unilateral and premature recognition of Croatia in December 1991, and in unconditional opposition to war against Iraq, even if backed by a UN Security Council resolution, in the fall and winter of 2002–3. Yet Germany's general preference for multilateralism persists in the context of special relationships, especially with France and the United States.

In Asia, Japan's policy reflects a strong preference for national autonomy within the constraints of markets and states. Maintaining rather than pooling national sovereignty is the core objective of government policy. The smaller states in northeast and Southeast Asia behave similarly, as South Korea and Taiwan illustrate. Japanese policy has facilitated the creation of regional production networks that tie together producers, subcontractors, and distributors across sectors and national borders in ways that protect Japan's control over core technologies. Of political importance in Japan and other Asian states are institutions and practices geared to rapid industrialization and broader economic and social development of the polity. Japanese security policies also reflect a national orientation: a deep preference for nonviolence. They are organized around the bilateral security relationship with the United States that has remained central for Japan for a half century. Ad hoc bilateral cooperation with other states and Asian security institutions are growing in significance, but they remain embryonic.

Technology and Production Networks in Asia and Europe

Asia's technology order is marked by rival networks of firms operating in markets that are organized along national, ethnic, and sectoral lines. Japanese networks tend to be closed and are given to slow, incremental changes. In building their regional production networks, Japanese corporations are typically reluctant to share technologies, either with other countries or with other corporations. The overseas Chinese offer an alternative: their networks tend to be commercial rather than technological. Since the late 1980s, however, some

Chinese networks have opened up to incorporate U.S. manufacturers. These more open networks lend themselves to quick and flexible decisions. Less protective of proprietary technologies, they are more ready to transfer technology to local enterprises. Although they lack the depth and breadth of Japanese and Chinese networks, Korean, American, and European corporations constitute alternative networks also suited to facilitate the flow of technology.[5]

What matters politically at the European level is the existence not of production networks in which technology is controlled or diffused but of an emerging European polity that attracts both Germany and the smaller states that depend on it. Contemporary European politics revolves primarily around the broadening of EU membership and the issues that fall under EU jurisdiction, rather than around the issue of national control over technology and production. In political terms, it matters little that German corporations have shown a proclivity for direct foreign investments that do not enhance technological capacities in southern, central, and eastern Europe. Transfer payments from the European Union to weak regions matter more. Europe has developed a specific institutional logic that differs in fundamental ways from the corporate and ethnic structures knitting Asia together. In precommercial technologies, for example, Europe has become such a substantial source of funding that the German government has curtailed national support for some technologies deemed of critical importance. Because of institutional differences, such a policy makes sense in Europe; it would be politically nonsensical in Asia.

Asia

Since the Meiji Restoration, Japan has developed an industrial structure that blends basic, intermediate, and high technology industries.[6] As Japan, unique among late industrializers, succeeded in moving to the technological frontier, its industrial orientation was reflected in a tight integration between R & D and shop floor activities. This was true in particular for technology imports. In the case of "turn-key" operations, Japan transformed the "know-how" of imported technology into the "know-why" of a technological process. For late industrializers, the shop floor is a battleground. Because many aspects of technology are tacit rather than fully specified, reverse engineering is often insufficient to unlock all aspects of a technology's deep structure. The shop floor is critical: that is where borrowed technology is customized to fit conditions specific to particular production processes and targeted markets.

Regionalization is leading Japan and Asia into a new era. For a variety of reasons, including high labor costs and environmental constraints, small and medium-size firms are losing the advantageous production conditions they had enjoyed in Japan. Foreign suppliers are becoming more important. As Mit-

5. Borrus, Ernst, and Haggard 2000, 14–31. Linden 2000, 221.
6. The following section draws on Katzenstein 2003b.

suhiro Seki writes, "Japan's full-set industrial structure . . . is under siege, and the nation is faced with the need to form close relationships with East Asia, especially China, for the survival of the fundamental industrial technologies that drive its high-tech sectors. We are entering the age of an Asian network in technology."[7]

Opening Japan's markets to foreign producers goes beyond the trade and investment liberalization that has been the focus of U.S. political pressures. "Opening" in this new context refers to a growing reliance on the basic technological capacities of Asian producers, tied initially to Japanese producers in tight production chains and eventually able to compete on their own. Japanese producers have responded vigorously to government incentive programs and, in contrast to U.S. firms, rely more readily on local and regional markets for procurement and sales.[8] The operations of Japanese firms tend to strengthen networks in Asian markets; the operations of American and Chinese firms keep networks in Asian markets open.[9]

This is not to suggest that Japanese firms share their technology freely. Yet evidence is accumulating that, over time, Japanese production networks are becoming more international as they mature and gain experience. Sensing a crisis in Japan's control over fundamental technologies in the small and medium-size firm sector, its large corporations have moved from developing basic technologies in-house, in the late 1980s, to reducing the risk of losing their multitiered supplier networks in early 2000.

The protection of technology by Japanese corporations is evident in their foreign operations. In detailed empirical studies, Hiroshi Itagaki and his collaborators have shown that barriers to the transfer of Japanese technology are lower in the United States than in East Asia.[10] That difference illustrates a shift in self-image, away from Japan as a self-reliant national economy that defends its autonomy in a hostile world, and toward a nation deeply embedded in different regional systems of production. Yet in East Asia, business practices frequently impede rather than accelerate the transfer of technology from Japanese firms to foreign producers. Asymmetric dependence, not symmetric interdependence, is characteristic of Asia's Japan-centered production networks.

In the apparel and electronics industries, Gary Gereffi has shown, the success of Japan and Asia's new industrial economies (NIEs) is part and parcel of the increasing diversification and integration of national economies. Regional production networks are key. These networks are part of more encompassing, producer- or buyer-driven commodity chains. "The successful export industries of Japan and the East Asian NIEs," writes Gereffi, "create hierarchical divisions of labor within and between regions. East Asian firms have mastered the art of

7. Seki 1994, 86, 3.
8. Encarnation 1999, 5.
9. Dobson 1997a, 17. Dobson 1997b, 243–45. Yue and Dobson 1997, 254–59.
10. Itagaki 1997, 367–72.

using networks as a strategic asset."[11] Japanese producers are strong in producer-driven chains, specifically in automobiles, electronics, and computers; U.S. buyers dominate in buyer-driven chains. The open character of Asian production networks in part reflects the presence of both types of chains. Gereffi concludes that these investment and trade networks lie "above" the interaction of discrete national systems of production but "below" the global economy.[12]

The regionalization of Japanese production networks has helped to accelerate economic change in Asia. Throughout the postwar period, and in particular after the oil shocks of the 1970s, "Japan's national security was premised on the security and stability of Southeast Asia, then a primary source of Japanese imports of petroleum, rubber, tin, and other critical natural resources."[13] In seeking to penetrate protected domestic markets, Japanese subsidiaries built up strong local ties. Local content in the products of Japanese foreign affiliates was relatively high, and Japanese firms supported some suppliers in the host country even at the expense of product quality and cost efficiency.[14] In this initial phase, Japanese producers occasionally exported intermediate technologies essential to the success of foreign assembly operations.[15]

In the wake of the sharp appreciation of the yen after 1985, a dramatic escalation in domestic costs prompted Japanese producers to move offshore. This development accelerated a de facto regional integration of some parts of the Asian economies into Japanese corporate structures. By 1992, more than nine thousand Japanese affiliates operated overseas, many of them in Asia. A new division of labor was taking shape, in which different countries became production bases and intrafirm trade took place across regional borders.[16] In this new system, Japanese producers achieve economies of scale and profitability through specialization.[17]

With varying degrees of success, Asia's newly industrializing economies are exploiting alternatives to the regionalization of Japan's developmental policies.[18] To some extent, Japanese corporations themselves provide Southeast Asian producers with opportunities to reduce technological dependence.[19] For example, rather than build up business ties with local firms, Japan's major corporations are forcing their parts suppliers, more or less gently, to regionalize their operations. Yet not all parts suppliers are able or willing to do so, and

11. Gereffi 1996, 76.
12. Gereffi 1996, 108–9.
13. Hatch and Yamamura 1996, 118.
14. Ernst 1997, 213.
15. Seki 1994, 99.
16. Ernst and O'Connor 1989, 42.
17. Between 1983 and 1987, Japanese profits in Asia were three times higher than in the United States and twice as high as in Europe. This profit gap widened further in the early 1990s. In 1993, profits from operations in Asia ran at 4 percent compared to zero profits in the United States and losses equivalent to 1 percent in Europe. *The Economist* 1995, 21–22. Profits are defined as recurring profit-to-sales ratios for overseas subsidiaries of Japanese manufactures.
18. Taylor 1995, 16.
19. Hatch and Yamamura 1996, 169–70, 177.

some of these firms enter into technology tie-ups with local firms to which they
sell their know-how for a fee. In 1993, Japanese technology exports to Asia exceeded technology exports to the United States by about 40 percent.[20]

A further regionalization of Japanese production networks in the 1990s required adjustments in corporate and government policies. The improved production and innovation capabilities of firms and the growth in East Asian
markets for electronic products and services pushed Japanese producers to adjust their strategies. The dynamic technical efficiency that Japanese corporations had previously achieved through organizing supplier networks inside
Japan had to be transferred to producers operating abroad, especially in China,
an essential provider of basic technologies.[21]

Yet the Japanese production system faces sharp limitations on the technology transfers that it generates. Generally speaking, since the mid-1980s large
Japanese corporations have been reluctant to share advanced technologies.[22]
Typically, both government and corporations make special efforts to counteract adverse shifts in technology—not only from positions of strength, from
which Japanese producers understandably wish to extract maximum profits,
but also from positions of anticipated weakness. In the early 1990s, for example, seeking to protect "technological national security," MITI announced a
plan aimed at strengthening domestic suppliers in the crisis-ridden casting and
forging industries. The program illustrated a sense of urgency "over the hem-
orrhaging of the nation's fundamental technologies."[23]

Concerned with the strength of Japan's technological base, the mission of
the renamed Ministry of Economy, Trade and Industry (METI) has become in-
exorably regionalized. Indeed, if METI wanted to support the operation of Japanese business abroad, it had little choice but to support industrial networks in
Asia. In the mid-1990s it developed a new plan to assist in the industrialization
of Cambodia, Laos, and Myanmar, which soon came to include all of Southeast
Asia. With headquarters in Bangkok, financed and staffed exclusively by METI,
this initiative supports stronger industrial linkages and liberal investment policies in East Asia.[24] More generally, METI has had to include in its mission "the
recovery and expansion of the Asian regional economy" as a whole, for example, by promoting imports from the region.[25] And it is seeking to facilitate tie-
ups between Japan's small and medium-sized firms and ASEAN corporations.
METI also plans to create a database of important technologies owned by local
firms in Southeast Asia, which it will distribute to Japanese firms, especially
smaller ones, planning to invest in the region.[26]

The rapidity of Japan's reorientation after 1985 and the need to control cost

20. Hatch and Yamamura 1996, 9, 163. Hatch 2000, 280.
21. Seki 1994, 3, 30–31, 99, 128, 130–32, 154–56.
22. Seki 1994, 17, 20–21, 23, 27. See also Dobson 1997b, 246. Yue and Dobson 1997, 258.
23. Seki 1994, 31.
24. Hatch 2000, 239.
25. Kohno 2003, 103–4.
26. Kohno 2003, 104–5.

and quality help explain why Japanese corporations continued to adhere to a centralized model of integrating local subsidiaries into their regional operations and were at best reluctant to transfer technology.[27] This is the central point of what one might call a Japan-centered market hierarchy, in which Asian suppliers are subordinate to Japanese firms as final product assemblers for exports, and must rely on high value-added Japanese components and equipment. In electronics and autos in particular, Asia has become an integrated production network for Japanese firms from which they can pursue global corporate strategies.

Asian producers benefit substantially from tie-ups with Japanese firms that create technological dependence, for they gain access to a network that promises markets and profits if not autonomy. Strings also function as ties: restrictive conditions on the use of technology are balanced by access to the customers, suppliers, distributors, and political allies of the Japanese manufacturer.[28]

Japanese technology is part of a larger package of relationships that loses much of its usefulness once it is severed from other elements of the network. These advantages were evident in the wake of the 1997 Asian financial crisis: Japanese companies used lower labor costs to partially offset higher material input costs, thereby delaying layoffs and creating goodwill among a more loyal workforce.[29] Indeed, the rationalization of overhead costs has encouraged employment *increases* in some industries. On balance, however, rationalization savings have been insufficient to outweigh the costs associated with the underutilization of plant capacities and the strains on cash flow. To keep themselves afloat, firms appear to have cannibalized their East Asian operations, moving to create more network openness, flexibility, and decentralization.

The role of technology in this system of control has become more important in recent years, but the system's basic logic has deeper historical roots. In his analysis of Japanese foreign investment in the 1960s and 1970s, Terutomo Ozawa noted the distinctive immaturity of Japanese foreign investment, as measured in terms of firm size and technological sophistication: small firms in traditional industries such as textiles were leading Japan's expansion into Asia.[30] Foreign investment became a way by which the ruling political coalition extended the basic institutional arrangements of the Japanese model. Technology is not helping Japan's neighbors to embark on autonomous development; instead, it tends to maintain Japan's preeminence.

Seeking to blunt protectionist forces in the U.S. Congress, Japanese corporations have put their new Asian production alliances into the service of a global strategy. The Japanese government has supported the regionalization of production networks with a host of trade, aid, investment, and cultural policies. Through regionalization, Japan has found a way to extend imbalanced

27. Hatch 2000, 236–44.
28. Hatch 2000, 132–33, 356.
29. Tachiki 2001, 5–13.
30. Ozawa 1979, 25–30, 76, 82, 199–200.

trade relations with all of its major trading partners on both sides of the Pacific. As in the 1960s and 1970s, Japan is externalizing its domestic arrangements into Asia. This time, however, it is a defensive move by Japan's business community.[31]

In parts of northeast and Southeast Asia, a technology order has thus evolved that reflects Japan's institutionalized political and corporate practices. It would be a mistake to frame the issue primarily in terms of deliberate strategizing by the dominant actors in Japan.[32] Regionalization is, rather, an extension of domestic practices, an interlocking system of state and corporate policies that Japanese actors largely take for granted and that is being adapted to new conditions in world markets. This explains why Japan's Asia policy has continued to closely link international public finance (such as aid, official export credits, export and investment guarantees) to private capital and financial flows (such as direct foreign investment, trade, bank lending).[33] In brief, Asia's regional technology order is shaped significantly by the institutional practices of Japan.

This does not mean that Japan determines Asia's technology order, and certainly alternatives exist to Japan-centered production alliances. Yet the structure of ownership and production in Asian business is generally defined by relationship-based networks. Korean conglomerates, for example, are owned by a handful of families. Centrally managed and vertically integrated, they segment the Korean economy and have been more successful than firms in Southeast Asia in extracting technology from Japanese producers. Because of changes in Korean politics and the 1997 Asian financial crisis, these conglomerates were in increasing disarray in the 1990s. The same cannot be said of Chinese firms. Controlled by a few individuals, their capital comes from family members and silent partners. Production occurs in networks of small and medium-sized firms, which cooperate to produce components and finished products without losing their independence. At times, these networks bring together Chinese firms with the technology of U.S. corporations. Clustered around producers based in Taiwan, Hong Kong, and Singapore, such networks are spreading, and they point to the emergence of non-Japanese alternatives to Japanese production structures. Finally, the emergence of China has made firms on the mainland serious competitors to Japan-centered production networks in Southeast Asia and improved greatly their bargaining position over the transfer of technology.

Asian governments also seek to lessen dependence through their national policies. Korea, for example, tried for decades to foster national technology programs through its largest firms. In imitating Japan, it hoped to lessen technological dependence on Japan. Yet in the mid-1980s, Korea's consumer goods industry imported from Japan crucial components for major exports, such as

31. Hatch 2000.
32. Hatch and Yamamura 1996, 22, 115–16.
33. Kato 2002, 81–82, 105–24, 147–48.

video cassette recorders, microwave ovens, fax machines, personal computers, and printers. And throughout the 1990s the Korean semiconductor industry remained heavily dependent on Japanese imports.[34] In contrast, Taiwan, Thailand, and Malaysia tailor their response to local circumstances and to economic networks run by overseas Chinese—thus sidestepping excessive dependence on Japanese producers.

Technonationalism has not lost its relevance for contemporary China. In the words of Ding Xinghao of Shanghai's Institute of International Studies, "Japan's view is always a flying geese formation with Japan as the head goose. Our memories are long, so we aren't about to fly in Japan's formation."[35] China is not yet in a position to define Asia's emerging technology order. But as its economic and political importance rises, it may well reach that level in some market segments in the near future. When it does, China will reinforce rather than challenge how Japan has dealt with problems of technology. China's goal is autonomous national development in an inherently hierarchical international division of labor. Powerful national and provincial governments with coherent political strategies to foster technological development are a natural means for enhancing China's competitiveness.

What holds for China does not apply to the overseas Chinese. Hong Kong is a hub around which the economy of Southeast Asia revolves as well as for corporations operating across the world economy. Michael Borrus suggests that the astonishing turnaround of the U.S. electronics industry in the early 1990s "has rested in large part on the growing technical sophistication and competitive strength of Asian-based producers in the China Circle, Singapore, and South Korea."[36] Confronted by a potentially crippling dependence on their Japanese competitors for precision components and other vital technologies, U.S. firms decided to make underlying technologies more open to firms in Chinese networks. They gradually turned their Asian production networks from simple assembly affiliates into producers that could compete effectively with the Japanese.[37] This policy exemplifies both a U.S. response to excessive dependence on Japanese suppliers and a move toward an emerging Chinese production network greatly strengthened by the decision of U.S. corporations.

The rapidity of that development resulted from the symbiosis of U.S. corporate strategies with both supportive government policies and local Asian investments. The hard disk drive industry is a good illustration.[38] It was the globalization of the operations of small firms like Seagate that assured their survival and propelled U.S. producers first to Singapore and then to locations throughout Southeast Asia. More established U.S. firms followed; Japanese firms followed later still, never posing a serious threat to U.S. domination of

34. Enos and Park 1987, 228–30. Smith 1997, 748–49.
35. Hatch 2000, 354.
36. Borrus 1997, 141.
37. Borrus 1997, 145–46.
38. McKendrick, Doner, and Haggard 2000.

the industry. The dual structure of the industry is still evident, with R & D located in Silicon Valley and production in and around Singapore.

Like Korea and Taiwan, Singapore pursues a strategy to capture advanced technology. The government's goal is not merely to receive imported technology but to develop a system aimed at quick adaptation, diffusion, and improvement. Although the specific mix of factors in the first-tier Asian political economies differs from country to country, all governments have relied on a strategy of capturing technology to accelerate the creation of competitive advantage in industries where no advantage initially existed. In second-tier economies, such as Malaysia, Thailand, Indonesia, and the Philippines, however, the chances for success are appreciably lower.

The rapidly growing, newly industrializing economies and other Asian investment channels offer an important avenue for sidestepping excessive reliance on Japan. Thailand and Malaysia, for example, tailor their response to the existence of overseas Chinese economic networks. First-tier Taiwanese firms have matured in their control over key technologies. They are themselves now riding herd on an extensive indigenous supply base that spreads technology to "thousands of small and medium-size design, component, parts, sub-assembly, and assembly houses" that have become part of a local production network and supply base.[39] Technical specialization has thus helped both U.S. firms and indigenous Asian producers to reduce their dependence on Japanese producers. In the coming decades, leadership in this industry could easily pass from U.S. and Japanese firms to indigenous Asian producers, particularly those located in the China Circle.

This view is not uncontested. For Walter Hatch and Kozo Yamamura, all the talk about Greater China, all the claims that an alternative manufacturing and financial network is being built up by and around China, is nothing but "idle chatter." In their view, Chinese networks are no more than a series of ad hoc deals. Handicapped in their ability to adopt new technology, even Taiwanese businessmen "have felt compelled to open wide their arms" to Japanese multinational corporations.[40] Chinese networks cultivate rent-seeking; Japanese networks, dynamic technological efficiency. In their view, the architecture of Asian regionalism is strictly hierarchical, with Japan at the apex. Japan controls the flow of aid and technologies and provides capital and intermediate inputs to producers in other countries. South Korea and Taiwan, though quickly closing the development gap, specialize in somewhat lower-tech products and remain dependent on Japan for key technologies.

Taiwan's meteoric rise in Asian production networks during the 1990s undercut such skepticism. Government policy and corporate investment came together in an industrial revolution in Taiwan's personal computer and chip industries. In less than two decades, Taiwan transformed itself from a low-wage

39. Borrus 1997, 152.
40. Hatch and Yamamura 1996, 96.

economy to the third largest producer of information technologies. It did so neither through a state-led industrial offensive nor through reliance on the unrestricted play of market forces. Instead, the government exploited the economic advantages it could derive from collaboration between Silicon Valley and the Hsinchu-Taipei region. Those connections were made possible first and foremost by the thousands of Taiwanese engineers returning home from the United States, especially in the 1990s. Highly skilled, these overseas Chinese were distinguished by strong ethnic and professional identities. As the largest group of Silicon Valley's foreign-born engineers, the Taiwanese and other overseas Chinese were also by far the largest group of foreign-born CEOs. Many of them are more comfortable than entrepreneurs from other Asian countries in setting up branch operations in Silicon Valley.[41] The group was a ready target as the Taiwanese government established a burgeoning venture capital market in the early 1980s to help build its own high-tech industry. Dollar for dollar, an investment in venture capital markets produces three to five times as many patents as an investment in R & D.[42] The outcome is a variety of networks linking Taiwanese firms and engineers as well as U.S. firms operating in Silicon Valley and Hsinchu-Taipei. A 2002 survey of Chinese and Indian engineers and executives working in Silicon Valley suggests the image of "brain circulation" rather than "brain-drain."[43]

Since the mid-1990s, the rise of the financial and manufacturing networks of Greater China has affected the strategy of Japanese corporations. As Japanese producers have been reluctant to diffuse their technology to Asian suppliers, Michael Borrus doubts there will be a quick turnaround in corporate strategies in favor of sourcing from an independent Asian supply base.[44] Dieter Ernst, on the other hand, sees Japanese corporations more rapidly opening their electronics production networks to extend the geographic coverage and the local embeddedness of regional production. In his view, Japanese corporations have a strong interest in developing and harnessing Asia's resources and technological capabilities.[45] In the 1990s, he writes, "The affiliates of Japanese higher level component suppliers thus increasingly have to rely on domestic Asian subcontractors, mostly through various contractual, nonequity arrangements such as consignment production and contract manufacturing."[46] This development, were it to occur on a large scale, would signal a historic shift. Change, however, will not be instantaneous. Ernst and Borrus do agree that throughout the 1990s, most key components were still sourced from Japan or from Japanese firms producing in the region.[47] One reason for the slowness of change is the accumulated weakness of Japan's business model in

41. Saxenian and Hsu 2001.
42. Saxenian and Li 2002, 18.
43. Richtel 2002, C6.
44. Borrus 1997, 149, 153–54.
45. Ernst 1997, 210–11, 218–36.
46. Ernst 1997, 223.
47. Ernst 1997, 223. Borrus 1997, 153–54.

an era of far-reaching transformations in the organization of regional production networks.[48]

The competitive networks that interlace Asia's political economies create a structural predisposition for openness. Japan's direct foreign investment in Asia is targeted, by sector and country, to harmonize with the structural transformation of Japan's economy. Even more important, the dependence of Asia (including Japanese Asian-based affiliates) on the U.S. market supports the continued openness of Asian regionalism. Japanese engagement in the rich U.S. and European markets remains unabated. And the financial and manufacturing networks of the overseas Chinese have been leading the way, in terms of both direct foreign investment and exports, since the late 1980s. Openness to global markets is the most likely path for Asian regionalism.

Whether Asia will retain a controlled regional technology order or evolve something new and more open will depend substantially on which of two views of Japan is closer to the truth. Should Japan falter, other Asian states, such as China, will take its place. Alternatively, high-technology industries dominated by U.S. or European producers could further anchor Asia in global hierarchies—in 1995, the United States still provided 71 percent of Japan's technology imports while taking only 29 percent of its technology exports.[49] Regional production alliances thus may broaden in geographical scope without necessarily supporting enhanced national autonomy. Even if Japan were to lose its established position, deeply entrenched characteristics of Asia's technology order would likely endure.

Maintaining or gaining control over technology is critical as Asian governments and corporate leaders seek to foster the development of national economies and the competitiveness of firms. A recent study by William Keller and Richard Samuels concludes that "despite considerable pressure to converge on more open, liberal norms, the Asian economies retained [after 1997] distinct approaches to innovation and technological innovation" through distinctive solutions that eschewed both technonationalism and technoglobalism.[50] All host countries welcome the economic growth and improved export performance that foreign investment and technology transfer can bring. But many also remain ambivalent. New economic linkages tend to be internal to the firm or part of complex and rapidly changing interfirm linkages that may or may not be conducive to autonomous growth and technological upgrading. Seeking to escape excessive dependence on Japan, Asia's newly industrializing economies thus exploit the leverage offered by international competition among foreign producers. By maneuvering in and out of different production networks, firms located in East Asia illustrate the political logic of Asian regionalism.

48. Ernst 2004.
49. Makihara 1998, 560.
50. Keller and Samuels 2003, 227.

Europe

On questions of technology, "Europeanization" refers to a multidimensional, dense bargaining system not fully dominated by any single national or European actor. The European dimension of industrial and technology policy has political traits that distinguish it from established national patterns. Sometimes the European Commission shapes industrial sectors directly, as is true of Europe's telecommunication policy. At other times, Europeanization has important indirect effects. The development of a European standard for a global system for mobile communication (GSM), for example, was from the very beginning developed at the European level with the active cooperation of industry. Flexible coordination among firms on a European scale replaced the hierarchical coordination of policy by national post and telecommunication monopolies.

Such direct and indirect linkages are evident in the financial support for R & D. While German business sharply reduced its funding for basic research in the early 1980s, European policymakers sought to counter that trend, supporting basic research with potential for commercial application. The Commission complemented national programs, but it was overly optimistic about stimulating marketable products.[51] European payments were substantial, in absolute terms, and they were exploited especially by large firms and by Germany's major centers for technology research. However, between 1987 and 1991, EC funding amounted to less than 2 percent of the total research funding of the federal government and less than 0.5 percent of Germany's total R & D expenditure.[52] It is not surprising that European R & D policy failed to reverse the German and European lag in high-technology products, specifically in electronics.[53]

The regional scope of technology policy extends beyond specific EU programs. In the 1970s, for example, Germany consciously stabilized the fledgling southern European democracies as they emerged from the shadows of fascism, a generation after Germany had made a similar transition. Active support for southern enlargement of the European Community was part of that policy. Germany also took a leading role in offering both political and financial support, thus setting an important precedent for eastern Europe after the end of the cold war.

German and European technology policies often operate at cross-purposes. With its large information technologies program, the European Union supports European industry against U.S. and Japanese competitors. At the same time, the German Federal Ministry of Research, as part of the Joint European Submicron Silicon Initiative program and a German-American industrial cooperation scheme, subsidizes the chip development of Siemens and IBM. And

51. Grande and Häusler 1994, 501.
52. Reger and Kuhlmann 1995, 164.
53. Van Tulder and Junne 1988, 125–55, 209–52. Roobeek 1990, 133–37.

individual German states, such as Nordrhine-Westfalia, support the investment plans of Japanese chip producers in Germany. Problems of coordination, both horizontal (in Germany) and vertical (in Europe), thus pose major barriers to effective technology policies. These problems are likely to increase as the Europeanization of technology policy advances. Economic and technological differences among European states are so large that the European Union cannot possibly achieve an economically optimal policy mix. For example, R & D expenditures in Germany are two hundred times larger than in Greece or Ireland, and the big European three (Germany, France, and Britain) account for 75 percent of total European expenditures on R & D.[54] On questions of technology, Germany is deeply embedded in European policy networks. Policy is caught between contradictory impulses: the German government cannot achieve its objectives by itself; and against the wishes of the German government, little can be achieved at the European level.

Contradictory policies are also encouraged by developments in the German corporate sector. In the electronics industry, for example, the federal government had to deal only with Siemens and a few other German firms in the 1960s and 1970s. Since then, escalating costs in product development and the lagging competitiveness of German producers have led to strategic alliances on a global scale and thus a loosening of ties between government and business. National programs seeking to enhance the competitiveness of national producers have become "leaky," and the efforts of national governments to create competition among producers is undermined by the growing cooperation between Siemens, IBM, and Toshiba.

Corporate investment policies were of central importance in the extension of a European-wide production system. Until the early 1970s, the foreign investment decisions of European producers were driven primarily by the incentives offered by host governments, as well as the prospect of producing in high-growth, protected markets. "Continental firms were inhibited from undertaking much international sourcing," writes Lawrence Franko, "by behavioral reflexes conditioned in more autarkic times, and by management structures adequate for tariff factories, but not for global strategies."[55] With a few notable exceptions, European producers did not participate in the move to offshore production that U.S. and Japanese corporations began to initiate in the late 1960s.

With the breakdown of the fixed exchange rate system in the early 1970s and the subsequent appreciation of the deutschmark, German producers reluctantly increased their direct foreign investment. Cost considerations became more important, and German firms began to build subsidiaries in southern Europe that were geared to exports.[56] German corporations typically favored foreign investment that increased the offshore processing trade of the

---

54. Grande and Häusler 1994, 507.
55. Franko 1976, 127.
56. Franko 1976, 127–28.

host country, especially in garments and textiles.[57] With a few exceptions, most notably in automobiles, German producers did not seek to create integrated production complexes across national borders, either in southern Europe in the 1970s or in eastern Europe after the end of the cold war.

Spain and Portugal emerged from authoritarian rule in the late 1970s with regulated economies and a record of structural change and growth comparable to that of the newly industrializing economies in Asia. They had a large number of state-owned enterprises, high levels of protection in manufacturing, and underdeveloped service sectors.[58] Their political strategies were geared primarily to European politics rather than to national technological developments. They sought quick entry to the European Community with long transition periods for inefficient agriculture and weak industries, and they sought substantial transfer payments from Brussels. Economic growth and political legitimacy through European integration were more important than technological autonomy.

These gradually liberalizing economies welcomed foreign investment. Spanish industrialization was driven by the growth of its domestic market. It received $2 billion between 1960 and 1974, concentrated primarily in autos, chemicals and plastics, food products, electrical machinery, and electronics—sectors that together accounted for more than 60 percent of the total profits of Spanish industry and 80 percent of technology payments. Most of the investments were from the United States and Switzerland (the European headquarters for U.S. corporations). Ten percent were from Germany. Of Spain's 154 top-ranked corporations in 1972, sixty had ties with U.S. and fourteen with German multinationals.[59] By 1980, the situation had changed greatly. Germany had become the leading supplier of investment goods, accounting for one-fourth to one-half of Spain's total imports from the European Community. In general, direct European investment was increasing faster than U.S. investment; France and Germany became the largest European investors in Spain.

Although technological dependence did not improve between 1976 and 1990, Spain was a net contributor to the European Union's R & D programs.[60] The inflow of European DFI accelerated sharply throughout the 1980s, from 0.4 percent of GDP in 1975 to 2.5 percent in 1990, with investment shifting into financial services. In the late 1980s, the imbalance between Spain's technology payments and receipts was much greater in its relations with Germany than with the United States.[61] By 1992, 85 percent of Spain's foreign investment came from EC member states. Even though foreign investment was

---

57. Fröbel, Heinrichs, and Kreye 1977, 33–36, 84–85, 91–97, 116–26, 290–91; and 1986, 56–58.
58. Eichengreen and Kohl 1997.
59. Baklanoff 1978, 43–44, 52–53. Muñoz, Roldán, and Serrano 1979, 166–69. Vaitsos 1982, 144–45.
60. Vaitsos 1982, 147–48. Herrera 1992, 221, 224–25. Wortmann 1991, 4.
61. Herrera 1992, 242.

motivated overwhelmingly by growth in local markets, and thus was import-sub-stituting in nature, foreign corporations were central to exports, especially in autos and chemicals. Portuguese developments were comparable: direct for-eign investment increased sharply in the 1960s, rising from less than 1 percent of gross capital formation to 27 percent by 1970; in 1973 foreign investment reached $110 million. In the last three years before Portugal's 1974 revolution, Germany was the largest foreign investor, with 26 percent of the total.[62]

By the mid-1990s German companies producing in Spain, Portugal, and Greece for the European market had become still stronger. One reason was partial privatization, which led to the sale of some major publicly owned cor-porations to foreign multinationals, such as Spain's SEAT to Volkswagen.[63] Be-cause of its low wage levels, Portugal, like the Southeast Asian states, exported primarily labor-intensive products (textiles, leather, apparel, food and bever-age, electronics). And apart from agricultural products, traditional manufac-tures dominated Greek exports.

In textiles and a few other sectors, German firms were able to benefit from low-cost producers, investing in outward processing. The subsequent increase in trade had no appreciably positive effect on the technology base of the Mediterranean economies in the 1970s.[64] As Germany's foreign investment increased in the 1980s, technological spillover became significant for the Mediterranean economies only above a high threshold, especially in capital-in-tensive industries. German chemical and pharmaceutical companies invested heavily in Spain in the 1970s and 1980s. By the early 1990s, Spain's costly in-dustrial policy in these sectors had come to rely on foreign companies.

Spain's development policies over the last two decades have had mixed re-sults, and Portugal's experience was similar. Their records resulted from a Ger-man investment strategy driven by considerations of cost and domestic market growth rather than by an attempt to enhance the technology profiles of the Mediterranean economies. The Mediterranean countries did not become ex-port platforms for serving the European market and acquiring foreign tech-nologies. Rather, they were locations for outward processing and, occasionally, for capital-intensive investments in selected industries. Technology transfer was not a salient policy objective, either for Germany or for the countries of south-ern Europe.

In the eyes of European elites, aid packages from Brussels were more im-portant than technology transfer for improving the infrastructure for sustained economic growth. Accession to the European Community was followed by the redistributive transfer payments of the Regional and Cohesion Funds, which helped accelerate economic growth and development. These transfer pay-ments were made possible by German aid. Throughout the 1980s and 1990s, Germany was the undisputed paymaster of the European Union, with a net

62. Baklanoff 1978, 136–38. Simões 1992.
63. Holman 1996, 158–59.
64. Fröbel, Heinrichs, and Kreye 1977, 308–9. Donges et al. 1982, 79, 82–83, 113.

contribution of about twelve billion ecu in 1995—roughly equal to the sum that Spain, Greece, and Portugal received as the largest net recipients from the EU budget.[65] Between 1994 and 1999, the European Union allocated a total of 138 billion ecu from its Structural Funds and 14.5 billion ecu from its Cohesion Funds to lessen regional inequalities. The three Mediterranean countries received more than half of the total allocation.[66] The result was a rapid transformation of the three Mediterranean states and increasing European equality and homogeneity in the 1980s and 1990s. The productivity and income gap separating Spain and Portugal from the rest of Europe has narrowed significantly.

Although such an explicitly political approach also characterized Germany's East European trade and technology policy after 1945, the eventual outcome after the European Union's 2004 eastern enlargement will differ. United Germany simply lacks the necessary financial clout. Before 1989, commercial relations were driven by West Germany's policy of national unification. During the cold war, Germany's trade negotiations with the East European members of the Soviet bloc had been matters of high diplomacy. Broad political interests, including the fate of German ethnic minorities, outweighed corporate interests. In the early 1970s, the European Community began to intrude on Germany's national prerogatives as it applied its common commercial policy. Since 1989, the European Union has enhanced international commercial diplomacy at the expense of a purely German policy, guided by a broader interest in the political and economic stabilization of eastern Europe and a strong commitment to the principle of free trade.

As was true of relations with southern Europe in the 1970s and 1980s, so relations between Germany and eastern Europe since 1990 have also been marked by the primacy of political over technological, and European over national, considerations. Although the developmental gap is larger than southern Europe's had been in the 1970s, eastern Europe finds itself similarly in a position of subordination. In terms of both per capita income and the relative share of agriculture in total production, for example, Barry Eichengreen writes that "the cohesion problem is somewhat more serious than it was with the Southern European enlargement, but not overwhelmingly so."[67]

Trade data record a dramatic reorientation from east to west. By 1996, Germany had become eastern Europe's leading trade partner, accounting for about a third of the region's trade with OECD countries and about 10 percent of German exports—more than Germany's trade with the United States. In this dramatic expansion of trade, technology played only a minor role. In industries where low labor costs rather than technology matter, East European exports have increased, from 24 to 32 percent of total exports. At the same time, the disadvantage of the East European economies in capital goods and tech-

65. *The Economist* 1997a, 51.
66. White 1997.
67. Eichengreen 1997, 342.

nological inputs remains high, despite a modest improvement in shipments from relatively specialized supplier firms and a rise in the share of science-based products to about 20 percent of overall exports.[68]

Faced with sharply increasing domestic costs in the 1980s and 1990s, German producers were active in taking advantage of new opportunities in the east. By 1995, for example, the top five hundred German firms employed over two hundred thousand workers in the four central European countries.[69] The bulk of German direct foreign investment still flows to wealthy OECD member states, but the share of other destinations is rising—although many of the German firms investing in eastern Europe are very small, well below the EU average. Central Europe accounts for nearly half of the non-OECD foreign employment of German producers. And Germany accounts for about two-thirds of the European Union's imports of offshore processing from central Europe.[70] Integration through subcontracting is generating a broad array of new corporate links between Germany and eastern Europe, stretching from an intra-industry division of labor without technology transfer, to intersectoral complementarities with technology transfer.[71]

To date, however, German direct foreign investment appears to have had little impact on the technological trajectory of eastern European economies. German business keeps a low profile, often for political reasons, and gives its subsidiaries plenty of slack. In many industrial sectors, the rapid expansion of trade between Germany and eastern Europe is attributable to non–equity-based activities, especially subcontracting and offshore processing. Although German producers invested 7.3 billion deutschmarks in central Europe between 1989 and 1995, many of the projects were small and sited very close to the former Iron Curtain. A distinctive border economy has been emerging along Germany's eastern border, a European version of the maquiladoras dotting the U.S.-Mexican border. The main determinant of German foreign investment is the availability of a well-trained and inexpensive labor force. Because they produce parts and components cheaply and with low transportation cost to final assembly locations, eastern manufacturers are readily integrated into western supply chains. Since 1989, no Asian-style production networks have sprung up.

Geographic proximity is especially important for Germany's small and medium-sized firms, which seek benefits from nearby low-wage areas but lack the resources to build regional production networks. Such firms own little technology that they can transfer. They typically rely on central European subcontractors as an extended workbench in a least-cost approach to the production of components. Furthermore, the location of outward processing investment is encouraged by the preferential tariff quotas of the European Union, for ex-

68. Guerrieri 1998, 140–42. Schmidt and Naujoks 1993, 13.
69. Dörrenbächer, Scheike, and Wortmann 1996, 4–5.
70. Lemoine 1998, 166.
71. Zysman and Schwartz 1998, 416–20. Lemoine 1998, 167.

ample in clothing, textiles, and shoes. Eastern European producers are now surpassing Asian countries as the preferred sites for outward processing. In many eastern European countries between 1988 and the mid-1990s, outward processing jumped from 10–20 percent of total exports to 40–60 percent.[72] This is true more in low-tech than in high-tech sectors. In electronics, for example, the workforce in eastern Europe lacks the skills to produce electronics goods to export standards.[73] The growing European economy holds the potential for border-spanning networks that might facilitate the flow of technology, but with few exceptions such networks did not grow up after the end of the cold war.

Since the mid-1990s, the character of trade and investment between eastern Europe and Germany has begun shifting, notably in Hungary and in the auto industry. As eastern European wage levels rise, "extended workbench" production is becoming less profitable. Offshore processing is declining. Low wages are no longer the main determinant of export performance. As cost advantages now shift further to the east, Hungary and Slovenia have less offshore processing trade than Bulgaria and Romania. Lead industries (cars and transport equipment, food, chemicals, machinery) are becoming less dependent on subcontracting arrangements. They have benefited from large direct foreign investments that seek to supply domestic markets and also enhance competitiveness in western markets.

Hungary is riding the crest of this wave. Hungarian firms are engaged in more than six thousand joint ventures with Germany.[74] Since foreign firms do not give up technology unless they can control its use, typically such joint ventures do not lead to the transfer of proprietary technology. Direct foreign investments, on the other hand, have encouraged a substantial modernization of Hungary's technological base. However, large foreign firms tend to adopt an enclave strategy: in a pattern reminiscent of Japan in Asia, GM, Ford, and Audi plants in Hungary tend to import components or entice their western suppliers to set up shop in Hungary. Multinational car producers use these networks to pressure unions, parts suppliers, and governments in the west to become more flexible and to agree to lower wages.[75] Skoda's Oktavia car, for example, is a product that can compete effectively in western markets. Productivity is around 90 percent of western levels and rising; labor costs are only 25 percent of those at VW's plants in Spain; and only 30 percent of the parts of the Octavia are purchased in the Czech Republic.[76] Magyar Suzuki is also noteworthy: it must meet EU local content requirements, and so it works with local suppliers that Suzuki helps to acquire the necessary licenses and technology.

It is too early to tell whether Hungary and the automobile industry will even-

72. Zysman and Schwartz 1998, 416–17. Pellegrin 2000, 7.
73. Zysman, Doherty, and Schwartz 1996, 43.
74. Miller and Templeman 1997.
75. Ruigrock and Van Tulder 1995, 130.
76. *The Economist* 1997b, 6–7.

tually revise the conclusion that direct foreign investment, like joint ventures and offshore processing, plays a limited role as a source of technological change. Generally speaking, however, German companies have been slow to build cross-regional production networks. Exports continue to grow rapidly, and European producers have begun to invest substantially in subsidiaries that they seek to control. Contract manufacturing and open networks of competitive suppliers are slow in coming and may never arrive.[77] A rapid transfer of technology remains improbable; the European experience looks profoundly different from the Asian trajectory.[78]

Asymmetries in the trade and investment relations of Germany and eastern Europe have been smaller in the 1990s than they were in the 1930s. German trade is less directed to small economies; trade concentration and vulnerability to ruptured trade relations has declined; commodity composition of trade has improved for smaller economies; and in the field of direct foreign investment—with the exception of the Czech Republic—vulnerability to the withdrawal of German capital has diminished. This experience parallels that of the smaller states in Western Europe after 1945. The institutionalization of various international and transnational relations has to some degree neutralized economic dependence. Politically, Germany is now linked to the smaller states through numerous multilateral European institutions. Specific domestic arrangements to cope with international economic dependence, such as democratic corporatism, have also helped. Both international and domestic political institutions have acted to counteract dependence and helped neutralize the fear of German hegemony. Technological dependence thus was of little political consequence compared to the eastern enlargements of both the European Union and NATO.

Relations between Germany and eastern Europe do not revolve around the creation of regional production networks that center on control over technology. More important to German firms are new opportunities for gaining the flexible production arrangements that international competitiveness requires. Eastern European firms require a broad and dynamically changing array of new linkages that are only peripherally concerned with technological upgrading. Since the end of the cold war, the German government has sought to further the integration of central and eastern Europe into NATO and the European Union. It has paid virtually no attention to technology transfer and emerging European production networks. Enlargement, not networks, is a core interest because it promises to stabilize Germany's eastern frontier and spread the costs of that stabilization among its allies. Enlargement is driven not by the search for autonomous national capabilities but by reform efforts to achieve the norms of capitalism, democracy, and civil rights spelled out by the European Union and NATO. Institutional not technological transfer is what matters.

77. Zysman, Doherty, and Schwartz 1996, 44–47.
78. Zysman, Doherty, and Schwartz 1996, 42.

This discussion of technology and production networks shows clear differences between Europe and Asia. European policies are driven by broader political considerations that are altogether absent in Asia. National autonomy is less important than the politics of a broader European context. In Asia, technology policy continues to reflect a strong preference for national autonomy within the constraints and opportunities of markets. National sovereignty is the core objective of government policy. Regional production networks link up producers, subcontractors, and distributors across sectors and national borders without regard to the possibility of building a European-style regional polity.

External and Internal Security in Europe and Asia

Europe's security order is undergoing a fundamental transformation. Political ferment is so great that the distinction between external and internal security has become almost nonexistent. Indicative of that shift is the use of both the European Union and NATO for state- and nation-building projects in central and eastern Europe as well as in the Balkans. The blurring of the line is also illustrated by the eagerness of NATO members, in response to the al Qaeda attacks of September 11, 2001, to invoke the collective defense provision in Article 5 of the NATO treaty.[79] In contrast to Europe's institutional turbulence, Asia's security order is marked by a striking degree of stability and continuity. In Asia, the principle of state sovereignty is observed both in theory and in practice. On questions of internal security, national law enforcement agencies cooperate on an ad hoc basis and in a manner of their own choosing. On questions of national security, states continue to rely primarily on bilateral defense treaties. Absent in Asia are the pooling of sovereignty and far-reaching multilateral arrangements that typify Europe's security order.

Europe

The changes in Europe's regional security institutions include NATO enlargement and the forging of cooperative security arrangements with former members of the Soviet bloc; a European union that is developing a common foreign and security policy; and the Organization for Security and Cooperation in Europe (OSCE) with a new, intrusive normative reach and highly circumscribed organizational competence. None of these institutions replaces the state as the central actor in Europe's security order, yet all of them reflect the willingness of national governments to participate in far-reaching experiments that tend to undermine the traditionally sharp distinction between external and internal security. Eschewing confederal and federal regional organizations, European governments created in the 1990s a novel set of multilateral

79. Lansford 2002, 60–83. Tuschhoff 2002, 2003.

security arrangements that modify substantially the nature of European state power.

NATO embodies two different principles that at times conflict. Multinational political cooperation is premised on the existence of sovereign member states. Integrated military operations can undermine that sovereignty.[80] With a treaty signed in April 1949, NATO was originally no more than a traditional defensive alliance directed against further expansion of the Soviet Union. After the outbreak of the Korean War in 1950, NATO transformed itself from a planning to an operational body. The executive branch features an integrated structure that is internationally organized. The operational capabilities are enhanced by a shared infrastructure including radar, airfields, and pipelines, as well as an integrated communications system.

NATO soon became more than a military alliance. Since the mid-1950s, the political elements of NATO have become more important, partly due to German prodding. Norms of cooperation and consultation have evolved on all substantive issues affecting the alliance and its members. Refurbishing NATO after the dramatic changes of 1989–91, therefore, was for its members a natural response. Since the end of the cold war, NATO has remained the most important security institution in Europe. The London Declaration of a Transformed North Atlantic Alliance, issued on July 6, 1990, envisaged many of the organizational changes subsequently adopted, and it affirmed the normative changes that the Conference for Security and Co-operation in Europe (CSCE)—a regional security organization created in 1975 to monitor and encourage compliance with the Helsinki Accord—had already begun to articulate. The declaration also revised the core of NATO's military strategy, forward defense and reliance on nuclear weapons. The 9/11 attacks raised new issues for NATO's security cooperation; and the unilateralist turn in U.S. foreign policy under the Bush administration, as well as the Iraq war, have fractured transatlantic relations in ways that will affect the future functioning of NATO.

In taking on new political tasks, NATO blurs distinctions among its roles. It is no longer simply a multilateral alliance providing for collective defense, as was true during the cold war. It is also an institution that manages security risks through the provision of negotiation fora that are inclusive, transparent, and predictable, and through policies that seek to contain nuclear proliferation and weapons of mass destruction. And it is a security community bound together by common values and the dependable expectation of peaceful change among members. As an alliance, NATO was poised to defend Western Europe and the United States against the threat posed by the Soviet Union. As a security community, it helped minimize European security dilemmas. As an institution managing insecurity, it has proved a helpful complement to national strategies designed to cope with new risks and threats.

It is not a quirk of history that NATO has been the most important institu-

---

80. Schwarz 1982, 8–11, 57–63. Fox and Fox 1967, 13–34.

tion to help guide the process of transition in Eastern Europe and the Commonwealth of Independent States (CIS).[81] NATO has always had a dual mission, one "outside" against its enemies, the other "inside" among actual or potential members. Since its inception, NATO had always made much of the fact that it was a community of values—Western, Christian, liberal, democratic, capitalist. The accession of Germany in 1955 and of Spain in 1982 proved that geostrategy was not enough to win membership; equally important was the credible commitment of the German and Spanish governments to the norms and values of liberalism and democracy. (This rule had one important exception: in the 1952 accession of Greece and Turkey, geostrategic and military considerations overrode liberal commitments.) During the cold war the inside dimension was subordinated to the outside one. In reinventing itself at the end of the cold war, however, NATO drew on the former, and assisting in the transition of the newly democratic states in eastern Europe and socializing them into new forms of civil-military relations became NATO's most important task. After the military campaign in Kosovo, the importance of state-crafting in southeastern Europe highlighted the growing importance of NATO's political mission.

In the early 1990s, it was far from clear that NATO would survive. There was great uncertainty as to how it would combine its military with its political mission in a new Europe. The first reform effort was the North Atlantic Cooperation Council of 1991, an important symbolic gesture at the time, which signaled the end of military blocs and the emergence of a new European security structure. Next came the Partnership for Peace of 1994, which was developed largely by General John Shalikashvili, first as Supreme Allied Commander in Europe and subsequently as chair of the U.S. Joint Chiefs of Staff. The Partnership for Peace promised to build the professional military ties that, in the Pentagon's view, had to precede any meaningful NATO enlargement. By deferring any new distinctions separating "ins" from "outs," it delayed all irrevocable decisions about Europe's security order. Every state that accepted the general principles of the Partnership for Peace could join and decide on its preferred level of participation. Finally, in the wake of President Vladimir Putin's unequivocal support of the Bush administration after the 9/11 attacks, the spring of 2002 saw the new Russia-NATO Council. The issues on the council's agenda are counterterrorism, ballistic missile defense, crisis management and peacekeeping, arms proliferation, cooperation on search-and-rescue missions and emergency planning, and management of airspace. Russia is far from NATO membership and cannot veto NATO decisions, but in the new council Russia and NATO members have an equal say.

The 1999 and 2004 NATO enlargements in the center (Poland, Hungary, and the Czech Republic) and the east (Bulgaria, Estonia, Lithuania, Latvia, Romania, Slovakia, and Slovenia) have raised serious issues regarding future links

81. Gheciu forthcoming.

with Ukraine and a further strengthening of links with Russia. The general evolution of NATO policy in the 1990s reflected a substantial shift in underlying
norms that made the domestic character of the state—democratic governance,
human rights, a free market economy—an integral part of Europe's security
order. In the process of enlargement, NATO thus transformed itself from a military alliance to a pan-European security order, which in the end will include
Russia, either de facto or de jure. It will also leave military engagements to ad
hoc coalitions of the willing, as was true of the 2003 war against Iraq. It is too
early to tell whether this security order will settle for security management, facilitating joint operations, and promoting trust in responding to risks, or
whether it will become a security community as in Western Europe, where dependable expectations of peaceful change have been fully institutionalized.

In addition to enlargement, NATO faced a second test with the war in
Kosovo. The war illustrated how deeply the United States remained involved in
European affairs, and how deeply fearful Russia and China are about general-
izing the new European security order on a world scale. Most important, NATO
responded as a military alliance to what was perceived as a massive humanitarian crisis. The war in Kosovo was shaped foremost by lessons NATO had learned
from Bosnia. Yugoslavian President Slobodan Milosevic's political ambition was
to be stopped this time around, if necessary by overwhelming military force
rather than through prolonged diplomatic negotiations. Strong agreement existed within NATO on the basic objective: opposing Milosevic by military
means. Even deeply skeptical members of the alliance, such as Greece and Italy,
agreed, persuaded by a barrage of reports attesting to a massive humanitarian
crisis in Kosovo in 1998–99. Their reactions were grounded in an understanding of NATO as a community of states that supported liberal democracy.
The risks for NATO were thought to lie not in calculated aggression but in the
adverse consequences of political instability in eastern Europe. Consensus
rather than traditional great power rivalry constituted a foundation for the
"contact group" of major western states and Russia, today's equivalent of the
nineteenth- century "concert of Europe." With the European Left in power in
most of the West European states, U.S. and NATO intervention received strong
political support, even though it was "out of area" and lacked the express consent of the UN Security Council. Confronted by Milosevic's determined resistance, NATO soon confronted a grave challenge, and the intensification of the
seventy-eight-day air campaign was increasingly justified in terms of NATO's
survival. When the war stopped, the decision to deploy ground troops appeared imminent.

Because of the extraordinary powers that UN Security Council Resolution
1244 placed in the hands of international organizations, NATO played a central role in the attempt to rebuild Kosovo after early June 1999. NATO committed not only to geostrategic containment of a threat but to rebuilding the
social and political institutions of part of Yugoslavia. The fall of the Milosevic
regime in the winter of 2000–2001, and the decision of the Serbian govern-

ment to hand Milosevic over to the International Criminal Tribunal in The Hague, helped stabilize political affairs in southeastern Europe as NATO began to cooperate with the new Belgrade government on reorganizing relations between Serbia and Kosovo.

The 9/11 attacks, and the wars in Afghanistan and Iraq, have redrawn NATO's security environment even more dramatically. The alliance was deeply split over the 2003 Iraq war. Even European NATO members who initially decided to join the U.S.-led coalition, at times against strong domestic opposition, such as Spain, Poland, Norway, the Netherlands, and Hungary, by the end of 2004 had decided to scale down their commitments or withdraw their troops altogether. NATO thus committed itself only to a very limited mission of training Iraqi security personnel and providing some equipment. It is too early to tell what will be the long-term consequences for NATO of the alliance's split over the Iraq war.

Often forgotten in acrimonious controversies over the war is the fact that since August 2003 NATO has been operating "out of area" in Afghanistan, thus meeting a long-standing demand of the United States. In October 2001 the alliance sent a small naval force to the eastern Mediterranean in support of the U.S. war against the Taliban regime. In 2002 opponents of the looming Iraq war such as Germany, Canada, and Turkey, and reluctant supporters, like the Netherlands, all NATO members, agreed to take over command of the peacekeeping operations in Afghanistan. In fact, all twenty-six NATO members contributed, and 95 percent of the nine thousand peacekeepers serving at the time of the October 2003 Afghan election were NATO troops. They were stationed around Kabul and in provincial capitals, mostly in the northern part of the country. Like the intensive sharing of intelligence and close police cooperation, this out-of-area deployment illustrates out of the limelight alliance cooperation and institutional adaptability in a new security environment.

If NATO is the first pillar of Europe's evolving security order, the European Union is the second. The recent history of the European Union illustrates how porous is the line that separates internal from external security. After the failure of the European Defense Community in 1954 and the two Fouchet plans of the early 1960s, Europe's security integration was left to NATO, the West European Union (WEU), and, eventually, the Conference on Security and Co-operation in Europe (CSCE) and the Organization for Security and Cooperation in Europe (OSCE). Only since the mid-1980s has the European Community begun to fashion a common foreign and security policy. Movement in that direction accelerated greatly after the wars in the Balkans and the events that followed 9/11.

After more than a decade of experience with European policy cooperation (EPC), the EC members in the 1980s intensified foreign policy consultation and joint actions. In its second and frequently overlooked part, the Single European Act of 1987 formally institutionalized the EPC. Article 30 of this EPC treaty removed legal barriers and created political space for the European

Community to forward integration in security matters, without in any way impairing closer cooperation under the auspices of NATO, the WEU, and the OSCE.[82]

The end of the cold war and German unification accelerated the institutionalization of a common foreign and security policy (CFSP), which became a "second pillar" of the 1991 Maastricht treaty, distinct from the European Community's decision rules codified in the "first pillar." The transgovernmental network that increasingly ties together the foreign policy bureaucracies of EU member states was strengthened further by the centralization of links between national governments in Brussels; by procedural changes in voting and budgeting rules; and by the articulation of collective expectations about greater consistency in the CFSP.[83] The move toward institutionalization has increased frictions between governments, because they fear that CFSP decisions may be more legally binding than those of the EPC: when EC (first pillar) and CFSP (second pillar) decision rules clash, those of the second pillar typically dominate. It remains unclear whether these clashes have been corrected by the move to more consistent institutionalization of policy adopted in the Treaty of Amsterdam (July 1997) and the ratification of the Treaty of Nice (February 2003).

The war in Kosovo galvanized the creation of a collective EU security identity. Like NATO enlargement and the normative changes articulated by the OSCE, the Europeanization of security policy illustrates the political ferment that is distinctive of Europe on questions of security. At its 1992 Petersberg meeting in Bonn, the WEU went far beyond the boldest of its previous European mandates, adopting guidelines for humanitarian efforts, peacekeeping operations, and military and civilian crisis management, including the deployment of combat forces. In the Treaty of Amsterdam of 1997, the European Union claimed more competence over the WEU. The wars in the Balkans, and the war in Kosovo in particular, gave European governments conclusive proof that they lacked the military capabilities necessary for keeping peace at Europe's borders. The United States quickly took over management of the war, providing two-thirds of the aircraft and flying about two-thirds of the sorties. The political debate in the U.S. Congress was openly critical of the Europeans' inability to keep their own house in order and questioned whether the war in Kosovo served U.S. interests.

Britain was not at the center of this Europeanization, but before the Kosovo war Prime Minister Tony Blair reset the agenda for European security cooperation. In a substantial change in policy, the British government initiated a joint plan with France. The St. Malo agreement of December 1998 declared that the European Union needed to acquire operational military capabilities. In its July 1999 Cologne summit, the European Union agreed to take over the crisis man-

82. Kirchner 1989, 2–4. Ifestos 1987, 56–58.
83. Smith 1996, 40.

agement tasks of the WEU, and defined its objective as creating a common European security and defense policy (ESDP). The European Union created a new Brussels-based political and security committee, generally known as COPS (after the French "Comité Politique de Securité") to coordinate matters on a daily basis; a new EU military committee, consisting of the national chiefs of staffs or their deputies; and a new EU military staff, drawn in part from the WEU's personnel. Finally, it made former NATO Secretary General Javier Solana the new High Representative for the European Union's CFSP. Five former observers of the WEU—Austria, Denmark, Finland, Ireland, and Sweden—gained full membership in the European Union's new security organization.

The Cologne summit also actively supported the countries that staffed Eurocorps, originally set up by France and Germany, to make it into a more effective military force. By November 1999, Eurocorps had become the European Rapid Reaction Force, which took over command of NATO forces in Kosovo in the first half of 2000. Even more important, at the December 1999 Helsinki meeting, the European Union committed itself to creating a force of sixty thousand by 2003, ready to be mobilized within sixty days, completely staffed by members of the European Union and equipped for a deployment of up to one year. This was an ambitious and costly commitment that the European Union is meeting, though not on its self-set deadline.

It is not clear how the transatlantic conflict over the second Iraq war will affect the willingness of key EU members to fund such a force. Defense expenditures of all EU members combined are little more than half of that of the United States. Because of many inefficiencies and duplications, military planners estimate that in times of crisis the European Union can deploy only onetenth of U.S. forces. Among specific military needs, some vital components such as the capability to suppress enemy air defenses are missing altogether. NATO assets will be essential for the operational significance of European security cooperation. Apart from all the military hardware, NATO has twelve thousand trained staff officers compared to one hundred working for the European Union. To duplicate NATO planning would simply be too expensive. It is thus unlikely that the European Union will seek to compete outright with NATO any time soon, and the consequence will be the persistence of a NATO bereft of the clear mandate it had during the cold war. The Bush administration, in particular, has lost interest in NATO because of new challenges after 9/11, its dramatic unilateral turn, and the strong opposition the United States has encountered from some European allies, especially on Iraq. In the absence of a common geostrategic threat, European governments will see less need for NATO, while accepting it as a useful institution for reassuring new members in central and eastern Europe.

Instead of competing with NATO, Europe will more likely complement NATO by building on the civilian power approach that has characterized Germany's stance in world politics since 1945. This is not to deny that occasionally the European Union favors limited military action, as it did in 2003 in Congo, and that it has expressed the intention of building a capacity for planning military operations. Its broader political approach to questions of security, however, prevails in most instances. Through enlargement, the European Union has stabilized large numbers of political regimes to its east and south. Compared with the United States, the European Union disburses four times the amount of economic aid worldwide, and it takes a more multilateral approach to the disbursement of that aid. Europe contributes ten times as many peacekeepers as the United States to UN peacekeeping operations around the world.[84] The United States may win the wars, but only with the help of European and other peacekeepers will it be able to win the peace that follows. Europe's insistence on a multilateral approach to security has strong support among democratic mass publics around the world. Indeed, the passing of a second UN Security Council resolution in February 2002, just prior to the U.S. attack on Iraq, might have swung about 20 percent of public opinion in most countries, including the United States, to support for a war a clear majority opposed—illustrating the illegitimacy of the unilateral path the United States chose.[85]

Along with NATO and the European Union, the OSCE is the third pillar of Europe's rapidly evolving security order. Although it lacks NATO's military capabilities and the political momentum of the European Union, the OSCE has articulated normative changes that have affected how the other two institutions operate. The OSCE emerged from a 1966 diplomatic initiative of the Soviet Union that was subsequently enlarged to include the United States and Canada as full participants. Subsequently, however, it was Germany that helped define the political content of the CSCE, which was ratified at the 1975 Helsinki summit.

The unanimity rule of the CSCE meant that no one party could simply force changes on any other. The CSCE evolved as a series of follow-on review conferences: no substantive results in Belgrade, 1977–78; a ground-clearing for the eventual 1986 Stockholm agreements on confidence building measures in Madrid, 1980–83; and expanded human and minority rights commitments and the institution of annual reviews in Vienna, 1986–89. Numerous expert meetings monitored, and at times amended, the 1975 Helsinki codification of the various dimensions of the European security order. Because of its unanimity rule, the CSCE replicated the unbridgeable gap in basic norms that had divided Europe since the late 1940s. Separated by clashing conceptions of legitimacy, East and West could agree only on one basic fact: a policy based on the threat of force posed unacceptably high risks in a nuclear age.

---

84. Moravcsik 2002.

85. In thirty-eight countries on average 53 percent opposed the war under all circumstances, 30 percent claimed to support it if sanctioned by the United Nations, and 8 percent supported unilateral action by the United States and its allies. In the United States corresponding figures were 21, 34, and 33 percent. See Gallup International (February 2003), www.gallup-international.com (accessed November 1, 2004).

Although the 1975 Helsinki Summit Final Act left the Soviet Union the option of using military force to maintain its control over Eastern Europe, it also enshrined principles of human rights, basic human freedom, and the free exchange of goods, persons, and ideas. These provisions led to unexpected results. Strong diplomatic pressures from the West on behalf of human rights, linked to other East-West negotiations, gave dissidents in the East a potent instrument for a prolonged, and in the end successful, attack on the Soviet empire from within. The Helsinki process had a deeply corrosive effect inside the Soviet bloc.[86] In the end, the military might of the Soviet empire could not stop "new thinking" and a fundamental reorientation of Soviet policy under Mikhail Gorbachev and Boris Yeltsin.[87]

Based on democratic norms and human rights that the overwhelming majority of European states embraced fully after 1989, the CSCE in the 1990s institutionalized the normative commitment to live by the values of liberal democracy and to seek change only by peaceful means. Intervention mechanisms that the CSCE created for itself in the early 1990s were, in the words of Gregory Flynn and Henry Farrell, "operationally modest but revolutionary in their normative implications. . . . The CSCE had endowed itself with a set of institutions that allowed it actively to engage in conflict prevention through a form of sub-state intervention."[88] Any state that wants to travel the road to Brussels, headquarters of NATO and the European Union, must meet the political and normative criteria that the CSCE has articulated.

Since 1993, the CSCE has mediated, on an ongoing basis, ethnic or minority conflicts in ten states and established thirteen Missions of Long Duration. The most significant exception to this pattern of involvement was Yugoslavia, whose government withheld visas for CSCE mediation personnel in 1993 and, in the same year, suspended the operation of the CSCE mission in the northern (Vojvodina) and southern (Kosovo) parts of the country. Yugoslavia thus opted out of the collective commitment to resolve issues of minority and human rights on the principles of democratic governance and the rule of law. This decision turned out to be central to the Kosovo war. The observance of human rights, rather than the principle of nonintervention, has become the cornerstone for Europe's security order. The supremacy of the principles of state sovereignty and nonintervention is now replaced by the insistence that legitimate European statehood is conditional. It rests on the collective recognition of the legitimate exercise of internal authority by democratic means. The democratic revolutions in Eastern Europe thus led also to a revolution in the normative foundation of Europe's security order.

Redubbed the Organization for Security and Co-operation in Europe in 1995, this security institution has also adapted itself to Europe's changing security environment within the context of international arms control. At its No-

---

86. Thomas 2001.
87. Herrman 1995.
88. Flynn and Farrell 1999, 514, 523.

vember 1999 Istanbul summit, the OSCE adopted the Charter for European
Security to adjust the 1990 conventional arms limitation to changed circumstances, replacing "bloc" with "national" limits on the number and geographic
concentration of weapons. Furthermore, NATO assured Russia that it would
refrain from stationing significant forces on the territory of new member states
and would reduce the number of NATO weapons systems by about eleven thousand (a key Russian demand). Other measures have increased transparency
and made it much more difficult to concentrate troops and weapons in particular geographic districts. Although far from perfect, the charter was a significant achievement in adjusting the OSCE to dramatic changes in European
security in the 1990s.

It is often overlooked that the Europeanization of internal security is a
process of great *political* importance, for it begins to fundamentally alter national control over the police and the courts. One by-product of the close cooperation among West European intelligence services after World War II was
a modest harmonization in police operations, especially in criminal investigations. In 1959, European governments enlarged this rudimentary system with
a treaty on international judicial assistance. Since then, the European record
of police cooperation and the internationalization of criminal investigation has
been "turbulent."[89] This is especially true since the mid-1970s, when governments began creating new regional arrangements designed to strengthen police cooperation.

Both formal and informal cooperative bodies have proliferated. Some have
evolved within existing institutions. To help contain a growing international
drug trade, for example, President Georges Pompidou's 1971 initiative helped
convince Interpol, staffed mostly by French police officials, to appoint several
liaisons at its headquarters in Saint-Cloud; these officers were responsible for
more closely coordinating police activity in different parts of Western Europe.[90]
European governments and police officials set up other cooperative arrangements. Spurred by a rash of highly visible acts by left-wing radicals, the most important of these responses was TREVI (Terrorism, Radicalism, Extremism, and
International Violence), an important part of the intergovernmental EPC.[91] A
standing conference of the ministers of interior and justice of the EC member
states, TREVI was not a part of the European Community, probably because governments wanted to sidestep parliamentary oversight. Ministers met, often on
the same day, both under the auspices of TREVI and in their capacity on the
Council of Ministers of Interior of the European Community.

TREVI was the result of a substantially British-German initiative in 1975, at
the height of a wave of Irish Republican Army bombings in Britain and terrorist
attacks in Germany. TREVI and its various working groups provided not only
for regular high-level contacts but also for institutionalized cooperation in

89. Fijnaut 1991, 105.
90. Bigo 1996.
91. Anderson et al. 1995, 53–56. Benyon et al. 1993, 152–64. Busch 1995, 306–19.

practical police work.[92] The institutionalization of European police cooperation under TREVI's auspices surpassed all previous efforts: operating out of the
limelight, TREVI's study groups added an important international dimension
to what may be the most national of policy domains in all governments, interior affairs and justice. TREVI originally restricted its working groups to the exchange of intelligence about potential attacks and suspected activists, but by
1985 it had broadened its work to include the analysis of techniques for fighting international crime. With the gradual elimination of European border controls, additional compensatory police actions within national territories
became a persistent need, to which TREVI's Comprehensive Action Program
of June 1990 responded.

This was to be the last major TREVI initiative. In the late 1980s, public perceptions of the dominant threat to European security began to shift away from
terrorism to immigration. Migration and border controls were the center of
the 1985 and 1990 Schengen accords, signed by all EU members except the
United Kingdom, Denmark, and Ireland.[93] The Schengen accords deal with a
broad range of sensitive issues, including the removal of control posts at internal European frontiers; the creation of common external border controls; coordination in regulating the pursuit of criminals across national borders; a
common policy dealing with questions of asylum, illegal immigration, and the
status of refugees; and joint action against drug smuggling and terrorism.
Schengen is two-tiered: a Council of Ministers meets biannually, while a Central Negotiation Group performs most of the practical work.[94] Its most important accomplishment is the creation of the Schengen Information System, an
integrated database holding about one million personal records.[95] In the
1990s, the European Council linked criminal justice and immigration issues,
creating a new policy field of internal security. In Article K1 of the Maastricht
treaty of 1991, the member states defined cooperation in the fields of justice
and home affairs as matters of "common interest" and an essential component
of the European Union.

On questions of internal security, the Central European Investigation Bureau (Europol) has been the most important initiative in the complex structure of the Maastricht treaty. It dates back to the European Regional
Conference established inside Interpol that German political pressure helped
bring about in the 1980s.[96] Europol in its initial phase was supposed to exchange information, and only later would member states grant it limited executive powers—the Maastricht treaty did not mark a bold initiative. The
history of Europol also illustrates, however, how far the Europeanization of security affairs moved governments toward a collective approach. Located in The

92. Katzenstein 1990, 23–27, 52–53. Sobieck 1994, 62–66.
93. Bigo 1996, 112–45, 196–208. Busch 1995, 319–32.
94. Benyon et al. 1994, 57–58.
95. Anderson et al. 1995, 56–63.
96. Anderson 1989, 118, 169–71. Anderson et al. 1995, 49–53. Busch 1995, 275–85.

Hague, Europol started its work in 1993 with the Europol Drug Unit. A full Europol convention was signed in July 1995.

Despite numerous political restraints and obstacles on issues of internal security, "the institutional knot has, in principle, been cut," writes Cyrille Fijnaut. "Police co-operation in Western Europe will become more and more an affair of the European Community."[97] Yet with the exception of issues of suspected financial "Euro-fraud," rhetoric and reality continue to diverge in the regionalization of Europe's internal security. Europol in its first stage (information exchange) is far removed from executive powers, and increased police cooperation under the provisions of Title VI of the Maastricht treaty has not vitiated its intergovernmental character. A central bureau for Europol, on the one hand, and national liaison bureaus, on the other, mark this underlying conflict about the future of European police cooperation. But after its 1999 ratification Europol was able to do more, especially in its fight against organized crime. And it is likely that eventually it will assume a greater role in counterterrorism efforts.

In reaching political agreement on changes in the European Union's institutional framework at the June 1997 European Council meeting, and in formally signing the Treaty of Amsterdam on October 2, 1997, EU member states took still another step to accelerate the Europeanization of their internal security policies. In the Amsterdam treaty European governments decided to move issues of free movement, asylum, and immigration into the Community's first pillar; the third pillar's provisions on police and judicial cooperation was anchored in the European Parliament; and the European Court of Justice was accorded a larger role. The structures and practices that have evolved under the Schengen accords are integrated, by means of a special protocol, into the Treaty of European Union. That protocol is complicated, especially because of a number of "opt-ins" applying to the United Kingdom and Ireland.[98] Still, the direction of Europeanization is unmistakable. The EU summit meeting in Tampere, Finland, in October 1999 was dedicated to exploring some of the major issues of internal security: asylum and immigration policy, the fight against cross-border crime, and proposals for a European judicial area. The European Union is now fully committed to creating an "area of freedom, security and justice," a legal space that rivals in its political significance the single market initiative of the late 1980s.

Asia

On questions of internal security, Asia features none of the far-reaching institutional mechanisms and has experienced none of the fundamental institutional change that mark Europe.[99] All governments perceive terrorism, illegal

---

97. Fijnaut 1993, 55.

98. These opt-ins permit both states to accept and implement only those measures that suit their national policies without abolishing their national border controls.

99. This section is adapted from Katzenstein and Okawara 2001/02, 2004, Okawara and Katzenstein 2001, and Friman, Katzenstein, Leheny, and Okawara forthcoming.

immigration, the smuggling of drugs and narcotics, and armed insurrection as increasingly important security threats.[100] In sharp contrast to Europe, however, Asian governments remain largely uninterested in political solutions at the regional level. The unintended consequences of national policing are dealt with on an ad hoc basis by the transnational links that connect different national police forces bilaterally. Regional initiatives, to the extent they occur at all, are very modest in scope, such as the programs that Japan's National Police Agency (NPA) is organizing. Regional organizations dealing with criminal justice issues are minuscule and politically not very significant.[101] Neither East nor Southeast Asia has evolved distinct regional institutions for issues of internal security.[102]

Take, for example, the smuggling of illegal immigrants, many of them Chinese—a problem to which Japan's police officials are forced to pay increasing attention. From a figure close to zero in 1990, arrests of illegal entrants had increased to 6,828 by the year 2000. According to police estimates, this is less than a quarter of the total number of illegal entrants (still a miniscule number in a country of about 140 million). By overstaying in Japan, another 271,000 foreigners are in violation of visa laws.[103] The NPA was slow to react to illegal Chinese entry: only since 1998 has it intensified its bilateral contacts with Chinese police officials. One reason was the extreme caution with which the NPA's Security Bureau had traditionally viewed cooperative ties with police officials from China. But by 1996 the Security Bureau's opposition had weakened, and since May 1997 the NPA has sought to intensify its cooperative ties at the deputy-chief level. Terrorism is a second example. The dramatic decline of the Japan Red Army, marked by the arrest of nine JRA members after 1995, did not end terrorism as a perceived threat to Japan. In the 1990s, Japan had to cope with some spectacular acts of terrorism both at home (Aum Shinrikyo's sarin gas attack in Tokyo's subway in 1995) and abroad (the attack on the Japanese embassy in Lima in 1996). It did so without dramatic changes in its counterterrorist policy. During the 1990s, concern shifted from the JRA to North Korea. Since 9/11, the NPA has also been paying attention to fundamentalist Islamic groups, even though no credible evidence has linked al Qaeda to Japan or northeast Asia. The reaction to 9/11 was to increase Japan's security role in Asia. The counterterrorism bill that passed the Diet on October 29, 2001, amounts to little more, in the words of David Leheny, than "an initiative to help U.S. action in this specific instance."[104] The law does very little to prepare either the Japanese government or the public for the eventuality that the U.S. war on terror may spread to Southeast Asia or the Korean Peninsula.

100. Friman 1996. Dupont 2001.
101. Katzenstein 1996, 68–71, 81–82.
102. Donnelly 1986, 628.
103. The interviews on security issues that I cite in this chapter were conducted, with the promise of anonymity of my respondents, on trips to Tokyo (January 1999 and January 2000) and Beijing (June 1998 and June 2000). The format for citation is: interview number-year, location, date conducted. Interview 10–99, Tokyo, January 13, 1999.
104. Leheny 2001–2, 24.

Japan's counterterrorist policy is marked by continuity and caution rather than by dramatic responses. Since 1993, the NPA has organized small seminars, attended by two or three police officials from three to five countries. These seminars provide technical assistance on counterterrorist measures.[105] Since 1995 it has hosted an annual two-week seminar on antiterrorism measures, attended by one or two high- or middle-level police officials from ten to twenty-five states, most in Asia-Pacific. In line with its policy on other security issues, the NPA thus has sought to increase trust through the strengthening of bilateral contacts with foreign police professionals and the systematic exchange of information. In sharp contrast to Europe, no regional institutions exist, beyond Interpol's Asian bureau, to help coordinate national policies.

In the absence of regional support, Japanese police seek to gather systematic intelligence abroad. Stationed at Japanese embassies all over the world, more than a hundred police officers cooperate with local police forces. In response to the Japanese embassy takeover in Lima, the Terror Response Team was set up in the spring of 1998, to be dispatched in future crises when Japanese nationals are threatened. The unit trains abroad, and it exchanges information with police forces in other countries. It complements the activities of seven metropolitan and prefectural assault teams, with about two hundred members, set up in 1996. Since 1997, the activities of these teams have been centrally coordinated by the NPA.[106]

Japan's antiterrorism policy shows that regional institutions play an insignificant role in Asia. This is also true of Interpol, headed between 1996 and 2000 by a former director general of the NPA's International Affairs Department, Toshinori Kanemoto. On antiterrorism, Interpol's main function is the posting of international arrest warrants. On questions of organized crime, Interpol does not provide the police with useful information. Regarding drug trafficking, its information, at best, duplicates what police officers learn through other channels. On questions of illegal immigration, Interpol is largely irrelevant.[107]

This is not to deny that, in recent years, issues of internal security in Asia show some incipient forms of multilateralism. Since 1989, the NPA has hosted an annual three-day meeting on organized crime. Funded by Japan's foreign aid program, this meeting is designed to strengthen police cooperation and facilitate the exchange of information. Confronting its third wave of stimulant abuse since 1945, Japan convened the Asian Drug Law Enforcement Conference in Tokyo in the winter of 1999 to address regional trafficking in methamphetamines. At that meeting, the director of the UN Office of Drug Control and Crime Prevention chastised the Japanese government for its limited commitment to a multilateral approach. The NPA was an observer at a May 1999

105. Interview 07–99, Tokyo, January 13, 1999.
106. Interview 07–99, Tokyo, January 13, 1999. *Daily Yomiuri*, August 13, 1997. *Japan Times*, August 30, 1997.
107. Interviews 06–99 and 10–99, Tokyo, January 13, 1999.

meeting at which five Southeast Asian countries and China formally approved an international anti–drug smuggling police strategy. In January 2000 it organized a conference, attended by officials from thirty-seven countries, on how police cooperation might stem the spread of narcotics.[108] The annual number of international meetings attended by senior NPA officials increased from two or three in the 1970s to ten in the 1990s.[109]

Because terrorism directly threatens the legitimacy of the state, it has provoked high-level political meetings of heads of state. Japan has supported the creation of regional institutions to complement its bilateral approach. In June 1997, for example, the NPA was instrumental in helping create the Japan and ASEAN Anti-Terrorism Network. This organization strengthens cooperative ties among national police agencies, streamlines information gathering, and coordinates investigations of acts of terrorism. Following up on an initiative taken by Prime Minister Ryutaro Hashimoto while traveling through Southeast Asia in January 1997, the NPA and the Ministry of Foreign Affairs jointly hosted in October 1997 the Japan-ASEAN Conference on Counterterrorism for senior officials from nine ASEAN countries.[110] In October 1998 the NPA and MOFA cohosted a joint Asian Pacific–Latin American conference on counterterrorism. Based on findings from the Peruvian hostage crisis, this gathering was designed to strengthen international cooperation on antiterrorist measures.[111]

These are tentative moves. On questions of internal security the absence of multilateral regional institutions in Asia-Pacific remains, in comparison to Europe, striking. A recent inventory of transnational crime lists several global institutions in which these issues are addressed, but with the exception of the Council for Security Cooperation in the Asia Pacific's working group on transnational crime for Asia-Pacific there exists only one regional organization, the ASEAN Ministry on Drugs.[112] Internal security remains firmly in the hands of national police forces, which typically engage one another on a bilateral and ad hoc basis.

For reasons of history, regional security institutions are also atypical.[113] Many Asian states gained their sovereignty only in the 1950s, after the collapse of the European empires, and they are intent on making the most of their newly gained sovereign powers. Furthermore, the legacy of the Chinese Revolution, as well as the Korean and Vietnam wars, also undermined any regionwide security order. Finally, the continued division of Korea and the difficult relations between China and Taiwan are powerful testimony to the staying power of some of the unresolved problems of the cold war.

Asia's regional security order remains substantially organized by the logic of power-balancing, bandwagoning, and threats, and it is shaped by the outlook

108. *Asahi Evening News*, January 28, 2000.
109. Interview 07–99, Tokyo, January 13, 1999.
110. Interview 07–99, Tokyo, January 13, 1999.
111. Okawara and Katzenstein 2001.
112. Shinn 1998, 170–71.
113. Press-Barnathan 2003.

of political and military elites in the United States, China, Russia, and the smaller powers in the region. The major exception to this generalization is Japan. The social and legal norms embedded in its polity, civil-military relations, and domestic politics constitute a significant break with the assumptions that inform balance-of-power politics.[114] Yet even Japan showed evidence of a growing "reluctant realism" in the 1990s.[115] Japan's inability to recognize its militarist past reinforces political suspicion throughout Asia, and its atypical national security policy has had remarkably little influence in reshaping Asia's regional security order.

This is a sharp contrast with China. China's leadership watched with mixed emotions the change in the U.S.-Japan security relationship in the 1990s. Condemnation of the upgrading of Japan's expanded regional security role in new guidelines adopted in September 1997 was swift. Beijing interpreted the changes as inherently more aggressive, in particular Japan's ambiguous stance on any outbreak of hostilities between Taiwan and the PRC. At the same time, many of China's leaders are fully aware of the stabilizing effects of the U.S.-Japan alliance.[116] Before 1995, Chinese policy elites were alarmed by the prospect that a fraying of the U.S.-Japan relationship might permit a unilateral remilitarization of Japan. After 1995, they were equally concerned by the consolidation of the U.S.-Japan relationship and the possible eventual creation under U.S. tutelage of a militarist and expansionary Japan. The indeterminacy inherent in all balance-of-power thinking is thus just as present for the Chinese government as it is for the United States and for other Asian governments.

The postcolonial states of Southeast Asia are ardent defenders of sovereignty. During the early years of statehood, many of these states confronted serious threats to the legitimacy of their regimes from communist guerrillas, ethnic minorities, and secessionist or irredentist movements. The norm of noninterference in domestic affairs is strongly held. It was embodied in the Treaty of Amity and Cooperation that ASEAN states signed in 1976 and, in sharp contrast to Europe, has been reconfirmed on numerous occasions. The political heterogeneity of Asian regimes has made it impossible for either ASEAN or the Asian Regional Forum (ARF) as the only regional security organizations in Asia to make democratic governance a key requirement for institutional membership. ASEAN has championed instead the virtues of soft authoritarianism and accommodation to nondemocratic regimes. It has resisted international pressures directed against the military regime in Burma in favor of constructive engagement, thus contradicting European notions of creating a security community among democracies. Often considered weak and ineffective in Europe, the OSCE would be for many Asian governments, and particularly for China, simply too intrusive and constraining to serve as a workable institutional

114. Katzenstein 1996, 99–152.
115. Green 2001.
116. Christensen 1999, 58–62. Interviews 01–98, 04–98 and 03–00, 04–00, Beijing, June 15 and 16, 1998, and June 13, 2000.

model. Unlike nations in Latin America, Africa, and central-eastern Europe, Asian states view human rights and election-watch commissions as unacceptable intrusions into their domestic affairs.

Yet ASEAN is the only regional institution in Asia that has attracted strong political support. It was formed in 1967, at a time when the internal security of newly independent states in Southeast Asia was severely threatened. "The major purpose of ASEAN," writes Yuen Foong Khong, was to insulate its members from the fate of South Korea and South Vietnam by creating "'national resilience' (precisely what was absent in Korea and Vietnam) and intra-ASEAN comity."[117] ASEAN evolved a distinctive style of conflict management, "the ASEAN way." In sharp contrast to Europe, it avoids legal agreements, prizing instead informality, consultations, and a consensus-building style that blurs the distinction between official (track one) and semiofficial (track two) dialogue. Other multilateral institutions in Asia Pacific, such as APEC, have subsequently emulated this style of conducting political business on multiple tracks.

After an unsuccessful Australian and Canadian initiative for an Asian analogue to Europe's OSCE, Asian governments took up a Japanese proposal they had initially rejected in 1991. In 1994 the ARF endorsed explicitly the principle of noninterference. The only multilateral security institution in Asia, the ARF is so weakly institutionalized that its twenty-one members are called "participants," thus avoiding the impression of institutional permanency. The ARF lacks a secretariat. Although it has a series of intercessional working groups that focus on confidence building measures and preventive diplomacy, the ARF meets only once a year, for about a day. In addition, there are other subregional security institutions, track two meetings, and ad hoc groups. But political commitment to these multilateral initiatives is guarded at best, and states continue to favor the traditional mixture of self-help, bilateral security arrangements, and a U.S.-centered alliance system.

States were interested in the ARF for several reasons. With balancing and bandwagoning as the norm, the ARF helps reduce the risk of costly arms races that might derail the region from its high-growth trajectory. The breakup of the Soviet Union and the possibility of a partial disengagement of the United States were politically unsettling, as was the presumed regional ascendancy of Japan. In the early 1990s, the ARF thus served the interests of its members by reducing uncertainty. Furthermore, ARF members have a considerable interest in Chinese objectives in the region, for example in the South China Sea. Many of the small states on China's periphery thus look to the ARF and more recent multilateral initiatives as useful mechanisms by which to influence those objectives through political engagement. In the words of Singapore's Lee Kuan Yew, "If you have a China out to make mischief, that increases the costs. Why not hoist the fellow on board?"[118]

117. Khong 1997, 295.
118. Quoted in Johnston 1999, 295.

The ARF's lack of institutionalization is partly due to the resistance of the Chinese government. Whatever incremental changes have occurred since 1993 are due largely to China's gradual acceptance of some aspects of the ASEAN way. The Chinese government puts a high premium on its international standing, which, it believes, is influenced in part by its conduct in regional institutions such as the ARF.[119] Some Chinese officials are increasingly convinced that multilateral strategies promise advantages in the pursuit of Chinese interests. "Multilateralism with Chinese characteristics" Paul Evans writes, "is decidedly state-centric, committed to conventional principles of sovereignty and noninterference, and dedicated to defending state interests against perceived challenges from non-state actors."[120] With U.S. policy since 9/11 focused explicitly on absolute security and unilateralism, in an odd reversal of roles China has come to champion cooperative security and Chinese-style multilateralism. However, China's approach to multilateral security retains a strong unilateral bent.[121] And China remains strongly opposed to discussion in regional institutions of controversial territorial or political issues such as the Spratly Islands or Taiwan.[122]

The ARF is more than an instrument in the hands of China, its most powerful member, and it is more than a way to balance various threats. Most Asian governments are unclear about which threats they may face and do not view the ARF as an institution for balancing against major powers within (China) or without (United States) the institution. Rather, the evolution of the ARF is being pushed by less powerful states, including Canada and Australia, which are firmly committed to strengthening Asia-Pacific's regional institutions rather than relying only on a balancing against power or threats.

However, as is true of APEC and ASEAN, one should not overestimate the role of the ARF. It does not address serious conflicts on the Korean Peninsula and across the Taiwan Strait. Long-standing ethnic conflicts in domestic politics are also beyond its scope, although they could easily have a profound effect on Asia's security order. The same is true of other formal governmental organizations such as APEC, ASEAN + 3, and the recent Shanghai Cooperation Organization. All of them facilitate consultations first known as the ASEAN way and also by its successor, the Asia-Pacific way. Weak as it is in comparison to NATO, the European Union, and even the OSCE, however, in Asia the ARF is the only "mechanism for defusing the conflictual by-products of power balancing practices" at the regional level.[123]

Institutionalization is occurring at the regional level more informally, in the proliferation of different arenas for debate and discussion that cover a broad

119. Interviews 03–98, 05–98, 06–98, 08–98, and 03–00, Beijing, June 15, 19, and 21, 1998, and June 13, 2000.
120. Evans 2005, 213.
121. Interviews 02–00, 03–00, 08–00, and 11–00, Tokyo, January 11 and 13, 2000.
122. Interviews 03–98, Beijing, June 15, 1998; 02–00 and 01–00, Beijing, June 13, 2000.
123. Khong 1997, 296.

spectrum of track one (government-to-government), track two (semi-governmental think tanks), and track three (private institutions) arrangements. How to count the number of different tracks is a matter of some disagreement. The lines separating them, furthermore, are blurred by the fact that government officials often attend track two meetings in a private capacity, thereby modifying the "private" character of these meetings, and that Chinese professors attending these meetings typically are members of the Communist Party. Discussions are also constrained by prior policies and by the information prepared before the meetings begin. Because no verbatim minutes are kept, none of the individuals who participate in the discussion can be assigned any direct responsibility. Paul Evans reports almost six hundred track two meetings on security affairs in the years 1994–2002.[124]

The institutionalization of what one might call discursive politics in Asia-Pacific takes different forms and serves different purposes.[125] Track two dialogues, for example, can provide a convenient venue for senior government officials to meet in relatively informal settings. Since 1993, Japan has cooperated with China, Russia, South Korea, and the United States in the North East Asia Cooperation Dialogue, with Japan cochairing its Study Project on Defense Information Sharing.[126] Since 1994 a Japanese research organization has cosponsored, with its American and Russian counterparts, the Trilateral Forum on North Pacific Security, also attended by senior government officials. Furthermore, since 1998, Japan has conducted semiofficial trilateral security talks with China and the United States.

On questions of Asian-Pacific security, perhaps the most important track two dialogues occur in the Council for Security Cooperation in the Asia Pacific.[127] CSCAP was created in 1993 and held its first meeting in 1994. Its membership was nearly coterminous with that of the ARF. It may be the most regular nongovernmental forum addressing issues of Pacific security. With its five working groups, CSCAP sponsors dialogues modeled after those in the Pacific Economic Cooperation Council, which since 1980 have brought together businesspeople, government officials in their private capacity, and academic economists.[128] National committees and international working groups are common to both. Besides ASEAN members, Australia, Canada, Japan, South Korea, the United States, China, and others have also joined CSCAP.

Track two activities offer governments a variety of informal venues to exchange information and to take stock of the evolving assessments of security issues.[129] Track two activities also help shape the climate of opinion in national settings in which security affairs are conducted. They can help in articulating

124. Evans 2005, 204 n. 8.
125. Katzenstein and Okawara 2004.
126. Fukushima 1999b, 35.
127. Interview 04–00, Tokyo, January 12, 2000. Simon 1998, 207–9. Stone 1997, 21–25.
128. Fukushima 1999a, 131, 154–55.
129. Interviews 03–00, Tokyo, January 11, 2000; 03–98, Beijing, June 15, 1998; and 06–00, Beijing, June 14, 2000.

new ideas for national decision makers. Over time, they may socialize elites, either directly or indirectly, to different norms and identities. They may also build transnational coalitions of elites that retain considerable influence in their respective national arenas. In brief, they have become an important aspect of Asian-Pacific security affairs. Future track three meetings may further enrich the discursive politics of Asian security.

Like China, the United States has given limited support to regional security institutions in Asia-Pacific. Prior to the late 1980s and the end of the cold war, U.S. policy supported multilateral arrangements in Asia-Pacific as complementary but subordinate to established bilateral security treaties. The growing U.S. toleration of and interest in the ARF reflects a change in policy. In striking contrast to U.S. policy in Europe, for example, since 1986, the Commander-in-Chief, Pacific Command (CINCPAC) has brought together on a regular basis military and civilian officials from about fifteen Asia-Pacific countries in a "seminar for East Asian security." The intent is to increase the level of reassurance and knowledge in the region. In 1994, the United States set up the Asia-Pacific Center for Security Studies in Honolulu, which offers a variety of short-term, midcareer courses, largely for professional military personnel. The U.S.-sponsored Pacific Air Force Chief of Staff Conference is held every other year. In the fall of 2000, Japan cohosted in Tokyo the U.S.-sponsored Pacific Army Management Seminar, which brings together officers from thirty to forty states. Since the mid-1980s, an incipient form of multilateralism, centering on the U.S. military, has become important for armed forces throughout Asia-Pacific.[130]

Japan's Self-Defense Force plays a circumscribed role in such regional meetings. At ARF sessions, the professional military is represented by the civilian bureaucrats staffing the Japan Defense Agency; members of the Self-Defense Force participate only in intersessional working groups when technical issues are being discussed.[131] The intersessional working group in which the Japan Defense Agency has been most involved, for example, deals with disaster relief; other Asian states staffed this working group with officials from their construction ministries.

The Self-Defense Force's minor role in Asian regional security was clear in the peacekeeping operation in East Timor. Japanese policy was based on the premise that East Timor and Kosovo, though regionally specific, raised more general issues of international security, requiring action by the international community rather than regional segmentation. Only in mid-November 1999, two and a half months after the East Timorese referendum of August 30, did the cabinet decided to send Japanese personnel to assist. In the absence of a declared cease-fire, the government was prohibited from sending peacekeeping or humanitarian aid missions to East Timor under Japan's 1992 Interna-

---

130. Interview 10–00, Tokyo, January 14, 2000.
131. Interview 10–00, Tokyo, January 14, 2000.

tional Peace Cooperation Law. Under the auspices of the United Nations High Commissioner for Refugees, the main contingent of a 150-member Air Self-Defense Force team left Japan in late November 1999 with relief for East Timorese refugees settled in West Timor camps. According to a top official, East Timor had requested that aid be delivered by "an Asian nation that is racially similar . . . instead of Australian troops."[132] Australia's active and high-profile role provoked opposition in many quarters of Asia-Pacific, whereas Japan's pursuit of quiet diplomacy and its $100 million support of an intervention force staffed by ASEAN member states shielded it from international criticism. It may in fact have helped to strengthen Japan's political position in Southeast Asia, despite its inability to contribute directly to the UN peacekeeping operation. Japan funded 95 percent of the cost of the operation, with Portugal contributing an additional $5 million and Switzerland $0.5 million.[133]

In sum, regional security institutions in Asia do not seriously encroach on the principle of noninterference in the affairs of sovereign states on issues of either internal or external security. At the same time, Asian regionalism has evolved different "tracks"—arenas for discursive politics that serve to reduce uncertainty and exchange information. These tracks may, with the passing of time, affect some of the underlying preferences of states.

Regional Orders in Asia and Europe

Both Germany and Japan are characterized by active policies that seek to enhance international competitiveness. The mainspring of their approaches to technology and production differs in what Kozo Kato describes as Japan's information-rich system of political institutions and Germany's quasi-corporatist polity.[134] In the case of Japan, technology and production are instruments for lowering the country's international vulnerability. Hence the Japanese government supports core technologies, collects information on technological and production advances made by foreign competitors, and seeks to advance its political objectives through numerous long-term programs. By contrast, economic security is not an objective of German policy. Keeping up with other industrial leaders, however, is a clear goal. Specifically, Germany seeks to defend its traditional position as the "good second" with a broad array of public policies. Rather than attempt to create the conditions for technological breakthroughs, German policy aims to further political institutions and programs at the European level.

In the area of information technology, these differences between Japan and

132. Maeda 1999.
133. This display of the parochial stinginess of European governments contrasts sharply with Japan's $240-million support for the peacekeeping operation in Kosovo. Interview 03–00, Tokyo, January 11, 2000.
134. Kato 2002.

Germany are readily apparent.[135] The "advanced information society," an organizing concept for Japanese policy, is an ambiguous structure that can motivate a wide variety of economic and social programs. Specifically, the Japanese government has aimed to support the technological progress of specific industry segments, in the hope of enhancing the international competitiveness of the entire industry. In Germany, policy is more concretely focused on firms and seeks a rapid and efficient integration of information technologies into the production process in both the manufacturing and service sectors. But German policy is also part of a more political approach to building a European polity in high technology. Japanese institutions are especially attuned to technological developments, which they follow closely, import freely, improve greatly, and seek to reintroduce into Asia under carefully monitored conditions. Contemporary Germany, by contrast, lacks the domestic institutions to shape regional technological trajectories on its own terms. It chooses instead to embed itself in regional institutions to achieve broader political purposes.

These national differences are conditioned by different regional contexts. Asian and European production networks leave the impression of important regional differences. European production networks are egalitarian not hierarchical; they enhance social homogeneity rather than heterogeneity. European regionalism is formal. It is reflected in collective political institutions operating at the regional level, including a common court, a commission issuing hundreds of binding regulations a year, a parliament, a common central bank and currency, and, soon, a limited collective military capacity for peace-keeping and peace-enforcement operations. Asian regionalism is informal. Despite institutions such as ASEAN and the Asian Development Bank, it operates predominantly through market institutions. Specific to Asian markets are ethnic networks that are partly competing and partly complementary, as, for example, in Japanese and Korean corporate networks and Chinese firms organized along family or clan groups. Informal networks have since the 1970s created new regional links and altered the patterns of Asian trade and investment.

Differences in national and regional political arrangements create different political capacities for change. At the level of the industrial sector, or for specific technologies, Japanese capacities are larger than German ones. This claim is illustrated by the fact that Japan's national production profile changed several times during the past half century, whereas Germany's remained largely unchanged. In Japan, leading industrial sectors frequently altered during that time period. In Germany machinery and machine tools, electrical equipment, chemicals, and automobiles remained the leading sectors throughout the second half of the twentieth century. Corporate linkages in Japan are primarily group based, in contrast to Germany's industry-based pattern. Such group-based linkages diffuse new technology rapidly across sector boundaries and fa-

135. Organization for Economic Co-operation and Development 1991, 8, 92, 98–99.

cilitate the incorporation of technologies developed in one sector into the products of another. At the regional level, the situation is reversed. Here, German political capacities for international collaboration exceed Japanese ones, as illustrated by Germany's active participation in substantial European technology projects.

The differences in European and Asian security orders are also apparent and parallel to those on economic questions. Over the decades, NATO has served both as a military alliance protecting Western Europe against the threat of Soviet attack and as a security community rooted in deeply shared values and a common identity. Cooperative security arrangements between NATO and the former Soviet bloc, as well as NATO enlargement, redefined the security agenda of European states throughout the 1990s. On questions of national security, European cooperation increased, first under the auspices of the West European Union, and subsequently under the common foreign and security policy of the European Union. Since 1999, the European Union has been moving to establish collective defense capabilities of its own. Finally, the Organization for Security and Cooperation in Europe has evolved substantially since its founding in 1975, and at no time more than in the early 1990s, when it was at the forefront of laying a radically new normative foundation for European security. In northeast and Southeast Asia, in sharp contrast, "national security policy" is precisely what the term conveys. Balance of power politics and bilateral defense arrangements are the norm. The Asian Regional Forum is the only significant institutional innovation, best seen within the context of a growing number of regionwide fora aimed at sharing information, reducing uncertainty, building trust, and thus affecting national objectives over the longer term.

A similar difference exists on questions of internal security. During the 1990s, the treaties of Maastricht and Amsterdam took account, in legal terms, of a regionalization in European police practices that had evolved since the early 1970s. The lines that separate internal from external security in Europe are increasingly blurred. Since the mid-1970s, antiterrorism has been at the center of European cooperation agreements, and the 9/11 attacks made those agreements even more central to national security. The tumultuous evolution of European institutions has led to both a shift in political priorities from external to internal security and a substantial intermingling of these policy sectors.

In East Asia, by contrast, the lines between internal and external security became not more but less blurred in the 1980s and 1990s. In comparison to the 1960s and 1970s, national security issues now have primacy—that is, as long as economic crises such as 1997 do not lead to widespread domestic upheavals. In contrast to Europe, immigration and asylum, drugs, terrorism, and organized crime are viewed as important but discrete issues of public policy. They are not defined, as they are in Europe, as demarcating a new field of internal security that requires new policy and institutional innovations at the regional level. Cooperation among national police forces still operates on an ad hoc basis, facilitated by a variety of annual meetings hosted by Japan's National Police Agency. Asia's regional security order thus has evolved without great institutional upheavals.

These differences in Europe's and Asia's security orders are due in part to the political strategies through which important states, here Germany and Japan, extend or fail to extend their regional reach. Both states seek to compensate in different ways for international weaknesses. German officials see legitimate rule as possible only within the context of institutions and legal norms that form a seamless web against all internal and external challenges to state security. German legalism, furthermore, is tightly linked to a strongly international strain in Germany's state identity. Multilateral and international policy approaches have great political appeal and enjoy great legitimacy. Japan adheres to different norms and follows a different course of action. It values social norms more than legal ones and prizes informal over formal contacts. This is also true of other Asian states. Now that they have consolidated a once-fragile domestic consensus (as was true of Japan in the 1950s and 1960s) and secured a once-tenuous grasp on power (as in South Korea in the 1950s and Southeast Asia in the 1960s and 1970s), Asian states remain deeply ambivalent about the regionalization of their security policies. Trying to make good on decades lost under socialism, China exemplifies this ambivalence.

Europe and Asia thus show marked institutional differences across issues of technology and security. Europe is undergoing fundamental institutional change, with far-reaching efforts to redefine state prerogatives and a preference for multilateralism; Asia is characterized by marginal adjustments, insistence on state sovereignty, and a preference for bilateralism. These striking consistencies in very different policy areas attest to pervasive institutional differences across regions.

CHAPTER FIVE

Porous Regions and Culture

Regions are made porous by the interaction of globalization and internationalization. These processes are open to different interpretations—think, for instance, of the different terms that we use in describing innovations such as the
World Wide Web or the Internet. The World Wide Web captures the radical
changes that globalization is bringing about. The cold war was about division;
the Web is about connection. During the cold war a hotline linked the White
House with the Kremlin as leaders attempted to stay in charge. On the World
Wide Web, we are all connected, and nobody is in charge. The Web creates new
social and economic benefits, as well as new risks and vulnerabilities. Technology itself is neutral. It empowers individuals for good and ill. And it is individuals—peace activists mobilizing against land mines, terrorists attacking the
United States—rather than governments whom the Web empowers.

We think about the Internet, by contrast, in the language of internationalization. "The idea that the Internet liberates you from geography is a myth,"
argues Martin Dodge.[1] Internationalization is shaped by the actions of national
governments. And indeed the Internet is a deliberate creation of the American national security state. In 1962, a classified RAND Corp. report proposed
a packet-switching network to protect the U.S. military from nuclear attack.
The idea was never implemented. A few years later, researchers working for the
Department of Defense backed a similar approach to address computing and
communication problems in the U.S. military. The Internet developed rapidly
in the interest of enhancing national security. Now, in an attempt to control the
information flowing across national borders, governments from Beijing to
Bavaria are trying to make the Internet into an intranet. In the case of China,
the U.S. government is funding an American-based computer network

1. *The Economist* 2001b, 18.

equipped with privacy servers to prevent the Chinese government from censoring local Internet users.[2]

China is not an isolated example. The 1996 Communications Decency Act was overturned by the Supreme Court a year after passage, and the U.S. approach has generally relied on self-regulation by the industry, which is making better filtering mechanisms available to parents seeking to protect their children. Democratic governments also act internationally. For example, national police forces in nineteen industrial states coordinated a crackdown on Internet pedophiles in December 2001.[3] As server technology increasingly focuses on geolocation, it is naive to dismiss such efforts to exercise state power as a quixotic fight with technological windmills, or an Orwellian effort at thought control. Even if they fail, states will continue attempts to shape the information revolution they helped bring about. With the coming of the Internet, "distance is dying; but geography, it seems, is still alive and kicking."[4]

In both its international and global manifestations culture illustrates the differences between regions. Japan's and Germany's cultural diplomacy and Europe's and Asia's popular culture markets point to the same conclusion: the porousness of contemporary regionalism is due to both international and global processes and various connections between the American imperium and these two regions.

Cultural Diplomacy of Japan and Germany

Cultural diplomacy reflects the logic of an international, not a global, world. Governments regard it as their special prerogative to represent the cultural achievements of their polity in the international society of states. The comparison of Japan and Germany supports this observation. It reflects also a great difference in the strength of the national and international elements in state identities. Despite that very noticeable difference, Japan and Germany both champion cultural exchange, building links between countries, and thus support a porous regionalism through their cultural diplomacy.

Japan

Only two decades ago, economics and technology appeared to have paved the road that would inevitably lead Japan back to "normal" great power status. Because it threatened to limit Japan's international appeal, cultural insularity was the only foreseeable bump in the road. To Joseph Nye, for example, Japan looked like a "one-dimensional economic power," with little political relevance

2. Lee 2001.
3. Hoge 2001.
4. *The Economist* 2001b, 20.

for other states.[5] In a similar vein, Ulf Hannerz argued that Japan put "culture on exhibit, in the framework of organized international contacts, as a way of displaying irreducible distinctiveness rather than in order to make it spread."[6] This opinion was held beyond the United States and Europe. One of China's leading film directors, Xie Jin, as well as many other Chinese commentators, argued that in contrast to Chinese and Western cultures, Japan lacked the religious and philosophical tradition necessary to sustain a leading role in international affairs.[7] Such views also find support in Japan. Akio Igarashi, for example, writes that "Japanization lacks a particular 'idea.'"[8] In this view, Japan cannot help but be culturally insular, inert and passive.

The evidence suggests a more complex pattern. Throughout most of the postwar years, the Ministry of Foreign Affairs and, since the early 1970s, the Japan Foundation have been the two central actors on questions of cultural diplomacy. The ministry and the government, more than the foundation, have a national vision of Japan's place in a changing world. That vision requires "explaining" to others the unique features of Japan that foreigners simply cannot grasp. In the 1960s that need to explain was driven by a sense of inferiority about Japan's "backwardness"; in the 1980s, by a sense of superiority because of Japan's extraordinary economic growth. Since then, there exists a growing sense of equality as Japan faces problems (demographic, financial, and otherwise) that also trouble other industrial states.

Japan's foreign cultural diplomacy is embedded in its general cultural policy. There have been two postwar turning points in Japan's cultural policies, and at both junctures international influences became increasingly important. One occurred in the late 1960s and early 1970s, the other in the early and mid-1990s. Both times, policy change resulted from the government's self-conscious attempt to reshape its international image. Cultural diplomacy became an instrument in the government's push to make Japan a more international state, celebrating culture as an attribute of a truly first-rate international power. To this end, the government decided first to favor more active support of culture, and subsequently to make the arts more visible in Japan's international affairs. Both policy innovations enhanced the slow process of opening Japan to outside influence.

After the late 1960s, increasingly aware of culture as a popular local and prefectural issue, elected officials made it a higher priority. The creation of the Agency for Cultural Affairs in 1968 was influenced also by international discussions in UNESCO and by an American model, the National Endowment for the Arts.[9] Under the auspices of the Ministry of Education, the agency is in charge of a state-defined meaning of "Japanese culture," typically of the "high" classical kind.[10]

5. Nye 1990, 166.
6. Hannerz 1989, 68.
7. Deng 1997, 386–87.
8. Igarashi 1997, 12.
9. Zemans 1999, 24.
10. McVeigh 1998, 133, also 144–46. The interviews on cultural issues that I cite in this chap-

Although several central government offices participate in Japan's cultural diplomacy, prefectural and local governments are increasingly involved. Territorial decentralization of power away from Tokyo has helped prefectures construct international links. In 1975, Kanagawa Prefecture was the first to open an international exchange office. Two decades later, all forty-seven prefectural governments had set up such offices, intent on cultural exchanges with adjacent China, Russia, and Southeast Asia. Prefectural governments have also established semigovernmental international exchange associations in each prefectural capital, and in eight metropolitan areas, which they fund and staff. In 1988, the Ministry of Home Affairs established the Council of Local Authorities for International Relations. In growing numbers, city and town halls have imitated these prefectural policies.

In creating the Japan Foundation in 1972, the Japanese government sought to modernize a policy machinery increasingly geared "to export official culture."[11] That fact alone put the Japan Foundation in a competitive relation with the lead domestic organization, the Agency for Cultural Affairs. Administratively, the Japan Foundation operates under the supervision of the Cultural Affairs Division of Ministry of Foreign Affairs. MOFA appoints its top officials, and the head of the foundation's administrative department is typically on loan from MOFA. In addition, the ministry has veto power over some key foundation appointments.[12] The Japan Foundation organizes a large number of programs dealing with people-to-people exchanges, language instruction and Japanese studies, the arts and performing arts, print media, film and television.

The Japan Foundation was set up to combat misunderstandings about both Japanese foreign policy and Japanese business practices overseas, and to counteract an underlying fear of isolation that remains a constant theme in Japan's diplomacy. According to Kenichiro Hirano, "There was a degree of aggressiveness in the Japanese approach to cultural exchanges during this period . . . even those who advocated mutual understanding through cultural exchanges thought little of the necessity for the Japanese to try to understand other peoples' cultures."[13] Article 1 of the law governing its operations prohibits the Japan Foundation from "introducing foreign cultures to the Japanese public."[14]

Contacts with business are close; the head of the Japan Foundation attends monthly meetings with the leadership of Keidanren, the premier association of business.[15] Business looks to cultural diplomacy to neutralize foreign criti-

---

ter were conducted, with the promise of anonymity of my respondents, on trips to Tokyo (October 1997, January 1999, January 2000, March 2001) and Berlin (May 2001). The format for citation is: interview number-year, location, date of interview. Interview 05–99, Tokyo, January 7, 1999, and 03–01, March 15, 2001.

11. Havens 1987, 346. Interview 08–00, Tokyo, January 7, 2000.
12. Interview 03–97, Tokyo, October 6, 1997. Interview 01–01, Tokyo, March 13, 2001.
13. Hirano 1988, 158.
14. Hirano 1997, 94.
15. Interviews 03–97, Tokyo, October 6, 1997; 06–01, Tokyo, March 19, 2001.

cisms of Japanese business. Business and government agree on one fundamental objective of cultural diplomacy: create a supportive climate abroad for Japanese firms. Yet the Japan Foundation was funded by the government (¥5 billion) with only a token (¥6 million) contribution by Keidanren. By 1995, the original endowment had increased twentyfold, to ¥100 billion. In addition to endowment income, the foundation receives annual allocations, especially funds from the government's overseas development budget. Yet the foundation's level of activity is relatively small. In the 1990s, its budget for external cultural affairs amounted to only about a third of the outlays of the German Goethe Institute and the German Academic Exchange Service or the British Council.

The Japan Foundation has operated under some serious disadvantages. Language teaching abroad is very important to Japan's cultural diplomacy. Between 1988 and 1998 the number of nonnative speakers trying to learn Japanese increased sharply, from 730,000 to 2.1 million (three-quarters of whom live in Asia-Pacific); since then that number has increased to 2.3 million in 2003. Compared, however, to German, which is learned by 15–20 million foreigners, mostly in Europe, this is a relatively small figure.[16] As a regional language with limited appeal, Japanese is a weak reed on which to build a cultural diplomacy that aims to export Japanese culture. In addition, and in sharp contrast to the U.S. government's commitment to spread the American way of life or the French government's efforts to help the cause of French civilization, until the late 1970s Japan's cultural diplomacy served as little more than a way to contain the resentment created by Japan's export offensive in world markets.

A broad definition of "cultural cooperation" that included economic development became a defining characteristic of Japan's cultural diplomacy. When the Japan Foundation was formed in 1972, Foreign Minister Takeo Fukuda insisted that "culture" not be part of its name. The foundation's work was to address the roots of obstacles to economic development, be they cultural, educational, or technological. This broad definition of culture permitted a dramatic change in the funding of the Japan Foundation. Starting in 1982, the government cut its direct contribution and funded the foundation largely through Japan's development aid budget. By 1987, 30 percent of the operating costs of the Japan Foundation came from subsidies for programs that assisted economic development.[17] With the economic motivations behind Japan's cultural diplomacy so strong throughout the 1980s, it is not surprising that on cultural matters, relations between Japan and Southeast Asia remained hierarchical rather than egalitarian.

In 1977, Fukuda, now prime minister, was the first to stress the importance of culture as an instrument for enhancing peace through nonhierarchical exchanges. Prime Minister Masayoshi Ohira (1978–80) articulated an even

---

16. University of Tokyo Study Group 1997, 37. *Look Japan*, July 2000, 25. Drifte 1996, 147.
17. Kawamura, Okabe, and Makita 2000, 20.

broader vision: Japan would have to explain itself to its partners but, he insisted, Japan would also have to learn from others. In the long term, international economic cooperation could succeed only in a system of give-and-take. One of the three pillars of Prime Minister Noboru Takeshita's 1988 Global Initiative was an expansion of cultural exchanges to encompass all forms of "cultural cooperation." Since then, virtually every prime minister has started a major cultural program: Morihiro Hosokawa's "Exchange That Will Build the Future of the Asia-Pacific Region" (1994), Tomiichi Murayama's "Peace, Friendship and Exchange Initiative" (1995), and Ryutaro Hashimoto's "Multinational Cultural Mission" (1997). Many of these initiatives, to be sure, remained little more than exercises in diplomatic rhetoric. But they indicate that Japan's cultural initiatives have placed new emphasis on balanced relationships with other countries. The speeches of Japan's prime ministers before the Diet document this gradual evolution of policy, and the importance of cultural themes increased in the 1980s and 1990s.[18]

With its greater international status and growing financial contributions to international organizations, Japan has practiced a form of status politics on the international stage. UNESCO is a good example. Japan's relations with UNESCO have had a very special meaning since the 1950s. It was the first international organization the "new" Japan joined after 1945, symbolizing Japan's fundamental transformation into a democratic and peace-loving country (the Japanese continue to support UNESCO very strongly at the grassroots to this day).[19] Almost two-thirds of MOFA's funding in support of cultural diplomacy is funneled through the Japan Foundation to UNESCO, which receives about a quarter of its total budget from Japan. Amid allegations that many votes had been bought or rigged, Koichiro Matsuura, Japan's ambassador in Paris, was the first Asian to be elected director-general of UNESCO in October 1999. His bid was supported by many Asian states and poorer countries. According to one senior member of the UNESCO staff, "Japan launched a full-scale diplomatic offensive. It reminded everyone, for example, that it is the largest foreign aid donor to sub-Saharan Africa—and that now it would like some return on its money."[20]

In the 1990s, Japan's cultural diplomacy also evolved along regional lines. Responding to a widespread perception of the growing importance of Asian regionalism, a 1989 Japan Foundation initiative led to the creation of the ASEAN Culture Center, in 1995 renamed the Japan Foundation Asia Center. The center was the first publicly funded organization charged with introducing other cultures to Japan.[21] It funds intellectual exchanges in Asia as well as programs to encourage a better understanding of Asia in Japan. The final report of a 1998 commission, convened with the express purpose of generating regional

18. Hirano 1988, 154–61. Wong 1991, 316–17.
19. Interviews 04–01 and 06–01, Tokyo, March 15 and 19, 2001.
20. Henley 1999.
21. Hirano 1997, 89, 95. Interviews 04–99 and 06–99, Tokyo, January 6 and 7, 1999.

cultural cooperation, recommended a course of action quite at odds with Japan's traditional approach: "Japan should place itself squarely in Asia and on equal footing with other Asian countries."[22] The terms of cultural engagement became more egalitarian in the 1990s. Through the work of the Asia Center, Japan's government began to see itself as an integral part of Asia-Pacific for the first time in the twentieth century.

Avoiding a narrow focus on East and Southeast Asia was central to Japan's cultural diplomacy. In terms of both the source and the level of funding, the creation of the Japan Foundation Center for Global Partnership in 1991 represented a very large financial commitment. Its creation increased the proportion of total foundation funds flowing to North American activities from 10 to 30 percent between 1989 and 1992, before dropping back to 19 percent by 1995.[23] With U.S.-Japan trade friction rising to dangerously high levels, the center was an effort to strengthen U.S.-Japanese collaboration in all fields.[24] In line with the redefined mission of the Japan Foundation, the center funds intellectual and grassroots exchange programs, as well as a fellowship program. It is less interested in high culture and more focused on collaborative problem solving. The Center for Global Partnership's priorities thus begin a shift away from the idea of exporting Japanese culture and toward global problem-solving capacities. The organization that is called the Center for Global Partnership in English is, in Japanese, literally the Japan-U.S. Center. In the thinking of Japanese government officials, internationalization, not globalization, is the correct context for a refashioned cultural diplomacy.[25]

The government is not the only actor in Japan's cultural diplomacy. Corporate philanthropy illustrates the deep entanglement of business. External economic frictions spurred a growing number of foundations dedicated to international exchange and cooperation. Ten such foundations were founded in the 1960s, 33 in the 1970s, 115 in the 1980s, and 28 in the years 1990–92.[26] The leading export market, the United States, was the most important foreign site for Japan's philanthropic foundations, especially in the 1980s. Examples include the Matsushita Foundation (1984), the Hitachi Foundation (1985), Toyota USA (1985), Ise Cultural Foundation (1986), Subaru of America Foundation (1984), and the Nakamichi Foundation (1982). U.S.-based Japanese foundations made charitable contributions in the United States totaling $30 million in 1986 and $500 million in 1991—the latter number exceeded U.S. corporate worldwide giving in 1990 by $100 million.[27] This sharp increase reflected a growing sense among Japan's corporate leaders that charitable giving was an essential cost of doing business in the United States. The donation rate

22. University of Tokyo Study Group 1998, 45.
23. University of Tokyo Study Group 1997, 42.
24. Zemans 1999, 57.
25. Interview 01–01, Tokyo, March 13, 2001. Interviews 04–99 and 06–99, Tokyo, January 6 and 7, 1999.
26. Menju and Aoki 1995, 145. Unfortunately no readily available data exist for the 1990s.
27. Katzenstein and Tsujinaka 1995, 98.

of these foundations is four or five times the average of corporate giving in Japan.[28] A change in the Japanese tax code in June 1990 made overseas, but not domestic, contributions tax deductible. "Generally speaking," writes Osamu Fujiwara, "Japanese companies are much more sensitive to social responsibilities in the United States than they are in Japan."[29]

Since the 1990s, furthermore, a growing number of citizen groups have gotten involved in program development and cultural diplomacy, in exchange for government funding. Quite often, leading officials of these organizations are former government officials. It is difficult to gauge accurately the importance of NGOs, for the simple reason that their numbers are very large. Estimates in the early 1990s put the number of all NGOs in Japan above five thousand, and that number has increased sharply since then.[30] Many of these groups focus primarily on learning about foreign cultures and secondarily on organizing exchanges and active cooperation. Haltingly in the 1980s, and more rapidly in the 1990s, a better understanding of foreign cultures became part of Japan's diplomacy. And after many decades of being clearly subordinated to economic considerations, by the 1980s the cultural elements of Japan's foreign policy acquired a more independent standing.[31]

After the Meiji Restoration, Japan embarked on a "cultural mission" to secure its position as a sovereign state in an international order dominated by the West, while also assuming the leading position in East and Southeast Asia. Since 1945, the government has refrained from celebrating an inherently superior Japanese race or Japanese values. Instead, cultural diplomacy initially served a dual purpose: to explain the specificity of Japanese culture and values to foreigners and to create a more stable economic environment for Japanese business abroad. Gradually, however, the purposes that had sustained Japan's cultural diplomacy for decades changed. International and regional elements of cultural diplomacy have become more important, reflected in new actors and new programs. Those responsible for cultural diplomacy now acknowledgethat culture is not the handmaiden of business and, more tentatively, that Japan must learn as well as instruct.

Germany

After the Holocaust, the German government reacted to the horrors of Nazi Germany not by shunning the concept of culture, as did the Japanese, but by making it a centerpiece of Germany's reestablishment in the community of states. "If culture was a secular grace," writes Charles Maier, "the state was the institutional channel for this sacrament."[32] In German, the concept of culture

28. Fujiwara 1992, 10, 15–16.
29. Fujiwara 1992, 16.
30. Interviews 01–01 and 06–01, Tokyo, March 13 and 19, 2001.
31. Hirano 1988, 159.
32. Maier 2002, 19.

has two different meanings. As recently as the 1950s, many Germans still distinguished culture from civilization—the inward appreciation of high art, science, and morality, on the one hand, and the outward manifestations of reasonably courteous behavior on the other. Civilization, not culture, was transportable.[33] Since the 1950s, Germany's diplomacy has helped give the concept of culture its second, international meaning, loosely translated as "cosmopolitan humanism" (*Bildung*).

On hearing the term "culture," instead of reaching for a revolver, as Josef Goebbels is reportedly to have joked, German politicians reach instead for their wallets. Culture is big business. The first comprehensive analysis of the economic importance of Germany's culture sector, in the late 1980s, concluded that it employed 680,000 persons and created annually a value-added of DM 40 billion, with the core of the culture industries accounting for about half of these. The culture business is substantially larger than aerospace or office equipment. The total cultural sector is comparable to energy in terms of value added, to agriculture and clothing and textiles in terms of employment, and to machinery in terms of investment.[34] Corporate philanthropy—9,500 foundations with assets exceeding DM 50 billion and annual outlays of about DM 830 million—accounted for only 5 percent of the DM 16 billion that the public sector pumped annually into all forms of culture in the late 1990s.[35] Germany's generous system of public subsidies for cultural affairs supported the initiatives in cultural diplomacy with which German governments sought to rehabilitate Germany after 1945.

After 1949, Germany's cultural diplomacy projected an image of "normality"—in contrast, for example, to French attempts to project the image of "national greatness."[36] Germans have traditionally subscribed to a sharp distinction between cultural and political nationhood. Germany's division after 1949 was a political act, and German culture remained both the foundation for eventual unification and a battleground for two "true" representatives of Germany and German culture during the cold war. Conspicuously absent was the explicit use of cultural propaganda in the interest of the state. During the 1950s, cultural diplomacy was viewed instead as an indirect support for German exports. "Learning German" and "buying German" were considered close cousins in an era when "made in Germany" became a badge of honor for the German trading state. Over the years, Germany's cultural diplomacy underwent significant change, from the celebration of economic products and language teaching in the 1950s and 1960s to dialogue and cooperation in the 1970s and 1980s to a hybrid combining both elements since unification in 1990.[37] The options had

33. Herf 1984, 224–27.
34. Bundesministerium des Innern 1990, 9–10.
35. König 1999, 30.
36. Znined-Brand 1997, 12.
37. Markovits and Reich with Carolyn Höfig 1997, 189–93. Znined-Brand 1997, 35–38, 43–45, 54–61, 72–75.

once been thought to be either "self-representation" or "dialogue"; in the
1990s "dialogue as self-representation" was increasingly taken for granted.[38]

In the first two postwar decades, Germany's cultural aim was to replace the
memory of Auschwitz and Buchenwald with that of Goethe and Schiller: in the
1950s by resuming external cultural contacts and language teaching, in the
1960s by strengthening Germany's cultural presence throughout the third
world. In this effort, Germany relied on the classic means of cultural diplomacy,
founding German schools abroad and fostering academic exchanges. In 1970,
under the leadership of Chancellor Willy Brandt, the Social Democratic Party–
Free Democratic Party (SPD–FDP) coalition government adopted new guidelines, broadening the concept of cultural diplomacy to include popular culture
and the introduction of foreign cultures into Germany. The machinery for cultural diplomacy in the foreign ministry was adapted to these new objectives,
and cultural diplomacy became an integral part of Germany's "active peace policy." In 1977, the government added an explicit European dimension to its cultural diplomacy, insisting that policy "must aid the political integration of
Europe in its cultural dimension."[39] The reform decade ended in 1980 with a
major conference, attended by representatives of forty-two nations, that gave
Germany's cultural diplomacy an explicitly international mission.

Although these changes had aimed at the legitimation of Germany in the
1970s, the SPD-led government insisted also on what it considered a well-bal-
anced pattern of self-representation abroad. At a time of great turmoil in domestic politics—widespread demonstrations, terrorist attacks, and the political
screening of applicants for civil service jobs—the government wanted to influence how Germany represented itself abroad. In the late 1970s, some cultural
programs provoked political controversy, with famous authors such as Günther
Grass and Heinrich Böll charging Bonn with undue interference in artistic
freedom. Such controversies continued, on and off, in the 1980s, under a conservative government led by Chancellor Helmut Kohl. The government tended
to favor the teaching of German abroad rather than the more encompassing
sense of cultural diplomacy of the 1970s, but practical policy supported both
approaches.

The end of the cold war, and the renewed interest in eastern Europe in Germany, consolidated the rebalancing of language and culture that had begun in
the 1980s. High demand for German as a language of business and trade, as
well as pent-up demand for traditional German culture, reinforced this reorientation. Policy, however, continued to favor a multilateral approach, insisting
whenever possible on working with numerous partner organizations abroad.
And policies supporting German culture and language were understood not
as substitutes for but as complements to the attraction of English and the appeal of American popular culture. In the 1990s, the different strands of Ger-

38. Herrmann 1994, 75. Werz 1992, 254.
39. Znined-Brand 1997, 57.

many's cultural diplomacy came together as united Germany rearticulated its role in Europe and in the world at large.

German unification highlights some of the cultural gaps that continue to divide East from West. United by a latent anti-Americanism, many on the right and left of the West German political spectrum viewed East Germany as the true heir of a German culture untainted by Western commercialism and cultural degradation. In contrast, East German artists and intellectuals by and large supported unification.[40] Yet the coming of a market economy cut East German culture loose from its political moorings. Worried about the collapse of the East German culture industry, the federal government granted a one-time subsidy of DM 900 million, enough to help East German cultural institutions survive but not enough to operate at their accustomed levels. Government policy continues to emphasize language teaching abroad, especially in eastern Europe. The foreign office has borrowed liberally from East German programs and practices without, however, relying on East German personnel. The result has strengthened Germany's cultural reach.[41] The daily ambivalences of German identity after unification thus are mirrored in Germany's cultural diplomacy.

On questions of culture and cultural diplomacy, it is an undue simplification to speak of Germany in the singular. In Germany's federal system, cultural affairs are the prerogative of individual states rather than the central government. At the federal level, cultural policy is made by a variety of ministries, among them Foreign Affairs, Interior, Finance, Education and Science, Women and Family Affairs, and Economic Cooperation and Development. Regional and local governments, and large numbers of independent organizations, implement policy within the guidelines of various public bodies. In 1998, the newly created office of State Minister for Cultural Affairs, what in the United States would be called the "culture czar," is a high-visibility appointment at the federal level without any substantial power base. Decentralization may be a hallmark of cultural diplomacy, but the federal government plays an important role. Confronted with widespread international skepticism about Germany's fledgling democratic institutions, in 1952 the Foreign Affairs Ministry had established a division of cultural affairs, making culture the "third pillar" of Germany's foreign policy, along with economics and politics, intended to improve the international climate. The Foreign Affairs Ministry's cultural division, with ten sections and one hundred employees, has under its direct supervision only the German schools that the government operates abroad.

For all other issues, the German government has relied on independent contractors under the indirect supervision of the Foreign Affairs Ministry.[42] German embassies have cultural attachés, who cooperate closely with other parapublic institutions that conduct much of Germany's cultural diplomacy.

40. Lepenies 1999b.
41. Interviews 02–01 and 04–01, Berlin, May 23 and 25, 2001.
42. Mitchell 1986, 75–77. Werz 1992, 249–50.

These include the Goethe Institute, the German Academic Exchange Service, the German Research Council, the Alexander von Humboldt Foundation, Inter Nationes, the Institute for Foreign Relations, and the Deutsche Welle, a German radio, television, and online program. These parapublic institutions give credence to the Foreign Affairs Ministry's insistence that its cultural diplomacy is not a handmaiden of either government or partisan policy.

In a speech he delivered as the first state secretary for cultural affairs of the SPD-FDP coalition in 1969, Ralf Dahrendorf called for "a shift of emphasis from a foreign policy of state to a foreign policy of societies."[43] There is, in fact, not much distance between the government's cultural diplomacy and what in Germany is called "societal foreign policy"—the foreign policies of various societal organizations. It is difficult to get an overall count of the organizations active in this policy domain. Apart from about a dozen federal ministries, sixteen states, scores of regions, and hundreds of cities and communities, perhaps as many as two hundred public, parapublic, and private organizations are involved in Germany's cultural diplomacy. Case studies of Germany's cultural diplomacy in Latin America and the Soviet Union have documented both the broad array of institutions involved and the variability across different regions and policy domains.[44] In the developing world, for example, policy focuses primarily on technology, vocational training, and the provision of information. Because it provides a large share of the budget of its partnership organizations, the Ministry for Economic Cooperation runs a much more centralized operation than does the Ministry of Foreign Affairs. It is also more sensitive to issues of technological change, including electronic media. In contrast, the Ministry of Foreign Affairs has barely begun to recognize the importance of new media for cultural diplomacy.[45]

The Goethe Institute is perhaps the most important of the parapublic institutions on which the federal government relies. Founded in 1951, its headquarters were for half a century in Munich, moving to Bonn after the 2001 merger with Inter Nationes (previously the government's main public relations organization). The main purpose of its programmatic activities had been to mediate between equal cultures with different traditions. Yet German unification and the "return" of the Eastern European countries to Europe prompted new guidelines in 1997. The Goethe Institute began to focus its activities once more on its core competencies—language, culture, and art—and it made, in part for budgetary reasons, a partial shift back to emphasize elite culture.

In the early 1990s, the Goethe Institute had about three thousand employees and ran 161 institutes in seventy-three countries, sponsoring about fourteen thousand events annually.[46] It favors a multilateral approach to cultural diplomacy and a dialogue format that not only "exports" German language and

43. Werz 1992, 254.
44. Scherfenberg 1984. Lippert 1996.
45. Interview 02–01, Berlin, May 23, 2001.
46. Interview 02–01, Berlin, May 23, 2001.

culture but also "imports" foreign culture. About one-fifth of its budget is spent on organizing events inside Germany, including language courses for foreign workers. By the mid-1990s, nine of its twenty-five language training centers were located inside Germany.

Both in the mid-1980s and the late 1990s, the Goethe Institute and the federal government's cultural diplomacy saw political controversies about the proper balance between political autonomy and government intervention, and about program content and funding priorities. Such occasional quarrels have never questioned the premise that Germany's cultural diplomacy should serve political not economic ends and be implemented by a partnership between public and private sectors. In the words of the general secretary of the Goethe Institute, Joachim-Felix Leonhard, "foreign cultural relations begin at home." Presenting a "good image abroad" is no longer the main impetus that drives Germany's cultural diplomacy.[47] In a major speech in 2000, Foreign Minister Joschka Fischer reiterated the central role of Germany's cultural diplomacy as "an integral element of a foreign policy that aims at the prevention of conflict and the securing of peace."[48] Cultural diplomacy is no longer a "third" pillar but an integral part of Germany's foreign and security policy.

National Overtures to the World

Differences in national approaches, rather than global convergence, are significant within the context of increasing openness to developments in world politics. Into the 1980s, Japan's cultural diplomacy served primarily economic ends. It remains deeply rooted in a distinctively national perspective, which for decades sought to instruct others to appreciate Japan's uniqueness. Yet, since the late 1970s, there have been unmistakable signs of change, pointing to a more open policy stance. This shift is indicated on the one hand by the growing role of prefectures and communities, nongovernmental organizations, and corporate philanthropy; and on the other by a broadening of policy focus from the UN and UNESCO to the United States and Southeast Asia. Japan's cultural diplomacy illustrates a national orientation and a gradual rise in the importance of Asia-Pacific. Like Japan, Germany's cultural diplomacy reflects processes of internationalization. From the beginning of the German Federal Republic, cultural diplomacy was an important tool of international rehabilitation. With the power of the German state heavily circumscribed, the habit of proceeding not alone but with domestic and foreign partners became deeply ingrained. What is striking about Germany, compared to Japan, is a more explicitly international purpose and context for cultural diplomacy. Yet both cases point to one central conclusion: internationalization creates national approaches that are open to the world.

47. Sittner and Steinfeld 2001. Interviews 02–01 and 04–01, Berlin, May 23 and 25, 2001.
48. Auswärtiges Amt 2000, 6.

Popular Culture in Asia and Europe

Cultural globalization also keeps Asia and Europe open. The products of Japan's profitable mass culture industries sell extremely well in Asian markets. In contrast to the traditionally insular approach of its government, Japan's dynamic capitalism has built a highly competitive popular culture industry, ranging from Japanese comic books (*manga*) and animated movies (*anime*), to Japanese forms of entertainment (karaoke), slot machines (*pachinko*), and fashion. Acting also as a filter for U.S. cultural products and practices, Japan is Asia's biggest success story in commodifying culture, and its market-oriented approach is beginning to create a collective consumer culture in the urban centers throughout East Asia.[49] In sharp contrast, Germany and Europe lack a dynamic popular culture industry that extends into regional and global markets and that competes with American products. Instead, we find in Europe a polity that seeks to stem, by political means and without much success, America's dominance in European culture markets.

The Regional Spread of Japanese Popular Culture

Japanese firms have been more adept at exporting mass culture than the Japanese state has been at exporting elite culture. "Image alliances" link the products of different media and find expression in innovative production well suited to compete in regional markets. Japan's popular culture, artistically creative and economically dynamic, is developing a broad appeal, especially in Asia-Pacific markets. Building on a long tradition of successfully importing cultural practices, from baseball to Christmas, Japan has a comparative advantage in acquiring cultural know-how from the West and then selling its cultural products, suitably localized, in overseas markets, especially in Southeast Asia.[50] In these markets, Japanese products have had no trouble being "understood."[51]

Since the early 1990s, Japan's mass culture has spread at an astonishing rate throughout Asia-Pacific. Between 1990 and 2002, foreign royalties from Japan's popular culture industries increased by 300 percent to $12.5 billion.[52] The new Asianism appearing in contemporary Japan is, in the words of Koichi Iwabuchi, the product of "constructing cultural similarity with the rest of Asia through popular culture and urban consumption." Japan's culture industry "is still less concerned with the direct export of Japanese cultural products than with how to rid cultural products of 'Japanese smell' and to make them acceptable in Asia."[53] In short, by translating Western leisure products and a lifestyle of urban consumerism, Japan's culture industries are creating a new

49. Shiraishi forthcoming.
50. Iwabuchi 1998, 165–66, and 2002.
51. Shiraishi 1997, 234–35.
52. Faiola 2003.
53. Iwabuchi 1994, 227–28.

sense of sameness between Japan and other parts of Asia and beyond. The young, in a burgeoning "middle-mass" society, are altering lifestyles in Japan's metropolitan areas and, with a short time lag, in major urban centers throughout East Asia. The urban middle mass is attracted neither by traditional folk art nor by Western high culture. This new middle mass operates in a space that is culturally open and relatively undefined. Its demands are not met by existing cultural frameworks or existing products.[54] Japanese producers are ready to meet that new demand. Developed in highly competitive domestic markets, Japanese print and electronic products reflect both imagination and quality, as well as scale economies and tie-ins across different media that create large numbers of spin-offs, clout in distribution and marketing channels, and large profits. "Ultimately," speculates Frederik Schodt, the success of Japan's popular culture "is emblematic of something much larger—perhaps a postwar 'mind-melt' among the peoples of industrialized nations, who all inhabit a similar (but steadily shrinking) physical world of cars, computers, buildings, and other manmade objects and systems."[55]

The spread of mass culture is facilitated enormously by the communications revolution that young customers in Asia-Pacific have embraced so readily, from Star TV and fax machines to personal computers, cellular phones, and personal pagers. The result projects Japanese images and values that differ sharply from the limited personal freedom, pervasive ethic of self-sacrifice, authoritarian relationships, and suppression of many signs of individuality that characterized Japan half a century ago. Japanese cultural products give clear expression to the values and aspirations of the contemporary Japanese middle mass—the freedom to pursue romantic inclinations and sexual impulses, the tensions between individuals and the organizations in which they live and work, the urge of a people living in cities to be one with nature. Since the mid-1990s, Japan's mass cultural products and lifestyle have become cutting edge throughout East Asia, offering a complement to or substitute for Hollywood.

Take popular music, for example. The influence of Japanese pop music is clear in the songs of Hong Kong stars like Jacky Cheung. Virtually unknown in Japan, Chiba Mika, a Japanese pop star groomed for East Asian markets, was one of the great successes in Taiwan, Southeast Asia, and China. Her career, "planned" for foreign markets, illustrates one facet of the broad appeal of Japanese cultural products.[56] The Japanese music industry, seeking to export "concepts," has made the production of Asian stars, what Sony calls "Asia Major," a centerpiece of its regionalization strategy.[57] Auditions held throughout Southeast Asia are part of a concerted corporate effort to open up the regional

54. Honda 1994, 76. Iwabuchi 1994, 239.
55. Schodt 1996, 339.
56. Sony Music Entertainment is using the same strategy to introduce a Colombian rock star, Shakira, to the U.S. market after she sold more than eight million records in Latin America. Orwall 2001.
57. Iwabuchi 1994, 237, and 1998, 170–73.

music market. But this is only part of the story. The initiative of local promot-
ers and the ready response of consumers has spread Japan's popular culture
far and wide. Using Hong Kong to reach all of Asia, rock stars borrow from Japanese hits and produce them for the Asia-wide market. New crossover styles
such as Mandopop have emerged, spurred by the huge Asian market, a large
Asian immigrant community in the United States, and the rise of the Internet.
An incipient regional popular culture results from dynamic market processes.

Japanese comics, or manga, illustrate a crossover of another type: the close
relation between the import and export of cultural products. Japan's culture
industries are acting as a transmission belt for cultural trends originating in the
United States. By incorporating and subtly changing U.S. products, Japanese
artists create a mass culture more accessible to consumers throughout Asia.
Adaptations can create entirely new art: Osamu Tezuka, for example, was
greatly influenced by Walt Disney and American cartoons. Yet he helped revo-
lutionize manga by extending story lines and introducing cinematic techniques into the images he drew. The result was a visualized narrative in over
three hundred books.[58]

Tezuka's genius for visual narration helped set in motion a large and dynamic Japanese industry that has increasingly been linked to export markets
in Asia-Pacific. Japanese filtering of American cultural products neutralizes
country-specific features, be they American or Japanese, creating a stronger regionwide appeal. One leading Japanese publisher has begun to train East Asian
cartoonists in Tokyo; they then work abroad, typically pirating Japanese products and spreading manga through domestic markets. With intellectual property rights now more rigorously enforced throughout Asia-Pacific, the growing
appeal of manga creates a large export market for Japanese corporations,
promising high profits and enormous growth. This is a genuine cultural and
commercial innovation, not merely a cultural fad.

Manga are more like visual novels than like comic books. As a Japanese art
form, visual storytelling has roots that go back a thousand years. Comics are
not only for kids. Boys and young men are the key market, it is true, and three-
quarters of all manga cater to them,[59] but manga target Japanese consumers
of different age groups, socioeconomic levels, and sexual orientations. Manga
has become a major feature of Japanese culture. Between 1980 and 2003, the
number of manga books or magazines published annually increased from 1 billion to 2.2 billion—40 percent of Japan's total print market in numbers of
copies sold, and 25 percent of gross revenues.[60] This amounts to fifteen manga
a year for every man, woman, and child in Japan. Manga typically run four hundred pages and are issued weekly. On a page-by-page basis, they are six times
cheaper than U.S. comics. On average, twenty new manga volumes are pub-

58. Shiraishi 1997, 237.
59. Schodt 1996, 82.
60. Schilling 2003. These are impressive figures despite the industry's seven-year slump.

lished every day, more than five hundred each month.[61] In highly competitive markets, manga artists and publishers frequently ascertain their readers' needs and interests through reader surveys. Series that do not meet with reader approval disappear rapidly.

Each successful manga goes through its own product cycle. One of the great hits of the 1990s, the *Sailor Moon* series, is a good example.[62] After three months of successful sales in manga form, it was made into an anime for television. At the same time, novelty goods and props that appeared in the manga were put on sale. After half a year, serialized installments came out in book form, generating much higher profits than the magazines had. A couple of months later, "film" comics, selected frames from the television animation, went on sale, and within a year the animation itself was sold on videotape. Finally, during both summer and winter school vacations, an anime version was released for screening in movie theaters. Musical renditions were staged. A video game based on the original manga appeared. And a collection of the original artwork was published in an expensive book form. During the first two years of *Sailor Moon*'s astonishingly successful run, more than five thousand novelty products and twenty video games reached the market.[63] In 1996, Dragon Ball Z, one of the most popular characters of Japanese anime, generated $2.95 billion worldwide in merchandise alone.[64] Saya Shiraishi's analysis suggests that the "image alliance" between manga and anime is the foundation for the multimedia product cycles that distinguish Japan's mass culture industry.[65] "Japanimation" is a translation of the characters and story lines of manga into anime.

Japanese manga have spread regionally. The enormous growth in Hong Kong's comic book industry, for example, was based on pirated editions of Japanese manga. Hong Kong comics are associated with the name of Tony Wong, the creator of *Jademan* comics. But by the early 1990s, the sales of local comics publishers had grown so much that they began to acquire licenses for the legitimate translation and marketing of manga. By 1993, Japanese manga controlled 50 percent of the Hong Kong market. Pirated Japanese manga were also an important factor in the development of Taiwanese comics. The Tong Li Publishing Company, run by Fang Wennan, "the self-appointed 'king of pirated *manga*,'" released over a thousand titles during a fifteen-year period.[66] Most of the smuggled comics were intended for rental shops, which declined in importance only in the 1990s as Japanese anime TV programs were broadcast every day, all day, not only on cartoon channels but also by the other networks. In addition, Taiwan and Hong Kong are gateways to China's enormous market, which has shown great receptivity to Japanese manga. The first foreign TV-

61. Schodt 1996, 19, 23. Shiraishi 1997, 237, 250. Natsume 2000, 2.
62. Kondo 1995, 6. See also Shiraishi 1997, 239–40, 253–54, 265, 270.
63. Kondo 1995, 6. Grigsby 1998.
64. Mullen 1997.
65. Shiraishi 1997, 235.
66. Schodt 1996, 306–7.

animation aired in China in the 1980s was Japanese; Japanese comics sell very briskly; and character merchandise is easily available all over the country, including in state stores.[67]

Japanese cultural products do not have universal appeal, however. In Thailand, one hears talk of Japanese cultural imperialism, and the Philippines has resisted the appeal of Japanese manga. In fact, the Philippine government imposes occasional bans on manga and anime because of their violence and sexual content. Developments in South Korea suggest, however, that the Philippines is a rare exception. For decades, the South Korean government imposed a total ban on the import of Japanese cultural products. Yet even before the tentative opening of the South Korean market to Japanese cultural imports in 1998 and its full liberalization in 2002, South Korea was deeply affected by Japanese manga and anime, which control 70 percent of the Korean market.[68] Korean animation TV stations rely largely on Japanese imports and, even before the market was opened, habitually violated the 30 percent limit on foreign animation products. A 1995 change in Korean policy aimed at increasing the domestic production of anime had only modest success.[69] Yet, in more recent years, South Korea has grown increasingly confident. In 1998 the government put in effect its first five-year cultural plan, and cultural exports (movies, videos, and television programs) have since doubled. The merging of Japanese and Korean popular culture is proceeding at great speed, despite unresolved issues stemming from contested historical memories.[70]

Saya Shiraishi concludes that "Japanese popular culture is becoming Asian popular culture."[71] After decades of phenomenal domestic growth, both manga and anime products are looking to export markets, primarily in Asia-Pacific but also globally, for future growth and profits. Pokémon showed Japanese firms that regional and world markets could produce enormous profits. This regional spread is greatly aided by overseas networks, and it draws strength from the young, who use the World Wide Web for pirating manga and anime products in Asia and for organizing fan clubs in the United States.

The process is not unidirectional. Japanese publishers deliberately support Taiwan's young artists, for example, by reserving 40 percent of the pages of the flagship journals they sell in Taiwan for local work. Foreign manga artists are gradually entering Japanese markets: Japanese firms have begun bringing Vietnamese artists to Japan, training them, and sending them back to Japanese subsidiaries in Vietnam. This parallels developments in the music industry. Japanese companies sign up Japanese singers, give them language training, and send them abroad to sing in foreign languages.[72] The export of Japanese popular culture creates countercurrents that are conducive to hybridization. Artis-

67. Shiraishi 1997, 268.
68. Chung 1997, 58–59.
69. Yu 1999, 38–39, 47–52.
70. Onishi 2004.
71. Shiraishi 1997, 236.
72. Interviews 06–99, Tokyo, January 7, 1999, and 09–00, Tokyo, January 7, 2000.

tic creativity remains central to the mass culture industry. As long as that creativity prevails, Japan's multinational image alliances will help its popular culture penetrate Asian markets, pulled in by the apparently insatiable demand of a new urban middle mass and able to replicate in different national contexts.

Japanese family television dramas, not Western soaps; Japanese horror movies, not Western versions with blond and blue-eyed characters; the familiar cuteness of Pokémon characters, not Mickey Mouse; and Japanese pop songs easily adapted to karaoke, not choreographed American bands—all of these cultural products sell in Asia because they resonate more fully with existing cultural repertoires.[73] Yet this regional popular culture is also spreading beyond Asia. Japanese manga revitalized Germany's stagnant comic book industry in the late 1990s, and Japanese children's series, like *Pokémon* and *Dragon Ball*, became big hits on German television. The most popular movie ever made in Japan, the anime *Spirited Away*, was a cowinner of the 2002 Golden Bear Award at the Berlin International Film Festival.[74] The 1990s was the decade of Japan's "Gross National Cool."[75] It belied the notion of a Japan lacking in "soft" power, as Joseph Nye had argued at the beginning of the decade.[76] Some of that soft power derives from Japan's century-old quest to translate and absorb foreign influences; some from the clever perfection of marketing strategies; and some from the creativity of brilliant artists. In a world of porous regions, popular culture makes Japan a lifestyle superpower that need not be a military or economic superpower.

German Popular Culture and Americanization

As Germany and Europe are awash in a sea of popular culture, most of it of American origin, the politics of popular culture in Europe focuses on imports rather than exports. "Americanization" has come to refer to the appropriation of American mass culture by different social strata, groups, and generations, and the processes by which these groups create their own subcultures.[77] Since World War II, the indisputable leadership of the United States has made the "American way of life" both salient and accessible for Germans and all Europeans. Americanization has connotations that are both positive (democracy, capitalism, affluence, modernity, tolerance, enlightenment) and negative (non-European, culturally inferior, superficial, materialist, profit-hungry). Concepts such as "self-Americanization,"[78] "self-colonization,"[79] and "cultural creolization"[80] all underline the active role that Germans play in the selection

73. Tadokoro 2000–2001, 24. Interviews 03–01 and 04–01, Tokyo, March 15, 2001.
74. Rosenbach 2001. Hammerstein 2001. Pilling 2002.
75. McGray 2002. Leheny forthcoming.
76. Nye 1990.
77. Jarausch and Siegrist 1997, 14–16.
78. Maase 1997, 223–26.
79. Wagnleitner 1994, 2.
80. Kroes 1996, 164.

and appropriation of the products of American mass culture. When Elvis Presley joined the U.S. Army in Germany in October 1958—crew cut, military demeanor, and all—German newspapers featured the headline "Elvis Presley is becoming German."[81] For the 341 million paperback novellas (*Groschenhefte*) that Germans bought in 1971, the most popular story line was, in the words of one of the publishers, "the German Western," written by German authors, many of whom had never been in the United States—a contemporary recapitulation of the enormously successful nineteenth-century author Karl May.[82]

Hollywood is the prime example of American domination of Europe's popular culture. The export of U.S. movies to Germany started slowly in the 1950s but gained strength with the generational changes of the 1960s. This trend also shaped mass television markets: by the mid-1970s, almost half of the movies shown on Germany's public television were American. In a report released in the mid-1980s, the European Commission estimated that in the future European television would broadcast 125,000 hours of new movies and entertainment shows annually, but European production would cover fewer than five thousand hours.[83] In 1987, 79 percent of global film and television exports originated in the United States.[84] Matters, however, turned out quite differently. In the 1990s, American studios began to price themselves out of television markets around the world, and local producers began to turn out television shows and movies on a substantial scale. In 2001, a Nielsen survey reported that 71 percent of the top ten programs in sixty countries were locally produced. American television shows were no longer hits on prime-time television, as foreign broadcasters developed programming that was competitive at the high end of the market.[85] At the low end, reality TV shows point to Europe as a possible future center of innovation in television.

This, however, is not true of Hollywood's impact. Despite some national subsidies, the European movie industry is less well funded and lacks the thematic inventiveness, technical wizardry, and firm control over global distribution networks that give Hollywood a strong edge in world markets. In four sample years in the 1990s, U.S. films accounted in all years and in all national markets for more than 50 percent of the most popular movies.[86] In 1998, the market share of U.S. movies was lowest in Italy and France (around 50 percent), highest in Britain, Belgium, and the Netherlands (80–85 percent), and ranged in the middle (between 65 and 75 percent) for all other European countries, including Germany.[87] In Germany less than one-fifth of movies shown in theaters are German productions. Domestic movies can occasionally claim as much as 40 percent of the market, as in France or Italy, but all European films are weak

81. Maase 1997, 219.
82. Haufler 1997, 405.
83. Bertlein 1989, 132.
84. Wagnleitner 1994, 249–51.
85. Kapner 2003, A8.
86. Laitin 2002, 68. Bertlein 1989, 131–32.
87. European Commission 2000a, 516.

outside their home markets. Despite the occasional international hit for the New German cinema with films such as the comedic farce *Good-bye Lenin,* attempts to use the German tax code to make Berlin-Babelsberg—in the 1930s and 1940s Hollywood's most avid imitator—an important center of Germany's and Europe's movie industry have failed miserably.[88]

This is not to deny the existence of numerous pockets of cultural innovation. William E. Schmidt noted that in the 1990s, perhaps for the first time in decades, there was some evidence that American hegemony over pop culture was being challenged by the emergence of a European sense of music, fashion, and style.[89] MTV Europe, for example, is modeled after the American television channel, yet it offers music and fashion that young Americans would hardly recognize. In the 1990s, European art films and German genre films showed cultural fusion at a level deeper than the mere disappearance of a distinctive German style in which the director writes the script, produces the movie, acts, and promotes. Light-hearted and entertaining, the German genre films were more American than the Americanized version of the new German cinema of the 1970s.[90] American popular culture, not indigenous European content, remains the single most pervasive cultural influence in contemporary Europe.

There is one exception to this generalization—in the world of popular music. Europe is part of a global market dominated by English-language songs, yet each European country has its own version of national pop music. In contrast to the movie industry, the European Union has three major companies (Britain's Thorn EMI, the Netherlands' Polygram, and Germany's BMG, or Bertelsmann Music Group) that together account for 40 percent of sales in world markets. European pop music is shaped by global trends, including developments in the United States, but it also has distinctive regional and national elements. When it originated in the 1950s, rock 'n' roll was distinctively American; its adaptation into Germany's working-class culture was a clear illustration of "self Americanization" at work. By the 1980s, however, German rock music had produced its own distinctive "New German Wave."[91]

The blurring of national boundaries has accelerated as a regional Europop style began to develop, combining Eurovision song contests with the disco sound of clubs in Ibiza, a favored vacation spot.[92] Swedish disco groups such as ABBA and the Italian "Eurobeat,"with its high-tech sound quality, convinced British recording studios that the time was ripe for producing not only for the American but also for the European market. Techno music originated in Detroit. In the early 1990s, Germany's techno music movement exploded with a timely political message of love, peace, and unity. By the end of the 1990s, the techno

---

88. Pauly 2001.
89. Schmidt 1993. Laitin 2002, 67–74.
90. Gemünden 1998, 211–13.
91. Dirke 1989.
92. Laitin 2002, 70–74.

sound of Berlin's annual musical spectacle, the Love Parade, was drawing 1.3 million ravers to Germany's capital. In 2002, the Love Parade went international with similar events staged in Vienna and Leeds. Techno music has evolved different national substyles, such as "jungle" in England and "trance" in Germany.

In most other popular music styles, which rely on lyrics, the border between Europe and America is blurred. European rap lyrics fall between mere imitation of and full emancipation from U.S. models.[93] In the European market, it is rare for non-English songs to succeed outside their domestic markets.[94] The pervasive influence of the English language is an important conduit for a regional pop music culture that is linked to the American market. This regional market does not act as a straitjacket. German recording artist Sash! (Sascha Lappessen) had five hits in 1997–98, with titles in three languages, none of them German.[95] About one-fifth of the top German hits are domestic, slightly more than the figure for European imports (around 15 percent) but well below the figure for U.S. imports (generally around 40 percent). The national origin of between a quarter and a third of the top hits is uncertain, illustrating the extent to which "origin" is of marginal importance to many listeners.[96]

In contrast to Japan, German popular culture has not succeeded in producing and marketing products with broad appeal in Europe. Yet German media giants have grown into some of the largest corporations in world markets—some with spectacular successes, such as Bertelsmann, and some with a resounding bankruptcy, such as Kirch. What unites these corporations is aggressive investment in rapidly growing media markets coupled with a total lack of interest in the content of the cultural message they deliver.

With annual revenues of about $15 billion in the year 2000, Bertelsmann was the third largest entertainment company in the world, behind Time Warner and Walt Disney.[97] Having nurtured relations with the cash-strapped AOL in the mid-1990s (eventually turning two small investments of $50 and $270 million into returns estimated respectively at $2.5 billion and $7–$8 billion), Bertelsmann rejected a merger proposal from AOL, losing out, luckily as it turned out, to Time Warner—which also beat Bertelsmann in its attempted acquisition of EMI. Yet with three hundred subsidiaries in fifty-four countries and about seventy-five thousand employees, Bertelsmann revenues continue to increase. The company is strong in magazines, books, and music, and by investing $9 billion in 2001, it increased from 37 to 67 percent its stake in Europe's largest television broadcaster, the RTL Group.

The collapse of global telecommunication markets found Bertelsmann still undecided between internationalization and globalization. In the early 1990s,

93. Androutsopoulos and Scholz 1999, 21.
94. In February 1999, for example, the top ten or top twenty listings in nine European countries listed 170 titles; of the twenty-two titles appearing on the lists of more than one country, only one was not sung in English.
95. Laitin 2002, 72.
96. Laitin 2002, 74.
97. Barnet and Cavanagh 1994, 68–111. Meyer-Larsen 2000, 107–21.

CEO Mark Wössner had insisted in an interview that "we are an international company. But not global."[98] His successor, Thomas Middelhoff, committed instead to globalization. After buying Random House in 1998, adding to its ownership of Bantam, Doubleday, and Dell, Bertelsmann became the largest English-language book publisher in the world. Its use of the Internet and e-trade resonate with the origins of Bertelsmann as a subscription-based book club. In 2001, Bertelsmann generated two-thirds of its revenues outside of Germany, a far larger number than AOL Time Warner's 20 percent. Although Bertelsmann survived the global shakeout of the telecom industry better than most, the firm's patriarch, Reinhard Mohn, dismissed CEO Middelhoff and the globalization strategy he had championed, reasserted family control, and returned the company to an international strategy.

Not all German media companies have operated so successfully. Leo Kirch, for example, controlled Germany's biggest commercial television networks and owned the rights to the world's largest library of programming and sports events, including the World Cup soccer tournament and Formula One racing. In 1996 Kirch acquired virtually all movie rights from the major Hollywood studios for the next ten years. Betting, mistakenly as it turned out, on the revolutionary impact of digital technology on TV viewing habits, Kirch invested about $6 billion in exchange for pay and pay-per-view rights to Hollywood's total production of movies and TV shows. Kirch's high level of debt left him no choice but to file for bankruptcy in the spring of 2002. The Kirch media empire was bought in 2003 by Haim Saban, a Hollywood-based Israeli billionaire who had made his fortune popularizing Japanese cartoons.

Whether successful or failing, Germany's media giants are interested in the medium to make money, not to develop a message. What is true for print media on a subnational scale holds also for Germany's high-tech electronic media, operating on a world scale. After 1991, for example, a Bavarian newspaper chain bought up much of the Czech Republic's regional press. Czech politicians and intellectuals were deeply worried about cultural annexation and possible German interference in Czech affairs. But the *Bayern-Kurier* was good at producing profitable regional papers, not at exporting conservative German political views.[99] Bertelsmann "is not known for openly promoting a political creed in its media. The main goal seems to be business growth, and not to operate as a leader of opinion."[100] The man who made Bertelsmann one of the world's media giants in the second half of the twentieth century, Reinhard Mohn, was not interested in publishing, printing, music, or the Internet. In the words of Richard J. Barnet and John Cavanaugh, "He could just as happily sell anything that wasn't disreputable. His passion is to create a successful corporate structure."[101]

Germany's place in popular culture markets must be viewed in a broader

98. Barnet and Cavanagh 1994, 79.
99. Jerábek and Zich 1997, 161–75.
100. Kleinsteuber and Peters 1991, 195.
101. Barnet and Cavanagh 1994, 85.

European context. A popular political joke, and a French nightmare, defines a European as a person who watches American soap operas on a Japanese television. Indeed, the most common cultural link across Europe is provided by American popular culture. The pervasiveness of American movies on European television, for example, perceived as an instance of cultural globalization, has prompted political responses at the European level that have failed to strengthen a distinctive European culture. The European Union has moved vigorously to facilitate the cross-border flow of audiovisual material. The 1989 Television without Frontiers Directive eliminated most legal barriers to the transmission and reception of television signals between EU member states, and imposed a controversial nonbinding quota regime on imports, seeking to reduce the exposure of mass audiences to the products of the U.S. entertainment industry.

U.S. programs enjoy inherent attractions: established market position; the historical preference of the European working class for U.S. cultural products (seen as less elitist than those created by European producers); and the internal size and heterogeneity of the U.S. market, which both permits economies of scale and offers space for cultural experimentation. The European Commission's clarion call for Europe's cultural defense was tactically astute: protection against "foreign cultural predators" was acceptable to national governments, the construction of a collective European cultural identity much less so. It created a political alliance with the European Parliament and with, rather than against, some of the most important member states, especially France and its cultural minister Jack Lang. The concept of a collective European popular culture—which did not exist, as two decades of failed policies demonstrated—was easily mobilized to "defend" Europe against the "outside" world.[102]

The first concrete manifestation of European policy was the MEDIA program. After years of tortuous negotiations, this program started in 1986. It sought to enhance the circulation of national film and television programs among member states, assisted by the Community with loans for low-budget films for Europe-wide distribution, joint audiovisual production among producers in small geographic or linguistic markets, and a scheme to refine translation and dubbing techniques appropriately called BABEL (Broadcasting Across the Barriers of European Languages). The funding of these initiatives amounted to no more than 0.13 ecu per EU citizen in the early 1990s.[103] The program hoped to increase the 20 percent figure for European films shown outside of the country of origin.[104] Europeanization did not mean transforming the content of movies through denationalization but rather making new national markets available for European producers.[105]

102. Theiler 1999, 73.
103. Theiler 1999, 77.
104. Bertlein 1989, 130.
105. Theiler 1999, 77.

The Treaty of Maastricht gave the European Union, for the first time, a mandate (albeit a weak one) in the area of cultural policy. Yet despite new directives that the EU Commission adopted for satellite transmission in August 1995 and for cable in September 1996, developments in the 1990s did not initiate a new era in audiovisual policy. The European Union's larger financial outlays funded an increased range of activities—special events, literature promotion, preservation of European heritage, promotion of exchanges in new cultural networks, and production and distribution of "high culture" movies. However, many legal restrictions and qualifications remain, including the veto power that all member states retain in this politically sensitive policy area.

In short, all attempts to create a pan-European television station with non-national "European programming" have failed. Viewers simply did not like European programs, and national governments were unwilling to secure Community-wide distribution of signals and adequate financial support. Only when the Commission learned to frame the issue in economic terms did national governments agree to cede some ground. In the 1990s the European Union sought to Europeanize production rather than consumption. The European Parliament and the Commission subsidized multinational coproductions in the hope of reducing national content over time. Lacking support from many member states, this policy also failed. EU policy has been reduced to boosting domestic output and subsidizing the circulation of audiovisual material throughout the Community. In this sense, the European Union's audiovisual policy resembles its cultural policy more generally: it facilitates the "horizontal" flow of products and information without having an effect on the "vertical" dimension of content that could create a different collective identity. Because European states guard their cultural sovereignty jealously—more jealously against political initiatives from Brussels than against movies from Hollywood—Europe remains "plurinational" rather than becoming "nonnational" or "European."

Since the end of the cold war, the salience of cultural conflicts in world politics has increased sharply. Distinctive of cultural processes in Asia, and specifically in Japan, is the dynamic spread of a profitable popular culture industry in Asia-Pacific markets. Although Europe's and Germany's indigenous popular culture industries are conspicuous largely by their absence in world markets, media corporations such as Bertelsmann have enjoyed enormous success abroad. Neither Japan nor Germany is defined today by a distinctive cultural message. For states that only sixty years ago opposed inclusive Western liberalism with an exclusive cultural nationalism, this triumph of the medium over the message signals an astounding change. In Germany, this outcome has ended the mistaken dichotomy between German "culture" and Western "civilization." In Japan, it has prepared the ground for a cosmopolitanism with a Japanese face.

A Very Distant World—Closed Regions in the 1930s

The cultural diplomacy of states and the global markets for popular culture point us to the porousness of contemporary regionalism. As we have seen in this chapter, the pressures for porousness are very strong. The cases confirm, furthermore, that Asia's and Europe's regionalism have different institutional structures. The difference is striking between Germany's internationalist-de-centralized and Japan's nationalist-centralized cultural diplomacy. And so is the difference between dynamic market developments in Asia and unsuccessful European efforts to shape popular culture through law and politics. The dynamics of contemporary regionalism create a world of regions similar in their porousness and dissimilar in their institutions.

A brief glance back at the 1930s underlines the distance that separates us from the closed regionalism of an earlier era. Then, Japan's identity was expressed in the language of national will, to be imposed on "the other" abroad, rather than of national consciousness, to be experienced by "the self" at home. Cultural diplomacy offered an avenue to project inherently superior Japanese values. In the early twentieth century, Japanese liberals were inspired by a vision of Japan as the one modern nation-state that could integrate Occident and Orient. In this view, Japan was a unique intermediary, equal in its relation with Western states and superior to other Asian states.

Japanese nationalists subscribed to a similar though more extreme view: Japan was inherently superior to *all* other states. It was Japan's task to change from a society importing culture from the West to one exporting culture to Asia. What united both conceptions was the idea of Japan's uniqueness, and during the interwar period Japan's foreign cultural relations were informed by this set of liberal and nationalist ideas.[106] Liberals promoted Japan's special cultural mission through small intellectual exchange programs championed by the Ministry of Education; the Ministry of Foreign Affairs focused instead on cultural projects in China, based on the view that Japan was to lead, China to follow.

Japanese liberals were drawn to culture as an alternative to the violence of World War I and the materialism associated with the idea of civilization. Japan's colonial state in Korea expanded Japanese influence in education, religion, historical consciousness, the mass media, and the arts, and enhanced the role of the regular police at the expense of the military police. Cultural policy became an instrument of an intrusive and active form of state power designed to prevent nationalist resistance to Japan's colonial rule. In its secular work Japan's colonial state competed with Christian missionaries, sent mostly from the United States, in intervening in the spiritual life of Koreans.[107]

Liberalism set the course, Japanese fascism followed. In the 1930s Japan

106. Shibasaki 1999, 32–62, 212–30; 1997, 39–40. Takahashi 1998.
107. Shin 2004, 8.

adopted a "cultural mission" to secure the nation's rightful position in an international order dominated by the West. The annexation of Manchuria was justified as an Asian alternative to Western practices, a demonstration that the East's harmonious Asianism was superior to the West's fractious liberalism. As a laboratory for a wider Asian empire, Manchuria was to consolidate Japan's leading position in East Asia.[108] The Society for International Cultural Relations (Kokusai Bunka Shinkokai, or KBS) expressed this dual impulse in Japanese policy. Created in 1934 to help improve fraying foreign relations, especially with the United States, and deal with other sovereign states, the KBS also became an important vehicle of cultural diplomacy in China.

Before 1937, the KBS expressed the view, shared by both liberals and nationalists, that Japan's culture was superior to that of its Asian neighbors. By 1940, it had shifted to an insistence on Japan's uniqueness as an instrument of propaganda to glorify Japan's war of aggression.[109] Japan's "new internationalism" differed from the one espoused by the Western status quo countries: it sought to unite several countries within a new Asian culture. Between the late 1930s and 1945, the Japanese media characterized the war in terms of cultural survival.[110] It was waged on behalf not only of Japan but of a billion Asians. In the language of one 1943 radio broadcast, "Our culture is that which teaches our way of happiness to every member of the Greater East Asia Sphere. . . . Our mission in this war is to teach the Imperial way. This war will expel the occidental concept of culture."[111]

Abroad, Japan's task was greatest in the Philippines, which had been influenced by American movies and music for so many years that it was not easy to return the Philippine people to their "original oriental ways."[112] In domestic politics, the Japanese government actively discouraged attention to Western culture and art and, to strengthen the authentic essence of Japan's unique culture, blocked Westernized art forms such as opera, classical music, and dance. After the Pacific War began, the Japanese government banned American and British movies, jazz, and baseball.[113]

Until the early 1970s, the Japanese government relied on the KBS, the Japan Foundation's predecessor, to deal with many aspects of its cultural diplomacy. Thoroughly complicit in Japan's militarist expansion, the KBS apologized after 1945 for the excesses of the late 1930s and 1940s.[114] However, it stood firmly by the principles of cultural nationalism that it had pursued. After Japan's disastrous defeat in the Pacific War, the KBS sought to ensure Japan's cultural survival. For the KBS, cultural diplomacy was an international means deployed in the pursuit of a national objective. Specifically, the KBS re-

108. Iriye 1997, 119–25.
109. Hirano 1988, 147–48. Interview 01–01, Tokyo, March 13, 2001.
110. Iriye 1997, 132–34.
111. McMurry and Lee 1947, 90.
112. McMurry and Lee 1947, 107–8.
113. Shillony 1981, 144–45.
114. Shibasaki 1999, 189–211.

mained committed to the export of Japanese culture and to international cultural exchanges that would spread Japanese and East Asian culture. The nationalist objective of cultural policy and diplomacy was adapted, not replaced. Continuity in policy from the 1930s to the 1970s is more striking than discontinuity.

Since the early 1980s, however, Japan's contemporary cultural diplomacy has changed greatly. Japanese nationalist sentiment remains strong and is clearly recognizable, but neither national closure to foreign cultural influences nor national propaganda is public policy any longer. For Japan, as for most other industrial states, the export and import of culture occurs in a world in which national cultures are integral parts of international, global, and transnational networks. Japan's contemporary cultural relations with other states differ greatly from those in the past. The dynamic spread of Japan's mass culture industries reinforces this important shift. Despite an internationally inaccessible language, a combination of exceptional artistic creativity and corporate savvy have made, in the words of Anne Allison, the "cuteness of capital and the commodification of intimacy" the hallmarks of Japan's cool cultural power.[115]

In Germany, the break of 1945 has been much sharper than in Japan. The history of Germany's cultural diplomacy dates back to the late nineteenth century and is grounded in a political tradition that prized culture as a constitutive aspect of German identity. Initially, Germany's cultural diplomacy focused on supporting German schools abroad.[116] In the late years of the rule of the kaisers, in a memorandum drafted for use inside the government bureaucracy, Chancellor Theobald von Bethmann-Hollweg embraced the potential political usefulness of an active cultural diplomacy. At the same time, he spoke in public against the advisability of the government expanding its reach into this policy arena.[117] This ambivalence was characteristic of the German empire's general political strategy, which vacillated between military and commercial expansion. After diplomatic fiascoes in 1905–6 and 1911, a liberal imperialist group pushed to strengthen Germany's international position through an energetic cultural offensive, rather than a risky military grasp for world power. To this end, about fifty "foreign associations" were founded between 1912 and 1914. A central task of these associations was to collect funds from private sponsors in order to strengthen Germany's cultural expansion abroad.[118] Imperialism and cultural diplomacy thus entered a symbiotic relationship.

After World War I, the German government made foreign cultural diplomacy an institutionalized part of the foreign office and an integral part of the foreign policy of the Weimar Republic. Left without traditional military instruments of statecraft, German political elites favored the development of new, cultural tools. Building on the institutional innovations of the Weimar Re-

115. Allison 2002, 4.
116. McMurry and Lee 1947, 39–47. Düwell 1981, 1976.
117. Kloosterhuis 1981, 10–13.
118. Kloosterhuis 1981, 16.

public, after 1933 Nazi Germany dramatically changed the instruments of cultural diplomacy for the purpose of political propaganda, in particular by intensifying contacts with ethnic Germans living abroad.[119] German associations and cultural clubs often became strong supporters of Germany's expansionist goals. For Josef Goebbels, a great admirer of Hollywood, the war against the United States was also a cultural war; Britain and France, by contrast, according to Goebbels, were able as European powers to generate authentic, if flawed, cultural products. The aesthetic appeal of fascism, most famously in the Nuremberg rallies of the Nazi Party and the films of Leni Riefenstahl, extended well beyond the borders of Nazi Germany. Staffed by French and francophone volunteers, the SS division "Charlemagne" was among the last troops defending Hitler's chancellery in the final days of the war, fired by anti-Communist feelings against Asiatic bolshevism, for sure, but also by the deeply engrained anti-Americanism of the French Right.[120]

In the 1930s and 1940s, Japan's and Germany's cultural politics were symptomatic of Asia's and Europe's more general closed regionalism.[121] The political economy and ideology of the Co-Prosperity Sphere were the culmination of Japan's historical experiences with a regional empire. The occupation and annexation of Taiwan, Korea, and Manchuria encouraged the Japanese government to create new combinations of industry, labor, and raw materials, and to invest in infrastructure, communications, transportation, and hydroelectric power. This geographically contiguous empire laid the foundation for a wave of industrialization in the 1930s. Addition of a Southeast Asian periphery to Taiwan, Korea, and Manchuria would have generated badly needed raw materials such as oil, rubber, and rice, to support an autarkic regional empire that could wage total war.

Yet Japan's attempt to make this imperial vision a reality was ill-fated. When militarists seized power in the 1930s, General Hideki Tojo relied on improvisation. Japan's annexation of Manchuria was defeated by China's strong nationalist opposition. The Co-Prosperity Sphere and the ideology of "Asia for Asians" were constructs created to address the mess Japan confronted in China and in Southeast Asia. Although Japan pacified Manchuria, its puppet regime in Nanking never enjoyed any legitimacy. Nor did Japanese terror succeed in breaking Chinese resistance. In Southeast Asia, Japanese rule was less brutal than in China. It granted nominal independence to Burma and the Philippines, and the promise of full independence for Indonesia was cut short only by Japanese surrender in 1945. Yet whatever legitimacy Japan may have enjoyed initially was lost through rampant corruption, coerced conscription of labor into the war effort and of women into sexual slavery, and the forced delivery of rice and raw materials. Japan's unsuccessful implementation of a bloc re-

119. McMurry and Lee 1947, 63–77.
120. Lepenies 1999a, 8.
121. Adapted from Katzenstein and Shiraishi 1997b, 373–78.

gionalism in the 1930s has nothing in common with the porous regionalism that characterizes contemporary Asia.

The same conclusion holds even more strongly for Germany's search for "living space" in the 1930s, reinforced by a Nazi doctrine of racial purity that was to create a New Order in Europe. Hitler's megalomaniac vision sought to transform political boundaries across Europe. Nazi Germany aimed to accomplish radical aims and so to supplant a liberal imperialism deemed both inferior and inauthentic. Germany's racial purification was to serve the purpose of dominating Europe, even if that entailed the incarceration, enslavement, and eventual mass murder of all political opponents, "social deviants," and Jews. This revolutionary objective was matched by a strategy of unlimited aggression. Hitler hoped for British and American acquiescence as he waged war on France and the Soviet Union over primacy on the European continent. That hope was based on a fundamental misunderstanding of the purpose and the power of the still-embryonic American imperium.

The coherence of Hitler's ideological vision required adjustment to geographical context. In eastern Europe the New Order was to be destructive colonization: ethnic cleansing; vast population resettlements; outright annexation; the creation of apartheid regimes; a rule of terror through the close cooperation of police forces, the Nazi Party, and the courts; and finally the Holocaust. In western Europe, the New Order rested on a less murderous rule. The Nazis embraced the notion of Germany at the center of an autarkic Europe, protectionist in its external orientation and strictly hierarchical in its internal organization. The importance of Germany's cartelized industries, its uncompetitive agricultural sector, and its exclusionary cultural practices all worked in the 1930s toward creating a region closed to external trade and currency transactions. In the 1940s the Nazis adjusted this closed region, under wartime conditions, to a credit and balance of payments arrangement that linked Germany to northern and western Europe.

Beyond the specific interests and ideologies motivating German and Japanese policies, Europe and Asia were ripe for protectionism during the interwar period. Technological change created mass production industries whose economies of scale were highly profitable for European and Asian corporations. The protectionism of the 1930s was a reaction to America's industrial supremacy in developing and exploiting new techniques of mass production. Only protection promised European and Asian producers a chance to compete with American producers in world markets.

This brief snapshot of the 1930s underlines the distance between now and then. Now, talk of bloc regionalism is totally misplaced. Porous regionalism characterizes current world politics. Then, Japan and Germany were captivated by the allure of regional empires that they would rule directly. Authoritarianism, militarism, and racism foreclosed in the 1930s the option that Allied victory reopened after 1945—that of informal rule by trading states linked to the American imperium and the serving of liberal ends in a world of porous regions.

CHAPTER SIX

Linking Regions and Imperium

Comparison between Europe and Asia highlights the differences in their institutional orders. Analysis of the relations among Europe, Asia, and the American imperium focuses on the vertical links that connect regions to the American imperium.[1] These two regions experience external influences differently, and they exercise different kinds of influence inside the American imperium. Subregionalism in Europe and Asia operates on a smaller geographic scale, both within and across state borders, while faithfully reflecting regional differences in institutional order. Just as core regional states shape and are shaped by their regional contexts, so the American imperium shapes and is shaped by porous regions. The United States is undeniably affecting regions, as chapter 2 illustrated with specific reference to the late 1940s, but equally significant is the fact that regions are affecting America. In this two-way Americanization, adaptation is mutual and interactive.

Connecting to the Center—Germany and Japan in the American Imperium

A vitally important link between regions and the American imperium is established through regional core states. In Europe and Asia, the conditions for those links were created by American policies that forced Germany and Japan to be free.[2] Despite this and other important similarities, Germany has evolved along more international, Japan along more national, lines. External influences make themselves felt in Germany in the form of Europeanization, in Ja-

1. For a discussion of the method of incorporated comparison see McMichael 1990, 1992, 2000a.
2. Montgomery 1957.

pan in terms of bilateral pressure. Moreover, the countries differ in the way they seek to influence the United States, Germany through its "societal foreign policy," Japan through markets, money, and middlemen.

Unconditional surrender in 1945 moved both countries into the emerging American imperium. Japanese and German national security depended largely on the protective umbrella that the United States extended for a half century over parts of East Asia and Western Europe. Neither country could or wanted to provide fully for its own national security. Both depended on the U.S. nuclear umbrella and its conventional military forces. And both benefited enormously from the liberal world economy that U.S. policies helped set up and maintain. The principle of liberal commercial exchange, rather than national autarky, was accepted gradually as the most appropriate way of organizing the international economy. Both countries became supporters of the United States and developed strong interests in maintaining an open international economy. During the cold war, in brief, Germany and Japan acted like peaceful civilian powers and prosperous trading states, responding similarly to a bipolar system of states and a liberal international economy.

The similarities in how these client states adapted to U.S. power offers a plausible explanation for the initial postwar years. Lacking a national nuclear deterrent, Germany and Japan looked, from the perspective of traditional realpolitik, woefully "incomplete." Furthermore, Germany's formidable army remains, even after unification, fully integrated into NATO, a security arrangement that leaves the German government without national control over its armed forces. Japan's pacifist stance and its longstanding commitment to limit defense spending to less than 1 percent of GNP, broken only on rare occasions, has left it with military forces that cannot fully guarantee its security.

After the failures of the command economies of the 1930s and 1940s, and following wartime destruction and defeat, the installation of market-based economies in Germany and Japan became an overriding objective of the U.S. government. Both countries maintained, however, some protective buffers against excessive market competition. Germany has consistently adhered to a liberal approach in product markets while developing the institutions of its vaunted "social market economy" in labor markets. Competition in Japanese product markets is tougher than in most other industrial states; and in the 1960s and 1970s enterprise unionism furthered what T. J. Pempel and Keiichi Tsunekawa have called "corporatism without labor."[3] Japan and Germany thus differ in important ways from the liberalism of Anglo-American polities.[4] In various sectors of the economy both countries typically rely on some institutions of coordination that are not market based.

These patterns have helped shape Japan's and Germany's distinctive politics, and Asia's and Europe's characteristic institutional structures. Historical

3. Pempel and Tsuenkawa 1979.
4. Hall and Soskice 2001. Albert 1993. Katzenstein 1978.

comparisons between 2005 and 1945 mislead us, for they ignore the effects of social and political interactions in the intervening decades. At the end of the cold war, for example, some authors wrote about Germany and Japan as emerging superpowers, evoking the United States and the Soviet Union in the 1950s and intimating a return to the international politics of the 1930s.[5] Neglecting the effects of the American imperium and the evolution of regional and national politics led to flawed analysis. Even historians are not immune to adopting such ahistorical perspectives. At the end of the cold war, for example, Arthur Schlesinger argued that Japan was well on its way to building the Greater East Asia Co-Prosperity Sphere, and Germany to achieving hegemony over the European continent, for which both had fought half a century earlier.[6] Newtonian metaphors, in which actors strain toward recurrent equilibria unaffected by domestic change and interactions within their respective regions and within the American imperium, are unhelpful for understanding Germany and Japan as regional states. In their regional aspirations Germany and Japan experienced different opportunities and constraints. European multilateralism afforded Germany some political slack in the American imperium—offset by the country's location on the main fault line of the cold war. Strong bilateral security arrangements with the United States provided little breathing room for Japan, but the situation was ameliorated by the lack of a direct geostrategic threat to Japan's territorial integrity and national security.

Pressuring Japan Bilaterally, Europeanizing Germany Multilaterally

When the outside world impinges on Japan, politicians and bureaucrats experience this as external pressure (*gaiatsu*) at the hands of the United States. In contrast, the supranational influences affecting modern Germany emanate not so much from Washington, D.C., as from Brussels.

In the case of Japan, external pressure comes largely from Washington. To gain better access to Japanese markets, American actors tend to pressure the Japanese bureaucracy and its ancillary political and social interests directly.[7] Foreign actors are included in domestic policy coalitions in which "nationalists" and "internationalists" seek to find compromises acceptable to both, as well as to impatient Americans who insist on changing traditional ways of doing business. The negotiation of voluntary export restraint agreements since 1955, and the Structural Impediment Initiatives (SII) talks designed in the late 1980s to open the Japanese economy to foreign producers, both illustrate a repetitive political process with predictable dynamics. Japan's persistent export surplus and cautious defense policy have continuously fueled external pressure.

5. Bergner 1991. Garten 1992.
6. Schlesinger 1989.
7. The discussion of Japan in the following pages draws on Katzenstein and Tsujinaka 1995. See also Schoppa 1997, 1999.

This pressure has become institutionalized in Japanese decision making. The American lobby in Japan has a predominantly public character, with the embassy, the representatives of twenty-seven U.S. states, and the American military supporting the activities of individual American corporations. Although a substantial amount of lobbying takes place indirectly, through an "old-boy network" and influential middlemen, the system is fundamentally driven by political pressure exerted by the U.S. government on the policy networks that link the Japanese government, the state bureaucracy, and the business community. American corporations seek to play the political game in Tokyo by Japanese rules, but they rely also on pressure tactics. For it is heavy pressure, especially heavy political pressure exerted by the U.S. government, that makes the gaiatsu system function.

Gaiatsu overcomes the immobilism that inheres in a Japanese policy system characterized by a decision-making style based on a bottom-up consensus. Because self-persuasion is so difficult, *naiatsu,* or internal pressure, is a rare commodity in Japan's political system. In the words of John Dower, *gaiatsu,* or "small violence," is often invited by government or business "to put pressure on the bureaucracy. Or, in certain circumstances, the bureaucracy itself may desire *gaiatsu* to strengthen its case against recalcitrant politicians or rival ministries. Whatever the case, it is apparent that a complex political dance is taking place."[8] External pressure has become an integral part of the shifting coalition of political forces that has led to the opening of Japanese markets during the last four decades, particularly when it has supported the domestic coalition favoring change. The end of the cold war and the decline in Japan's economic fortunes have changed the nature of this Japanese dance in two distinct ways. First, Japan has become less deferential to U.S. trade demands, just as, with the economic rise of China, both the need and the success rate for U.S. pressure politics has declined. Second, under the impact of internationalization and globalization, Japan has developed a system of "permeable insulation" as a way to manage the speed and the effect of growing openness on a case-by-case basis.[9]

In contrast, Germany experiences a less intrusive and more pervasive form of transnational, specifically European and North Atlantic, influence. In the late 1960s a German political scientist, shaped by the experience and sensibilities of postwar Germany, coined the term "transnational relations."[10] The political experience of the Federal Republic made this a "natural" category of analysis. With unconditional surrender in May 1945, the German state ceased to exist. The country was partitioned and occupied. And it participated in a variety of innovative institutions designed primarily to constrain a possible resurgence of German power.

In the late 1940s and early 1950s, for example, European states put their, and Germany's, coal and steel industries under the supervision of the Euro-

8. Dower 1988, 26.
9. Schaede and Grimes 2003, 4.
10. Kaiser 1971.

pean Coal and Steel Community. This amounted to an internationalization of a possible military-industrial complex in the Federal Republic. A few years later, the European Atomic Energy Community, or Euratom, sought the same outcome for the nuclear industry. These institutions gave expression to an innovative European answer to the continent's traditional German question. Hindsight tells us that the direct effects of these institutions on Germany's economic potential were limited; much more consequential was the unforeseen influence of a customs union, the European Economic Community, which eventually evolved into today's European Union. The gradual growth of a multitiered European polity has profoundly shaped German politics.

A growing number of policy issues, and many features of German politics, are increasingly affected by Europeanization. At times that process is public and creates political debates. German subsidies to ailing firms in the former GDR, and the size of Germany's financial contribution to the EU budget, were examples in the 1990s. But this is not the core of Europeanization. The European Council, Commission, and Parliament together affect thousands of issues, most of them minute, touching on all aspects of German economic and social life. *External* pressure does not capture the dynamics of this process, for Germany is, generally speaking, an active proponent of Europeanization. And when it lags on particular issues in implementing European directives, regulations, and decisions, the self-understanding of Germany as a European state is an important barrier to the notion, harbored in some political quarters and by groups disadvantaged by specific decisions, that Germany is caving in to external pressure.

The importance of Europeanization was clearest in the politically delicate relations between two core institutions, justice and banking. Since the 1960s, the European Court of Justice has argued successfully that European law supersedes national law. Innovative legal procedures have guaranteed individuals access to the court on specific issues. And they have ensured that national and European courts do not work at cross-purposes. With some reluctance, Germany's powerful Constitutional Court has generally acknowledged the primacy of the European Court of Justice and European law over the Constitutional Court and German law.

A related example is the Europeanization of the German Bundesbank. Since 1979, Germany's powerful Bundesbank had run Europe's monetary policy, de facto. With the possible exception of the Constitutional Court, the Bundesbank's prestige overshadowed all other German institutions. Yet the German government accepted, indeed embraced, European monetary integration. Europeanization reduced the Bundesbank to the status of a regional branch of the European Central Bank. In its policies, the ECB is designed to imitate the Bundesbank, yet the ECB represents as much a French as a German political victory. Since the 1960s, successive German governments have supported monetary integration as the culmination of a gradual political unification that would guarantee the coordination of national economic policies. French governments pushed for monetary integration without political unification. German unification and the "stability pact" that was part of the European Monetary Union provided the political issues that finally made a compromise between Germany and France possible. German public opinion was deeply concerned about relinquishing the deutschmark, perhaps the country's strongest source of economic pride, but in the broad center of German politics the surrender of monetary sovereignty received strong electoral support. During the 1990s, running for office on a cautiously anti-European platform proved to be a recipe for failure outside of Bavaria.

Throughout the cold war, Germany's participation in NATO was also a conduit of transgovernmental influence. In the 1950s, Germany's controversial rearmament was made palatable to a hostile public and suspicious European neighbors only through NATO command of West Germany's armed forces. Keeping the Americans "in," the Russians "out," and the Germans "down" were in the words of NATO's first secretary general, Lord Ismay, the three main purposes of the organization. Things turned out differently. As the first alliance in history with a peacetime standing defense force, NATO kept Germany "in," not "down." In all of the practical aspects of military policy, including nuclear targeting, German defense officials became partners and eventually were asked to assume leading positions in the Western alliance. Professional contacts between Germany's military and those of its European and American partners created links that, over time, have transformed Europe and the North Atlantic region into a security community. Many Germans regarded NATO as a nuisance and its operations and bases as an environmental hazard in the 1970s and 1980s. A significant minority of Germans, especially in the early 1980s, objected to NATO as dangerous and destabilizing. But because Germany was an integral part of NATO, the public did not perceive NATO influence as external pressure. In the 1990s, Germany actively supported NATO's enlargement, the bombing campaign in Serbia, and peacekeeping operations in Bosnia, Kosovo, and Afghanistan.

Japan's and Germany's Access to America

Japan and Germany are not only targets for external pressure, they also seek to exercise international influence beyond their national borders. Japan typically works through markets, money, and middlemen. In the American imperium, Japan seeks influence through low-key lobbying and a strategy of cultivating favorable public opinion. Germany relies instead on its societal foreign policy (*gesellschaftliche Aussenpolitik*). The most important institutions in Germany typically engage partner organizations in other countries, conducting their own foreign relations. German politics thus accords important roles in foreign affairs to many of Germany's major private and parapublic institutions. These differing ways to exercise influence abroad intersect in different ways with how America accommodates outside influence.

Since the arrival of the first settlers, the United States has been shaped by geopolitical and economic rivalries among Europe's leading powers. Slavery and continental expansion were profoundly shaped by external influences.[11] Neither the conflict between Mexico and the United States, nor that between Native Americans and white settlers, was a "domestic" matter of building a national state and economy—instead, both involved numerous empires. And the unregulated expansion of white settlers at the frontier occurred in the context of an inflow of European capital and labor that helped create a national market for the continent's rich natural resources.

Recent U.S. history continues to illustrate the close links between the United States and the world. The creation of an enormously powerful national security state in the United States was a direct result of the military threat posed by fascism in World War II and communism during the cold war. A large defense budget and a powerful Department of Defense, for example, have a profound effect on Congress, the character of regional economies in the United States, the structure of higher education, and the subjects treated by Hollywood's movie industry. Foreign trade also connected the United States closely to the world economy, and in the evolution of U.S. politics differences in the economic competitiveness of sectors and regions mattered profoundly. Unlike in the nineteenth century and the late 1920s and early 1930s, since World War II the United States has in general favored free trade, as protectionist forces in Congress have failed to create a viable coalition. Since the 1970s, this free-trade consensus has frayed, and the conflict over trade policy has now moved inside both major parties. The connections between the United States and the world are evident in many other fields, going far beyond security and economic affairs to affect issues such as human rights, women's rights, and the environment.

The openness and decentralization of the U.S. polity help build connections to different parts of the American imperium. Such connections can reassure allies who are nervous about the preponderance of U.S. power. Openness means that information about U.S. policy is easily obtained, and decentralization makes possible participation in the give-and-take of Washington politics. Within the U.S. polity, consultation and conflict resolution exist both during the formulation of policy and during policy implementation. Transgovernmental and transnational politics thus are integral parts of an U.S. imperium that is structurally predisposed to be porous.

Britain has traditionally wielded considerable influence in Washington. During the early postwar years, British access was evident on a broad range of issues affecting Europe, including the occupation of Germany, the crisis in the eastern Mediterranean, and the economic crisis of 1947. More generally, Britain played the game of Washington politics effectively, preserving many Commonwealth connections in an era of decolonization. Insisting on its own

11. Katznelson 2002. Bolton 1933.

"special relationship," Canada, too, was much more effective in the 1950s and 1960s in influencing U.S. policy than its relative power might lead one to expect.[12] As Thomas Risse-Kappen has documented, the NATO allies participated in the Washington policy process to further their interests, at times with considerable success.[13] Participation in U.S. domestic policy has undoubtedly facilitated bargaining and compromise in the American imperium.

Different countries participate in different ways. Unlike Britain's and Canada's direct interventions, Japan's overtures have been coy, as Japanese officials seek indirect access.[14] The Japan lobby in the United States is largely private, with individual corporations, business associations, and the Japan External Trade Organization as central actors. Japan's lobbying received much attention in the early 1990s, and studies stressed its size, breadth, and effectiveness.[15] A knowledgeable and well-known lobbyist himself, Ira Wolf argued then that, with the possible exception of Israel, "there is little doubt that the Japan lobby in the United States is the largest and most effective foreign effort to influence legislation, policy making, and public attitudes in this country."[16]

The Japan lobby has grown steadily. Starting with only one lobbyist in 1951, by 1957 Japan employed as many in Washington as other client states such as West Germany, Taiwan, and Israel. By 1962, it had moved into the number one position in terms of financial outlay, which it has not relinquished since. Japanese lobbying maintained a low profile for many years and recorded very few legislative successes. Japanese lobbyists rarely lobby for private companies or the government. Rather, the Japan lobby gathers information and gives advice both to Americans and Japanese. It has avoided making substantial contributions to political action committees, investing instead in "old boys"—that is, in well-placed officials, many of them former members of the U.S. government, who enjoy excellent access to key decision makers. This lobbying strategy is consistent with the pattern of networking and buying of access that is common in Japanese domestic politics.

By the early 1990s, the Japan lobby was spending a great deal of money on low-profile activities. Japan's fifteen consulates in the United States, for example, regularly hired local public relations firms to advise them on how to create a public climate favorable to Japan's political objectives.[17] Furthermore, *Business Week* estimated that in the late 1980s, Japanese corporations spent $45 million annually in the United States on public relations, $140 million on corporate philanthropy, and $30 million on academic research grants.[18] Suzanne Alexander reports that Japanese philanthropy increased from $30 million in

12. Bow 2003.
13. Risse-Kappen 1995.
14. Katzenstein and Tsujinaka 1995.
15. Choate 1990. Morse 1989.
16. Wolf quoted in Pempel 1991, 43.
17. Lee 1988, 142.
18. Farnsworth 1989, F6. Pat Choate 1990, xviii, gives an estimate that is about 30 percent higher.

1986 to $300 million in 1990 and $500 million in 1991.[19] Academic research proved particularly vulnerable to Japanese funds. In the late 1980s, up to 80 percent of the studies on U.S.-Japan relations conducted at American universities and research institutes were reported to have been financed at least in part by Japanese corporations, foundations, or government agencies.[20]

In a book written before Ross Perot selected him as his running mate in the 1992 U.S. presidential election, Pat Choate argued that the "Japanese penetration of the American political system is now so deep that its integrity is threatened. In their own country the Japanese call this sort of money politics 'structural corruption.' In this case, it means that so many advocates of Japan's position are involved in decision making that the ultimate outcome is structurally biased in Japan's favor."[21] This is overstating the case. But the attention to image building and the creation of a favorable public climate continue to be a distinctive feature of Japan's transnational relations with the United States.

Germany seeks access in an entirely different manner. Postwar Germany did not enjoy hard-core sovereign rights or an unproblematic sovereign status. It was instead what Wolfram Hanrieder called a "penetrated political system."[22] Transnational relations preceded and conditioned diplomatic relations after 1945, and in times of crisis these relations were probably more important than were U.S. security guarantees. Associative transnational links impeded, but did not prevent, dissociative government policies.[23] For example, close German-American business and labor relations placed "narrow" limits on the dissociative policy of French president Charles de Gaulle. Complex transnational connections with the United States and other partners in the American imperium took place at numerous sites, both in Washington and in the institutions governing the imperium.

Germany's characteristic form of engaging the United States and other partners differs greatly from Japan's informal money politics, which is only a short step removed from market considerations. In the societal foreign policy system, all of the major institutions in Germany conduct their own foreign relations, including IG Metall, the largest industrial union in the world; employer and business associations; scientific organizations and cultural foundations; publicly funded research institutes; think tanks of all ideological stripes; and Germany's churches. All of these links created a plethora of formal, institutional connections. Created after 1949 to help democratize Germany and attached to each of the major parties, Germany's party foundations are the political nucleus of this system. With the passing of time, and the growth of funding, these foundations have opened offices all over the world and engaged ideological allies in common projects. Focusing specifically on high culture, one inventory

19. Alexander 1991.
20. Farnsworth 1989, F6.
21. Choate 1990, xx.
22. Hanrieder 1967.
23. Link 1977, 4, 11; 1978, 117–18.

of German institutions operating in the United States runs almost fifty pages.[24] Unlike their Japanese counterparts, these institutions cover a broad spectrum of issues, are highly visible, seek to engage partner organizations in other countries, and prefer to operate multilaterally rather than bilaterally.

This brief discussion illustrates the systematic differences between Germany and Japan. Germany was exposed to a pervasive process of Europeanization, whereas Japan's involvement in Asian organizations has left hardly a trace. While there has been a substantial amount of journalistic and scholarly debate on the external pressure brought to bear on Japan by the United States, a summary book on U.S.-German relations does not contain a single chapter devoted to the subject.[25] With the exception of Marxist writings that interpret the relationship in the language of neoimperialism, the literature focuses on interdependence and transnational relations, not external U.S. pressures on Germany or unobtrusive German influence in the United States. In sum, Germany and Japan are supporter states mediating between Europe, Asia, and the United States. Yet the terms on which they engage the American imperium differ greatly.

Connecting to the Periphery—Subregionalism in Europe and Asia

Porous regions are connected vertically to various smaller geographical areas. Characteristic differences in Asian and European institutions are sufficiently strong that they are also apparent in subregional politics.

Political geographers have pointed to the link between these two kinds of regionalism. For Allen Scott space is acquiring a new significance, as "supra-state" and "infra-state" regionalism interact in novel ways.[26] World regions of continental proportions are linked to a mosaic of smaller subnational regions that are engines of economic growth and social change. Each of these regions is organized around a metropolitan core. Silicon Valley and Route 128 are prime examples in the United States, as are the "new economic zones" in Asia and some Euro-regions. Regions reflect processes operating from "above," "below," and "within."[27] Subnational regions provide a layered arrangement of different scales, creating both constraints and opportunities. The "new" regionalism of the 1990s reflected spontaneous economic and social processes "from below" rather than a planned process "from above" that was characteristic of the old regionalism of the 1950s and 1960s.[28] Institutional differences between Europe and Asia are noteworthy. Europe's microregions combine polit-

24. Weidenfeld 1996.
25. Knapp 1975.
26. Scott 1998, 1–4, 10–11, 68–73, 138–40. Fawcett and Hurrell 1995, 2, make the same argument for the relationship between "micro-regional" schemes for economic integration and "macro-economic" blocs encompassing East Asia, Europe, and the Americas. See also Storper 1997.
27. Hettne 1999a; 1999b 7. Hurrell 1995, 38–39. Grugel and Hout 1999, 9.
28. Hettne 1999b, 7.

ically engineered Euro-regions with high-technology initiatives typically funded by the European Union and some of its member states. In Asia, microregions result from policies, tolerated or orchestrated by central governments, that seek to exploit local initiatives in the creation of special production zones that give maximum play to unfettered market forces.

Asia

Subregionalism in Asia takes two different forms: economic zones and growth triangles. Economic zones provide fiscal incentives and good infrastructure, which simplify business practices and increase profits. Growth triangles are created by the informal or formal agreement of neighboring states to pool complementary comparative advantages, for example in labor and raw materials (Indonesia), manufacturing facilities (Malaysia), and logistical support (Singapore) in the Singapore–Riau Islands–Johore growth triangle. Asian subregionalism has created investment corridors that link high-growth economies up and down the western shores of the Pacific. They account for the bulk of Japanese companies with production facilities in East Asia. Subregionalism offers an instrument for economic development that is not politically and legally constraining. "This subregionalism," writes James Mittelman, "is more spontaneous, springing from within and below."[29] Subregions are essential ingredients for the spread of production chains across Asian borders and are a vital complement to the family and ethnonationalist networks that criss-cross Asia-Pacific.

This subregionalism is linked to the rise of an Asia-wide system of urban capitalism, in which fewer than a dozen centers are the locus for as much as 90 percent of international finance, transportation, tradable manufacturing, and information networks.[30] These urban centers spill into adjacent areas: Hong Kong into the Pearl River delta, Singapore into nearby Indonesian islands, Taiwanese manufacturing across the strait to Fujian, Japanese capital into the areas surrounding Kuala Lumpur and Bangkok. In the interest of economic competitiveness, cross-border economic transactions outweigh national sovereignty. Special development zones become buffers against the sharp conflicts that separate metropole from hinterland.[31] This is not just a matter of recent urbanization. In several instances, these "natural" economic territories have existed for many decades, if not centuries. Whatever their source, the growing importance of "natural economic territories" (NETs) is one of the defining characteristics of Asian regionalism. Driven by private investment, facilitated by common cultural practices, and supported by government policies that remove barriers, NETs are a patchwork of smaller subregional groupings involving the territories of several countries.

29. Mittelman 1998, 29.
30. Shiraishi forthcoming.
31. Rohlen 1995, 2, 13–15.

Asia's subregionalism is more a zone of contact than a pastiche of smaller territories.[32] Governments have tried to enlarge these zones of contact in recent decades, thereby sidestepping the need to reach formal and time-consuming multilateral understandings: "NETs allow states to proceed along their own paths of economic growth and development without the need to agree on overarching regional goals."[33] Subregionalism has evolved through unilateral policies with which governments, sometimes fostering and sometimes responding to grassroots economic pressures, have sought to advance their economic and political interests. In the words of Michael Borrus, we are witnessing in Asia "the apparent emergence of coherent sub-regional trade and investment patterns that lie 'below' the aggregate regional picture but 'above' the interaction between states, a kind of parallel in the productive sphere to the region's noted 'investment corridors.' "[34]

Northeast Asia exhibits the potential for similar subregional developments, for example, along the Yellow Sea rim that connects Kyushu with Korea's west coast and China's northern coastline. In the early 1990s, there existed in northeast Asia an alliance favoring both localism and cosmopolitanism: the combination of Chinese labor and entrepreneurship, Russian raw materials and land, and Japanese capital and technology. At Tumenjiang, the intersection of Russia, North Korea, and China, a new hub was to be created. Facilitated by the end of the cold war, the growing importance of markets in China and Russia, and the increasing ease of international exchange, actors were looking for subregional cooperation while facing poor prospects for increased revenue transfers from central governments. But progress has been hindered by a lack of complementary economic and political interests in various locales. Economic relations remain primarily bilateral in nature, and government cooperation continues to be hindered by unresolved security issues.[35] The ambitious Tumen River project, for example, has been all but abandoned.

At the same time, an unofficial regionalism is flowering. When the Beijing government decided in 1988 to delegate the monitoring of cross-border trade to the provinces, new trade grew suddenly and dramatically between the Chinese northeast and the Russian Far East. The Chinese province of Heilongjiang, with its 3,000-kilometer border, has no problems with the growth of cross-border trade with Russia's three largest East Asian cities: Vladivostok, Khabarovsk, and Blagoveshchensk. Meanwhile, Dalian's development zone opened in 1984. In 1988, the entire Liaodong Peninsula was designated an export-processing zone. Its backers argue that further investment might rectify the serious imbalance between the southern coast and northern China. Jilin Province continues to insist that Tumenjiang be established as China's second growth node, thus helping the province's capital to become the region's rail-

32. Liu 2000, 21.
33. Jordan and Khanna 1995, 435.
34. Borrus 1994, 5.
35. Rozman 2004.

road center. Similarly, Heilongjiang is pushing hard to have its capital, Harbin, become the transportation node with Russia's Far East.[36]

This microregionalism is not linked to Japan, even though Japan has an interest in developing a subnational regionalism surrounding the Sea of Japan. In the 1990s, a coalition of prefectures from "backdoor Japan," including Ishikawa, Niigata, and Hokkaido prefectures, lobbied Tokyo for a greater measure of decentralization. Sister city programs, academic conferences, and local political initiatives lacked the backing to overcome the fallout from Japan's collapsing bubble economy and the 1997 Asian financial crisis. The Sea of Japan never became a new hub of Asian subregionalism.

Southeast Asian subregional cooperation has received much more government assistance. The growth triangle connecting Indonesia, Malaysia, and Singapore, for example, is the region's oldest. It is slightly misleading to call the triangle a market-driven process, since, in the words of Shannon Smith, "governments often intervene to shape comparative, and competitive, advantage and market forces . . . [it] is essentially no more than a pragmatic context for bilateral cooperation."[37] Indonesia and Malaysia also form a growth triangle with Thailand, building on existing trade links that governments wish to strengthen. This is true also of the "Golden Quadrangle" that connects northern Thailand, China's Yunnan Province, northern Burma, and Laos.[38] New market opportunities are especially attractive for illicit trade. The "Golden Triangle" connecting Burma, Thailand, and Laos, for example, is the world's second most important site for opium production. Illicit trade is typically organized by drug lords or run by corrupt government or military officials.[39]

China's economic development zones connect to different subregions: a northern zone adjacent to Japan and Korea; a southern zone close to Indonesia, Malaysia, and Singapore; and, most important, a central zone around Hong Kong, Shanghai, and Taiwan. From this center, Asian regions radiate outward as a set of concentric circles around Hong Kong: Greater Hong Kong (Hong Kong, Macao, and Guangdong); Greater South China (Greater Hong Kong plus Taiwan and the southeastern coast of the PRC up to Shanghai); Greater Nanyang (Greater South China plus Singapore and overseas Chinese in the rest of Southeast Asia); and All China (Greater Nanyang, the PRC, and overseas Chinese worldwide).[40] Whatever its specific form, the importance of China's special economic zones for the dynamic growth of Asia-Pacific's subregions is beyond doubt.

---

36. Russian suspicion of the rise of China runs deep, fed by a fear of the sheer vitality of China's economic resurgence and the demographic imbalance between the two countries' borderlands: one hundred million Chinese and eight million Russians, divided by a border stretching over more than twenty-five hundred miles. And that fear is reinforced by the lack of competitiveness of the main economic actors in the Russian borderlands: inefficient, decrepit, and corrupt state enterprises, often producing for the military, interlaced with petty or organized crime.

37. Smith 1997, 382.

38. Jordan and Khanna 1995, 450–60.

39. Dupont 1999.

40. Harding 1993, 666–67.

The special zones have both political and economic rationales. The government of the PRC created them adjacent to Hong Kong and across the Taiwan Strait not only as engines of economic growth and development but also as instruments to facilitate China's eventual reunification.[41] From those beginnings, the cross-regional Chinese economy has expanded steadily to encompass long stretches of the Chinese coastline. In Shenzen, for example, the central government has relaxed many controls, permitting the emergence of a society that in the 1980s and 1990s was increasingly gravitating to Hong Kong rather than to Beijing.[42] With the Yangtze River basin and Shanghai outstripping growth in southeastern China in the 1990s, in the interest of balance the central government permitted in 2004 the alliance of nine provinces located in the Pearl River delta region radiating northeast from Hong Kong.[43]

Special economic zones are important sites for the development of contacts with overseas Chinese networks. Early on in the development process, Shenzen had a relatively poor physical and legal infrastructure and a heavy political and bureaucratic presence:

> To operate in such a realm requires not only deep cultural and linguistic competence, but a network of relationships that substitute for the guarantees that rule of law, a secure system of property rights, and a neutral administration provide elsewhere but that are lacking here. The success of the Overseas Chinese networks in extending production systems into China derives precisely from their ability to provide alternative forms of social and material capital for building stable relationships in this legal no man's land.[44]

Over the short term, Asian subregionalism has contributed to a remarkable increase in intra-Asian trade and investment that has begun to diminish the heavy reliance of Asian producers on the U.S. market. Over the longer term, the development of China's special economic zones and Asia's regionalism will be affected profoundly by whether government policies continue to favor coastal regions or shift the loci of development inland. This choice is fundamental: between a coastal-Mediterranean and a continental-Sinocentric pattern of economic, cultural, and political life.

Europe

Subregionalism in Europe involves the actions of political units such as Catalonia, Rhône-Alpes, or the various German states that operate directly below the level of central governments. It is a vital political force in many countries, for territorial politics retains great salience in Europe. That salience has been

41. Harding 1993, 666–72. Weidenbaum and Hughes 1996, 85–89.
42. Rohlen 1995, 16.
43. Bradsher 2004.
44. Berger and Lester 1997, 132.

intensified by European integration, and it is not, as in Asia, defined primarily by unofficial, cross-border market transactions. It is instead closely linked to the creation of the European Union's single market. For two reasons, the harmful distributional consequences of market integration have required compensatory political action. First, the European Union operates under an institutional mandate to create convergence, not divergence, in the economic fortunes of its member states. Second, relatively poor states have demanded that market deepening be coupled with the transfer of significant EU resources to Europe's poorer regions.

The origin of the Community's regional policy dates back to the accession of the United Kingdom and Ireland in 1972. In Britain, only England's southeast reached the Community per capita income; all other areas were below the average, in some cases by as much as 20 percent. All of Ireland counted as a development region under the Community's initial plan. A regional development fund was created in 1973, and a Community regional policy gradually began to take shape. Even in rich countries such as Germany, the new regulatory regime for regions has encroached on the political turf of *Länder* (states). Political backlash was strong. During the negotiations for the 1997 Treaty of Amsterdam, the German Länder compelled Chancellor Helmut Kohl to veto greater EU competencies in environmental, social, and cultural affairs, policy fields under their direct jurisdiction. The German Länder also insisted on direct representation in EU decision-making bodies whose actions deal with these policy fields. In contrast to informal market processes in Asia, European regionalism operates through formal political institutions involving tough political bargains at the highest levels.

Quite apart from Brussels politics, however, European regionalism also exists as an economic and political force. Regional autonomy movements in Scotland, the Basque country, Catalonia, Flanders, Brittany, and the Jura, for example, have been attracting attention for decades. These movements are grounded in a revival of local languages and cultures. In France, for example, the languages of Breton, Occitan, Basque, Corsican, and Alsatian have been revived since a socialist government took over in 1997; Gaelic is gaining in Scottish and Welsh schools and Friulian in Northern Italy; Dutch radio stations broadcast in Frisian and Limburgs, Finnish stations in Saami; Basque is making a comeback in Spain's north, and in Catalonia, Catalan prevails over Spanish. About 10 percent of Europeans speak a regional language that differs from their official national language.[45]

Some regional elites and members of the Commission thought in the 1980s, erroneously as it turned out, that a "Europe of the Regions" might grind down the power of national governments by applying pressure from above and from below.[46] A variety of Euro-regions and cross-border regional associations has grown up—some outside of the purview of the Community, such as the region

45. Simons 1999.
46. Newhouse 1997.

between the Jura mountains, the Black Forest, and the Vosges, and some inside, such as the Sar-Lor-Lux region that connects the border regions of France, Luxembourg, and Germany. Others include Alps-Adria, the Lake Geneva Council, Upper Rhine Cooperation, and the Conference of Coastal Regions. As the Community acquires regional functions, territorial politics is adapting with a dense associational network. But this network should not lead us to mistake the conceptual language of Euro-region for a transformed political reality. Instead of a Europe of the regions, what has evolved is a Europe with regions.[47]

Since the early 1990s, the European Union has had its own Committee of Regions.[48] The Council of Ministers and the European Parliament must consult this committee on issues that touch on regional or local affairs. Because it has only advisory powers, however, the influence of the committee has been modest. By 1999 subnational governments had opened over 160 offices in Brussels. German and Spanish regions are particularly well represented. These offices do not play a formal role in European policy, but they are part "of the subterranean political world of multi-level governance" that operates below and beyond EU treaties.[49] Europe's stronger regions failed to get a more important role for regions written into the new EU constitution. Still, some have worked out regular consultative arrangements with the Council of Ministers. Particularly interesting is what is known as the "Four Motors for Europe Group." Four powerful and self-confident regions (Baden-Würtemberg, Lombardia, Catalonia, and Rhône-Alpes), often in active cooperation, are pushing their views of Europe within their national political systems and, on issues that matter, conducting their own European policies. This multiplicity of channels illustrates how the European Union works as a system of multilevel governance that goes well beyond traditional interstate bargains.

European regions also play a central part in the EU budget. The admission of Greece, Portugal, and Spain, and the creation of a single market in the 1980s, prompted the European Union to commit itself to counteract the growth of interregional inequality that market integration would create. At least for the 1970s and 1980s, there is strong evidence of persistent regional differences, even more so when we include the poorer Mediterranean countries in the calculations.[50] Each of the European Union's major institutional innovations has been accompanied by political agreements extending regional development funding, typically secured in tough bargaining among governments that need something to show their domestic constituencies.

The European Union's eastern enlargement brings new claimants. The share of structural funds in the European Union's total budget has increased from less than 5 percent in 1975 to 9 percent in 1987, 30 percent in 2002, and

47. Kohler-Koch 1998, 232. Anderson 1990.
48. Hooghe and Marks 2001, 81–118.
49. Marks, Haesly, and Mbaye 2002, 1, 14–15.
50. Dehesa and Krugman 1992, 11–41.

an estimated 39 percent for an enlarged European Union in the year 2006. In 2002, the European Union allocated thirty-one billion euros to the regions; for the years 2000–2006 it expects to spend, in real terms, about 213 billion euros or 0.2 percent of its GDP.[51] Expenditures for cohesion increased at the expense of the common agricultural policy, which was considered too wasteful and adverse to regional cohesion. In the overall allocation of funds, national governments have been the dominant actors; in the implementation of specific programs, however, the Commission and the regions have played an important role. The allocation of regional funds is increasingly concentrated in poor regions. Seventy percent of the structural funds are spent in regions with a GDP below 75 percent of the EU average. These regions contain 22 percent of the EU population.[52]

We should not overdraw the differences between Asia's and Europe's subregionalism. In Asia subregionalism is primarily market-driven, but it rests, as in Europe, on a political foundation. Subregionalism connects countries with different political systems and trade and investment laws. Income differences between the richest and poorest economies are so large that changes in trade flows can have massive repercussions. Geographical distance and poor infrastructure create high transaction costs for supranational, regionwide integration schemes. And political structures and interests differ widely. Because the negotiation of formal economic integration schemes would be very difficult under such circumstances, subregionalism is an attractive solution to an operational problem in Asia-Pacific.[53] Meanwhile Europe's political approach features its own brand of regional production networks. Producer communities in specific industrial districts are related in dense networks that support flexible quality production.[54] Geographically concentrated, small-scale producers have built institutions that provide for collective learning and the creation of trust. Typically they are active in design and production and, occasionally, in finance and marketing. Compared to Asia-Pacific, these European production networks are egalitarian not hierarchical. They tend to enhance social homogeneity rather than heterogeneity.[55] And European production networks are often spontaneous rather than the result of government policies seeking to create cross-border investment corridors.

Nevertheless, the politics of European subregionalism is generally formal and motivated by political efforts to ameliorate the inequalities brought about by market integration. The market-driven process of Asian subregionalism is informal, adheres to economic incentives aimed at maximizing national growth through participation in the world economy, and has proved to be economically effective and politically attractive.

51. Allen 2000, 244. Hooghe and Marks 2001, 84–85.
52. Hooghe and Marks 2001, 83–85, 93–118.
53. Tang and Thant 1994, 7–8.
54. Piore and Sabel 1984. Locke 1995. Herrigel 1996.
55. Zysman, Doherty, and Schwartz 1996, 29–33.

Agriculture—An Extension of the Argument

This characteristic difference in subregionalisms is mirrored in the economic sector that remains most closely linked to land. The production, distribution, and marketing of agricultural products remains of vital importance in both Europe and Asia. The common agricultural policy (CAP) provided the foundation for the economic bargain between Germany's interest in unrestricted access to the European market for industrial production and France's interest in garnering financial resources to modernize French agriculture. The CAP was a political cornerstone of the EEC from its very beginning. The lack of competitiveness of West German agriculture made it an economic deadweight to Europe. European farming became heavily protectionist, and prices stayed well above those of the world market. Just before the reforms of 1992, agricultural subsidies consumed about 60 percent of the European Union's total budget, twenty-four times more than agriculture's share in the Community's GDP. They inflated food prices by 7 percent and nonagricultural prices by about half as much.[56]

A complex system of shadow prices and large subsidies made the CAP cumbersome. Its objective was to guarantee even small and marginal farmers a standard of living comparable to that in an ever more affluent broader society. By the 1970s, subsidized domestic surpluses encouraged a vast export drive on world markets, in direct competition with U.S. exports. During the 1990s, three developments diminished the importance of the CAP: half-hearted reforms at the Community level; renationalization of agricultural policy; and grudging concessions to the demands of the European Union's main trading partners, primarily the United States. Cumulatively, these developments have stopped European agriculture from spiraling out of budgetary and political control. Still, a rapidly diminishing slice of the electorate was bought at a very high price. That price was not calculated in the marketplace but in politics: at the national level where parties compete for marginal votes, and at the Community level where member states defend national interests. In the political economy of European agriculture, politics looms very large.

Asian agriculture offers an instructive contrast. Like Korea, Japan has a bifurcated food system. The traditional, highly protected, and subsidized rice economy, supported by an electoral system that has been the mainstay of LDP power, is eroding very gradually. It is increasingly complemented by a liberalization first brought about by a global food regime under U.S. leadership and supplemented or supplanted by production complexes organized by transnational corporations. These complexes are spreading throughout Asia-Pacific and have made Japan the most import-dependent food economy in the world. The national rice regime is gradually crumbling under the pressure of demographic and dietary changes, coalitions of consumers and producers that favor

56. Keeler 1996, 127.

cheaper and more profitable food imports, and international negotiations aiming at a further opening of the Japanese economy.[57]

The internationalization of food supplies—for example in feed grain, livestock, and processed flour products—has rested on two pillars. One was the surplus food regime under U.S. leadership. Concessionary and commercial sales of surplus food products, especially of feed grains and wheat, kept food prices low, helped change dietary habits, accelerated the move from countryside to city, and kept industrial wages low, thereby supporting Japan's and South Korea's export-led drive on world markets. Although the heyday of this system has passed, some of its main elements remain in place. As late as 1989, Japan and South Korea were the two top importers of U.S. agricultural products.[58] Yet the political and institutional weight of Japan's rice economy is locked into a slow, irreversible, decline.

The second pillar is a regional system of food supplies centering on Asia-Pacific, organized by the offshore investments of Japanese, Australian, Southeast Asian, Chinese, and U.S. agribusiness.[59] Southeast Asia in particular is beginning to rival the United States in agricultural exports, supplying East Asia's food requirements in a regional division of labor. In the Philippines, for example, 55 percent of farmland is devoted to export crops for the Japanese market. In Thailand between 1961 and 1989, mangrove forests declined by half, in part to fuel an ecologically unsustainable expansion of shrimp farming for the Japanese market. As Derek Hall has shown specifically for shrimp production, the regionalization of some food trade is driven by disastrous environmental degradation affecting production sites, often in a very short time.[60] Enormous ecological pressures have accompanied the conversion of the Australian beef industry from extensive grazing to intensive lot-feeding, while Australia has become Japan's dominant supplier. In the interest of achieving economies of scale, meanwhile, Japan has outsourced the animal protein complex and parts of food-processing to neighboring feed-supply zones.

This regional food regime is increasingly supplemented by Japan's global sourcing of its food imports. Japanese demand is supporting the rise of "new agricultural countries" such as Thailand and Indonesia for corn, Brazil for soybeans, and South Africa, China, Argentina, and Australia for coarse grains. Global and regional sourcing by agribusiness is replacing bilateral deals involving the disposal of surplus foodstuff by governments. Offshore sourcing of food imports is driven by long-term factors, among them the high costs of Japanese agriculture, the appreciation of the yen, Tokyo's tax policy, and the expectation of further liberalization of Japanese food imports.

The politics of European subregionalism seeks to counteract the inequali-

57. Hall forthcoming.
58. McMichael and Kim 1994, 33.
59. McMichael 2000b.
60. Hall 2002.

ties that attend deeper market integration, even at the cost of making Europe less porous. In Asia-Pacific, subregionalism is establishing export platforms that create new links, both within the region and with the world, at the cost of intensifying territorial and social inequalities. In Europe, the annual redistribution of tens of billions of dollars is accomplished through an institutionalized system of power sharing. National governments decide on the overall allocation of funds and pool their sovereign competences with the Commission. Regions, localities, and a host of nonstate actors are involved in the implementation of specific programs. Asia's subregionalism rests, by contrast, on national development strategies that seek to exploit cross-border complementarities without complicated political negotiations. Both Asian and European regionalism give ample economic and political space to the activities of subregions, and in the way they fill that space we recognize characteristic differences between the two regions.

Two-Way Americanization

The vertical links that core regional states establish within their regions, and the connections between regions and their subregions, point to pervasive adaptation and interaction. This is true also for the vertical links that link porous regions to the American imperium.

Webster's International Dictionary tracks the evolution in the meaning of the term *Americanization* over time. In its fifth edition (1936) the terms means "to assimilate to the Americans in customs, speech etc; to bring in conformity with, or to develop, American methods or characteristics." The eighth edition (1973) defines the term as "instruction of foreigners (as immigrants) in English and in U.S. history, government, and culture." These are one-way versions of Americanization: America changes others, abroad or at home. But this is a restricted view of the world, and it describes only half of an interactive process. We must recognize also the reverse process: others change America, at home and abroad.

Two-way Americanization involves a broad range of social and political practices that cover both the spontaneous spread of American products, values, and practices, through markets and informal social networks, and the explicit economic and political strategies of corporations, other formal organizations, and the U.S. government. It also offers an idiom in which to debate American and non-American concerns. Jonathan Zeitlin distinguishes among different types of interaction: at one extreme, the simple diffusion of best practice from America; at the other, locally effective ensembles of interdependent elements that absorb American influences and recombine at the behest of self-reflective actors.[61] Two-way Americanization is profoundly interactive.[62] This book has

---

61. Zeitlin 2000, 16–17.
62. Nolan 1994, 5, 12. Gemünden 1998, 17.

tracked interactive regional processes in the case of Germany in Europe and Japan and Asia, and in different institutional contexts we find an unending process of interaction between regional power and regional context. The same holds for the American imperium. America shapes a world of regions, which in turn remakes America.

Americanization is a two-way street on questions of popular culture, technology, and national security, the three empirical domains covered in chapters 4 and 5. In popular culture, it resembles a cross-fertilization that is remote from conventional politics. Particular styles and fashions, fads, and novel forms of artistic expression diffuse by being appropriated, adapted, and transformed, and then they are exchanged or sold once again. This process typically bypasses governments and occasionally even formal markets. Technology, broadly understood, is also a part of national culture, though it can become a deeply politicized issue when it touches issues governments consider to be national security interests. Typically, though, technology is harnessed by corporations, often large and powerful ones, operating in world markets. The flow of technology mixes diffusion and appropriation, yielding coevolution. Finally, on questions of internal and external security, Americanization is regulated by states and tends to promote both imitation and blowback.

Popular Culture—Cross-Fertilization

From shopping malls[63] to intellectual and artistic currents,[64] Americanization is prominent in the realm of culture. Which American cultural exports succeed and which fail, what are the terms of success and failure, how individuals and groups abroad interpret new modes of expression in their own cultural milieu—answers to these questions reflect a complex mixture of the hierarchical and egalitarian elements that characterize Americanization. European avant-garde and contemporary American popular culture have been deeply intermingled, both in mutual admiration and in criticism. The United States rather than France, Italy, or Germany, acquired a taste for french fries, pizza, frankfurters, and hamburgers, and succeeded in marketing these products all over the world.

Americanization is sometimes viewed as undermining indigenous culture.[65] This is a curiously imbalanced view. To the extent that Europe has a common culture, it is either American[66] or anti-American.[67] In the field of popular culture, Americanization often enriches and invigorates local cultures rather than undermining them. Musical imports from the Caribbean, for example, help create in the United States a new art form, rap, that finds its way to France

63. Kroes 1996.
64. Pells 1997.
65. Ermarth 1997, 318.
66. Riding 2004.
67. Markovits 2004.

and offers African immigrants there a new medium, previously unavailable, to write and sing in French—and thus they become part of and enrich French culture.

The movie industry is an important center of cultural Americanization. The profit motive has provoked Hollywood to produce nationally what can be sold globally. International marketing success and ethnic diversity and multiculturalism are important parts of America's self-image.[68] Although it is undeniably American, Hollywood is substantially owned by foreigners. In the early 1990s, only three of the seven major Hollywood studios—Disney, Paramount, and Warner Brothers—were controlled by U.S. corporations. Rupert Murdoch's News Corporation owned Twentieth Century Fox; Sony was in charge of Columbia Pictures; Matsushita Electric Industrial Company took over Universal Pictures; and Italian financier Giancarlo Parretti bought MGM/UA. The American recording industry is also largely foreign owned. Most U.S. recording companies have been taken over by foreign corporations: Sony (Columbia and Epic), Matsushita (MCA and Geffen), Thorn EMI (Capitol), Bertelsmann (Arista and RCA), and Polygram (Mercury, PLG, and A&M).

In the American center of the global entertainment industries, ownership does not equal control, as Sony and Matsushita learned the hard way. Having conquered the consumer goods industry in the 1980s, these firms aimed at vertical integration, from hardware to software, to lock in their competitive advantage on a global scale. The difficulties they experienced in adjusting to Hollywood were enormous. National ownership has had little impact on the way films are conceived and made in Hollywood. Many of Hollywood's most famous directors and actors are non-American, and many Hollywood films are made about America by non-Americans.[69] "Odds are good," writes James Verniere, "that your favorite American movie classic was directed by someone from somewhere else."[70] In terms of ownership and artistic talent, Hollywood is both in America and of the world.

In this open system, cultural imports—for example, from Japan and Asia—matter. For Kazuo Ogura, an "Asian restoration" is a conscious political project based on the resurrection of imagined Asian values.[71] Although politically significant, the cultural impact of this restoration is probably less important than the spontaneous manner through which, for example, Chinese transnational cultural flows create new forms of modernity. Asia is a source of vigorous cultural production. The influence of Japanese manga, for example, is showing

68. Cowen 2002, 95.

69. Poland's Roman Polanksi (*Chinatown*), Czechoslavakia's Milos Forman (*One Flew over the Cuckoo's Nest, The People vs. Larry Flynt*), Taiwan's Ang Lee (*Crouching Tiger, Hidden Dragon, Ride with the Devil*), England's Sam Mendes (*American Beauty*), and Germany's Roland Emmerich (*Independence Day*) and Wolfgang Petersen (*Airforce One*) illustrate the importance of the influx of distinguished foreign moviemakers for Hollywood's success.

70. Verniere 1999.

71. Ogura 1993, 40.

up in various aspects of U.S. pop culture: Hollywood movies, MTV videos, and especially children's television cartoons, which are typically repackaged Japanese anime with manga roots. By 2001, anime-style programming occupied the majority of cartoon time slots in the afternoon and Saturday morning schedules of the WB, Fox, and the Cartoon Network.[72] The growing appeal of Japanese anime for U.S. audiences is enhanced by what Kenji Sato has called Japan's "ethnic bleaching," a visual self-denial that has suffused Japanese society, especially since 1945.[73] The Westernized appearance of its characters has increased manga's competitiveness in Western markets.[74]

Hollywood is beginning to turn to Japanese manga for characters and plot lines that it can no longer get from U.S. comics. In the case of Disney's highly successful *Lion King*, the similarities with Osamu Tezuka's renowned 1966 TV series *Jungle Emperor*, shown in the United States under the title of *Kimba the White Lion*, were so strong as to give some credence to the suggestion of artistic theft.[75] To high acclaim, Disney's art-film unit, Miramax, has dubbed Hayao Miyazaki's *Princess Mononoke*, until recently the largest box-office success of all time in Japan. With the production costs of movies growing, it appears likely that, leaving aside the artistic ingenuity of the Japanese industry, anime will cut into the revenues and profits of live-action movies while establishing itself in a secure market niche.[76]

Japan is a formidable presence in global culture markets—but this is not to argue that American popular culture will become Japanized. Sony and Matsushita, after all, failed to create strong links between the consumer electronics industry, which they had come to dominate, and Hollywood as a source for content. Now, American ignorance of geography is legendary, and less than half of the American population can find the United Kingdom, France, South Africa, and Japan on a map. Americans' foreign language competence declined dramatically during the twentieth century.[77] Still, it remains true that, thousands of miles from the United States's more cosmopolitan coasts, youngsters in the American heartland watching children's television on Saturday morning are unwittingly exposed hour after hour to the commercial savvy and artistic ingenuity of a Japanese industry. What is now apparent for children's TV may well become a broader trend. The completion of the shift from analog to digital technology will render moviemaking less costly, and Hollywood's special effects monopoly will decline. New national and regional nodes of production are likely to appear, from Japan to India and, eventually, perhaps Europe.

72. Burress 1997. Rutenberg 2001.
73. Sato 1997.
74. Schodt 1996, 62.
75. Kuwahara 1997. Hughes and Clements 1997.
76. Lyman 2000.
77. Paarlberg 1995, 48–49.

Technology—Coevolution

Technology is an aspect of culture closely linked to science and the economy. The United States emerged from World War II with undisputed global technological leadership. In the 1970s and 1980s, one study reports, about two-thirds of the international supply of disembodied proprietary technology was of U.S. origin, with Great Britain running a distant second.[78] The top-ranked American research universities attract foreign students and young scholars early in their careers, and many of them choose to stay. American corporations are adept at translating scientific discoveries into technological know-how that can be converted relatively quickly into marketable products. Other societies may be better at one stage or another of this three-stage process; only the United States has a strong position in all three. On questions of technology, Americanization expands through markets, and does so with a high degree of elasticity. Insinuating itself into different markets all over the world, American technology is absorbed, even by those who oppose it. It thus alters societies, both undermining and reconstituting them.[79]

This widely held view is little more than a first approximation of a more complex and interesting reality. Summarizing various studies dealing with the Americanization of technology after 1945, Jonathan Zeitlin insists that wholesale imitation of American technology and practices is the exception, with innovative hybrids through piecemeal borrowing and selective adaptation being the norm.[80] Americanization is more about the learning capacity of local actors than about the diffusion of standardized American technologies. Indeed, Zeitlin replaces the concept of Americanization with American engagements, with its multiple and actively charged connotations.[81] Other scholars of technology have come to similar conclusions.[82] In this view, it is not so surprising that at the beginning of the twenty-first century, the tide is beginning to turn in physics and some other fields long dominated by American scientists: foreign advances in basic science now often rival or surpass those made in the United States. "Europe and Asia are ascendant, analysts say, even if their achievements go unnoticed in the United States."[83]

Since technological Americanization is a two-way street, concepts like "made in the U.S.A." and "American know-how" are rapidly becoming obsolete.[84] Foreign producers have transformed some of America's leading industries. By

---

78. Ernst and O'Connor 1989, 29. This estimate is based on an imperfect statistical indicator, the national technological balance of payments, which covers only a part of international technology flows, including the sale of patents, licensing agreements, provision of know-how, and technical assistance.

79. On the role of American manufacturing and financial corporations, see, respectively, Servan-Schreiber 1968 and Dore 2000.

80. Zeitlin 2000.

81. Zeitlin 2000, 5.

82. Bjarnar and Kipping 1998, 6, 12. Djelic 1998, 2–3, 274–75.

83. Broad 2004, A19.

84. Pollak 1992, 48.

the early 1990s Japan had become a world leader in scores of important technologies, making deep inroads in areas in which U.S. firms had held unassailable positions only a few decades earlier. Indeed, the concept of "Japanization" is theoretically as open as the concept of "Americanization." It originally referred to the particular talent of Japanese firms to create large productivity gains, first in the export of manufactured goods, including cars, car parts, and electrical products. In the automobile industry, specifically, it referred to "lean production" and the combination of productivity with flexibility and quality. Adoption of the "Japanese model" was spurred by direct foreign investment, especially after the mid-1980s. But like the American model, the Japanese one is not uniform, and it means different things to different local actors. Motives for embracing the Japanese model differ. The British government sought to encourage the introduction of new industrial relations practices. In the United States, Japanese firms scrambled to open production facilities in a market that threatened to disappear behind protectionist walls. The Japanese government favored direct foreign investment as an attractive way of recycling a large trade surplus.

Japanization is now taking on a different appearance even in automobiles.[85] During the 1980s, Japanization became the term to characterize the shift from an old to a new production paradigm, yet the scope of this process could not be demarcated with any precision. "The notion of Japanization," Tony Elger and Chris Smith conclude, "has become a label for a fairly open-ended agenda of investigation rather than a set of strong claims about the scope and character of the spread of Japanese production techniques."[86] Japanization became an open-ended process of diffusion, emulation, and the adoption of a distinctive pattern of production. It does not yield either a copy of the original or a replica of existing local patterns. The combining of original and replica can be the consequence of deliberate organizational design, of an ongoing process of gradual change in shared cognitive schemas and normative orders, and of political conflict that is driven by competing interests. Japanization creates something new in the intensively studied American automobile industry.[87]

Americanization and Japanization illustrate powerful processes that accelerate the spread of civilian technological innovation. Similarly, in defense-related production, leading-edge military technologies can no longer be developed solely at home. Since the 1970s, the growing complexity and sophistication of modern weapons has required sourcing with foreign suppliers, breaking the preference for autarky that had marked the American military-industrial complex. In the years 1986–90, the total number of licensed production and coproduction or codevelopment programs was 50 percent greater than in 1971–75 and 200 percent greater than in 1961–65.[88]

85. Elger and Smith 1994b, 37–38.
86. Elger and Smith 1994a, 7.
87. Boyer et al. 1998. Freyssenet et al. 1998. Westney 1999, 385, 402–3.
88. Brooks 2005, 82

But for the United States since the mid-1970s, these measures of the two-way flow of technologies were less important than production at the sub-component level, among lower-tier producers, in dual-use industries.[89] In information technology, for example, the core of the so-called revolution in military affairs, 39 percent of interfirm alliances connected U.S. producers with European and Japanese firms. International subcontracting of production and production by foreign affiliates of U.S.-based multinational companies also increased sharply—a source of considerable worry for the Defense Department throughout the 1980s. One empirical study established that 13 percent of all procurement at the subcontractor level involved foreign firms in 1988; for the most electronics-intensive weapon system, the Verdin communication system, 40 percent of second-tier procurement was allocated to 163 foreign subcontractors located in twenty-six countries.[90] The efficiency gains of these international corporate alliances were considerable, and they were not lost on U.S. policymakers. Polities that are bypassed by such technological processes, such as the Soviet Union in the field of national defense in the 1980s, pay a high price for technological insularity.

Security—Imitation and Blowback

It is on questions of security that Americanization is politically most visible. Because the U.S. "war on terror" is in its early stages, I focus here instead on the "war on drugs." The illegal shipment of drugs to an American market with an insatiable appetite has had devastating effects by spreading addiction, undermining public health, and creating an incarceration crisis of tragic proportions. For decades the United States has waged a war on drugs largely unsuccessfully. European initiatives such as the formation of the Pompidou Group of 1971 were a direct response to the persuasive arguments and implicit threats of the United States. Later, in the 1980s, pressure from the Reagan administration was also important in redirecting the attention and resources of European police forces to international drug trafficking.[91] In the case of Japan, Americanization took the form of bilateral pressure. U.S. concern about drugs rose at a time of intense trade friction between the two countries, and so the Japanese government was in no position to oppose U.S. initiatives after 1985, even though Japan was relatively free of heroin and cocaine.

The Americanization of the war on drugs has been both direct and indirect. The United States has taken the lead in defining international legal norms, concluding international agreements, and placing its agents abroad, thereby shaping methods of law enforcement worldwide. The Drug Enforcement Agency has a large overseas presence. In the late 1980s, it operated sixty permanent offices in forty-three countries and had a less permanent presence in

89. Brooks 2005, 83, 85–87.
90. Brooks 2005, 90–91.
91. Friman 1997, 2.

an additional twenty-seven.[92] An international war on drugs—whether fought with the active cooperation of police officials in the host country, with their tacit approval, or without their knowledge—has created a U.S. presence in frequently fragile political regimes, especially in Latin America; and it has a pervasive influence on regional efforts at crime control.[93] Americanization also has taken indirect forms. In drug enforcement policy, the DEA's approach has been popularized, especially by American television shows broadcast in many countries. By the end of the 1980s, most European police forces had followed the U.S. example by adopting special antidrug police units, imitating American-style procedures, and sanctioning these new police operations through the courts and legislatures.[94]

Two-way Americanization allows for substantial differences in response. For example, the United States views drugs as a risk to its national security, interprets the supply of drugs as a criminal problem, relies on the military to address the problem, adopts a repressive policy against producers and sellers, and prefers a unilateral approach. In contrast, Germany views drugs as a risk to its internal security, interprets the supply of drugs as a problem of economic development, bypasses its military in addressing the issue, focuses on alternative economic development strategies for producer states, and prefers a multilateral approach.[95] Analogously, American immigration policy frames the issue in terms of security and focuses almost exclusively on border controls. German policy takes a less targeted approach, incorporating issues of economic aid and labor markets.[96] Similar differences are observable in American and German antiterrorism policies.[97] In a new era in which states often confront unspecific risks rather than specific threats, the war on drugs points to a persistent divergence in policy approaches. The United States has strong effects on others, and others are having strong effects on the United States both in their production and export strategies and in their various policy approaches.

On questions of military security, Americanization refers to the standard that the U.S. military sets worldwide. In 2002, the United States was offering military training and education to about one hundred thousand foreign soldiers, mostly officers, serving in the armies of 133 countries.[98] By conventional financial measures, the U.S. military is larger and better equipped than the next dozen or so militaries combined. The United States is the armory of the world and leads in military research and development; during the last half century, it has been by far the largest weapons exporter in world markets. U.S. military bases cover the globe. The financial support, technical proficiency, training, and professionalization of the American military are unsurpassed.

92. Nadelmann 1993. Anderson 1989, 160–65.
93. Anderson et al. 1995, 119, 130.
94. Nadelmann 1995, 272.
95. Friesendorf 2002, 167–68, 185.
96. Scheller 2002, 65–66.
97. Katzenstein 2003c.
98. Johnson 2004, 132.

And its organization is widely emulated—when national militaries in central-eastern Europe had to be rebuilt after the cold war, the American pattern was the norm, and the American military helped the reform process. Most important, its war-fighting capability is very impressive, as a series of successful military campaigns in the Gulf War, Bosnia, Kosovo, Afghanistan, and Iraq have demonstrated in recent years.

Yet as is true of culture and technology, Americanization in national security is also a two-way street. U.S. military supremacy creates its own opposition. Chalmers Johnson refers to "blowback" to capture the unintended consequences of U.S. policies.[99] The attacks of 9/11 illustrate how the world can remake America. For Americans, September 11 was a second "day of infamy." Out of a clear blue sky, enemies staged a surprise attack on the United States more devastating than the one on Pearl Harbor, whose image it evoked. For more than half a century, with a broad arsenal of sophisticated weapons systems, U.S. security policy had aimed to prevent another surprise attack. The mountain of rubble in lower Manhattan and the charred Pentagon symbolize the power of blowback and the shattering of the American yearning for invulnerability. Yet publicly reported Saudi intelligence sources state that since 1979, as many as twenty-five thousand young Saudis have received military training or experience abroad, most with the intent of waging an Islamic holy war.[100] The government let these young radicals leave unhindered, and from them fighters were recruited for wars in Afghanistan, Chechnya, Kosovo, and Bosnia. From among these fighters terrorists were recruited and trained who bombed U.S. targets in Saudi Arabia, Kenya, Tanzania, and Yemen, killing hundreds of Americans and non-Americans. September 11 made Americans more security-conscious and conservative. Many now see the waging of preemptive war as a legitimate form of self-defense. The unilateralism and assertiveness of current American foreign policy thus finds broad public support. National security and the reaction to 9/11 thus offer a dramatic illustration of something also true of popular culture and technology: the American imperium has the capacity to shape a world of regions. But that world has the capacity to react, often with a complex mixture of admiration and resentment and occasionally with violent fury—thus remaking America.

In 1941, in the darkest hours of Germany's and Japan's conquests, Henry Luce acknowledged the internationalism of the "American Century." His celebration of the power of American ideas, ideals, and products was prescient. For Luce, an authentic vision required a projection of American power free of geographic boundaries. Neither the "absurd sound of distant cities" like "dear old Danzig" nor "the brassy trumpeting of majestic words" like "democracy and freedom" were for Luce compelling reasons to go to war. An internationalism that would make American interests synonymous with the "world environment

---

99. Johnson 2000, 8.
100. Jehl 2001.

in which she lives" was the force propelling America to fight.[101] In his movie *Citizen Kane,* released in the same year, Orson Welles offered an enactment and critique of Luce's vision. Because the American imperium acts not only through the military and coercive power of the state but also through commerce and culture, Welles later wrote that "if Luce's prediction of the American Century will come true . . . it will make Germany's bid for world supremacy look like amateur night."[102]

101. Luce 1941, 20–24.
102. Quoted in Kaplan 2002, 168.

CHAPTER SEVEN

The American Imperium in a World of Regions

Our contemporary world of regions does not float freely. It is embedded in the American imperium. When U.S. governments see vital security and economic interests at stake, the United States supports the creation of regional powers, as it did in Germany and Japan—but not in any other world region. Regions can be peaceful and rich, or war-prone and poor. They can grow, as Europe did with the enlargement of the European Union after the cold war. Or they can shrink, as APEC did in Asia-Pacific in the wake of Asia's 1997 financial crisis. Regions can be relatively closed to international and global processes, as in the 1930s, or relatively open, as in the 1990s. And different regions vary in their importance for American power and purpose.

The American imperium, I argue, is defined by the intersection of territorial and nonterritorial dimensions of power, which parallel aspects of reality highlighted by theories of internationalization and globalization. Globalization and internationalization intermingle in creating conditions favorable to porousness; and characteristic differences distinguish Asian from European regionalism. And what of the rest of the world? The Americas are open to the dual imprint of the U.S. imperium, yet there is no regional supporter state. The United States has been involved only sporadically in the affairs of South Asia and Africa. And these regions lack core states that strongly support the United States. Meanwhile the U.S. strategic interest in the Middle East, where Israel and Saudi Arabia are close allies, has not replicated Europe's or Asia's porous regionalism. In the Middle East, territorial conflicts have overwhelmed all other issues. Neither Israel's position at the center of U.S. domestic politics, nor the cultural and institutional distance that separates Saudi Arabia from the values and institutions of the United States, has helped to resolve the intractable conflicts in that region.

American Imperium

In the making since the American Revolution, the American imperium has matured fully only since the middle of the twentieth century. In 1945, U.S. military expenditures were three times as large as those of the next five powers combined, and the U.S. GDP was about 50 percent larger. Fifty years later, after the collapse of the Soviet Union, the U.S. defense budget was larger than those of the next nine states combined, and its GDP amounted to 70 percent of the total GDP of the next five powers.[1]

Statistics can be misleading. They suggest, for example, that Soviet economic production was about a quarter of U.S. production at the end of World War II.[2] After the loss of twenty million of its citizens in World War II, compared to "only" four hundred thousand U.S. casualties, the Soviet Union may well have been much weaker than production statistics indicate. Half a century later, Japan's GDP stood at about 60 percent of American GDP; yet the financial crisis building in Japan throughout the 1990s made that country much weaker than the statistics suggested. Furthermore, statistics tell us little about a state's inclinations in foreign policy. In the first half of the nineteenth century, for example, the United States "overexpanded" from a position of relative economic backwardness; in the second half it "underexpanded" while attaining economic primacy over Britain and Germany.[3] The economic lead that the United States enjoyed over Europe and Asia declined between 1950 and 1970 as Western European and East Asian states rebuilt their war-torn economies. Since then, changes in the relative economic power of the United States, measured in material terms, have been small. Huge, in contrast, have been shifts in the beliefs about the decline (in the 1970s and 1980s) and rise (since the early 1990s) of America's power.

Most Americans believe that the United States, by its history and very nature, cannot be imperial, let alone imperialist. Ruling an empire is not part of America's business, all but a small group of tough-minded realists hold. Business is, and so is the defense of freedom.[4] The concept of empire belongs to the Old World not the New. Before 1914, there existed two kinds of empire: old land empires and new maritime ones.[5] The expansion of Russia, Austria-Hungary, the Ottomans, and China over a contiguous land mass differed from the colonial acquisitions of the British, French, Dutch, Spanish, Portuguese, and later the Germans, Japanese, and Americans. In the first case, states were empires; in the second, states had empires. The internal crises of the first group and conflicts among the second led to the "Thirty Years War" of 1914–45, to

1. Ikenberry 2001, 279–80.
2. Lundestad 1990, 40.
3. Zakaria 1998.
4. Ferguson 2004.
5. Maier 2002, 28–29.

the bipolar system in which the United States and the Soviet Union vied for global preeminence between 1947 and 1989, and, after the collapse of the Soviet Union in 1991, to a world defined by an American imperium. Yet most Americans remain deeply uncomfortable with the term.

Statistics and the commonsensical understandings of Americans are of little help in shedding light on the nature of American power in a world of regions.[6] American power has both territorial and nonterritorial dimensions. Direct control over territory, for example in the form of military bases, is an important feature of America's imperium. The cold war and the war on terror provided the need and the opportunity to operate military bases in scores of countries. At the same time, the United States has pushed hard to lower barriers impeding the flows of goods, capital, and services across state borders. Throughout the second half of the twentieth century, free access to society and economy was a programmatic interest of the United States, and a source of nonterritorial power. The American imperium involves the convergence of territorial and nonterritorial power.

The territorial base of the U.S. imperium is unmistakable. The first American empire was "the long and contested incorporation of continental territory based on settlement colonialism."[7] The United States expanded for more than a century, waging a relentless war on the indigenous population. The 1803 Louisiana Purchase doubled the size of the United States, and annexations of small territories in 1810 and 1813 and the Florida Cession followed soon after. A generation later, President James Polk completed the manifest destiny of continental expansion. On the heels of the 1845 annexation of Texas, Polk arranged for the Oregon purchase in 1846. Under a flimsy pretense, he then turned on Mexico, which had rejected previous U.S. offers to buy California. At the conclusion of the Mexican-American War in 1848, the victorious United States annexed California and the entire Southwest, doubling in size once more. A one-term president, and a realist who used military force to achieve his political objectives, Polk was the Bismarck of the United States. Yet there is no monument on the Washington Mall commemorating his achievements. Banished from U.S. collective consciousness, Polk's presidency points to the deep ambivalence with which Americans view territorial conquest.

The slowing of territorial expansion after the Civil War, Fareed Zakaria argues, was due to the weakness of the central institutions of the U.S. state, which could not provide muscle adequate to America's expansive nationalism.[8] Between 1898 and 1917, finally, the United States succumbed to the temptation of empire, European-style. In those two decades the United States joined the worldwide scramble for colonies, starting with the Spanish-American War and the acquisition of the Philippines in 1898, and ending with a string of occupa-

6. For two reviews of a torrent of recent books on the subject see Ikenberry 2004 and Dueck 2004.
7. Kramer 2002, 1316.
8. Zakaria 1998.

tions and acquisitions in Central America and the Caribbean. By European standards, the American empire was puny. But it was large enough to roil the likes of Mark Twain and the Anti-Imperialist League, who saw America's exceptional role in world politics sullied by colonial acquisitions.

America's universal nationalism is a powerful force; it gave Mark Twain the strength of his moral outrage, and it denied Polk the fame he surely would have garnered as head of any European state. It is a mistake, and a big one, to see the American imperium as being constituted only by its territorial dimensions. American values and institutions are reflected in a unique American self-image, a specific way of life, and a creed of exceptionalism—all central to the ascendance and perpetuation of the American imperium. The open, egalitarian democracy of the New World offers a sharp contrast to the closed, class-ridden authoritarianism of the Old World. To become American is a matter of individual choice not of state doctrine or communal experience. What links America and the world is a superior idea. Yet the gap between lofty ideals and mundane reality is large and persistent, especially where issues of race and class intersect. Although the idea of an open society unites America, racial hierarchies and class inequalities divide it. American foreign policy cycles between these two poles.

For George Washington, as he said in his Farewell Address, America's mission is "to give to mankind the magnanimous and too novel example of a people always guided by an exalted justice and benevolence."[9] Thomas Jefferson invoked an "Empire of Liberty" and argued as he retired from public office in March 1809 that America was the "solitary republic of the world, the only monument to human rights, . . . the sole depository of the sacred fire of freedom and self-government, from hence it is to be lighted up in other regions of the earth, if other regions of the earth shall ever become susceptible to its benign influence."[10]

In speeches delivered at the beginning of the Gulf War and in response to the September 11 attacks, respectively, George Bush the elder and George Bush the younger responded in similar terms. America was fighting because it was part of something larger, because the threat to decency and humanity had to be stared down, here and now, by Americans and for the world. In his State of the Union address delivered to Congress a few days after the bombing of Iraq began, George Bush the elder insisted that

> we are engaged in a great struggle. . . . We are Americans: part of something larger than ourselves. For two centuries we've done the hard work of freedom. . . . What is at stake . . . is a big idea: a new world order where diverse nations are drawn together in common cause to achieve the universal aspirations of mankind—peace and security, freedom and the rule

9. Washington 1896, 23.
10. Tucker and Hendrickson 1990, 7.

of law. . . . For two centuries America has served the world as an inspiring example of freedom and democracy.[11]

A decade later, in his 2002 State of the Union address, his son sounded a similar theme:

> America will lead by defending liberty and justice because they are right and true and unchanging for all people everywhere. No nation owns these aspirations, and no nation is exempt from them. We have no intention of imposing our culture. But America will always stand firm for the non-negotiable demands of human dignity: the rule of law; limits on the power of the state; respect for women; private property; free speech; equal justice; and religious tolerance. . . . Steadfast in our purpose, we now press on. We have known freedom's price. We have shown freedom's power. And in this great conflict, my fellow Americans, we will see freedom's victory.[12]

From the first to the forty-third president, then, America has always been a new Jerusalem, "a city upon a hill."

This sense of America's exceptional mission in the world was part of the U.S. Constitution and the creation of popular sovereignty, through a democratic politics that is simultaneously united in the notion of a democratic public and divided through the separation of powers. In this constitutional design, the Declaration of Independence and the Federalist Papers articulate the two core principles: power rests in "the people" as an ultimate source of authority, and it moves incessantly in competition among the different branches of government and segments of civil society. Popular sovereignty can tend toward various outcomes, two in particular: democratic self-control that looks inward, and an expansiveness that looks outward. The idea of a universal republic is at the core of this tendency toward limitless expansion, designed to usher in an era of peace and prosperity among democracies.[13] In the first half of the nineteenth century, America's open frontier provided the outlet for such expansive tendencies. Jefferson expressed this notion best when he insisted that expansion was "the indispensable concomitant of a stable, secure, and prosperous Empire of Liberty."[14] In a letter addressed to his successor and neighbor, James Madison, Jefferson favored extreme measures, the acquisition or conquest of Cuba and Canada. An enlarged United States would have "such an Empire of Liberty . . . no constitution was ever before so well calculated as ours for extensive empire and self-government."[15]

11. Quoted in Schweigler 1991, 6–7.
12. http://www.gpo.gov/congress/sou/sou02.html.
13. Hardt and Negri 2000, 166–67.
14. Tucker and Hendrickson 1990, 162.
15. Brodie 1975, 563.

In the competing visions of the Progressive movement at the outset of the twentieth century, the tension between the territorial and nonterritorial dimensions of the American imperium was especially stark.[16] Both visions agreed about curbing the immense power of U.S. trusts through antitrust legislation and creating a broad political regulation of the capitalist economy. But there was a sharp clash over the kind of world the United States could and should inhabit. Teddy Roosevelt spoke for imperialism as a solution to the closing of America's frontier. Woodrow Wilson stood for an internationalist ideology of peace that would banish European state practices from world politics once and for all. Wilson's legal utopianism was an extension of U.S. constitutional principles and a direct affront to established European state practice. Roosevelt's populist imperialism, steeped in civilizational and racial imagery, was close cousin to that of the European powers.

The tension between the territorial and nonterritorial imperatives of American foreign policy was also of central importance after 1945. The Atlantic Charter of 1941 gave ringing endorsement to an anticolonial political program that the United States sought to carry out by granting the Philippines independence in 1946. In the following years, America's strong anticommunism often made the U.S. government falter in its commitment to the anticolonial cause, at times with disastrous consequences, as in Indochina. After 1945, moreover, the American imperium required territorial bases. The Soviet Union and the People's Republic of China were surrounded by U.S. military installations. Throughout the cold war, the U.S. military deployed hundreds of thousands of troops in Europe and Asia. In September 2001, 280,000 military and civilian personnel and their dependents were stationed in Europe, 150,000 in East Asia and the Pacific, and another 45,000 worldwide.[17] The redeployment that President Bush announced on August 16, 2004, will over the coming decade return sixty to seventy thousand troops and another one hundred thousand civilian employees and family members, mostly from Europe, to the United States.

Throughout the cold war, the tension between the territorial and nonterritorial imperatives of U.S. foreign policy never disappeared. The nuclear revolution at the outset of the cold war, and the threat of terrorist attacks after its end, diminished the immunity that the United States had enjoyed by virtue of geographical location. The reduction in military forces stationed abroad after the end of the cold war, particularly in Europe, has been reversed by the war on terrorism commenced after the attacks of September 11, 2001. New bases proliferate in the Middle East and Central Asia, likely staging areas for the U.S. Air Force and special ground forces.

The continued relevance of territory, however, should not blind us to the centrality of the nonterritorial basis of the American imperium. With the

16. Hunt 1987, 126–35. Trubowitz 1998, 31–95.
17. Johnson 2004, 156–60.

spread of democracy, Henry Nau argues the exceptionalism of American democracy has been diminishing.[18] Just as the old aristocracies of Russia, Prussia, and Austria were bound together in a relatively peaceful Concert of Europe after 1815, so the democracies of North America, Western Europe, and East Asia now share so many basic values that, for now, war between them has become unthinkable. Significant political differences exist between different forms of democracy and different types of capitalism, but the divisiveness of these differences is less important than the lived reality that drives democratic politics. A "banana war" between the United States and the European Union may provoke diplomatic tension, even commercial conflict. But few of the pundits who use war metaphors to spice up their TV talk shows and newspaper columns believe that they are capturing reality. War is no longer an instrument of foreign policy in relations among the major industrial democracies. The deep divisions between the United States and many European states over the 2003 Iraq war illustrate the point. The United States may be from Mars and Europe from Venus,[19] but it is now inconceivable that either side would prepare for a possible war against the other.

Nonterritorial rule rooted in similar values and institutions is even more central for the American imperium than it was for the British Empire.[20] To be sure, after their unconditional surrender, Japan and Germany were briefly occupied and ruled directly by U.S. and Allied troops. Compared to Britain's well-developed institutions of formal empire, however, the American imperium is marked by the absence of formal control over foreign territories. And compared to the paucity of Britain's investment in imperial institutions, the United States has developed a plethora of such institutions, including the WTO, the IMF, and the World Bank.[21] John Ikenberry goes so far as to call such institutions the infrastructure of a "constitutional order" at the international level.[22] Through these institutions, the most important democratic, capitalist states in world politics have joined the American imperium "by invitation."[23] Liberal values and imperial rule merge in what Raymond Aron aptly called "the imperial republic."[24]

The dynamic and distinctive trait of the U.S. imperium is its nonterritorial power. As Samuel Huntington argued long ago, the American imperium is organized around economic and social functions rather than the acquisition of territory.[25] It is powered by the spread of transnational organizations that have evolved out of American groups, both governmental and nongovernmental. Access to foreign societies is as important as accords with foreign governments.

18. Nau 2002.
19. Kagan 2003.
20. Ferguson 2002.
21. Lundestad 1990, 38.
22. Ikenberry 2001.
23. Lundestad 1986, 1999.
24. Aron 1974.
25. Huntington 1973, 342–43.

American expansion is based less on the control of foreign people and resources than on the deployment of American people and resources. Typical of American expansion is not the acquisition of foreign territory and the power to control but the penetration of foreign society and the ability to operate there freely (as neo-Marxist theories of neocolonialism have rightly emphasized). This form of expansion is quintessentially American: segmented and pluralist. The mechanisms of U.S. expansion are a mixture of coercion, competition, and emulation. "The United States," Huntington concludes, "could, with hearty enthusiasm, become expansionist, but it could not, in good conscience, become colonialist."[26]

The balance between territorial and nonterritorial power is shaped by the domestic interplay of political coalitions and institutions. The open frontier and sectional conflict, for example, were for Frederick Jackson Turner the two pivots of U.S. politics. The former is central for the nonterritorial, the latter for the territorial power of the American imperium. In Turner's words, America's sections are a "shadowy image" of the European nation-state "denatured of its toxic qualities."[27] In continental America, the world economy accentuates uneven growth and development among different sections. Distinctive of the United States is the primacy of economic interests at the "macroregional" level. Since the Civil War, racial, ethnic, religious, and cultural divisions have tended to occur instead at the "microregional" level of neighborhood and city.[28]

Economic interests are obvious at crucial junctures in American history. With imperialists and anti-imperialists debating the issue of overseas expansion in the 1890s, the industrial Northeast defeated the agrarian South, with the West playing a swing role. U.S. policy changed sharply from inward- to outward-looking, as it became committed to opening new markets in Latin America and Asia and spreading its liberal ideology. Colonial acquisitions, the construction of a modern navy, and the use of the tariff as a bargaining tool followed. In the 1930s, a coalition that united the urban Northeast with the South excluded the nationalists from the rural West. Breaking sharply with past policies, the New Deal enhanced the government's role, both in economic and in international affairs. In the 1980s, the rustbelt Northeast lost out to a newly forged coalition of the growing Sun Belt regions in the South and West. The Reagan administration initiated a more assertive foreign policy that modernized the armed forces and established a more visible American presence overseas, while also fostering investment in new technology sectors of a less regulated economy at home. Each of these three sectional realignments represented the victories of new political coalitions uniting two of America's three great regions at the expense of the third: Northeast and West in the 1890s, Northeast and South in the 1930s, and South and West in the 1980s.[29]

26. Huntington 1973, 345.
27. Cited in Trubowitz 1998, 13.
28. Trubowitz 1998, 13.
29. Trubowitz 1998, xiv.

Sectional politics, although important, is not the only process that shapes the expansionist tendencies of the American imperium. Changing coalitions among different economic,[30] financial,[31] or industrial[32] sectors follow a similar political logic. Economic interests shape coalitional responses to the impact of international and domestic developments that impinge differently on different segments of business, banking, and industry. A different perspective focuses on the political process of coalition formation as the main determinant, overriding economic interests.[33] In this formulation, coalitions form around other issues and drag economically antithetical forces into political alliance, as did Bismarck's marriage of Iron and Rye in 1879. There is, in brief, nothing unique about the domestic political struggles that motivate the expansiveness of America's imperium.

Coalitional politics interacts with the institutions of American democracy—most directly with federalism and party politics, less directly with the separation of powers among the three branches of government. Critics of democracy have argued that democratic institutions are not well suited to the requirements of a world power that needs to set strategic priorities and think in ways that transcend the insights of an electorate typically ill-informed about the politics of distant lands and ill-advised about the long term. Driven by populist passion or political indifference, according to this view, democratic institutions overreact to or underplay the foreign challenges that the American imperium faces.

Defenders of a democratic foreign policy disagree. For them, the executive's position and the conduct of foreign policy are strengthened by legislative oversight, bureaucratic subordination, and electoral pressures. Consent for the mobilization of resources to achieve foreign policy goals strengthens the position of America's democratic government. The transparency of democratic politics at home assures that government commitments are credible. Gaining public support for foreign policy is a complicated and costly process, particularly in a democracy with many veto points and gatekeepers. Foreign governments learn quickly that foreign policies stick once arrived at through democratic means. Furthermore, in contrast to Britain, for example, U.S. democracy is uniquely advantaged by its capacity to concentrate power in the hands of the president—assuring that the implementation of foreign policy is somewhat insulated from the short-term pressures and passions of democratic politics.[34]

Finally, the balance between territorial and nonterritorial power is also shaped by the purposes of policy and the political coalitions and identities they reflect. Policy purposes come in multiple stripes: realism versus idealism, power versus liberty, pragmatism versus principle. So do coalitions and identities: the commercial realism of Hamiltonians, the moralist internationalism of Wilso-

30. Frieden 1988. Shafer 1994.
31. Ferguson 1984.
32. Kurth 1979.
33. Gourevitch 1977, 1986.
34. Waltz 1967.

nians, the opportunistic pacifism of Jeffersonians, and the muscular parochialism of Jacksonians.[35] And so do the strategies these coalitions and identities favor: unilateralism vs. multilateralism, isolationism vs. internationalism.[36]

Typically, these tendencies divide political parties, but not always. After the cold war, for example, important foreign policy divisions existed within both parties as well as between them, creating, in the words of Norman Podhoretz, "strange bedfellows" among Republicans and Democrats.[37] Neoconservatives, who urged intervention in other countries when core American values were at risk, found themselves aligned with interventionist human rights liberals. Traditional conservatives championing the norms of nonintervention found support among a Left still heeding the lessons of Vietnam. In contrast to the political alignments formed between the early 1930s and the mid-1950s, floating fragments were available for recombination into a more enduring constellation in the 1990s. It remains to be seen whether the war on terrorism, the doctrine of preventive war, and tax cuts despite rapidly increasing budget deficits—the policy mix with which the Bush administration reacted to the attacks of 9/11—have shifted the center of American politics and recombined America's political fragments into a durable but polarized pattern.

Porous Regions in Europe and Asia

Besides the territorial and nonterritorial influence of the American imperium, regions are also shaped by distinctive political practices emanating from distinctive regional settings. Technology and production illustrate particularly well processes of globalization, while internal and external security illuminate processes of internationalization. Yet it is quite clear that elements of both globalization and internationalization are deeply intermingled in both cases. Rather than demonstrate the primacy of one over the other, the interaction of both processes makes this a world of porous regions.

Technology does not typify globalization only. Throughout history states have rarely left new communication and transportation technologies unregulated for long. Once technologies become commercially viable, the largest and most successful companies typically enlist the help of states. Enforceable property rights, not unregulated markets, become the rule. Similarly, big and small states alike have sought to keep within their borders those technological innovations that they judge to be of vital interest. China guarded jealously the secrets of silk production, Switzerland those of watchmaking. Even when such policies proved futile, after centuries in the case of China and after a couple of decades in the case of Switzerland, they were considered legitimate.[38]

35. Mead 2001. Nau 2002, 43–85.
36. Lake 1999, 293–98.
37. Podhoretz 1999.
38. Nelson 1990, 15.

Since the beginning of the nineteenth century, first Britain and then the United States have parlayed their technological prowess into international primacy. Through imitation and innovation, Japan and Germany have also attempted, unsuccessfully, to exercise domination over Asia and Europe. Directly relevant to both military strength and economic competitiveness, technology matters. It cannot be left to unregulated global markets.

Very few multinational corporations are globally footloose and truly transnational. In today's supposedly global economy, between two-thirds and three-quarters of corporate assets are owned, jobs are held, and sales continue to be made, in home markets.[39] It is thus no accident that research and development remains concentrated in the home markets of the world's largest corporations.[40] U.S. corporations, for example, increased their overseas R & D expenditures from a mere 7 percent in 1977 to slightly above 10 percent by the mid-1990s; figures for German and Japanese multinationals were considerably smaller.[41] Furthermore, technology reflects specific institutional relations within and between state and society, and its transfer is unavoidably slowed by the institutional barriers of national experience and expertise. Technology is a *specific* knowledge, skill, or method that improves the production and distribution of goods and services. It is embodied in different forms: in machinery, individual cognition, organizational and institutional structures, and behavioral patterns.

Issues of state security do not reflect only international processes. Increasingly, governmental and nongovernmental actors alike must address global issues that defy the logic of the traditional arrangements that link states. Globalization connects individuals, groups, and states through multiple channels that bypass traditional government diplomacy and transcend traditional military affairs. Global processes deeply affect human and societal insecurity broadly understood, both at the individual and at the global levels. The new security agenda includes terrorism, illegal migration, international refugees, drug trafficking, nuclear smuggling, organized crime operating at a global level, the spread of infectious disease, and environmental degradation. These issues are creating new security threats and a new kind of global politics that transcends and subverts state sovereignty. The September 11 attacks on the World Trade Center and the Pentagon, planned and executed by a global network of terrorists, illustrates the centrality of globalization for security.

The security that is at stake, moreover, is no longer restricted to the state. Globalization creates new insecurities. New forms of cyber-warfare could attack the high-tech strategies of defense ministries in the most powerful states. The equivalent of the Cuban missile crisis is the global computer virus that might destroy, in a matter of hours, programs and data on millions of computers

39. Borrus 1997, 143. Dörrenbächer 1999, 32–34. Hirst and Thompson 1996, 18–98.
40. Doremus et al. 1998, 89, 107, 109, 114.
41. By contrast, foreign firms expanded their R & D activities in the United States at a much faster rate, from 4.8 percent of total company-financed R & D in 1977 to 11.2 percent in 1988. See Howells and Wood 1993, 22–23. Pollak 1992, 48. Pauly and Reich 1997, 13–15.

worldwide at a cost of hundreds of billions of dollars. The "love bug" computer virus created by two Filipino graduate students in 2000 was an early illustration of the global vulnerability of a connected world. Globalization empowers people for both good and ill. Security can be enhanced—by mobilizing a political constituency for the banning of land mines, for example—or it can be diminished, by facilitating communications among a far-flung network of terrorists. Globalization also fosters trade in illegal drugs approximating half a trillion dollars annually, just under 10 percent of total world trade—a number that exceeds the value of the international oil trade in the late 1990s and approaches the amounts involved in money laundering, which is estimated at 2 percent of global GDP.[42]

The politics of technology and regional production, and of external and internal security, deeply intermingle international and global processes: "globalization with borders" is an apt description.[43] Yet as I argued in chapters 4 and 5, regionalization occurs in distinct European and Asian orders. Germany *in* Europe, Japan *and* Asia—a shorthand formulation captures these institutional differences. Across various issues, Asia and Europe show distinctive, recognizably different regional patterns of policy and politics.

European regionalism centers on state bargains and legal norms, Asian regionalism on market transactions and ethnic or national capitalism. This finding agrees with the views of other analysts, who point to persistent institutional differences across world regions. "Looking across regional trade regimes in the world," writes Peter Hall, "one finds very different levels of institution-building."[44] Similarly, Miles Kahler observes that "the Pacific region, whether defined to include the United States and Canada or limited to East Asia, represents a profound anomaly for any argument that posits a strong relationship between economic interdependence and institutional strength."[45] Regional institutions and political practices are distinctive.

In both economic and security affairs, Europe's regionalism is more transparent and intrusive than Asia's. The legislative history of the European Union on economic issues, for example, one part of its *acquis communitaire,* has no analogue in Asia. Even in the wake of the massive dislocations caused by the Asian financial crisis of 1997, ASEAN agreed to a financial surveillance regime much less transparent and intrusive than corresponding mechanisms in Europe. The same is true in security affairs. In the early 1990s, for example, changes in the political understandings of human rights in Europe, brought about in the OSCE, laid the conceptual and political foundation for intrusive rights protection and election monitoring. Limited exceptions notwithstanding, Asian regionalism honors instead the principle of nonintervention and adheres to traditional understandings of state sovereignty. In Asia, lack of respect for hu-

42. McFarlane 1999, 175–76.
43. Borrus and Zysman 1997.
44. Hall 1997, 3.
45. Kahler 1995, 107–8.

man rights and democratic procedures does not constitute grounds for curtailing engagement, as the case of ASEAN and Burma illustrates. At the same time, the ethnic organization of Asian capitalism makes transactions in both domestic and regional markets more susceptible to a volatile and at times explosive identity politics.

In institutional terms, therefore, Asian and European regionalism differ substantially. Jeffrey Frankel and Miles Kahler talk of Asia's "soft" regionalism, which is centered on ethnic and national identity capitalism operating in markets, as compared to Europe's "hard" regionalism based on politically and legally defined arrangements.[46] Across the duration of the cold war James Kurth saw in the Atlantic Alliance and the Pacific Basin two different paradigms of international relations that juxtaposed, respectively, international liberalism and international mercantilism on the one hand, and extended and finite deterrence on the other.[47]

How can we explain these differences between Asia and Europe? Differences in state power, regime type, and state structures shape the different institutional forms and practices of European and Asian regionalism.[48] European regionalism is conditioned by the relative equality of Germany and the other major European states; by the relations among similar political regimes; and by well-functioning state bureaucracies in virtually all EU members. In Asia, by contrast, Japan and, increasingly, China tower over their neighbors; Asia features a large number of different types of political regimes; and many Asian states lack the bureaucratic capacity to commit themselves credibly to intrusive forms of regional integration. Asian regionalism thus occurs through market networks constituted by ethnically or nationally organized firms or groups of firms, creating a vibrant, high-growth, and prosperous regional economy. European regionalism evolves instead through "big bang conferences" among states that are transforming the European polity into a multilevel governance system.

The degree of power imbalance in the two regions is striking.[49] In 1990, German GDP amounted to about one-quarter of the GDP of the European Community; the corresponding figure for Japan, compared to the East Asian Economic Caucus (EAEC) countries, was three times larger.[50] Over the previ-

46. Frankel and Kahler 1993, 4.

47. Kurth 1989. See also Boyer 2003. Duffield 2003. Grieco 1999. Mjøset and Nordhaug 1999. Beeson and Jayasuriya 1998. Kahler 1995. Higgott 1995.

48. The argument developed in the following pages draws on Katzenstein 1997a.

49. Katzenstein and Shiraishi 1997b, 365–66.

50. Estimates for Japanese and Chinese GDP differ widely depending on whether they are calculated at purchasing power parity or market prices. There is no simple answer as to which exchange rate calculation is more appropriate. Purchasing power parity gives a better indication of comparative levels of total consumption; market exchange rates indicate greater power in the international economy, which is of primary concern in this analysis of regionalism. Using purchasing power parity GDP figures for the year 2000 in 1990 dollars ranks China ($4,330 billion) ahead of Japan ($2,669 billion) for a ratio of 100:63. Using market prices sharply reverses the picture as Japan ($4,667 billion) ranks far ahead of China ($1,080) for a ratio of 100:27. On a per capita basis, using either measure, Japan is far ahead of China, by a factor of six for purchasing parity power GDP and by a factor of forty for market GDP. See McNicoll 2005, 57–58.

ous two decades, Germany's share had decreased from 27 to 25 percent; by contrast, Japan's share increased from 57 to 73 percent. By 2000, after a decade lost to the economic cost of unification in the case of Germany and economic stagnation in the case of Japan, the German figure had declined slightly to 24, and the Japanese figure to just under 70 percent. Furthermore, economic equality is much greater in Europe than in Asia. In both 1970 and 1990, the per capita GDP income in the wealthier EC member states exceeded that in the poorer states by a factor of three. In the EAEC, the corresponding factor increased from nine to twenty-nine. Other statistical indicators also illustrate the contrast between European homogeneity and Asian heterogeneity.[51]

Regime type also matters in the shaping of different types of regionalism. Europe is populated by democracies of different stripes. Whether majoritarian, presidential, prime ministerial, monarchic, corporatist, consociational, or transitional, they all adhere to the basic precepts of democracy: regular elections, free speech and a free press, and civil liberties defended by an independent judiciary. Furthermore, European states have insisted for decades that only democracies can participate in its regional institutions, as the Greek colonels learned after staging their coup d'état in 1967. After the cold war, European states adhered to this precept with iron conviction as they embarked on European enlargement. Asian polities, by contrast, exhibit a broad spectrum of regimes "from Communism to Confucianism, from constitutional monarchies to military dictatorships, from personalized rule to bureaucratic governance, from democratically elected governments to single-party rule."[52] Between 1975 and 1986, Asian states that subsequently joined the EAEC and APEC did not make any significant progress toward democratization—a striking contrast to Spain, Portugal, and Greece, and the southern enlargement of the European Community in the 1980s. In the 1990s, all of the central and eastern European states seeking EU membership made great strides in democratic practices. Since the mid-1980s, developments in South Korea, Taiwan, the Philippines, and, since 1997, Indonesia, have, broadly speaking, also been moving in the direction of institutionalizing democratic politics. No such developments, however, can yet be observed in the national politics of the People's Republic of China, Vietnam, North Korea, and Burma.

Similarity in regime type facilitates a political-legal regionalism in Europe, dissimilarity an ethnic- and market-based one in Asia. Reconciliation between France and Germany eventually made that partnership the engine of Europeanization. No comparable political development has brought Japan and China closer together in the last two decades. China's resurgence and Japan's faltering economic performance have, if anything, made the tangled relations

51. Alan Siaroff has documented a large number of different economic dimensions—including total population, GDP per capita, total GDP, stock of foreign investment, hosting of multinational corporations, total external assets or debts, and research development spending—that shows Asia as marked by asymmetric dependence, Europe by symmetric interdependence. Siaroff 1994, 14–15. See also Feng and Genna 2003.

52. Carnegie Endowment Study Group 1994, 14.

between the two countries even more complex. And Japan has also failed to achieve deeper reconciliation with its other neighbors in East Asia.

Finally, differences in European and Asian regionalism are due to the character of state structures. Some types of states are simply better suited to deal with public law and political institutions as the preferred vehicles for regionalism. I shall call them "Weberian states"; they exhibit highly rationalized forms of bureaucratic and legal rule. Despite some important variations, the European states, with one significant exception, all belong to the same Weberian species, making possible a regional politics built around law and institutions.

Prior to the 2004 EU enlargement, only Greece was singularly ill-equipped for full participation. Greece was admitted to the European Community primarily for ideological reasons. Widely considered as the cradle of European culture and civilization, Greece simply could not be excluded once the colonels were deposed in 1974. Yet the interaction between social and state structures that shaped modern Greece in the nineteenth and twentieth centuries showed strong traces of centuries of Ottoman rule. "Greek constitutionalism at the time of the founding of modern Greece," writes Vassiliki Georgiadou, "had little to do with the liberal-bourgeois constitutional order in Western Europe. . . . Despite the formal constitutional anchors of state and government, the political regime had enormous difficulties to institutionalize Roman law principles and uncontested property rights."[53] Traditional regional and local power brokers—local bureaucrats, clerics, the military—created a state that on the surface may have resembled Western Europe but in its core retained strong elements of Ottoman autocracy and corruption. The bloated Greek civil service and public economy; the absence, until very recently, of a regional system of government; the absence of reliable statistics; and the institutional limitations of the state bureaucracy are some of the political characteristics that make the modern Greek state quite different from a typical Weberian state. Greek preparation for the 2004 summer Olympic Games illustrated this difference, to the evident discomfort of many international sponsors.

On all of these dimensions, furthermore, Greece differs qualitatively from the other southern European states. Under the impetus of European integration, Spain and Portugal have effected a far-reaching transformation. It would be too strong to argue that Greece has not. Greece is changing and gradually converging toward a European profile. But change is slow and painful for both Greece and its European partners. It is difficult to conceive of EU-style institutional practices if all member states were to operate along Greek lines. The European hesitation to admit Turkey to full membership in the European Union is rooted not only in the human rights record of the Turkish government, the opposition to large-scale labor migration, and the fear of Islamic fundamentalism, but also in EU members' firsthand experience with Greece as a distant cousin of the Ottoman Empire.

53. Georgiandou 1991, 4–5, author's translation.

Asian regionalism is shaped by the character of Asian states. Southeast Asian states, for example, are heirs to British, Dutch, French, Spanish, and U.S. colonialism. Social forces penetrate these postcolonial states deeply and thus create intricate network structures. Their informal politics, writes Haruhiro Fukui, is as much defined by "the rule of men" as by "the rule of law."[54] Furthermore, these states have inherited the colonial tradition of "the rule by law" rather than the European tradition of "the rule of law." East and Southeast Asian states are constituted legally. But the relation between state and society is governed as much by informal, social norms as by formal, legal expectations. As Natasha Hamilton-Hart has argued, sharp differences in state capacities, for example between Singapore and Indonesia, pose a major barrier to the institutionalization of regional cooperation in Asia.[55] On questions of capital accounts, for example, Singapore's ample governing capacities make it much less dependent on regional financial cooperation than are Indonesia and some of its other Southeast Asian partners. In this view, the Weberian state of Singapore is perhaps as much an exception in Southeast Asia as the non-Weberian Greek state is in Europe.

Why this difference between Western Europe and East Asia since 1945? War and the threat of war was endemic to Asia:[56] the Chinese civil war, the Korean War, the Vietnam War, military confrontation over the formation of Malaysia, the Vietnamese occupation of Cambodia, a series of local guerrilla wars, and a cold war that threatened to turn hot on the Korean Peninsula and across the Taiwan Strait. In two different ways, strong states took control over the rise of successful export-oriented sectors.

First, war and the preparation for war helped greatly in the development of central bureaucracies. East Asian states developed strong structures with close links to business, able to adopt and fully implement the policy reforms necessary to push their economies away from import substitution and toward export-led growth. Asian Communism required the mobilization of all possible resources to enhance both the coercive and the civil powers of the state. Opposing the Communist threat enjoyed broad popular support and put left oppositional forces on the defensive. State legitimacy was grounded in performance rather than representation. There existed important differences among the East Asian states in the historical foundations on which modern state structures were built, the timing of export-led growth, and the various links to the American imperium. But the overall outcome was remarkably similar.

Second, war and the threat of war made capital readily available to most of the East Asian states. In the interest of state security, governments improved roads, railways, ports, and airports—also essential for improved economic performance. American aid and procurement orders during the Korean and Vietnam wars were of critical importance in moving these states onto a high-growth

54. Fukui 2000, 3.
55. Hamilton-Hart 2002, 175–80.
56. Stubbs 1999, 2005. Zhu 2000, 2002.

trajectory. Finally, the Vietnam War was crucial in creating export markets for Asian products. With the United States pursuing an inflationary policy of fighting a war against communism abroad and against poverty at home, in the 1960s the American market developed an insatiable appetite for cheap consumer products from Asia, which it has not lost since. Between 1965 and 1972, Japanese exports to the United States grew at an annual rate of 21 percent.[57] The redirection of trade in northeast and Southeast Asia was no less dramatic. War and the threat of war have been of critical importance to strong developmental states riding the waves of East Asia's vibrant economies.

What is true of East Asia in general is true of Japan in particular. This may be one reason why contemporary Japanese state theory has insisted on coining a series of neologisms that seek to transcend the dichotomies of strong/weak and public/private when theorizing about politics. Rule by a powerful bureaucracy, legitimated by the long-term LDP domination of Japanese politics, is an important part of a polity that links state and society in complex ways. It is difficult to describe these relationships between state and society with established categories that distill European experiences. Moreover, no evidence suggests that the powerful combination of a strong developmental state with a pervasive style of informal politics is disappearing either in Japan or in Asia. Instead, informal politics is likely to survive money politics the way it survived repressive politics: by adaptation.[58] Japan specialists thus emphasize the network character of the Japanese state and the requirements of reciprocity in the building of a political consensus that combines political efficacy with a mixture of economic efficiency and inefficiency. Although autonomous in some ways, the Japanese state is both embedded in civil society and penetrated by it. It has the potential, that is, for both strength and weakness.[59] And that state has cultivated its talents in riding rather than overriding market developments.

Network structures that vitiate the distinction between public and private spheres inside Japan are replicated in and externalized to Asia. Unsurprisingly, a nation of networks creates regional integration through market networks. "In large part," write Walter Hatch and Kozo Yamamura, "Japanese business and political elites have 'schmoozed' their way to power. They have, in other words, mastered the fine art of networking in Asia."[60] Somewhat less colloquially, U Nyun, executive secretary of the UN Economic Commission for Asia and the Far East (ECAFE), coined the term "Asian Way" to describe an amalgam of the teachings of Buddha, Confucius, and Mohammed. Michael Haas has identified informal discussions, consensus decision making, and pragmatic incrementalism as three core aspects of the Asian Way that have become diplomatic norms.[61] Rather than insist on the uniqueness of a specific set of Asian values, the Asian Way charac-

57. Stubbs 1999, 348.
58. Dittmer 2000, 306.
59. Rohlen 1989.
60. Hatch and Yamamura 1996, 131.
61. Haas 1989, 4–10.

terizes one part of the normative foundation that distinguishes Asian politics.[62] Pooling exclusive state sovereignties, European-style, in international institutions in the interest of regional integration assumes the monopoly of force as the defining element of state power and politics. This assumption derives from the European historical experience and the specific character of European state structures. Different structures have made Asian states less supportive of and less susceptible to processes of regional integration in legal institutions.

Self-generated, characteristic practices in Asia and Europe differ; and these differences are explicable in terms of state power, regime type, and state structure. Institutional practices in Asia and Europe interact in the American imperium with international and global processes. In the middle of the twentieth century, as I argued in chapter 2, American policy self-consciously created Germany and Japan as client states that eventually matured into supporter states. It backed multilateralism in Europe and bilateralism in Asia, thus laying the foundation for different regional orders. During the waning years of the twentieth century, globalization and internationalization reinforced the porousness of these two regions. But do similar connections link other regions to the American imperium?

The Americas

Latin America and Canada,[63] close to the center of the American imperium, are less shielded from the territorial and nonterritorial powers of the United States than are other regions.[64] Mexico and Cuba to the contrary notwithstanding, the Americas is the world's only region without a regionwide postcolonial, postwar, or revolutionary rupture. U.S. private economic interests dominated the Americas before U.S. worldwide preeminence, and by and large these interests have supported established elites. American preference for free regional markets is tied closely to American domination and undisguised resistance to the free flow of labor and regional imports in sensitive economic sectors. Finally, the Americas do not have a Germany or a Japan, one or two central regional powers that also act as steady supporters of America. Compared to Asia and Europe, this constellation yields a distinctive regionalism that interacts with the American imperium on the basis of informal rule, patron-client relations, coercive diplomacy, and military interventions.

62. Dupont 1996.
63. I would like to thank Brian Bow and Kevin Strompf for their excellent research assistance, including the drafting of a number of memos that helped me greatly in fleshing out my ideas.
64. Because I have a different purpose, I deviate here from the conceptualization of regional and country specialists who tend to view their topic under the rubric of "U.S. relations with"—Latin America, Mexico, or Canada. This book's regional focus incorporates also Central America and the Caribbean, vitally important to my characterizations of the nature of the American imperium. And it is attuned to more recent, regionwide political and economic currents not captured well by an analysis that focuses on a set of bilateral relations.

Throughout the last two centuries, the United States has been intent on securing the western hemisphere against outside interference. In recent decades, deep U.S. involvement in the overthrow of the Salvador Allende
government in Chile on September 11, 1973, and strong U.S. support of right-
wing dictatorships in Central America in the 1980s were in line with the behavior of a traditional imperial power. More recently Central America was the
model for journalist Robert Kaplan's advocacy of U.S. global "supremacy by
stealth," with CIA operatives and Special Forces operating beyond the political
control of Congress.[65] Grudging toleration of Communist Cuba a few miles
off the shore of Florida, however, points to some limits of that supremacy.
The Americas, one might think, should feature European-style regionalism.
They do not. The overwhelming presence of the United States dwarfs all other
states and has prevented the emergence of states both supportive of American
purpose and power and central to the region's political affairs. Moreover, U.S.
governments have felt deep ambivalence about supporting a more fully institutionalized regionalism that other states might use as a shield against the
United States.

Since the beginning of the nineteenth century, the Americas have been intimately tied to the "Western Hemisphere Idea."[66] Central to the idea is a distinctive sovereignty norm with two defining characteristics: the principle of
nonintervention belongs to the world of international politics, and the principle of representative government (and subsequently more broadly conceived
human rights) belongs to the world of global politics. The acceptance of intrusive election monitoring in the 1990s suggests that, more than in Asia, and
perhaps even Europe, in the 1990s state sovereignty in the Americas came to
incorporate an explicitly global dimension. "Human rights and representative
government," writes Arturo Santa-Cruz, have been "fundamental in validating
the claim to sovereign statehood."[67] The Western Hemisphere Idea can thus
be seen as a specific articulation of the nonterritorial aspects of the U.S.
imperium.

This is not to deny the obvious: the exercise of U.S. power through both military interventions and trade and investment was central to the evolution of the
Americas. From the perspective of the United States, James Kurth has put the
matter succinctly: "The essential purpose of any inter-American security system
has always been not so much inter-American as anti-European."[68] Insulating
the United States and the Americas from European wars and entanglements
has been a core interest since the beginning of the American republic. The inter-American system offered an effective block against the leading land power
on the European continent: imperial Germany at the beginning of the twentieth
century, Nazi Germany in the 1930s and 1940s, and the Soviet Union during

65. Kaplan 2003.
66. Whitaker 1954, 1.
67. Santa-Cruz 2003, 26.
68. Kurth 1990, 9.

the cold war. By 1900, the United States had become the dominant trader and investor in the Americas; unsurprisingly, Latin American states have tended to look to Europe as a natural balancer against an overbearing United States. Spain, in particular, has been a refuge for the opponents of Latin American regimes, thereby counterbalancing Latin America's heavy dependence on the United States. The inter-American system was never based on a congruence of interests that might have supported the growth of regional political institutions. It was based instead on bargains that served the different vital interests of Latin America and the United States, at the expense of the peripheral interests of the other.[69]

In its approach to the Americas, the Janus-faced U.S. imperium has often surrendered to its territorial impulses. International constraints were minimal. At the beginning of the nineteenth century, the Monroe Doctrine excluded European states from direct territorial control over Latin America. At the beginning of the twentieth, the Roosevelt corollary legitimated preemptive intervention to prevent European states from gaining indirect control through financial means. The absence of "reasonable efficiency and decency in social and political matters," inability to keep political order, and failure to honor international obligations, announced Teddy Roosevelt in 1904, might constitute grounds for U.S. military intervention.[70] By 1900 it was the United States, not Europe, that posed the greatest threat to the states of Latin America. The American imperium showed its territorial ambitions, starting with the Spanish-American War in 1898 and the subsequent annexations of Puerto Rico and Cuba. The pattern was reinforced by occupations of Haiti (1915–34), the Dominican Republic (1916–24), and Nicaragua (1912–33); interventions in the Mexican Revolution and in northern Mexico; the creation of Panama (1903); and the building and administration of the Panama Canal. For the Americas, the American Century began with the United States playing the old European game of acquiring a territorial empire and all but forgetting the new game enshrined in the nonterritorial Western Hemisphere Idea.

In the twentieth century, U.S. power and purpose in the Americas rested on two pillars. The corollary of the first Roosevelt administration and the Good Neighbor Policy of the second typify, respectively, the territorial, international pillar and the nonterritorial, global pillar. Both characterized the U.S. imperium in the Americas throughout the twentieth century. Mexico in the 1930s, Guatemala in the 1950s, Cuba in the 1960s, and Nicaragua in the 1980s illustrate the territorial, international pillar; the Good Neighbor Policy of the 1930s, the Alliance for Progress of the 1960s, and the move to a free trade area at the turn of the twenty-first century represent the nonterritorial, global one. At times, both merged into an Americanization that did not simply emanate from the United States—instead, it connected government and business elites

69. Kurth 1990, 24.
70. Roseperry 1989, 99.

and oppositional movements across national borders.[71] Foreign trade and enclave economies first, and domestic markets and nationalist, militarist, or populist regimes later, have given the United States the instruments to wield its
influence south of its border. Often experienced as life-threatening constraint
by rural communities, ethnic minorities, and groups whose aspirations went
unmet, U.S. influence was simultaneously a welcome opportunity for a new urban middle class and working population that prospered from deep economic
linkages with the United States.

The neoliberal Washington consensus of the 1980s and 1990s posed a great
challenge, especially to the governments of weaker states in the Americas struggling to avoid economic meltdown and social marginalization. As the Americas experiment with approaches to regionalism and regionalization, a chasm
separates the new economic regionalism from the new security threats.[72] The
new economic regionalism is occurring in the center of the Americas: the North
American Free Trade Agreement, Mercosur, and the proposed Free Trade Area
of the Americas (FTAA). The new security threats—terrorism, narcotics, immigration, environmental degradation—are concentrated on the periphery,
in Central America, the Caribbean, and the depressed Andean countries.

Four summit meetings of the Americas held in 1994, 1998, 2001, and 2004
consolidated the commitment to common political and economic principles.
They enhanced military confidence-building measures among historical rivals
in the Southern Cone, as well as collective peacekeeping operations in Central
America and the Caribbean. At the same time, some traditional security conflicts persist, such as the 1996 border war between Ecuador and Peru. Other
security threats are on the rise, such as transnational drug and arms trafficking, terrorism, corruption, and guerrilla insurgency. The fine line separating
military and criminal violence is blurred. As "Crimintern" replaces Comintern
this requires cooperation among law enforcement agencies at least as much as
among militaries.[73] In the absence of a state acting as an anchor supportive of
the central purposes of American power in the region, U.S. policy oscillates
widely between disengagement and unilateralism rather than developing a
consistent security stance.

Regionalism in the Americas also exists north of the United States. Canadians used to define themselves in terms of what they are not. In the words of Seymour Martin Lipset, "Canadians are the world's oldest and most continuing
un-Americans."[74] Over time Canada has evolved a European-style welfare state
that is deeply divided along ethnic lines. Various markers of Canadian national
identity point to important differences from the United States: a nonrevolu-
tionary break with Britain, a stronger labor movement, a more generous welfare state, an official enshrinement of French-English biculturalism, a greater

71. Roseperry 1989, 80–121.
72. Johnson 2001.
73. Farer 1999, xv–xvi.
74. Lipset 1990, 53.

openness toward multiculturalism, less violence, and smaller prisons. There exists also a clear one-sidedness in knowledge about and interest in each other. The highest-rated Canadian television comedy show ever produced, *Talking to Americans,* featured interviews with people in the United States designed to highlight their ignorance of Canada. Canadians worry about the effects of the diffusion of U.S. popular culture on Canadian culture, in part because the deep split between English Canadians and French Canadians makes Canadian identity problematic. Hoping for more autonomy, the Quebecois in particular have proved enthusiastic about North American economic integration, which has greatly reduced Quebec's dependence on the rest of Canada. Protected by their French language against the threat of cultural assimilation, the Quebecois have less favorable views of the United States than do anglophone Canadians, a gap that dramatically widened on the subject of the 2003 Iraq war.

Before the assertion of congressional power in the 1970s undermined the advantages of the earlier informal coordination of trade policy, Canada had shown little interest in a North American free trade zone. Eventually, a Canada-U.S. free trade agreement appeared to be the only way to head off increasing U.S. protectionism, imposing institutional restraints on the arbitrary recourse to U.S. "trade remedy" law.[75] Canada's exports to the United States doubled in the 1990s. Eighty-two percent of Canada's exports are destined for the United States, and 71 percent of imports originate there. Much of this trade, as in automobiles, is intraindustry and intrafirm. The trade partnership is highly asymmetric. Bilateral trade accounts for only 2.5 percent of U.S. GDP, compared to 35 percent of Canadian GDP.[76]

Security relations are remarkable for a basically unprotected border of over five thousand miles. Karl Deutsch noted long ago that the demilitarization of the U.S.-Canadian border in 1819 symbolized a pluralistic security community defined by peaceful change.[77] Today, at 425 official crossing points, only 334 agents police the border, compared to nine thousand assigned to the U.S.-Mexican border.[78] Stricter controls along the Mexican border have not stopped hundreds of thousands of illegal immigrants from crossing, and a dramatic increase in personnel could not seal the U.S.-Canadian border. In the aftermath of 9/11, the issue of border control is paramount for Canada's economic well-being and for U.S. security. Both countries are now cooperating on the December 2001 thirty-point Smart Border plan. At the same time, Canada has deflected Mexican attempts to establish trilateral consultations on issues of border security.

Since the United States conquered and annexed almost half of Mexico's territory in its westward expansion in the 1840s, Mexico has always looked with great suspicion at the colossus to its north. This suspicion is expressed in its National Museum of Intervention. Unlike Canada, Mexico has traditionally

75. Bow 2003, 238. Gruber 2000.
76. Fagan 2003, 36.
77. Deutsch 1957, 34.
78. Andreas 2003, 8.

lacked in Washington either informal access or an institutionalized framework for cooperation and dispute resolution. The financial crisis of 1982 and the economic and political liberalization that followed brought important changes: Mexico's accession to GATT, the increasing political salience of legal and illegal Mexican immigration in U.S. politics, the creation of NAFTA, and an increasingly integrated cross-border economy. Today nearly twenty-one million U.S. citizens are of Mexican heritage, and seven to eight million of those citizens were born in Mexico.[79] They are an important source of remittances to and investments in Mexico, an increasingly important political constituency in U.S. politics, and a vital part of a transnational community linking Mexico to the United States.

Since the first Mexican debt crisis of 1982, Mexico's fortunes have become increasingly tied to those of the United States, culminating in the 1994 North American Free Trade Agreement. Mexico changed from its traditional policy of import substitution to trade-led development. Between 1990 and 2000, U.S.-Mexican trade increased more than fourfold, from $58 to $247 billion.[80] Direct foreign investment increased by a factor of six, from $2.5 to $14.6 billion.[81] Yet, despite these changes, Mexican job growth since 1994 has been restricted to the maquiladora sector and the border economy. Even there, almost half of the seven hundred thousand jobs created between 1994 and 2000 have since been rationalized away; Mexican wages have stagnated and in 2002 were below the 1993 level; and inequalities between large and small businesses, rich and poor, and the north and south of Mexico have widened.[82] NAFTA has also helped the cause of political liberalization, breaking the pattern of one-party dominance.

Growing dependence on the United States has increased Mexico's willingness to participate in multilateral, regionwide institutions as a way to balance U.S. influence. Topping the security agenda between Mexico and the United States is the cross-border flow of illegal migrants and illicit drugs. Increasing economic trade and migration have led to a dramatic increase in border policing. Especially since the 9/11 attacks, the United States and Mexico deal with each other across a "borderless economy and a barricaded border."[83]

Canada and Mexico are too proximate to and too dependent on the United States to play the roles of both supporter states and regional powers. NAFTA, deeply controversial in both Canada and Mexico, has remade North America. Because the international shocks of 1981–82 created a profound crisis of legitimacy for governing elites, Canada in 1985 and Mexico in 1990 overcame their long-standing aversion to free trade with the United States.[84] NAFTA is

79. Tulchin and Selee 2003, 5.
80. United States Census Bureau 2004.
81. World Bank 2004.
82. Pastor and Wise 2003. Weiner 2003.
83. Andreas 2003, 14.
84. Golob 2003.

driven by Canada's problematic relations with the United States rather than by broader political concerns, and it reflects U.S. hopes for a social and economic stabilization of Mexico and improved U.S. access to Mexico's oil reserves rather than a Mexican attempt to shape the politics of the western hemisphere. This is not to deny NAFTA's substantial impact. In the 1990s Mexico's low-cost imports displaced many Asian suppliers in U.S. markets. Offshore sourcing and cross-border production have been far reaching and helped reorganize North American intraindustry trade. U.S. relations with its neighbors surely are of vital importance. But they have not permitted these two countries to speak to the interests of the region at large while also supporting U.S. values and interests.

Further removed geographically, Brazil and Argentina are furtively more opposed to U.S. purposes in the Americas than are Canada and Mexico. Mercosur expresses this opposition. It is a politically defensive form of regionalism supported by the countries of the Southern Cone to stabilize their political relations and to defend themselves against the U.S. neoliberal agenda. Plans for a South American Community bolster those defenses. Even though the United States is deeply attached to a plan for hemispheric regionalism—embodied initially in NAFTA—Mercosur has succeeded in establishing itself, as illustrated by economic cooperation agreements signed with Chile, Bolivia, the European Union, and Canada.

Economic initiatives such as NAFTA and Mercosur offer competing models for hemispheric integration under the provisions of the Free Trade Area of the Americas. There is no state or group of states supportive of U.S. purposes that seeks to broker a compromise between the two models, and it remains to be seen how they can be made compatible in an arrangement that aims at market liberalization and domestic economic reforms. NAFTA is a free trade area. Mercosur charts a new model located somewhere between NAFTA and a common market. NAFTA is a more comprehensive and detailed agreement, whereas Mercosur is a simple and evolving one with an ambitious goal. NAFTA adheres to a legalized process, for example, on issues of accession and dispute resolution, while Mercosur adheres to a political process more open to interventions and evasions. Mercosur is amenable to informal tradeoffs and open to a political dynamic for coordinating policy. In sum, "NAFTA represents a mostly contractual approach based on legal dynamics, and Mercosur represents a participatory approach based on political dynamics."[85] Regionalism in the Americas thus offers a hybrid of European and Asian elements.

The United States and Brazil are the leading proponents of these two approaches, and an eventual FTAA, if it is to occur, must somehow integrate elements from both. The absence of a supporter state and the lack of a bipartisan consensus in Washington on how to deal with the Americas leaves U.S. policy wavering. The gradual enlargement of NAFTA through special bilateral agreements with Chile and a few other countries competes with the creation of a mul-

85. Bernier and Roy 1999, 87.

tilaterally negotiated, and possibly cumbersome, FTAA. Because of its diversified trade and investment links, Brazil has traditionally favored a multilateral
over a regional approach, and it has a strong preference for subregional
arrangements such as Mercosur over a U.S.-led hemispheric arrangement.[86]

Yet even though policy is based on competing approaches, international and
global processes push porous regionalism in the Americas. Even before serious
negotiations had commenced on a region-wide free trade agreement in 1998,
Latin American states had slashed their tariffs. Between 1985 and 1997, on average, tariffs fell from 40 to 11 percent, with maximum tariffs falling from more
than 80 to 40 percent. Most countries cut tariffs by half. These reductions have
squeezed much of the "water" out of the tariff schedules of Latin American
states; plenty of "muscle" remains in both tariff and nontariff barriers.[87] Still,
most hemispheric trade remains concentrated in a few key bilateral relationships, such as those between Mexico and the United States and Brazil and Argentina.[88] Chile's policy of seeking advantageous free-trade agreements with
Mercosur in 1996 and with the United States in 2000 illustrates the likely tug-
of-war in a hemispheric FTAA. The United States will push, and Brazil will resist, market opening and liberalization. Governments with progressive policy
agendas, as in Brazil and Argentina, or more radical ones, as in Venezuela, face
enormous political costs if they adhere to the Washington consensus. The
hemispheric consensus of the 1990s on the benefits of porous regionalism persists but remains fragile.[89]

Central America also reflects the dual imprint of the American imperium.
For much of the 1980s, writes James Mahoney, "the United States was directly
or indirectly linked with death squads, paramilitary units, and counterrevolu-
tionary organizations that helped oversee the repression and killing of thousands of civilians in the region."[90] With the collapse of the Soviet Union and
the end of the cold war, those brutal conflicts have ended. Yet the underlying
social and economic causes have not. Poverty, inequality, unemployment, lack
of access to arable land, migration, and environmental degradation have not
improved. Border disputes and disagreements over migration continue to fes-
ter between El Salvador and Honduras and between Nicaragua and Costa Rica.
Since 9/11, the spread of violent crime and lawlessness appears even more
threatening. Kidnappings, narcotics smuggling, murders, and robberies have
increased as the military has withdrawn from society and as governments have
failed to beef up police forces and the judiciary. NAFTA has restricted dramatically the options available to Nicaragua, El Salvador, Costa Rica, Honduras,
and Guatemala, the member states of the revitalized Central American Common Market. A free trade agreement would have to be based on the principle

86. Soares de Lima 1999, 136.
87. Hufbauer, Schott, and Kotschwar 1999, 69.
88. Devlin, Estevadeordal, and Garay 2000, 157.
89. Grugel 1996, 158–59, 162–63. Weiner 2003.
90. Mahoney 2001, 259.

of reciprocity, but given the large differences in tariff levels, this would seriously undercut the Central American Common Market. The limited capacities of governments in this region are unlikely to be bolstered soon by incorporation, on favorable terms, into growing markets.

This description captures only one part of Central America's reality. Policies creating economic openness provide the second part. The Caribbean Community and Common Market and the Andean Pact are two of more than thirty "minilateral" schemes for economic cooperation that sprang up in Latin America in the 1990s.[91] Subregional arrangements promise strength in numbers, an asset for small states that must bargain with larger economic groups. Subregional arrangements signal a willingness to submit to the disciplining effects of international economic accords in order to encourage the streamlining of production across national borders, and thus to avoid exclusion from larger economic groups in the Americas and in the world economy. The Andean Pact, for example, serves few of its members' economic interests, but it strengthens the hand of member states interested in negotiating with other groups of states. The risk of defection persists. Colombia, Venezuela, and Ecuador trade mostly within the Andean Pact, Peru and Bolivia mostly outside.[92] The Caribbean Community and Common Market enjoys tariff-free access to the rich U.S. market, an advantage that NAFTA neutralized when it granted Mexico similar benefits. Indeed, Mexico is diverting both trade and investment away from the Caribbean. As nonreciprocal preferences are being eliminated by economic reorganization under U.S. leadership, the Caribbean states have little choice but to remain a haven for offshore financial services, for tourists, and for illicit drugs, with little prospect of stemming the flow of out-migration.

The Americas are dominated by the United States, and they lack a core regional power largely favorable to U.S. purpose and power. Just as Europe and Asia are divided into different subregions, so are the Americas. Different political visions and interests exist between particular states, such as the United States and Brazil, and in general between governments committed to, and opponents protesting in the streets against, deepening market integration and liberalization. Because of U.S. power, NAFTA is probably a closer approximation to the evolving FTAA than is Mercosur. The perception is widespread that the FTAA is a technocratic acronym for the hegemonic exercise of power, in which the United States determines the rules and reaps the benefits of international trade liberalization inside the region while strengthening its position outside.

Between the establishment of the United States (1781–89) and the American Civil War (1861–65), the "Philadelphia system" in early-nineteenth-century U.S. politics differed from the European Concert system and a deteriorating Sinocentric order in Asia.[93] Today, the Americas are evolving a regional order that also differs from Europe's and Asia's. The free market regionalism that is

91. Smith 2001, 47. Devlin, Estevadeordal, and Garay 2000, 159.
92. Grugel 1996, 153–55.
93. Deudney 1995.

emerging in the Americas is rule based, though shallower than Europe's. NAFTA's Free Trade Commission is not the European Council of Ministers, and expert panels for dispute settlement are no match for the European Court of Justice. A free trade area is far removed from a single market with free labor mobility and common external tariffs, a common currency, and a legal order of close to one hundred thousand pages of intrusive regulations and directives. Compared to Asia, however, the free market regionalism of the Americas infringes more on the autonomy of medium-sized and small states that simply cannot hide from overwhelming U.S. power. These states have no recourse to a regional power. Rather than assume a regional leadership comparable to that of Germany and Japan, Brazil and other core states are wavering between hesitant support of and quiet opposition to the United States. Free market regionalism leaves no room for either the redistributive aspects of the European Union or the benign tutelage that regional powers exert at times in Asia. Instead, political actors must cope with the informal rules, patron-client relations, coercive diplomacy, and military interventions that comes with their immediate exposure to the U.S. imperium.

Extending the Argument to South Asia, Africa, and the Middle East

How might this book's argument be applied to other world regions? Globalization and internationalization and the regional porousness they create affect all regions of the world. The vertical relations that link regions with other political entities, however, differ, and so does the basic institutional form of different regional orders. Just as variety in condiments enhances the taste of food, so variety in institutional form creates raw material for continued political conflict and innovations in cooperation. Institutional variety offers a large and evolving repertoire for action and the possibility for learning and adaptation, and so it matters greatly for the long-term evolution of world order.

In the short term, however, institutional variety is less important than the presence or absence of core regional states that support U.S. power and purpose. These states are the hinges that connect regions to the American imperium. Supporter states in Asia and Europe, the world's two most important regions, stabilize the current world order. Their absence in the Americas is consequential for that region's evolution, but it does not have worldwide ramifications. For more than half a century the American imperium has played a role as both the world's and its own region's preeminent state. Other regions, South Asia, Africa, and the Middle East, have oppositional, client, or lackey states at their core. But they do not have regional supporter states. The consequences for world order vary with the region's centrality in the American imperium as measured by the statistical indicators summarized in table 1.

With the end of the cold war, large numbers of U.S. troops were withdrawn from Europe and Asia and, in smaller numbers, stationed in and around the

Table 1. Regions in the American Imperium

	U.S. Active Duty Personnel Abroad[1]			U.S. Crude Petroleum Imports[2]		
	(Annual Averages)			(Thousands of Barrels)		
	1959–1961	1979–1981	1999–2001	1960	1980	2000
Europe[a]	375,656	326,335	115,239	—	116,208	219,769
East Asia	203,681	120,758	97,074	26,720	137,551	54,002
South Asia[b]	855	1,417[c]	695[c]	—	—	—
Middle East/ North Africa[d]	23,160	6,235	15,323	114,626	954,951	1,390,785
Sub-Saharan Africa	1,328	223	268	—	337,639	498,460
Latin America	27,581	14,214	8,674	188,880	306,811	1,139,981

	U.S. Trade ($US Million)[3]					
	Exports	Imports	Exports	Imports	Exports	Imports
	1962		1980		2000	
Europe[a]	7,405	4,544	71,038	50,455	183,009	257,511
East Asia	3,105	2,320	41,412	57,215	193,238	442,930
South Asia[b]	974	347	2,708	1,603	4,614	18,328
Middle East/ North Africa[d]	1,302	432	15,884	36,453	28,486	46,978
Sub-Saharan Africa	358	439	5,461	19,333	5,874	23,614
Latin America	3,675	3,968	38,745	38,915	167,525	210,769

	U.S. Foreign Assistance ($US millions)[4]			Foreign Travels of the U.S. Secretary of State[5]		
	(Annual Averages)			(Number of Visits, Percentage of All Visits)		
	1958–1962	1978–1982	1997–2001	1957–1965	1977–1985	1997–2004
Europe[a]	499.0	319.8	1,672.4	70 (60%)	106 (41%)	190 (44%)
East Asia	730.1	354.9	465.1	16 (14%)	28 (11%)	52 (12%)
South Asia[b]	778.5	583.1	372.1	4 (3%)	3 (1%)	18 (4%)
Middle East/ North Africa[d]	595.1	1,958.1	2,138.3	8 (7%)	71 (21%)	96 (22%)
Sub-Saharan Africa	124.4	698.2	1,999.0	0 (0%)	6 (2%)	30 (7%)
Latin America	347.5	556.6	1,172.0	12 (10%)	39 (15%)	44 (10%)

Sources:
[1]Calculated from U.S. Department of Defense, "Personnel Statistics," www.web1.whs.osd.mil. Does not include military personnel afloat for South Asia, Middle East/North Africa, and Sub-Saharan Africa.
[2]American Petroleum Institute, *Basic Petroleum Data Book*, vol. 24, no. 1, Washington, D.C., 2004.
[3]Calculated from International Monetary Fund, *Direction of Trade Statistics*, Washington, D.C. Various issues.
[4]Calculated from USAID, "U.S. Overseas Loans and Grants, Obligations, and Loan Authorizations," qesdb.cdie .org/gbk/index.html.
[5]Calculated from U.S. Department of State, www.state.gov/r/pa/ho/trvl.

Notes:
[a]Includes Eastern Europe and Soviet Union/CIS.
[b]Includes Afghanistan.
[c]Includes Diego Garcia.
[d]Includes Turkey.

Middle East. U.S. oil imports increased sharply between 1960 and 1980 from the Middle East, and since the early 1980s from Latin America. Asia has displaced Europe as the leading trade partner of the United States, and Latin America is quickly closing the gap that separates it from Europe as the second most important trading partner of the United States. The United States is disbursing less foreign aid in Asia and more in other parts of the world, including eastern Europe, with sharp increases recorded also in Africa and Latin America. Over time, the attention of U.S. diplomacy, as indicated by the travels of the secretary of state, has shifted from Europe to the Middle East, while holding steady across the other world regions.

These figures are useful in charting the changing importance of different regions to the United States. Generally speaking, India and South Asia were marginal to U.S. foreign policy in the second half of the twentieth century. They lack crucial raw materials and, in sharp contrast to Europe and Asia, they lacked geostrategic significance throughout the cold war. The formation of the Baghdad Pact in 1955 and the U.S. reaction to the Soviet invasion of Afghanistan in 1979 precipitated the two major tilts of U.S. foreign policy toward Pakistan before 9/11, thereby reinforcing a split in the region. American interest centered for decades on limiting Soviet influence, supporting economic development, and constraining nuclear proliferation and the spread of missile technology. During the cold war, events rather than grand strategy dictated U.S. foreign policy. After the Soviet invasion of Afghanistan the United States gave Pakistan billions of dollars in economic and military aid to funnel U.S. military supplies to the mujahideen. U.S. support may have hardened Pakistan's position on Kashmir and thus impeded a thaw between the two main states in the region. The policy was repeated after the 9/11 attacks, without this time leading to a deterioration of U.S.-India relations.

Like South Asia, Africa has been a low priority for American foreign policy—with the possible exception of the antiapartheid movement in the 1970s and 1980s. This is not to deny the potential importance of Nigerian oil or the strategic importance of the Horn of Africa and South Africa. Still, in terms of economic aid, trade, troop deployments, and visits by various U.S. secretaries of state, Africa ranks near the bottom of U.S. strategic and economic interests. In the early decades of the cold war U.S. attention was fully focused on Europe and Asia.[94] Subsequently, a policy of limited arms transfers, technical assistance, and economic aid was designed to forestall political upheavals that might have opened Africa to Soviet influence, as in Sierra Leone in 1958, the Congo in 1960, and Angola in 1975. The ill-fated, UN-sponsored American intervention in Somalia in 1993 prompted temporary disengagement. The United States was, however, at the forefront of creating in 1997 the African Crisis Response Initiative, which trains African troops for regional peacekeeping

94. Marte 1994, 49–106, 141–44.

missions.[95] Spurred by both security and economic considerations and rein-forced by the pressures of the religious right of the Republican Party, U.S. aid policy has targeted selected African states for special assistance. After 9/11 the United States has commenced a broad set of more or less clandestine initiatives to secure its military and economic presence in numerous African states. With good reason James Fearon and David Laitin speak of such interventions as a type of "postmodern imperialism."[96]

These descriptions and the figures in table 1 conceal, however, a structural feature central to my argument: the importance of a state or small group of states offering steady support for American purpose and power while also play-ing an important role in the region's affairs. South Asia and Africa lack such a core regional state. India is too big to play the part in South Asia, and until very recently South Africa under apartheid was too isolated and Nigeria too trou-bled to do the same in Africa. Instead the United States has ruled as in the Americas: informally, through patron-client relations, and relying on coercive diplomacy or military intervention.

South Asia lacks regional supporter states. India's dominant position has convinced its neighbors that regional cooperation would only consolidate In-dia's leading role. In recent years India has attempted, with some success, to counteract that regionwide perception. Under the Gujral doctrine, since the mid-1990s India has explicitly put relations with its neighbors on the basis of nonreciprocity.[97] At the same time, however, India adopted a new "Look East" policy as it saw its economic future linked to developments in East Asia. India became a "full dialogue partner" of ASEAN in 1995, joined the Asian Regional Forum in 1996, began participating in ASEAN summit-level meetings in 2002, and began negotiation on an ASEAN-India free trade area in 2003. Advances in South Asian regionalism by the most important regional organization, the South Asian Association for Regional Cooperation, are blocked by Pakistan's exclusion and the lack of compromise over Kashmir, the region's most serious security conflict. The South Asian Association for Regional Cooperation is use-ful for facilitating an informal exchange of information, and it offers a venue for Indian and Pakistani leaders to meet when bilateral meetings are politically too costly at home. Still, Jeffrey Key concludes, among the regional organiza-tions of the world, this one "is the most moribund."[98] And for several reasons— the marginality of South Asia to the United States, the repeated tilts of U.S. for-eign policy in favor of Pakistan, and a nonaligned tradition in Indian foreign policy dating back to the Bandung conference of 1955—India as the world's largest democracy has not evolved into a steady supporter of the United States.

Africa also lacks a regional supporter state. Liberia has the strongest ties to

95. Keller 1997, 308. Rothchild 2000, 169.
96. Fearon and Laitin 2004, 7. Barnes 2004.
97. Ayoob 1999, 257.
98. Key 1998, 99.

the United States, yet it does not play the part. Established in 1816 by the American Colonization Society, the independent republic of Liberia was declared as early as 1847, with a constitution and political institutions modeled after the United States. Americo-Liberians, even though they constituted only 5 percent of the population, ran the country's politics until the military coup of 1980. U.S. diplomatic support and occasional port calls by the U.S. Navy helped protect Liberia's independence; they did not, however, stop Britain and France from pressuring the Liberian government to cede large tracts of land to Sierra Leone and Ivory Coast. In 1926, the Firestone Corporation signed a 99-year lease on 1 million acres of land for a rubber plantation; in 1989, the company was still employing eight thousand people in Liberia. In 1959, the U.S. and Liberian governments signed a mutual defense pact, and Liberia became an African communication node for the United States during the cold war. Financial support for Liberia increased greatly in the first half of the 1980s, as it became a staging area for clandestine CIA operations in Libya and the shipment of war materials to Angola's UNITA rebels. The end of the cold war, however, ended this special relationship. The United States conducted limited interventions in 1990, 1992, and 1996 to evacuate U.S. citizens and other foreign nationals, but it kept its distance from both sides in Liberia's protracted and bloody civil war. After the cold war ended, the special relationship between the United States and Liberia did not translate into sustained political engagement—replicating the experience of Africa at large.[99]

Unlike in South Asia and Africa, in the Middle East America's vital economic and security interests have always been at stake. Historically there have been several potential regional supporters.[100] Iran had the power resources and was committed to Western-style modernization, but before the revolution of 1979 it could not play the part for one simple reason: it was not "Arab." Egypt was the heart of pan-Arab nationalism, especially in the 1950s and 1960s, and with the Camp David agreement joined the U.S. side. The Arab League ostracized Egypt for a decade. By the late 1980s, the estrangement had subsided, but the harsh rule of the Mubarak regime, in particular its intense conflict with political Islam, limited Egypt's room for maneuver.

That leaves Saudi Arabia and Israel. The contradictions between America's interest in stable oil supplies, and thus a stable Saudi Arabia, and its unflinching support of Israel, especially after the 1967 war, have done nothing to make the territorial issues centering on the Arab-Israeli conflict less intractable. Furthermore, Saudi Arabia's quasi-feudal regime is so distant from the democratic practices of American politics that close ties between politicians, such as the Bush family and the royal House of Saud, and economic sectors, such as the oil industry, substitute for the absence of compatible values. Saudi wealth has promoted the cause of radical Islam, through the funding of mosques and

99. Adebajo 2002. Ellis 1999.
100. I would like to thank Marc Lynch for his astute observations from which I borrow freely here.

movements. Fifteen of the nineteen men who attacked the World Trade Center and the Pentagon on 9/11 were citizens of Saudi Arabia, a key U.S. ally in the Middle East. And prior to the emergence of al Jazeera Saudi Arabia exercised far-reaching control over the media, in part through a few London-based, Saudi-owned newspapers. Saudi Arabia has played the role of regional pivot, but in ways largely antithetical to American values.

American-Israeli relations show an opposite pattern, excessive political proximity. In the 1990s, for a brief moment, leading Labor and Likud politicians toyed with the idea of Israel becoming a regional state by joining the Arab League in order to spread peace and prosperity throughout the region. But this was largely talk, and not very serious talk at that. The reason is simple. Over time, Israel has become an inextricable part of U.S. electoral politics. It is unthinkable for a presidential candidate of either party to run on a platform that appears to dilute U.S. support for Israel. Deeply divided over sacred territories, and either too distant or too close to the United States, neither Saudi Arabia nor Israel can play the role of regional supporter of the United States.

At the beginning of the twentieth century, First Lord of the Admiralty Winston Churchill decided that Britain would defend its naval supremacy against Germany with a new generation of dreadnought battleships. Powered by oil not coal, these ships suddenly made the Middle East a region of great geostrategic significance.[101] With the passing of the British Empire, U.S. interest in securing the "postwar petroleum order" has tended to be in tension with guaranteeing Israel's security.[102] Middle East oil was central to postwar reconstruction in both Europe and Asia. Between 1970 and 2000, dependence on Middle East oil, as a percentage of total consumption, was halved in Western Europe and declined moderately in Japan. It increased more than fourfold in the United States. Admittedly, in 2000, Saudi Arabia was the only Middle Eastern state among the top five oil suppliers of the United States, behind Canada and ahead of Venezuela, Mexico, and Nigeria. But in today's global markets the geographic origin of a barrel of oil is less relevant than who exercises price leadership and, because of the size of its proven reserves, Saudi Arabia plays that part.

Over many decades, successive U.S. administrations have expended enormous political capital in the Middle East. During the cold war, U.S. policy helped push hard-line secularist governments opposed to Israel, such as Gamal Abdel Nasser's Egypt, Hafiz al-Assad's Syria, and, before 1980, Iraq under the Baath Party, into the Soviet orbit. After the Iranian Revolution of 1979, the United States stepped up its defense commitments in the region, making the Persian Gulf a region of "vital interest," supporting Iraq's Saddam Hussein in his war against Iran, and permitting Kuwaiti tankers to fly U.S. flags and enjoy the protection of U.S. Navy escorts against hostile Iranian fire. In 1991, the

101. Khalidi 2004, 84–85.
102. Yergin 1991, 409–30.

United States fought its first war against Iraq, in response to its invasion of Kuwait in 1990. Arab armies fighting Iraq under U.S. command "marked the final collapse of the Arab unity project."[103] When the United States chose to attack Iraq again in 2003, its improvised and ineffectual occupation policies helped reunite Arabs in opposition to the United States.

The status quo–oriented, conservative Saudi Arabian regime cannot play the role of U.S. supporter state. Like the other Gulf states, it puts itself at risk by too open an alignment with the United States. Nasser's vision of a pan-Arab identity constrained Saudi Arabia's foreign policy options, and Iraq was a serious warning. The Iraqi monarchy joined the 1955 Baghdad Pact, which helped bring about the downfall of the regime soon thereafter.[104] The lesson was not lost on Saudi Arabia, which for years thereafter distanced itself from formal defense relationships with the United States.[105] In 1958, Saudi Arabia essentially stopped military purchases from the United States, and in 1962 the Saudi government refused to renew the lease on Dahran air base, which the United States had begun using during World War II. In this period, also, the Saudi government began to emphasize its Islamic identity as a counter to Nasser's radical Pan-Arabism. Between 1962 and 1967 Saudi Arabia and Egypt fought a proxy war in Yemen, with direct, substantial involvement of the Egyptian army, a conflict settled only after Nasser's decisive defeat in the Six-Day War with Israel in 1967. This shifted the balance of power toward Saudi Arabia and other status quo powers in the Gulf.

The mid-1970s' deal between Saudi Arabia and the United States traded Saudi price leadership in OPEC against an American security guarantee.[106] American support also became vital for economic reasons. The United States was one of the leading consumers of oil and the most important destination of Saudi foreign investment. The Saudi oil industry had been created by American corporations. In 1944 Standard Oil of California and Texaco formed the Arabian American Oil Company (Aramco); before the Saudi government purchased the company on friendly terms in the 1970s, it was the largest single U.S. foreign investment.[107] The Iranian Revolution, the Soviet invasion of Afghanistan, and the Iran-Iraq War in 1980 committed the United States more explicitly to the defense of Saudi Arabia and the Gulf states. But it took the immediate threat of Iraq's invasion of Kuwait in 1990 to push Saudi hesitation into open alliance with the United States. Within a decade, however, hesitation reasserted itself, because of the strength of the Islamic movement inside Saudi Arabia, unequivocal U.S. support for Israel during two Palestinian uprisings, and the political fallout of the September 11 attacks. This history shows no opportunities for Saudi Arabia to emerge as a regional supporter of the United States.

103. Hudson 1999, 13.
104. Barnett 1996, 415–22.
105. Gause 1996, 304.
106. Spiro 1999.
107. Bahgat 2001, 3.

Over the last half century, America's complex "special relationship" with Israel has been deeply antithetical to its special relationship with Saudi Arabia. Because Israel was the target of a regionwide coalition, it simply could not assume the role of regional supporter of the U.S. government. U.S. support for a Jewish state predates Israel's independence. American diplomatic pressure was very important for the original UN partition plan in 1947.[108] The U.S. security commitment grew decisively after the 1967 war. Although the two nations have clashed numerous times—over Israeli settlements in the occupied territories, various U.S. arms deals with Arab countries, and Israeli tactics during two Palestinian uprisings—during the last half century, in the words of Steven Spiegel, "no matter how high tensions between the two governments might rise, no administration since 1948 has wavered from a fundamental commitment to the security and survival of the State of Israel."[109]

The Six-Day War had a transformative effect on both Israeli domestic politics and Israeli-U.S. relations. The tense months leading up to the 1967 war increased the Israeli extremist camp's legitimacy and credibility. Within a matter of years, the Likud Party, founded in 1973, emerged from extremist isolation to become a legitimate contender for power. Occupation of the West Bank renewed debate about the Jewish identity of the Israeli state and the extent of Israel's territorial claims. The call for a "Greater Israel" gave Likud an issue that cut across Israeli society, including traditional supporters of the Labor Party, and polarized Israeli society. Especially in the 1990s, the participation of Likud in Israeli politics complicated negotiations with Arab states over the exchange of land for peace.

Israel's close relations with the United States are secured by a formidable lobby that presses elected U.S. officials to favor Israel. Congressional support is important in determining financial and military aid policies, but on most matters of foreign policy Congress acts as, at best, a loose constraint on the president and the executive branch. More important than Congress and finance is the arithmetic of the electoral college. It is extremely difficult for any presidential candidate to win an election without at least one of three crucial states: New York, California, and Florida. The Jewish vote is potentially decisive in each, which is why some observers think of Israel as the fifty-first state of the Union. These domestic political factors operate within the context of underlying, shared values and a common identity. That context includes, specifically, a shared Judeo-Christian heritage, historical memories of the Holocaust, and common democratic institutions and values. Since 9/11, this foundation has been strengthened by the shared experience of being targeted by Arab militants. Before 9/11 and the U.S. occupation of Iraq, the systematic denial of basic rights to Palestinians living in the occupied territories weakened, for many Americans, Israel's identity as a Western state. Now that Americans share in the

108. Brands 1994, 19–30.
109. Spiegel 1985, 381.

experience of Arab terrorism, the alliance has become stronger. Since 1967, Americans have found in Israel the virtues on which Americans pride themselves—democracy, self-reliance, pragmatism, idealism, a frontier mentality, military toughness—and which many Americans now see being challenged by a common, implacable foe in the Middle East. Yet the forces that make for an ever closer alliance have prevented Israel from playing a central role in its region. In terms of culture, Israel is a foreign body in the Middle East. Because the United States has lacked suitable regional intermediaries it has dealt with recurrent problems in the Middle East as it has in the Americas, South Asia, and Africa—with a mixture of informal rule, patron-client relations, coercive diplomacy, and military intervention.

The intractable Middle East and the search for an activist response to the attacks of 9/11 have moved U.S. foreign policy in a radically new direction. Unilateralism and preemptive war, always latent in the repertoire of U.S. foreign policy, have been declared the country's national security doctrine. The war to remove Saddam Hussein from power in 2003 was planned and initiated without a compelling, immediate threat and without genuine and widespread international support. The Bush administration relied on faulty and possibly fabricated intelligence to convince Congress and the American people, though not many of its allies, to go to war.

One important reason for the war is, however, very much in line with a central argument of this book. A democratic and capitalist regional supporter might redefine the politics of the entire region. From this perspective it is not far-fetched to look to the revival of a democratic, secular Iraq as a magnet for reorienting the politics for the entire Middle East. Unlike Saudi Arabia, Iraq has the size and cultural weight to play the part, and unlike Israel it is culturally an insider not an outsider in the region. The creation of supporter states in Europe and Asia is one of the great accomplishments of U.S. foreign policy in the second half of the twentieth century—making Germany and Japan U.S. anchors in Europe and Asia. Why not, asked the Bush administration, duplicate this model in Iraq and for the entire Middle East? In answering that question with an unprovoked attack on Iraq, U.S. foreign policy overlooked the special circumstances that permitted regional supporter states to emerge elsewhere. Contemporary regionalism does not yield the optimistic conclusion that there exists an abundance of potential regional powers that can offer strong support for American purposes.

The historical analogy of Iraq in 2003 with Germany and Japan after 1945 is, in the words of Suzanne Nossel, "beguiling but false."[110] America then was different from America now. After 1945, America stood for liberalism, internationalism, multilateral cooperation, a serious commitment to human rights, and economic democratization that assigned the state a serious role—all principles that are anathema to the deep conservatism of the Bush administra-

110. Nossel 2004, 134.

tion.[111] Furthermore, American occupation of Germany and Japan did not aim at "nation" building.[112] Both countries had fully formed national identities, sophisticated though faulty political structures, powerful state apparatuses, and highly developed economies. What American intervention built were democratic governments within the context of existing state structures.[113] In sharp contrast to Iraq, American occupation policies were not perceived as loathed, successors to those of European imperial powers. After 1945 American occupation policies enjoyed broad legitimacy, internationally and in Germany and Japan; after the first phase of the Iraq war, worldwide anti-Americanism was running at levels not seen in decades, and many Iraqis wanted the United States to leave as soon as possible.

Just as America differed then and now, so did Germany and Japan then differ fundamentally from Iraq now. Citizens in both countries had been socialized to accept a strong state. Germany could draw on a liberal, federal, and democratic tradition; had lived under a brutal dictatorship for only a dozen years; was not on the verge of breaking up into different ethnic camps; was not fighting a guerrilla war against U.S. forces; and was under an occupation regime carefully prepared for three years prior to Germany's final surrender. These factors also operated in Japan, along with other radical differences compared to Iraq: an emperor symbolized continuity in an era of dramatic change; the basic structures of government were intact at both national and local levels; no mobs and gangs terrorized society in the crucial weeks of power transition; the society was cohesive despite a wide range of deeply held views; no expatriates hoped to seize power on the back of the military occupation; without oil, Japan did not invite war profiteering; economic reconstruction was pro-state and antiforeigner rather than, as in Iraq, antistate and proforeigner; and the American occupation consisted of only five thousand military and civilian personnel. The American effort to accomplish, with ample means, limited though extremely difficult tasks in Germany and Japan was haphazard and successful.[114] The American effort in Iraq, undertaken with limited means, aims at far more ambitious objectives, is equally extraordinary, and risks a political disaster of major proportions.

The American occupation of Germany and Japan yielded democracy under conditions that have little in common with Iraq. The occupations of Okinawa and South Korea did not yield democracy. There, the requirements of security and empire easily trumped the American desire to establish democracy, and the deployment of the U.S. military lasted more than half a century. They offer a more plausible though less appealing historical parallel for the U.S. occupation of Iraq. America's search for empire in the cities and deserts of Iraq is risky business. For there exists a world of difference between America's ge-

111. Dower 2003a.
112. Ferguson 2004, 70.
113. Khalidi 2004, 167–68.
114. Ferguson 2004, 69–78.

nius for running an imperium in a world of porous regions and America's occasional proclivity to succumb to the temptation of empire.

Predicaments and Possibilities of Imperium

American foreign policy is jeopardized when it neglects the dynamics of regions. Just as the American imperium is changing regions, they in turn are changing the imperium. Various processes to which Japan contributes help create "a civilization in the making" in Asia, and Europeanization is creating a novel kind of "civilian" polity in Europe.[115] Such processes point to the need to focus attention on two-way processes of change. Viewing the world in terms of binary distinctions—us-them, rational-irrational, modern-traditional, East-West—is wrongheaded. It evokes regions and the people that inhabit them as neatly bordered units. This way of thinking produces little more than a clash of ignorance.[116] Current world politics is both more complicated and more interesting.

At times it is also less novel than we might want to believe. For almost a decade after the onset of the cold war the United States was committed to multilateralism in Europe. But it also tried to reorganize the international system unilaterally by eliminating the Soviet Union and constructing a global order that would include a reformed Eastern bloc. Gregory Mitrovich has reminded us that both Democratic and Republican administrations considered this enormous task to be eminently feasible.[117] U.S. foreign policy was considerably more assertive than we now remember. Through the aggressive application of psychological warfare, American policy aimed at rolling back the Soviet Union from Eastern Europe and eliminating Communist control within the Soviet Union. U.S. military superiority would deter the Soviet Union from responding militarily to American provocations. A multilateral system was to garner international support, assure the victory of American interests and values, and avoid the devastations of World War III. Rollback abroad and McCarthyism at home made Reinhold Niebuhr reflect on the irony of the American predicament: "If virtue becomes vice through some hidden defect in the virtue; if strength becomes weakness because of the vanity to which strength may prompt the mighty man or nation; if security is transmuted into insecurity because too much reliance is placed upon it; if wisdom becomes folly because it does not know its own limits—in all such cases the situation is ironic." In ironic situations, Niebuhr argued, the person involved bears some responsibility that is related to an unconscious weakness. An ironic situation must be resolved once actors become aware of it, either through contrition or through "a desperate accentuation of the vanities to the point were irony turns into pure evil."[118]

115. Yamazaki 1996.
116. Said 2001. Thornton 2002. Clifford 1988.
117. Mitrovich 2000, 1–13.
118. Niebuhr 1954, viii.

There exists no general threat to the state system as the basic organizing principle of international politics. Everywhere, states retain at least minimal sovereignty. Yet internationalization and globalization are embedding states and other actors everywhere in regions and are having a profound impact on the agenda of world politics. This is one step in the direction that Hedley Bull speculatively called the "neo-Medievalism"[119] of contemporary international politics: a move, more or less halting in different regional settings, toward multiple, nested centers of collective authority and identity. American power and purpose interact with global and international processes to create that world of regions.

The American imperium is both an actor and a system. This dual face was exemplified by the regional cast of American foreign policy at the onset of the cold war and by an ongoing process of two-way Americanization. The American imperium thus helps to shape the politics of all of the world's major regions. At the same time that imperium is a system that no longer dictates regional outcomes (with the possible exception of Central America). Power thus inheres both in America and in a world of regions that it must engage.

Debates over the desirable course of U.S. foreign policy either celebrate or deplore the unilateral assertion of U.S. military power that marked the reaction of the Bush administration to the September 11 attacks. They view the world after 9/11 either as confirming the unstoppable ascent of American power or as ending an American era.[120] These debates remind us that U.S. power is defined by its formidable capabilities as well as by the consent and cooperation it must elicit from others. The main failings of the foreign policy of the Bush administration are that it undermines the long-term basis of U.S. power through its reckless fiscal policy. Furthermore, its unilateralism and high-handedness diminishes the consent and cooperation that remains indispensable to America's imperium. Militarist and unilateral impulses of the New Rome risk sucking America into a futile search for stability. The wall (*limes*) that the Roman Empire built on its northern frontier to keep out the Germanic tribes did not limit Rome's appetite for order beyond the wall. The pacification of unstable borderlands all over the world is an elusive and corrosive goal. Throughout history, imperial overexpansion has exacted an enormous price. There is little reason to believe that it might not do so once more.

U.S. governments make important choices about the balance between territorial and nonterritorial powers, and the unilateral and multilateral means by which that power is deployed. The American imperium often reflects contradictory impulses. The question of how to strike a proper balance has often elicited intense partisan disagreements. But the political center was held comfortably by a bipartisan coalition of liberal internationalists and pragmatic realists. The proper balance between hard and soft power translated into smart

---

119. Bull 1977, 254–55.
120. Kagan 2003. Kupchan 2002.

power: America's voice was not too loud, and its ears were not too small; and when occasionally it brandished a big stick, it did so for the most part with support from core regional powers.

Since the September 11 attacks, an unusual coalition has come together inside the Bush administration, uniting assertive nationalists with democratic imperialists, to wield military power unilaterally. Enticed by America's unrivalled military might and dismayed by the prospect of a novel vulnerability (novel, at least, to Americans), since 9/11 U.S. policy has moved with great zeal to wager two bets simultaneously: that military power, unilaterally and preemptively exercised, can guarantee American security in a changing world of regions; and that American ideas and ideals are readily exportable to all regions of the world. Gone is a foreign policy that adorns the rhetoric of transformation with the practice of accommodation. Half-baked hegemony has been superseded by the aspiration to bring about fundamental change by force of the sword and the inherent attraction of American democracy. In this sea change, pessimistic realism joins optimistic idealism in the conviction that America will make the world a more secure and better place.

This drastic change in policy runs counter to the dynamics of a world of regions. That world is too complex and contains too many elements of potential resistance. Furthermore, despite the enormous political success the United States enjoyed in reconstructing Germany and Japan, twentieth-century history records only very limited accomplishments elsewhere.[121] Finally, in sharp contrast to nineteenth-century Britain, the American electorate evidently lacks the appetite to spend a lifetime of service in distant countries serving "noble causes"—not to speak of billions of dollars and thousands of body bags. Americans, writes Niall Ferguson, "lack the imperial cast of mind. They would rather consume than conquer."[122] Within a year of announcing its new security doctrine in September 2002, the Bush administration was forced, with evident reluctance, to start taking account of the international and domestic actors who had resisted its shift in grand strategy.

A lopsided policy that relies on the exercise of territorial control through military conquest, unilateralism, and preemption risks converting the American imperium, in the words of British historian Michael Mann, into a "military giant, a back-seat economic driver, a political schizophrenic and an ideological phantom."[123] Such a policy is profoundly misguided. It overlooks the central characteristic of the American imperium: the scope and weight of its nonterritorial power. The war to defend the imperium is also a war to preserve and extend the strategy of openness.[124] It is not American dictates to the world that are its most important and enduring source of power. It is the American ca-

---

121. Carothers 1999, 171, 181–82, 250–51, 308, 332.
122. Ferguson 2004, 29; 2002. The one-sidedness and limitations of Ferguson's arguments are clinically dissected by Chibber 2005.
123. Mann 2003, 13.
124. Bacevich 2002, 225–44.

pacity to generate and tolerate diversity in a loose but shared sense of moral order.

A world of porous regions is what we now see. Total defeat in war was the precondition for Japan's and Germany's belated conversion to the American way of informal, liberal rule. Unlike Britain, they have been regional intermediaries that felt neither too close to the United States nor too distant from their regional neighbors. Germany and Japan could not remember a glorious imperialist past, nor recall superpower status at the end of World War II, nor could they draw on a historically deep "special relationship" with the United States.[125] And their total military defeat in World War II undermined the self-confidence that sustains Britain's obsession with its "myth of difference" from Europe in the era of its national decline.[126] Germany and Japan, in brief, are core regional states that have supported the purpose and power of the United States. In the second half of the twentieth century, that conversion gave porous regionalism its dual political significance in the American imperium: as a buffer against an overweening United States when its power seemed to rise too fast, and as a support for an overtaxed United States when its power appeared to decline too much. This unending recalibration in military capabilities, economic and cultural ties, and political legitimacy holds forth the promise for durable links between Asia, Europe, and the American imperium.

Incessant recalibration requires a nuanced understanding of world politics. Yet too often we yield to slogans or overly simple cognitive maps—the democratic peace, the clash of civilizations, the end of history, the end of sovereignty, the new anarchy.[127] This urge for simplification in the face of complexity, though understandable, is misguided. It is understandable because all of us look for a compass that gives a clear direction. It is misguided because there exists no single point in world politics that fixes the direction of the needle. Pretending otherwise risks sinking the ship on its maiden voyage. In this book I have identified two markers, imperium and regions, and tracked the various currents that flow between them. Oscillating between both, the compass needle does not create blurred vision leading to catastrophe. It defines the width of the channel through which we can steer a safe passage.

Prediction is a notoriously risky business in the study of world politics. In two foundational studies of international relations, Kenneth Waltz bet that the Soviet Union would last for a century, and Robert Keohane predicted the disappearance of U.S. hegemony during our lifetime.[128] A dream for some and a nightmare for others, America as the New Rome is an improbable prospect. It is true, however, that in a world of regions, the New World is remaking the old world of Europe and the ancient world of Asia. But so are those old worlds, in their own ways, remaking the New. American power is broad, but it lacks depth.

125. Fox 1944. Waltz 1967.
126. Medrano 2003, 214.
127. Fry and O'Hagan 2000.
128. Waltz 1979, 95. Keohane 1984, 244.

It is spectacular, but it is insufficient. The American imperium will fail if it tries to impose its partial vision of order on an infinitely complex and unruly world. It can succeed only, in Walt Whitman's celebrated phrase, as the "world nation"—as the inclusive center of the global and international currents that are shaping a diverse world of regions.

BIBLIOGRAPHY

Abdelal, Rawi. 1998. "The Politics of Monetary Leadership and Followership: Stability in the European Monetary System since the Currency Crisis of 1992." *Political Studies* 46, no. 2: 236–59.

Acharya, Amitav. 1990. "A Survey of Military Cooperation among the ASEAN States: Bilateralism or Alliance?" *Occasional Paper,* No. 14. Toronto: Centre for International and Strategic Studies.

Acheson, Dean. 1949. "Statement on the North Atlantic Treaty." *Department of State Bulletin* 20, no. 508: 385.

——. 1969. *Present at the Creation: My Years at the State Department.* New York: W. W. Norton.

Adebajo, Adekeye. 2002. *Building Peace in West Africa: Liberia, Sierra Leone, and Guinea-Bissau.* Boulder: Lynne Rienner.

Aggarwal, Vinod. K. 1993. "Building International Institutions in Asia-Pacific." *Asian Survey* 32, no. 11 (November): 1029–42.

Akamtsu, Kaname. 1961. "A Theory of Unbalanced Growth in the World Economy." *Weltwirtschaftliches Archiv* 86, no. 2: 196–217.

Albert, Michel. 1993. *Capitalism vs. Capitalism: How America's Obsession with Individual Achievement and Short-Term Profit Has Led It to the Brink of Collapse.* New York: Four Walls Eight Windows.

Alexander, Suzanne. 1991. "Japanese Firms Embark on a Program of Lavish Giving to American Charities." *Wall Street Journal* (May 23): B1.

Allen, David. 2000. "Cohesion and the Structural Funds." In Helen Wallace and William Wallace, eds., *Policy-Making in the European Union,* 4th ed., pp. 243–66. Oxford: Oxford University Press.

Allison, Anne. 2002. "The Cultural Politics of Pokemon Capitalism." Paper presented at the annual meeting of the Association for Asian Studies, Washington, D.C., April 4–7.

Alter, Karen. 1996. "The European Court's Political Power." *West European Politics* 19, no. 3: 458–87.

———. 1998a. "Explaining National Court Acceptance of European Court Jurisprudence: A Critical Evaluation of Theories of Legal Integration." In Anne-Marie Slaughter, Alec Stone Sweet, and J. H. H. Weiler, eds., *The European Court and National Courts—Doctrine and Jurisprudence*, pp. 227–52. Oxford: Oxford University Press.

———. 1998b. "Who Are the Masters of the Treaty? European Governments and the European Court of Justice." *International Organization* 52, no. 1 (Winter): 121–48.

Anderson, Jeffrey J. 1990. "Skeptical Reflections on a Europe of Regions: Britain, Germany, and the ERDF." *Journal of Public Policy* 10: 417–47.

Anderson, Malcolm. 1989. *Policing the World: Interpol and the Politics of International Police Co-operation*. Oxford: Oxford University Press.

Anderson, Malcolm, et al. 1995. *Policing the European Union*. Oxford: Clarendon.

Andreas, Peter. 2003. "A Tale of Two Borders: The US-Canada and US-Mexico Lines after 9–11." In Peter Andreas and Thomas J. Biersteker, eds., *The Rebordering of North America: Integration and Exclusion in a New Security Context*, pp. 1–23. New York: Routledge.

Androutsopoulos, Jannis, and Arno Scholz. 1999. "On the Recontextualization of Hip-Hop in European Speech Communities: A Contrastive Analysis of Rap Lyrics." Paper presented at the Workshop on Americanization and Popular Culture in Europe, Centro S. Franscini, Monte Verità, Ascona, Switzerland, November 10–14.

Aoki, Masahiko. 1988. *Information, Incentives, and Bargaining in the Japanese Economy*. Cambridge: Cambridge University Press.

Arase, David. 1995. *Buying Power: The Political Economy of Japan's Foreign Aid*. Boulder: Lynne Rienner.

Armstrong, Kenneth A. 1998. "Legal Integration: Theorizing the Legal Dimension of European Integration." *Journal of Common Market Studies* 36, no. 2 (June): 155–74.

Aron, Raymond. 1974. *The Imperial Republic: The United States and the World, 1945–1973*. Englewood Cliffs, N.J.: Prentice-Hall.

Arrighi, Giovanni. 1997. "Globalization and Capital Accumulation." Paper presented at the conference on States and Sovereignty in the World Economy, University of California, Irvine, February 21–23.

Ash, Timothy Garton. 1994. "Journey to the Post-communist East." *New York Review of Books* (June 23): 13–20.

Auswärtiges Amt. 2000. *Forum: Zukunft der Auswärtigen Kulturpolitik*. Berlin (July 4).

Axtmann, Roland. 2003. "State Formation and Supranationalism in Europe: The Case of the Holy Roman Empire of the German Nation." In Mabel Berezin and Martin Schain, eds., *Europe without Borders: Remapping Territory, Citizenship, and Identity in a Transnational Age*, pp. 118–39. Baltimore: Johns Hopkins University Press.

Ayoob, Mohammed. 1999. "From Regional System to Regional Society: Exploring Key Variables in the Construction of Regional Order." *Australian Journal of International Affairs* 53, no. 3: 247–60.

Bacevich, Andrew J. 2002. *American Empire: The Realities and Consequences of U.S. Diplomacy*. Cambridge: Harvard University Press.

Bahgat, Gawdat. 2001. "Managing Dependence: American-Saudi Oil Relations." *Arab Studies Quarterly* 23, no. 1: 1–14.

Baklanoff, Eric N. 1978. *The Economic Transformation of Spain and Portugal*. New York: Praeger.

Barkenbus, Jack. 2001. "APEC and the Environment: Civil Society in an Age of Globalization." *AsiaPacific* 51 (March): 1–8.

Barnes, Sandra T. 2004. "Global Flows: Terror, Oil and Strategic Philanthropy." Presidential Address to the African Studies Association, New Orleans, November 12.

Barnet, Richard J., and John Cavanagh. 1994. *Global Dreams: Imperial Corporations and the New World Order.* New York: Simon and Schuster.

Barnett, Michael N. 1996. "Identity and Alliances in the Middle East." In Peter J. Katzenstein, ed., *The Culture of National Security: Norms and Identity in World Politics,* pp. 400–47. New York: Columbia University Press.

Bates, Robert H. 1996. "Letter from the President: Area Studies and the Discipline." *APSA-CP: Newsletter of the APSA Organized Section on Comparative Politics* 7, no. 1: 1–2.

Bates, Robert H. 1997. "Area Studies and the Discipline: A Useful Controversy?" *PS: Political Science and Politics* 30, no. 2 (June): 166–69.

Bates, Robert H., et al. 1998. *Analytic Narratives.* Princeton: Princeton University Press.

Beeson, Mark, and Kanishka Jayasuriya. 1998. "The Political Rationalities of Regionalism: APEC and the EU in Comparative Perspective." *Pacific Review* 11, no. 3: 311–36.

Beisheim, Marianne, Sabine Dreher, Gregor Walter, Bernhard Zangl, and Michael Zürn. 1999. *Im Zeitalter der Globalisierung? Thesen und Daten zur gesellschaftlichen und politischen Denationalisierung.* Baden-Baden: Nomos.

Benyon, John, J. L. Turnbull, A. Willis, R. Woodward, and A. Beck. 1993. *Police Cooperation in Europe.* Leicester: University of Leicester, Centre for the Study of Public Order.

Benyon, John, J. L. Turnbull, A. Willis, and R. Woodward. 1994. "Understanding Police Cooperation in Europe: Setting a Framework for Analysis." In M. Anderson and M. Den Boer, eds., *Policing across National Boundaries,* pp. 46–65. London: Pinter.

Berger, Suzanne, and Richard K. Lester, eds. 1997. *Made by Hong Kong.* Hong Kong: Oxford University Press.

Bergner, Jeffrey T. 1991. *The New Superpowers: Germany, Japan, the U.S., and the New World Order.* New York: St. Martin's.

Bernard, Mitchell. 1996. "Regions in the Global Political Economy: Beyond the Local-Global Divide in the Formation of the Eastern Asian Region." *New Political Economy* 1, no. 3: 335–53.

Bernier, Ivan, and Martin Roy. 1999. "NAFTA and Mercosur: Two Competing Models?" In Gordon Mace, Louis Bélanger, et al., *The Americas in Transition: The Contours of Regionalism,* pp. 69–91. Boulder: Lynne Rienner.

Bertlein, Reihold F. 1989. "Europäischer Film und Kulturelle Eye-Dentity." In Kulturpolitsche Gesellschaft, ed., *Kultur-Markt Europa: Jahrbuch für Europäische Kulturpolitik,* pp. 129–39. Cologne: Volksblatt Verlag.

Bhagwati, Jagdish. 1992. "Regionalism versus Multilateralism." *World Economy* 15, no. 5 (September): 535–55.

Biddle, Sheila. 2002. *Internationalization: Rhetoric or Reality?* ACLS Occasional Paper No. 56. New York: American Council of Learned Societies.

Bigo, Didier. 1996. *Polices en Réseaux: L'Expérience en Européenne.* Paris: Presses de la Fondation Nationale des Sciences Politiques.

Bjarnar, Ove, and Matthias Kipping. 1998. "The Marshall Plan and the Transfer of US

Management Models to Europe: An Introductory Framework." In Matthias Kipping and Ove Bjarnar, eds., *The Americanization of European Business: The Marshall Plan and the Transfer of US Management Models,* pp. 1–17. London: Routledge.

Block, Fred. 1977. *The Origins of International Economic Disorder.* Berkeley: University of California Press.

Bolton, Herbert E. 1933. "The Epic of Greater America." *American Historical Review* 38 (April): 448–74.

Borneman, John, and Nick Fowler. 1997. "Europeanization." *Annual Review of Anthropology* 26: 487–514.

Borrus, Michael. 1994. "MNC Production Networks and East Asian Integration: A Research Note." Paper presented to the Berkeley Roundtable on the International Economy, University of California, Berkeley.

———. 1997. "Left for Dead: Asian Production Networks and the Revival of U.S. Electronics." In Barry Naughton, ed., *The China Circle: Economics and Electronics in the PRC, Taiwan, and Hong Kong,* pp. 139–63. Washington, D.C.: Brookings Institution.

Borrus, Michael, Dieter Ernst, and Stephan Haggard. 2000. "Introduction: Cross-Border Production Networks and the Industrial Integration of the Asia-Pacific Region." In M. Borrus, D. Ernst, and S. Haggard, eds., *International Production Networks in Asia: Rivalry or Riches?,* pp. 1–30. London: Routledge.

Borrus, Michael, and John Zysman. 1997. "Globalization with Borders: The Rise of Wintelism as the Future of Global Competition." *Industry and Innovation* 4, no. 2 (December): 141–66.

Borstelmann, Thomas. 1999. "Jim Crow's Coming Out: Race Relations and American Foreign Policy in the Truman Years." *Presidential Studies Quarterly* 29, no. 3: 549–69.

Bow, Brian. 2003. "The Missing Link: Transgovernmental Networks, Bargaining Norms, and Issue-Linkage in US-Canada Relations." PhD diss., Cornell University.

Boyer, Robert. 1996. "The Convergence Hypothesis Revisited: Globalization but Still the Century of Nations?" In Suzanne Berger and Ronald Dore, eds., *National Diversity and Global Capitalism,* pp. 29–59. Ithaca: Cornell University Press.

———. 2003. "European and Asian Integration Processes Compared." *CEPREMAP Working Paper No. 0302.* Paris: Centre d'Etudes Prospective d'Economie Mathématique Appliquées à la Planification.

Boyer, Robert, E. Charron, U. Jürgens, and S. Tolliday. 1998. *Between Imitation and Innovation: The Transfer and Hybridization of Productive Models in the International Automobile Industry.* Oxford: Oxford University Press.

Bracken, Paul. 2000. "The Second Nuclear Age." *Foreign Affairs* 19, no. 1: 147–56.

Bradsher, Keith. 2004. "Chinese Provinces Form Regional Economic Bloc." *New York Times* (June 2): W1, W7.

Brands, H. W. 1994. *Into the Labyrinth: The United States and the Middle East, 1945–1993.* New York: McGraw-Hill.

Bredow, Wilfried von. 1996. "Bilaterale Beziehungen im Netzwerk Regionaler und Globaler Interdependenz." In Karl Kaiser and Joachim Krause, eds., *Deutschlands neue Aussenpolitik,* pp. 109–115. Munich: R. Oldenbourg.

Breslin, Shaun, and Richard Higgott. 2002. "Regions in Comparative Perspective." In Shaun Breslin et al., eds., *New Regionalisms in the Global Political Economy,* pp. 1–19. New York: Routledge.

Brick, Andrew B. 1992. "The Emergence of Greater China: The Diaspora Ascendant." *The Heritage Lectures* No. 411. Washington, D.C.: The Heritage Foundation.

Bright, Charles, and Michael Geyer. 1987. "For a Unified History of the World in the Twentieth Century." *Radical History Review* 39: 69–91.

Broad, Robin. 1999. "Footloose Financial Flows in the 1990s: Where, What, Why, and How to Tame Them?" *International Studies* 1, no. 1 (Spring): 114–18.

Broad, William J. 2004. "U.S. Is Losing Its Dominance in the Sciences." *New York Times* (May 3): A1, A19.

Brock, Lothar, and Mathias Albert. 1995. "Entgrenzung der Staatenwelt: Zur Analyse weltgesellschaftlicher Entwicklungstendenzen." *Zeitschrift für Internationale Beziehungen* 2 (December): 259–85.

Brodie, Fawn M. 1975. *Thomas Jefferson: An Intimate History*. New York: Bantam.

Brooks, Stephen G. 2005. *Producing Security: Multinational Corporations, Globalization, and the Changing Calculus of Conflict*. Princeton: Princeton University Press.

Brzezinski, Zbigniew. 1997. *The Grand Chessboard: American Primacy and Its Geostrategic Imperatives*. New York: Basic Books.

Bull, Hedley. 1977. *The Anarchical Society: A Study of Order in World Politics*. New York: Columbia University Press.

Bumiller, Elisabeth. 2002. "Bush Affirms U.S. Role in Asia in New 'Pacific Century.'" *New York Times* (February 19): A8.

Bundesministerium des Innern. 1990. *Kultur-Staat—Wirtschaft, Zukunftsperspektiven der Kulturpolitik: Dokumentation über das Symposium des Bundesministers des Innern am 6. Dezember im Wissenschaftszentrum in Bonn*. Stuttgart: Kohlhammer.

Burress, Charles. 1997. "San Francisco's Manga Man." *San Francisco Chronicle* (February 2).

Buruma, Ian. 1994. *The Wages of Guilt: Memories of War in Germany and Japan*. New York: Farrar, Straus, and Giroux.

Busch, Heiner. 1995. *Grenzenlose Polizei? Neue Grenzen und polizeiliche Zusammenarbeit in Europa*. Münster: Westfälisches Dampfboot.

Buzan, Barry, and Ole Wæver. 2003. *Regions and Powers: The Structure of International Security*. Cambridge: Cambridge University Press.

Camilleri, Joseph A. 2000. *States, Markets, and Civil Society in Asia Pacific: The Political Economy of the Asia-Pacific Region*. Vol. 1. Northampton, Mass.: Edward Elgar.

Capie, David H., Paul M. Evans, and Akiko Fukushima. 1998. "Speaking Asian Pacific Security: A Lexicon of English Terms with Chinese and Japanese Translations and a Note on the Japanese Translation," *Working Paper*. Toronto: University of Toronto–York University Joint Centre for Asia Pacific Studies.

Carnegie Endowment Study Group. 1994. *Defining a Pacific Community*. New York: Carnegie Endowment for International Peace.

Carothers, Thomas. 1999. *Aiding Democracy Abroad: The Learning Curve*. Washington, D.C.: Carnegie Endowment for International Peace.

Chase, Kerry A. 2003. "Economic Interests and Regional Trading Arrangements." *International Organization* 57, no. 1 (Winter): 137–74.

———. 2005. *Trading Blocs: States, Firms, and Regions in the World Economy*. Ann Arbor: University of Michigan Press.

Checkel, Jeffrey. Forthcoming. "International Institutions and Socialization in Europe: Introduction and Framework." *International Organization*.

Chibber, Vivek. 2005. "The Good Empire: Should We Pick Up Where the British Left Off?" *Boston Review* (February/March): 30–34.

Choate, Pat. 1990. *Agents of Influence: How Japan's Lobbyists in the United States Manipulate America's Political and Economic System.* New York: Knopf.

Christensen, Thomas J. 1999. "China, the U.S.-Japan Alliance, and the Security Dilemma in East Asia." *International Security* 23, no. 4 (Spring): 49–80.

Chung, Daekyun. 1997. "Nationalization and Naturalization: Practice and Process of the Korean Incorporation of Japanese Culture." *Journal of Pacific Asia* 4: 47–64.

Clifford, James. 1988. *The Predicament of Culture: Twentieth Century Ethnography, Literature, and Art.* Cambridge: Harvard University Press.

Clover, Charles. 1999. "Dreams of the Eurasian Heartland: The Reemergence of Geopolitics." *Foreign Affairs* 78, no. 2 (March–April): 9–13.

Cohen, Benjamin J. 1998. *The Geography of Money.* Ithaca: Cornell University Press.

Cohen, Joshua, and Charles F. Sabel. 2003. "Sovereignty and Solidarity: EU and US." In Jonathan Zeitlin and David M. Trubek, eds., *Governing Work and Welfare in a New Economy: European and American Experiments,* pp. 345–75. Oxford: Oxford University Press.

Conant, Lisa. 2002. *Justice Contained: Law and Politics in the European Union.* Ithaca: Cornell University Press.

Cowen, Tyler. 2002. *Creative Destruction: How Globalization Is Changing the World's Cultures.* Princeton: Princeton University Press.

Crone, Donald. 1993. "Does Hegemony Matter? The Reorganization of the Pacific Political Economy." *World Politics* 45, no. 4 (July): 501–25.

Cumings, Bruce. 1990. *The Origins of the Korean War.* Vol. 2, *The Roaring of the Cataract, 1947–1950.* Princeton: Princeton University Press.

——. 1993. "Rimspeak; or, The Discourse of the 'Pacific Rim.'" In Arif Dirlik, ed., *What Is in a Rim? Critical Perspectives on the Pacific Region Idea,* pp. 29–47. Boulder: Westview.

——. 2000. "The American Ascendancy: Imposing a New World Order." *The Nation* 270, no. 18 (May 8): 13–20.

Dalton, Russell J., and Richard C. Eichenberg. 1998. "Citizen Support for Policy Integration." In Wayne Sandholtz and Alec Stone Sweet, eds., *European Integration and Supranational Governance,* pp. 250–82. Oxford: Oxford University Press.

Dehesa, Guillermo de la, and Paul Krugman. 1992. "EMU and the Regions." In *Group of Thirty's Occasional Papers,* pp. 1–59. Washington, D.C.: Group of Thirty.

Deng, Yong. 1997. "Chinese Relations with Japan: Implications for Asia-Pacific Regionalism." *Pacific Affairs* 70, no. 3 (Fall): 373–91.

Deudney, Daniel H. 1995. "The Philadelphia System: Sovereignty, Arms Control, and Balance of Power in the American States-Union, Circa 1787–1861." *International Organization* 49, no. 2 (Spring): 191–228.

Deutsch, Karl W. 1944. "Medieval Unity and the Economic Conditions for an International Civilization." *Canadian Journal of Economics and Political Science* 10, no. 1 (February): 18–35.

——. 1981. "On Nationalism, World Regions, and the Nature of the West." In Per Torsvik, ed., *Mobilization, Center-Periphery Structures, and Nation-Building: A Volume in Commemoration of Stein Rokkan,* pp. 51–93. Bergen: Universitetsforlaget.

Deutsch, Karl W., et al. 1957. *Political Community and the North Atlantic Area.* Princeton: Princeton University Press.

Devlin, Robert, Antoni Estevadeordal, and Luis Jorge Garay. 2000. "Some Economic and Strategic Issues in the Face of the Emerging FTAA." In Jorge I. Dominguez, ed., *The Future of Inter-American Relations,* 153–96. New York: Routledge.

Dirke, Sabine von. 1989. "A New German Wave: An Analysis of the Development of German Rock Music." *German Politics and Society* 18 (Fall): 64–81.

Dirlik, Arif. 1993a. "Introducing the Pacific." In A. Dirlik, ed., *What Is in a Rim? Critical Perspectives on the Pacific Region Idea,* pp. 3–11. Boulder: Westview.

———. 1993b. "The Asia-Pacific in Asian-American Perspective." In A. Dirlik, ed., *What Is in a Rim? Critical Perspectives on the Pacific Region Idea,* pp. 305–29. Boulder: Westview.

Dittmer, Lowell. 2000. "Conclusion: Asian Informal Politics in Comparative Perspective." In Lowell Dittmer, Haruhiro Fukui, and Peter N. S. Lee, eds., *Informal Politics in East Asia,* pp. 290–308. Cambridge: Cambridge University Press.

Djelic, Marie-Laure. 1998. *Exporting the American Model: The Post-War Transformation of European Business.* Oxford: Oxford University Press.

Dobson, Wendy. 1997a. "Crossing Borders: Multinationals in East Asia." In W. Dobson and C. S. Yue, eds., *Multinationals and East Asian Integration,* pp. 3–27. Ottawa and Singapore: International Development Centre and Institute of Southeast Asian Studies.

———. 1997b. "East Asian Integration: Synergies between Firm Strategies and Government Policies." In W. Dobson and C. S. Yue, eds., *Multinationals and East Asian Integration,* pp. 223–47. Ottawa and Singapore: International Development Centre and Institute of Southeast Asian Studies.

Dörrenbächer, Christoph. 1999. *Vom Hoflieferanten zum Global Player: Unternehmensreorganisation und nationale Politik in der Welttelekommunikationsindustrie.* Berlin: Edition Sigma, Rainer Bohn Verlag.

Dörrenbächer, C., I. Scheike, and M. Wortmann. 1996. *Die Top 500 Deutschen Tochter- und Beteiligungsgesellschaften in den Visegrad-Ländern.* Berlin: FAST.

Donges, Jürgen B., et al. 1982. *The Second Enlargement of the European Community: Adjustment Requirements and Challenges for Policy Reform.* Tübingen: J. C. B. Mohr (Paul Siebeck).

Donnelly, Jack. 1986. "International Human Rights: A Regime Analysis." *International Organization* 40, no. 3 (Summer): 599–642.

Dore, Ronald. 2000. *Stock Market Capitalism: Welfare Capitalism—Japan and Germany versus the Anglo-Saxons.* New York: Oxford University Press.

Doremus, Paul N., William W. Keller, Louis W. Pauly, and Simon Reich. 1998. *The Myth of the Global Corporation.* Princeton: Princeton University Press.

Dower, John. 1988. "Psychological Aspects of Contemporary U.S.-Japan Relations." Unpublished paper.

———. 2003a. "A Warning from History: Don't Expect Democracy in Iraq." *Boston Review* (February–March): 6–8.

Drifte, Reinhard. 1996. *Japan's Foreign Policy in the 1990s: From Economic Superpower to What Power?* New York: St. Martin's.

Dueck, Colin. 2004. "New Perspectives on American Grand Strategy." *International Security* 28, no. 4 (Spring): 197–216.

Düwell, Kurt. 1981. "Die Gründung der Kulturpolitischen Abteilung im Auswärtigen Amt 1919/20 als Neuansatz." In Kurt Düwell and Werner Link, eds., *Deutsche Auswärtige Kulturpolitik seit 1871,* pp. 46–61. Cologne: Böhlau.

Duffield, John. 2003. "Asia-Pacific Security Institutions in Comparative Perspective." In G. John Ikenberry and Michael Mastanduno, eds., *International Relations Theory and the Asia Pacific,* pp. 243–70. New York: Columbia University Press.

Dulles, John Foster. 1952. "Security in the Pacific." *Foreign Affairs* 30, no. 2 (January): 175–87.

Dupont, Alan. 1996. "Is Three an 'Asian Way'?" *Survival* 38, no. 2: 13–33.

———. 1999. "Transnational Crime, Drugs, and Security in East Asia." *Asian Survey* 39, no. 3 (May–June): 433–55.

———. 2001. *East Asia Imperiled: Transnational Challenges to Security.* Cambridge: Cambridge University Press.

Economist, The. 1995. "Japan and Asia: A Question of Balance." (April 22): 21–22.

———. 1997a. "The EU Budget: Just Small Change?" (October 18): 51–52.

———. 1997b. "A Survey of Business in Eastern Europe." (November 22): 1–22.

———. 2001a. "The Cutting Edge." (February 24): 80.

———. 2001b. "Geography and the Net: Putting It in Its Place." (August 11): 17–20.

Eichengreen, Barry. 1997. "Comment." In Stanley Black, ed., *Europe's Economy Looks East: Implications for Germany and the European Union,* pp. 342–45. New York: Cambridge University Press.

Eichengreen, Barry, and Richard Kohl. 1997. "The State and the External Sector in Eastern Europe: Implications for Foreign Investment and Outward-Processing Trade." Paper presented at the conference "Will There Be a Unified European Economy?" Vienna, June 5–6.

Eisenhower, Dwight D. 1963. *The White House Years: Mandate For Change, 1953–1965.* Garden City, N.Y.: Doubleday and Company.

Eisenstadt, Shmuel N. 2000a. "Multiple Modernities." *Dædalus* 129, no. 1 (Winter): 1–29.

———. 2000b. *Die Vielfalt der Moderne.* Weilerswist: Velbrück Wissenschaft.

Elger, Tony, and Chris Smith. 1994a. "Introduction." In T. Elger and C. Smith, eds., *Global Japanization? The Transnational Transformation of the Labour Process,* pp. 1–30. London: Routledge.

———. 1994b. "Global Japanization? Convergence and Competition in the Organization of the Labour Process." In T. Elger and C. Smith, eds., *Global Japanization? The Transnational Transformation of the Labour Process,* pp. 31–59. London: Routledge.

Ellis, Stephen. 1999. *The Mask of Anarchy: The Destruction of Liberia and the Religious Dimension of an African Civil War.* New York: New York University Press.

Elster, Jon. 2000. "Rational Choice History: A Case of Excessive Ambition." *American Political Science Review* 94, no. 3 (September): 685–95.

Emmerson, Donald K. 1993. "Part Two: Scenarios and Regimes." *NBR Analysis* 4, no. 2 (July): 18–35.

Encarnation, Dennis J. 1999. "Introduction: Japanese Multinationals in Asia." In D. J. Encarnation, ed., *Japanese Multinationals in Asia: Regional Operations in Comparative Perspective,* pp. 3–13. New York: Oxford University Press.

Enos, J. L., and W. H. Park. 1987. *The Adoption and Diffusion of Imported Technology: The Case of Korea.* London: Croom Helm.

Epstein, Joshua M. 1987. *Strategy and Force Planning: The Case of the Persian Gulf.* Washington, D.C.: Brookings Institution.

Ermarth, Michael. 1997. "'Amerikanisierung' und deutsche Kulturkritik 1945–65."

In K. Jarausch and H. Siegrist, eds., *Amerikanisierung und Sowjetisierung in Deutschland 1945–1970*, pp. 315–34. Frankfurt: Campus.

Ernst, Dieter. 1997. "Partners for the China Circle? The East Asian Production Networks of Japanese Electronic Firms." In B. Naughton, ed., *The China Circle: Economics and Electronics in the PRC, Taiwan, and Hong Kong*, pp. 210–53. Washington, D.C.: Brookings Institution.

——. 2001. "The Internet's Effect on Business Organization: Bane or Boon for Developing Asia?" *AsiaPacific Issues* 48 (January).

Ernst, Dieter, and David O'Connor. 1989. *Technology and Global Competition: The Challenge for Newly Industrialising Economies.* Paris: Organisation for Economic Co-operation and Development.

Esman, Milton. 1986. "The Chinese Diaspora in Southeast Asia." In Gabriel Sheffer, ed., *Modern Diasporas in International Politics*, pp. 130–63. New York: St. Martin's.

European Commission. 1996. *Top Decision Makers Survey, Summary Report: Directorate-General X, Survey Research Unit.* Brussels: European Commission.

——. 2000a. *Panorama of European Business 1999.* Luxembourg: European Commission.

——. 2000b. *Standard Eurobarometer: Public Opinion in the European Union.* No. 52. Brussels: European Commission.

——. 2001. *Europeans and Languages: A Eurobarometer Special Survey.* http://europa.eu .int/comm/dgs/education_culture/index_en/htm.

Evans, Paul. 2005. "Between Regionalism and Regionalization: Policy Networks and the Nascent East Asian Institutional Identity." In T. J. Pempel, ed., *Remapping East Asia: The Construction of a Region*, pp. 195–215. Ithaca: Cornell University Press.

Evers, Hans-Dieter, and Markus Kaiser. 2001. "Two Continents, One Area: Eurasia." In Peter W. Preston and Julie Gilson, eds., *The European Union and East Asia: Interregional Linkages in a Changing Global System*, pp. 65–90. Northampton, Mass.: Edward Elgar.

Fagan, Drew. 2003. "Beyond NAFTA: Towards Deeper Economic Integration." In D. Carment, F. O. Hampson, and N. Hillmer, eds., *Canada among Nations 2003: Coping with the American Colossus*, pp. 32–53. Toronto: Oxford University Press.

Faiola, Anthony. 2003. "Japan's Empire of Cool: Country's Culture Becomes Its Biggest Export." *Washington Post Foreign Service:* A01.

Fairbank, John King, and Merle Goldman. 1998. *China: A New History.* Cambridge: Belknap Press of Harvard University Press.

Farer, Tom 1999. Introduction to Tom Farer, ed., *Transnational Crime in the Americas: An Inter-American Dialogue Book*, pp. xiii–xvi. New York: Routledge.

Farnsworth, Clyde H. 1989. "Japan's Loud Voice in Washington." *New York Times* (December 10): F1, F6.

Fawcett, Louise, and Andrew Hurrell. 1995. "Introduction." In Louise Fawcett and Andrew Hurrell, eds., *Regionalism in World Politics: Regional Organization and International Order*, pp. 1–6. Oxford: Oxford University Press.

Fearon, James D., and David D. Laitin. 2004. "Neotrusteeship and the Problem of Weak States." *International Security* 28, no. 4 (Spring): 5–43.

Feng, Yi, and Gaspare M. Genna. 2003. "Regional Integration and Domestic Institutional Homogeneity: A Comparative Analysis of Regional Integration in the Americas, Pacific Asia, and Western Europe." *Review of International Political Economy* 10, no. 2 (May): 278–309.

Ferguson, Niall. 2002. *Empire: The Rise and Demise of the British World Order and the Lessons for Global Power.* New York: Basic Books.

———. 2004. *Colossus: The Price of America's Empire.* New York: Penguin.

Ferguson, Thomas. 1984. "From Normalcy to New Deal: Industrial Structure, Party Competition, and American Public Policy in the Great Depression." *International Organization* 38, no. 1 (Winter): 41–94.

Fijnaut, Cyrille. 1991. "Police Co-operation within Western Europe." In M. Farrell, ed., *Crime in Europe*, pp. 103–20. London: Routledge.

———. 1993. "The Schengen Treaties and European Police Co-operation." *European Journal of Crime* 1, no. 1: 37–56.

Fishlow, Albert, and Stephan Haggard. 1992. *The United States and the Regionalisation of the World Economy.* Paris: OECD.

Flynn, Gregory, and Henry Farrell. 1999. "Piecing Together the Democratic Peace: The CSCE and the 'Construction' of Security in Post-Cold War Europe." *International Organization* 53, no. 3 (Summer): 505–36.

Folly, Martin H. 1988. "Breaking the Vicious Circle: Britain, the United States, and the Genesis of the North Atlantic Treaty." *Diplomatic History* 12, no. 1: 59–77.

Fox, Edward Whiting. 1971. *History in Geographic Perspective: The Other France.* New York: W. W. Norton.

Fox, William T. R. 1944. *The Superpowers: The United States, Britain, and the Soviet Union—Their Responsibility for Peace.* New York: Harcourt, Brace.

Fox, William T. R., and Annette B. Fox. 1967. *NATO and the Range of American Choice.* New York: Columbia University Press.

Frankel, Jeffrey A. 1997. *Regional Trading Blocs in the World Economic System.* Washington, D.C.: Institute for International Economics.

Frankel, Jeffrey A., and Miles Kahler. 1993. "Introduction." In J. A. Frankel and M. Kahler, eds., *Regionalism and Rivalry: Japan and the United States in Pacific Asia*, pp. 1–18. Chicago: University of Chicago Press.

Franko, Lawrence. 1976. *The European Multinationals: A Renewed Challenge to American and British Big Business.* New York: Harper and Row.

Freyssenet, Michel, Andrew Mair, Koichi Shimizu, and Giuseppe Volpato, eds. 1998. *One Best Way? Trajectories and Industrial Models of the World's Automobile Producers.* Oxford: Oxford University Press.

Frieden, Jeff. 1988. "Sectoral Conflict and Foreign Economic Policy, 1914–1940." *International Organization* 42, no. 1 (Winter): 59–90.

Friedman, Thomas L. 1999. "Dueling Globalizations: A Debate between Thomas L. Friedman and Ignacio Ramonet." *Foreign Policy* 116 (Fall): 110–27.

Friesendorf, Cornelius. 2002. "Drogenhandel: Unterschiede der deutschen und amerikanischen Anti-Drogenpolitik." In Christopher Daase, Susanne Feske, and Ingo Peters, eds., *Internationale Risikopolitik: Der Umgang mit neuen Gefahren in den internationalen Beziehungen*, pp. 167–190. Baden-Baden: Nomos.

Friman, H. Richard. 1996. "Gaijinhanzai: Immigrants and Drugs in Contemporary Japan." *Asian Survey* 36, no. 10: 964–77.

———. 1997. "Europeanization and the U.S. War on Drugs." Paper presented at the conference on Europeanization in International Perspective, University of Pittsburgh, September 19–21.

Friman, H. Richard, and Peter Andreas. 1999. "Introduction: International Relations and the Illicit Global Economy." In H. Richard Friman and Peter Andreas, eds., *The*

Illicit Global Economy and State Power, pp. 1–24. Lanham, Md.: Rowman and Little-field.

Friman, H. Richard, Peter J. Katzenstein, David Leheny, and Nobuo Okawara. Forth-coming. "Immovable Object? Japan's Security Policy." In Peter J. Katzenstein and Takashi Shiraishi, eds., *Beyond Japan: The Dynamics of East Asian Regionalism.* Ithaca: Cornell University Press.

Fröbel, Folker, Jürgen Heinrichs, and Otto Kreye. 1977. *Die neue internationale Arbeit-steilung: Strukturelle Arbeitslosigkeit in den Industrieländern und die Industrialisierung der Entwicklungsländer.* Hamburg: Rowohlt.

——. 1986. *Umbruch in der Weltwirtschaft—Die globale Strategie: Verbilligung der Arbeits-kraft/Flexibilisierung der Arbeit/Neue Technologien.* Hamburg: Rowohlt.

Fry, Greg, and Jacinta O'Hagan. 2000. *Contending Images of World Politics.* New York: St. Martin's.

Fujiwara, Osamu. 1992. *Philanthropy: Learning from America. IIGP Policy Paper* No. 74E (February). Tokyo: International Institute for Global Peace.

Fukui, Haruhiro. 2000. "Introduction: On the Significance of Informal Politics." In Lowell Dittmer, Haruhiro Fukui, and Peter N. S. Lee, eds., *Informal Politics in East Asia,* pp. 1–19. Cambridge: Cambridge University Press.

Fukushima, Akiko. 1999a. *Japanese Foreign Policy: The Emerging Logic of Multilateralism.* Basingstoke: Macmillan.

——. 1999b. "Japan's Emerging View of Security Multilateralism in Asia." In Ralph Cossa and Akiko Fukushima, *Security Multilateralism in Asia: Views from the United States and Japan,* edited by Stephen Haggard and Daniel Pinkston. San Diego: University of California Institute on Global Conflict and Cooperation.

Gallagher, John, and Ronald Robinson. 1953. "The Imperialism of Free Trade." *Economic History Review,* 2nd. ser., 6, no. 1: 1–15.

Gambe, Annabelle. 1997. "Competitive Collaboration: Western Liberal and Overseas Chinese Ethnic Entrepreneurship in Southeast Asia." *Forschungsberichte aus dem ISW* 22 (November).

Garrett, Geoffrey. 1998. *Partisan Politics in the Global Economy.* Cambridge: Cambridge University Press.

Garten, Jeffrey E. 1992. *A Cold Peace: America, Japan, Germany, and the Struggle for Su-premacy.* New York: Times Books.

Gates, Hill. 1996. *China's Motor: A Thousand Years of Petty Capitalism.* Ithaca: Cornell University Press.

Gause, F. Gregory, III. 1996. "From 'Over the Horizon' to 'Into the Backyard': The US-Saudi Relationship and the Gulf War." In D. W. Lesch, ed., *The Middle East and the United States: A Historical and Political Reassessment,* pp. 299–312. Boulder: Westview.

Geertz, Clifford. 1980. *Negara: The Theatre State in Nineteenth-Century Bali.* Princeton: Princeton University Press.

Gemünden, Gerd. 1998. *Framed Visions: Popular Culture, Americanization, and the Con-temporary German and Austrian Imagination.* Ann Arbor: University of Michigan Press.

George, Stephen. 1994. *An Awkward Partner: Britain and the European Community.* 2nd ed. Oxford: Oxford University Press.

Georgiadou, Vassiliki. 1991. *Griechenlands nicht-kapitalistische Entwicklungsaspekte im 19. Jahrhundert.* Frankfurt: Peter Lang.

Gereffi, Gary. 1996. "The Elusive Last Lap in the Quest for Developed-Country Status." In James H. Mittelman, ed., *Globalization: Critical Reflections*, pp. 53–81. Boulder: Lynne Rienner.

Gheciu, Alexandra. Forthcoming. *NATO in the 'New Europe': International Socialization and the Politics of State-Crafting after the End of the Cold War.* Stanford: Stanford University Press.

Gienow-Hecht, Jessica C. E. 2000. "Shame on US? Academics, Cultural Transfer, and the Cold War—A Critical Review." *Diplomatic History* 24, no. 3: 465–94.

Gilpin, Robert. 1975. *U.S. Power and the Multinational Corporation.* New York: Basic Books.

———. 2000. *The Challenge of Global Capitalism: The World Economy in the 21st Century.* Princeton: Princeton University Press.

Gilpin, Robert, with the assistance of Jean M. Gilpin. 2001. *Global Political Economy: Understanding the International Economic Order.* Princeton: Princeton University Press.

Godement, François. 1999. *The Downsizing of Asia.* New York: Routledge.

Golob, Stephanie R. 2003. "Beyond the Policy Frontier: Canada, Mexico, and the Ideological Origins of NAFTA." *World Politics* 55, no. 3 (April): 361–98.

Gordon, Donald, et al. 2002. "Teaching International Studies from a Regional Perspective: An ISP Symposium on *Power, Wealth and Global Order: An International Relations Textbook for Africa.*" *International Studies Perspectives* 3, no. 3 (August): 235–57.

Gourevitch, Peter. 1977. "International Trade, Domestic Coalitions, and Liberty: Comparative Responses to the Crisis of 1873–1896." *Journal of Interdisciplinary History* 8 (Fall): 281–313.

———. 1986. *Politics in Hard Times: Comparative Responses to International Economic Crises.* Ithaca: Cornell University Press.

Grande, Edgar, and Jürgen Häusler. 1994. *Industrieforschung und Forschungspolitik: Staatliche Steuerungspotentiale in der Informationstechnik.* Frankfurt: Campus.

Gray, Colin S. 1977. "The Geopolitics of the Nuclear Era: Heartland, Rimlands, and the Technological Revolution." *Strategy Paper* (National Strategy Information Center) No. 30. New York: Crane, Russak.

Green, Michael J. 2001. *Terrorism: Prevention and Preparedness; New Approaches to U.S.-Japan Security Cooperation.* New York: Japan Society.

Greene, Kevin. 1986. *The Archeology of the Roman Economy.* Berkeley: University of California Press.

Grieco, Joseph M. 1999. "Realism and Regionalism: American Power and German and Japanese Institutional Strategies during and after the Cold War." In E. Kapstein and M. Mastanduno, eds., *Unipolar Politics: Realism and State Strategies after the Cold War,* pp. 319–53. New York: Columbia University Press.

Grigsby, Mary. 1998. "Sailormoon: Manga (Comics) and Anime (Cartoon) Superheroine Meets Barbie: Global Entertainment Commodity Comes to the United States." *Journal of Popular Culture* 32, no. 1: 59–80.

Group of Lisbon, The. 1995. *Limits to Competition: The Group of Lisbon.* Cambridge: MIT Press.

Gruber, Lloyd. 2000. *Ruling the World: Power Politics and the Rise of Supranational Institutions.* Princeton: Princeton University Press.

Grugel, Jean. 1996. "Latin America and the Remaking of the Americas." In Andrew

Gamble and Anthony Payne, eds., *Regionalism and World Order,* pp. 131–67. New York: St. Martin's.

Grugel, Jean, and Wil Hout. 1999. "Regions, Regionalism, and the South. " In J. Grugel and W. Hout, eds., *Regionalism across the North-South Divide: State Strategies and Globalization,* pp. 3–13. New York: Routledge.

Guerrieri, Paolo. 1998. "Trade Patterns, FDI, and Industrial Restructuring in Central and Eastern Europe." In John Zysman and Andrew Schwartz, eds., *Enlarging Europe: The Industrial Foundations of a New Political Reality,* pp. 130–56. Berkeley: University of California, International and Area Studies, a BRIE/Kreisky Forum Project.

Gungwu, Wang. 1994. "Empires and Anti-empires: Asia in World Politics." In G. Lundestad, ed., *The Fall of Great Powers: Peace, Stability, and Legitimacy,* pp. 235–58. Oxford: Oxford University Press.

Gurowitz, Amy I. 1999. "Mobilizing International Norms: Domestic Actors, Immigrants, and the Japanese State." *World Politics* 51, no. 3 (April): 413–45.

Haas, Ernst. 1966. "International Integration: The European and the Universal Process." In *International Political Communities: An Anthology,* pp. 93–129. New York: Doubleday, Anchor Books.

Haas, Michael. 1989. *The Asian Way to Peace: A Story of Regional Cooperation.* New York: Praeger.

Hall, Derek Andrew. 2002. "Dying Geese: Japan and the International Political Ecology of Southeast Asia." PhD diss., Cornell University.

——. Forthcoming. "Regional Shrimp, Global Trees, Chinese Vegetables: The Environment in Japan-Asia Relations." In Peter J. Katzenstein and Takashi Shiraishi, eds., *Beyond Japan: The Dynamics of East Asian Regionalism.* Ithaca: Cornell University Press.

Hall, Peter. 1997. "The Political Challenges Facing Regional Trade Regimes." *La Lettre de la Régulation* 22 (September): 1–4.

Hall, Peter, and David Soskice. 2001. "An Introduction to Varieties of Capitalism." In Peter A. Hall and David Soskice, eds., *Varieties of Capitalism: The Institutional Foundations of Comparative Advantage,* pp. 1–68. New York: Oxford University Press.

Hall, Peter A., and Sidney Tarrow. 1998. "Globalization and Area Studies: When Is Too Broad Too Narrow?" *Chronicle of Higher Education* 44, no. 20 (January 23). D4.

Hall, Robert. 1948. *Area Studies: With Special Reference to Their Implications for Research in the Social Sciences.* New York: Social Science Research Council, Committee on World Area Research Program.

Hamilton, Gary G. 1996. "Overseas Chinese Capitalism." In Tu Wei-ming, ed., *Confucian Traditions in East Asian Modernity: Moral Education and Economic Culture in Japan and the Four Mini-Dragons,* pp. 328–42. Cambridge: Harvard University Press.

——. 1999. "Asian Business Networks in Transition: or, What Alan Greenspan Does Not Know about the Asian Business Crisis." In T. J. Pempel, ed. *The Politics of the Asian Economic Crisis,* pp. 45–61. Ithaca: Cornell University Press.

Hamilton, Gary G., and Robert C. Feenstra. 1997. "Varieties of Hierarchies and Markets: An Introduction." In Marco Orrù, Nicole Woolsey Biggart, and Gary G. Hamilton, eds., *The Economic Organization of East Asian Capitalism,* pp. 55–94. Thousand Oaks, Calif.: Sage.

Hamilton, Gary G., and Cheng-Su Kao. 1990. "The Institutional Foundations of Chinese Business." *Comparative Social Research* 12: 135–51.

Hamilton, Gary G., Marco Orrù, and Nicole Woolsey Biggart. 1987. "Enterprise

Groups in East Asia: An Organizational Analysis." *Shoken Keizai* 161 (September): 78–106.

Hamilton, Gary G., and Tony Walters. 1995. "Chinese Capitalism in Thailand: Embedded Networks and Industrial Structure." In Edward K. Y. Chen and Peter Drysdale, eds., *Corporate Links and Foreign Direct Investment in Asia and the Pacific*, pp. 87–111. New York: Harper Educational.

Hamilton-Hart, Natasha. 2002. *Asian States, Asian Bankers: Central Banking in Southeast Asia*. Ithaca: Cornell University Press.

Hammerstein, Konstantin von. 2001. "Schluss mit Eiapopeia." *Der Spiegel* 10: 74–76.

Hampton, Mary. 1995. "NATO at the Creation: U.S. Foreign Policy, West Germany, and the Wilsonian Impulse." *Security Studies* 4, no. 3 (Spring): 610–56.

Hannerz, Ulf. 1989. "Notes on the Global Ecumene." *Public Culture* 1, no. 2: 66–75.

Hanrieder, Wolfram F. 1967. *West German Foreign Policy, 1949–1963: International Pressure and Domestic Response*. Stanford: Stanford University Press.

Harding, Harry. 1993. "The Concept of 'Greater China': Themes, Variations, and Reservations." *China Quarterly* 136 (December): 660–86.

Hardt, Michael, and Antonio Negri. 2000. *Empire*. Cambridge: Harvard University Press.

Hassner, Ron E. 2003. "To Halve and to Hold: Conflicts over Sacred Space and the Problem of Indivisibility." *Security Studies* 12, no. 4 (Summer): 1–33.

Hatch, Walter. 2000. "Rearguard Regionalization: Preserving Core Coalitions in the Japanese Political Economy." PhD diss., University of Washington, Seattle.

———. 2002. "Regionalizing the State: Japanese Administrative and Financial Guidance for Asia." *Social Science Japan Journal* 5, no. 2: 179–97.

Hatch, Walter, and Kozo Yamamura. 1996. *Asia in Japan's Embrace: Building a Regional Production Alliance*. New York: Cambridge University Press.

Haufler, Daniel. 1997. "Amerika, Du hast es Besser? Zur Deutschen Buchkultur nach 1945." In Konrad Jarausch and Hannes Siegrist, eds., *Amerikanisierung und Sowjetisierung in Deutschland, 1945–1970*, pp. 387–408. Frankfurt: Campus.

Havens, Thomas R. H. 1987. "Government and the Arts in Contemporary Japan." In Milton C. Cummings Jr. and Richard S. Katz, eds., *The Patron State: Government and the Arts in Europe, North America, and Japan*, pp. 333–49. New York: Oxford University Press.

Hein, Laura, and Mark Selden. 2000. "The Lessons of War, Global Power, and Social Change." In Laura Hein and Mark Selden, eds., *Censoring History: Citizenship and Memory in Japan, Germany, and the United States*, pp. 3–50. Armonk, N.Y.: M. E. Sharpe.

Helleiner, Eric. 1994. "Regionalization in the International Political Economy: A Comparative Perspective." *Eastern Asia Policy Paper No. 3*. Toronto: University of Toronto-York University, Joint Centre for Asia Pacific Studies.

Hemmer, Christopher, and Peter J. Katzenstein. 2002. "Why Is There No NATO in Asia? Collective Identity, Regionalism, and the Origins of Multilateralism." *International Organization* 56, no. 3 (Summer): 575–608.

Henley, Jon. 1999. "UNESCO's New Head Vows to End Corruption." *The Guardian* (October 21).

Henrikson, Alan K. 1975. "The Map as an Idea: The Role of Cartographic Imagery during the Second World War." *American Cartographer* 2, no. 1: 19–53.

———. 1980. "The Creation of the North Atlantic Alliance, 1948–1952." *Naval War College Review* 33, no. 3: 4–39.

Henwood, Doug. 2003. "Beyond Globophobia." *The Nation* (December 1): 17–20.

Herf, Jeffrey. 1984. *Reactionary Modernism: Technology, Culture, and Politics in Weimar and the Third Reich.* Cambridge: Cambridge University Press.

Herrera, Juan José Durán. 1992. "Cross-Direct Investment and Technological Capability of Spanish Domestic Firms." In J. Cantwell, ed., *Multinational Investment in Modern Europe: Strategic Interaction in the Integrated Community*, pp. 214–55. Brookfield, Vt.: Edward Elgar.

Herrigel, Gary. 1996. *Industrial Constructions: The Sources of German Industrial Power.* Cambridge: Cambridge University Press.

———. 2000. "American Occupation, Market Order, and Democracy: Restructuring the Steel Industry in Japan and Germany after World War II." In J. Zeitlin and G. Herrigel, eds., *Americanization and Its Limits: Reworking Management and Technology in Europe and Japan after World War Two*, pp. 340–99. Oxford: Oxford University Press.

Herrman, Robert. 1995. "Ideas, Identity, and the Redefinition of Interests: The Political and Intellectual Origins of the Soviet Foreign Policy Revolution." PhD diss., Cornell University.

Herrmann, Karin. 1994. "Auswärtige Kulturarbeit—Magd oder Muse?" In Hilmar Hoffmann and Kurt Jürgen Maaß, eds., *Freund oder Fratze? Das Bild von Deutschland in der Welt und die Aufgaben der Kulturpolitik*, pp. 73–78. Frankfurt: Campus.

Herz, John H. 1983. *From Dictatorship to Democracy.* Westport, Conn.: Greenwood.

Hettne, Björn. 1999a. "The New Regionalism: A Prologue." In Björn Hettne, András Inotai, and Osvaldo Sunkel, eds., *Globalism and the New Regionalism*, pp. xv–xxxvi. New York: St. Martin's.

———. 1999b. "Globalization and the New Regionalism: The Second Great Transformation." In Björn Hettne, András Inotai, and Osvlado Sunkel, eds., *Globalism and the New Regionalism*, pp. 1–24. New York: St. Martin's.

Hicks, George, and J. A. C. Mackie. 1994. "Overseas Chinese: A Question of Identity." *Far Eastern Economic Review:* 46–48.

Higgott, Richard. 1995. "Economic Co-operation in the Asia-Pacific: A Theoretical Comparison with the European Union." *Journal of European Public Policy* 2, no. 3 (September): 361–83.

Hirano, Kenichiro. 1988. "International Cultural Conflicts: Causes and Remedies." *Japan Review of International Affairs* 2, no. 2 (Fall/Winter): 143–64.

Hirano, Kenichiro. 1997. "Japan's Cultural Exchange Approaches." In Charles E. Morrison, Akira Kojima, and Hans W. Maull, eds., *Community-Building with Pacific Asia*, pp. 88–97. New York: Trilateral Commission.

Hirst, Paul, and Grahame Thompson. 1996. *Globalization in Question: The International Economy and the Possibilities of Governance.* Cambridge: Polity Press.

———. 2002. "The Future of Globalization." *Cooperation and Conflict* 37, no. 3 (September): 247–65.

Hochberg, Leonard J. 1986. "The Geography of Revolution: The Cases of England, the United States, and France." PhD diss., Cornell University.

Hoge, Warren. 2001. "Nineteen Countries Join in Raids on Internet Pornography." *New York Times* (November 29): A11.

Holman, Otto. 1996. *Integrating Southern Europe: EC Expansion and the Transnationalization of Spain.* London: Routledge.

Honda, Shiro. 1994. "East Asia's Middle Class Tunes in to Today's Japan." *Japan Echo* 21, no. 4: 75–79.

Hooghe, Liesbet, and Gary Marks. 2001. *Multi-Level Governance and European Integration*. Lanham, Md.: Rowman and Littlefield.

Horn, Ernst-Jürgen. 1990. "West German Technology in the 1980s: Perceptions, Evidence, and Policy Issues." In G. Heiduk and K. Yamamura, eds., *Technological Competition and Interdependence: The Search for Policy in the United States, West Germany, and Japan,* pp. 64–84. Seattle: University of Washington Press.

Horne, Gerald. 1999. "Race from Power: U.S. Foreign Policy and the General Crisis of 'White Supremacy.'" *Diplomatic History* 23, no. 3: 437–61.

Howells, Jeremy, and Michelle Wood. 1993. *The Globalisation of Production and Technology*. London: Belhaven Press.

Huber, Evelyne. 2003. "The Role of Cross-regional Comparison." *APSA-CP: Newsletter of the APSA Organized Section on Comparative Politics* 14, no 2: 1–6.

Hudson, Michael C. 1999. "Arab Integration: An Overview." In M. C. Hudson, ed., *Middle East Dilemma: The Politics and Economics of Arab Integration,* pp. 1–32. New York: Columbia University Press.

Hudson, Wayne, and Geoffrey Stokes. 1997. "Australia and Asia: Place, Determinism, and National Identities." In Geoffrey Stokes, ed., *The Politics of Identity in Australia,* pp. 145–57. Cambridge: Cambridge University Press.

Hufbauer, Gary C., Jeffrey C. Schott, and Barbara R. Kotschwar. 1999. "U.S. Interests in Free Trade in the Americas." In Albert Fishlow and James Jones, eds., *The United States and the Americas: A Twenty-First Century View,* pp. 58–78. New York: W. W. Norton.

Hughes, David, and Jonathan Clements. 1997. "Arts: Manga Goes to Hollywood." *The Guardian* (April 14).

Hui, Po-Keung. 1995. "Overseas Chinese Business Networks: East Asian Economic Development in Historical Perspective." PhD diss., State University of New York, Binghamton.

Hui, Victoria Tin-bor. 2004. "Toward a Dynamic Theory of International Politics: Insights from Comparing Ancient China and Early Modern Europe." *International Organization* 58, no. 1 (Winter): 175–205.

Hunt, Michael. 1987. *Ideology and U.S. Foreign Policy*. New Haven: Yale University Press.

Huntington, Samuel P. 1968. *Political Order in Changing Societies*. New Haven: Yale University Press.

———. 1973. "Transnational Organizations in World Politics." *World Politics* 25, no. 3 (April): 333–68.

———. 1996. *The Clash of Civilizations and the Remaking of World Order.* New York: Simon and Schuster.

———. 1999. "The Lonely Superpower." *Foreign Affairs* 78, no. 2 (March–April): 35–49.

Hurrell, Andrew. 1995. "Regionalism in Theoretical Perspective." In L. Fawcett and A. Hurrell, eds., *Regionalism in World Politics: Regional Organization and International Order,* pp. 37–73. Oxford: Oxford University Press.

Ifestos, Panayotis. 1987. "European Political Cooperation (EPC): Its Evolution from 1970 to 1986, and the Single European Act." *Journal of European Integration* 11, no. 1 (Fall): 47–62.

Igarashi, Akio. 1997. "From Americanization to 'Japanization' in East Asia?" *Journal of Pacific Asia* 4: 3–19.

Ikenberry, G. John. 2001. *After Victory: Institutions, Strategic Restraint, and the Rebuilding of Order after Major Wars.* Princeton: Princeton University Press.

———. 2004. "Illusions of Empire: Defining the New American Order." *Foreign Affairs* 83, no. 2 (March–April): 144–54.

International Labor Organisation. 2002. *Employment and Social Policy in Respect of Export Processing Zones (EPZs)*. Geneva: International Labor Organisation, Committee on Employment and Social Policy.

Iriye, Akira. 1992. *China and Japan in the Global Setting*. Cambridge: Harvard University Press.

———. 1997. *Cultural Internationalism and World Order*. Baltimore: Johns Hopkins University Press.

Isaacson, Walter, and Evan Thomas. 1986. *The Wise Men: Six Friends and the World They Made*. New York: Touchstone.

Isard, Walter. 1956. *Location and Space-Economy: A General Theory Relating to Industrial Location, Market Areas, Land Use, Trade, and Urban Structure*. New York: Technology Press of Massachusetts Institute of Technology and John Wiley and Sons.

Itagaki, Hiroshi. 1997. "Conclusions and Prospects." In H. Itagaki, ed., *The Japanese Production System: Hybrid Factories in East Asia*, pp. 366–79. London: Macmillan.

Iversen, Torben and Thomas R. Cusack. 2000. "The Causes of Welfare State Expansion: Deindustrialization or Globalization?" *World Politics* 52, no. 3 (April): 313–49.

Iwabuchi, Koichi. 1998. "Marketing 'Japan': Japanese Cultural Presence under a Global Gaze." *Japanese Studies* 18, no. 2: 165–80.

———. 1999. "Return to Asia: Japan in Asian Audiovisual Markets." In Kosaku Yoshino, ed., *Consuming Ethnicity and Nationalism: Asian Experiences*, pp. 177–99. Honolulu: University of Hawaii Press.

———. 2002. *Recentering Globalization: Popular Culture and Japanese Transnationalism*. Durham: Duke University Press.

Jackson, Patrick Thaddeus. 2001. "Occidentalism: Rhetoric, Process, and Postwar German Reconstruction." PhD diss., Columbia University.

Jarausch, Konrad H., and Hannes Siegrist. 1997. "Amerikanisierung und Sowjetisierung: Eine Vergleichende Fragestellung zur Deutsch-Deutschen Nachkriegsgeschichte." In Konrad Jarausch and Hannes Siegrist, eds., *Amerikanisierung und Sowjetisierung in Deutschland, 1945–1970*, pp. 11–46. Frankfurt: Campus.

Jehl, Douglas. 2001. "Holy War Lured Saudis as Rulers Looked Away." *New York Times* (December 27): A1, B4–B5.

Jerábek, Hynek, and Frantisek Zich. 1997. "The Czech Republic: Internationalization and Dependency." In Peter J. Katzenstein, ed., *Mitteleuropa: Between Europe and Germany*, pp. 149–91. Providence, R.I.: Berghahn Books.

Johnson, Chalmers. 1997. "Preconception vs. Observation, or the Contributions of Rational Choice Theory and Area Studies to Contemporary Political Science." *PS: Political Science and Politics* 30, no. 2 (June): 170–74.

———. 2000. *Blowback: The Costs and Consequences of American Empire*. New York: Henry Holt.

———. 2004. *The Sorrows of Empire: Militarism, Secrecy, and the End of the Republic*. New York: Henry Holt.

Johnson, Kenneth L. 2001. "Critical Debates: Regionalism Redux? The Prospects for Cooperation in the Americas." *Latin American Politics and Society* 43, no. 3 (Fall): 121–38.

Johnston, Alastair Iain. 1999. "The Myth of the ASEAN Way? Explaining the Evolution of the ASEAN Regional Forum." In Helga Haftendorn, Robert O. Keohane, and Celeste A. Wallander, eds., *Imperfect Unions: Security Institutions in Time and Space,* pp. 287–324. London: Oxford University Press.

Jones, Eric. 1987. *The European Miracle: Environments, Economies, and Geopolitics in the History of Europe and Asia.* Cambridge: Cambridge University Press.

Jordan, Amos A., and Jane Khanna. 1995. "Economic Interdependence and Challenges to the Nation-State: The Emergence of Natural Economic Territories in the Asia-Pacific." *Journal of International Affairs* 48, no. 2 (Winter): 433–62.

Jowitt, Kenneth. 1992. *New World Disorder: The Leninist Extinction.* Berkeley: University of California Press.

Kaelble, Hartmut. 1990. *A Social History of Western Europe, 1880–1980.* Savage, Md.: Barnes and Noble.

Kagan, Robert. 2003. *Of Paradise and Power: America and Europe in the New World Order.* New York: Alfred A. Knopf.

Kahler, Miles. 1995. *International Institutions and the Political Economy of Integration.* Washington, D.C.: Brookings Institution.

Kaiser, Karl. 1971. "Transnational Relations as a Threat to the Democratic Process." *International Organization* 25, no. 3: 706–20.

Kammen, Michael. 2003. "Clio, Columbia, and the Cosmopolitans: Beyond American Exceptionalism and the Nation-State." *History and Theory* 42 (February): 106–15.

Kang, David. 2003a. "Getting Asia Wrong: The Need for New Analytical Frameworks." *International Security* 27, no. 4 (Spring): 57–85.

——. 2003b. "Hierarchy and Stability in Asian International Relations." In G. John Ikenberry and Michael Mastanduno, eds., *International Relations Theory and the Asia-Pacific,* pp. 163–89. New York: Columbia University Press.

Kang, David C. 2003/04. "Hierarchy, Balancing, and Empirical Puzzles in Asian International Relations." *International Security* 28, no. 3 (Winter): 165–80.

Kao, John. 1993. "The Worldwide Web of Chinese Business." *Harvard Business Review* 71 (March–April): 24–36.

Kaplan, Amy. 2002. *The Anarchy of Empire in the Making of U.S. Culture.* Cambridge: Harvard University Press.

Kaplan, Lawrence S. 1981. "NATO: The Second Generation." In L. S. Kaplan and R. W. Clawson, eds., *NATO after Thirty Years,* pp. 3–29. Wilmington, Del.: Scholarly Resources.

——. 1984. *The United States and NATO: The Formative Years.* Lexington: University Press of Kentucky.

Kaplan, Robert D. 2003. "Supremacy by Stealth." *Atlantic Monthly* (July–August): 65–83.

Kapner, Suzanne. 2003. "U.S. TV Shows Losing Potency around World." *New York Times* (January 2): A1, A8.

Kasza, Gregory J. Forthcoming. *Japan's Welfare Policies in Comparative Perspective.* Ithaca: Cornell University Press.

Katada, Saori N. 2001. *Banking on Stability: Japan and the Cross-Pacific Dynamics of International Financial Crisis Management.* Ann Arbor: University of Michigan Press.

Katada, Saori N., Hans W. Maull, and Takashi Inoguchi, eds. 2004. *Global Governance: Germany and Japan in the International System.* Aldershot: Ashgate.

Kato, Kozo. 2002. *The Web of Power: Japanese and German Development Cooperation Policy.* Lanham, Md.: Lexington Books.

Katzenstein, Peter J. 1978. *Between Power and Plenty: Foreign Economic Policies of Advanced Industrial States.* Madison: University of Wisconsin Press.

———. 1985. *Small States in World Markets: Industrial Policy in Europe.* Ithaca: Cornell University Press.

———. 1990. *West Germany's Internal Security Policy: State and Violence in the 1970s and 1980s.* Ithaca: Cornell University, Center for International Studies, Western Societies Program.

———. 1996. *Cultural Norms and National Security: Police and Military in Postwar Japan.* Ithaca: Cornell University Press.

———. 1997a. "Introduction: Asian Regionalism in Comparative Perspective." In P. J. Katzenstein and T. Shiraishi, eds., *Network Power: Japan and Asia,* pp. 1–44. Ithaca: Cornell University Press.

———. 1997b. "United Germany in an Integrating Europe." In P. J. Katzenstein, ed., *Tamed Power: Germany in Europe,* pp. 1–48. Ithaca: Cornell University Press.

———. 1997c. "The Cultural Foundations of Murakami's Polymorphic Liberalism." In Kozo Yamamura, ed., *A Vision of a New Liberalism? Critical Essays on Murakami's Anticlassical Analysis,* pp. 23–40. Stanford: Stanford University Press.

———, ed. 1997d. *Tamed Power: Germany in Europe.* Ithaca: Cornell University Press.

———. 2000. "Varieties of Asian Regionalisms." In P. J. Katzenstein, N. Hamilton-Hart, K. Kato, and M. Yue, *Asian Regionalism,* pp. 1–34. Ithaca: Cornell University, Center for International Studies, East Asia Program.

———. 2001. "Area and Regional Studies in the United States." *PS: Political Science and Politics* (December): 789–91.

———. 2002. "Regionalism and Asia." In Shaun Breslin, Christopher W. Hughes, Nicola Phillips, and Ben Rosamond, eds., *New Regionalism in the Global Political Economy,* pp. 104–18. New York: Routledge.

———. 2002a. "Area Studies, Regional Studies, and International Relations." *Journal of East Asian Studies* 2, no. 1 (February 2002): 127–38.

———. 2003a. "Regional States: Japan and Asia, Germany in Europe." In Kozo Yamamura and Wolfgang Streeck, eds., *The End of Diversity? Prospects for German and Japanese Capitalism,* pp. 89–114. Ithaca: Cornell University Press.

———. 2003b. "Japan, Technology, and Asian Regionalism in Comparative Perspective." In Giovanni Arrighi, Takeshi Hamashita, and Mark Selden, eds., *The Resurgence of East Asia: 500, 150 and 50 Year Perspectives,* pp. 214–58. London: Routledge.

———. 2003c. "Same War—Different Views: Germany, Japan, and Counter-Terrorism." *International Organization* 57, no. 4 (Fall): 731–60.

———. 2003d. "*Small States* and Small States Revisited." *New Political Economy* 8, no. 1 (March): 9–30.

Katzenstein, Peter J., and Nobuo Okawara. 2001/02. "Japan, Asian-Pacific Security, and the Case for Analytical Eclecticism." *International Security* 26, no. 3 (Winter): 153–85.

———. 2004. "Japan and Asian-Pacific Security." In J. J. Suh, Peter J. Katzenstein, and Allen Carlson, eds., *Rethinking Security in East Asia: Identity, Power, and Efficiency,* pp. 97–130. Stanford: Stanford University Press.

Katzenstein, Peter J., and Takashi Shiraishi, eds. 1997a. *Network Power: Japan and Asia.* Ithaca: Cornell University Press.

Katzenstein, Peter J., and Takashi Shiraishi. 1997b. "Conclusion: Regions in World Politics, Japan and Asia—Germany in Europe." In Peter J. Katzenstein and Takashi

Shiraishi, eds., *Network Power: Japan and Asia,* pp. 341–81. Ithaca: Cornell University Press.

Katzenstein, Peter J., and Rudra Sil. 2004. "Rethinking Asian Security: A Case for Analytical Eclecticism." In J. J. Suh, Peter J. Katzenstein, and Allen Carlson, eds., *Rethinking Security in East Asia: Identity, Power, and Efficiency,* pp. 1–33. Stanford: Stanford University Press.

Katzenstein, Peter J., and Yutaka Tsujinaka. 1995. "'Bullying,' 'Buying,' and 'Binding': US-Japanese Transnational Relations and Domestic Structures." In Thomas Risse-Kappen, ed., *Bringing Transnational Relations Back In,* pp. 79–111. Cambridge: Cambridge University Press.

Katznelson, Ira. 2002. "Rewriting the Epic of America." In I. Katznelson and M. Shefter, eds., *Shaped by War and Trade,* pp. 3–23. Princeton: Princeton University Press.

Kawamura, Yoko, Maki Okabe, and Toichi Makita. 2000. "The Concept of 'Region' as a Framework for Interchange: Japanese-German Comparison of National Participation in Regional Cultural Cooperation [Koryu no Wakugumi to Shiteno 'Chiiki' no Ninshiki: Chiiki Bunka Kyoryoku ni Taisuru Kokkateki Kanyo no Nichidoku Hikaku]." Paper presented at the conference on Contemporary Thought on International Cultural Relations, May 19, Tokyo.

Keeler, John T. S. 1996. "Agricultural Power in the European Community: Explaining the Fate of CAP and GATT Negotiations." *Comparative Politics* 28, no. 2: 127–49.

Keller, Edmond J. 1997. "Rethinking African Regional Security." In David Lake and Patrick M. Morgan, eds., *Regional Orders: Building Security in a New World,* pp. 296–317. University Park: Pennsylvania State University Press.

Keller, William W., and Richard J. Samuels, 2003. "Continuity and Change in Asian Innovation." In W. W. Keller and R. J. Samuels, eds., *Crisis and Innovation in Asian Technology,* pp. 226–41. Cambridge: Cambridge University Press.

Kennan, George F. (Mr. X). 1947. "The Sources of Soviet Conduct." *Foreign Affairs* 25, no. 4 (July): 566–82.

——. 1994. "The Failure in Our Success." *New York Times* (March 14): A17.

Keohane, Robert O. 1984. *After Hegemony: Cooperation and Discord in the World Political Economy.* Princeton: Princeton University Press.

Keohane, Robert O., and Joseph S. Nye. 2001. *Power and Interdependence.* 3rd ed. New York: Longman.

Key, Jeffrey E. 1998. "Beyond 'Tilting Both Ways': A New Post-Cold War South Asia Policy." *Asian Affairs* 25, no. 2: 89–102.

Khalidi, Rashid. 2004. *Resurrecting Empire: Western Footprints and America's Perilous Path in the Middle East.* Boston: Beacon Press.

Khong, Yuen Foong. 1997. "Making Bricks without Straw in the Asia Pacific?" *Pacific Review* 10, no. 2: 289–300.

Kim, B. Sang Joon. 1965. "The United States and SEATO." PhD diss., Yale University.

Kimball, Warren F. 1984. *Churchill and Roosevelt: The Complete Correspondence.* Vols. 1–2. Princeton: Princeton University Press.

Kindleberger, Charles. 1969. *American Business Abroad.* New Haven: Yale University Press.

Kirchner, Emil J. 1989. "Has the Single European Act Opened the Door for a European Security Policy?" *Journal of European Integration* 13, no. 1 (Autumn): 1–14.

Kleinsteuber, Hans J., and Bettina Peters. 1991. "Media Moguls in Germany." In Jeremy Tunstall and Michael Palmer, eds., *Media Moguls,* pp. 184–205. London: Routledge.

Kloosterhuis, Jürgen. 1981. "Deutsche Auswärtige Kulturpolitik und Ihre Trägergruppen vor dem Ersten Weltkrieg." In Kurt Düwell and Werner Link, eds., *Deutsche Auswärtige Kulturpolitik seit 1871,* pp. 7–35. Cologne: Böhlau.

Knapp, Manfred. 1975. "Zum Stand der Forschung über die deutsch-amerikanischen Nachkriegsbeziehungen." In M. Knapp, ed., *Die deutsch-amerikanischen Beziehungen nach 1945,* pp. 7–85. Frankfurt: Campus.

König, Dominik Freiherr von. 1999. "Leistungen und Vielfalt der Kulturstiftungen: Petersilie im Maul des Karpfen?" In *Kulturstiftungen als Impulsgeber in einem Zusammenwachsenden Europa,* pp. 26–41. Bonn: Bundesverband Deutscher Stiftungen.

Kohler-Koch, Beate. 1998. "Leitbilder und Realität der Europäisierung der Regionen." In B. Kohler-Koch, ed., *Interaktive Politik in Europa: Regionen im Netzwerk der Integration,* pp. 232–53. Opladen: Leske + Budrich.

Kohno, Masaru. 2003. "A Changing Ministry of International Trade and Industry." In Jennifer Amyx and Peter Drysdale, eds., *Japanese Governance: Beyond Japan Inc.,* pp. 96–112. London: Routledge.

Kondo, Hisashi. 1995. "Manga Go Global." *Pacific Friend* 23, no. 2 (June): 2–9.

Koopmans, Thijmen. 1991. "The Birth of European Law at the Cross Roads of Legal Traditions." *American Journal of Comparative Law* 39, no. 3 (Summer): 493–507.

Kramer, Alan. 1991. *The West German Economy.* New York: Berg.

Kramer, Paul A. 2002. "Empires, Exceptions, and Anglo-Saxons: Race and Rule between the British and United States Empires, 1880–1910." *Journal of American History* 88, no. 4 (March): 1315–53.

Krasner, Stephen. 1995. "Compromising Westphalia." *International Security* 20, no. 3: 115–51.

Kroes, Rob. 1996. *If You've Seen One, You've Seen the Mall: Europeans and American Mass Culture.* Urbana: University of Illinois Press.

Kume, Ikuo. 1998. *Disparaged Success: Labor Politics in Postwar Japan.* Ithaca: Cornell University Press.

Kupchan, Charles A. 2002. *The End of the American Era: U.S. Foreign Policy and the Geopolitics of the Twenty-first Century.* New York: Alfred A. Knopf,

Kurth, James. 1979. "The Political Consequences of the Product Cycle: Industrial History and Political Outcomes." *International Organization* 33, no. 1 (Winter): 9–33.

———. 1989. "The Pacific Basin versus the Atlantic Alliance: Two Paradigms of International Relations." *Annals of the American Academy of Political Science* 505 (September): 34–45.

———. 1990. "The Rise and Decline of the Inter-American System: A U.S. View." In Richard J. Bloomfield and Gregory F. Treverton, eds., *Alternative to Intervention: A New U.S.-Latin American Security Relationship,* pp. 9–25. Boulder: Lynne Rienner.

Kurzer, Paulette. 2001. *Markets and Moral Regulation: Cultural Change in the European Union.* Cambridge: Cambridge University Press.

Kuwahara, Yasue. 1997. "Japanese Culture and Popular Consciousness: Disney's *The Lion King* vs. Tezuka's *Jungle Emperor.*" *Journal of Popular Culture* 31, no. 1 (Summer): 37–48.

Laffan, Brigid. 1998. "The European Union: A Distinctive Model of Internationalization." *Journal of European Public Policy* 5, no. 2: 235–53.

Laitin, David D. 1997. "The Cultural Identities of a European State." *Politics and Society* 25, no. 3: 277–302.

——. 2002. "Culture and National Identity: 'The East' and European Integration." In Peter Mair and Jan Zielonka, eds., *The Enlarged European Union: Diversity and Adaptation*, pp. 55–80. London: Frank Cass.

Lake, David A. 1999. *Entangling Relations: American Foreign Policy in Its Century*. Princeton: Princeton University Press.

Lake, David A., and Patrick M. Morgan. 1997. "The New Regionalism in Security Affairs." In D. A. Lake and P. M. Morgan, eds., *Regional Orders: Building Security in a New World*, pp. 3–19. University Park: Pennsylvania State University Press.

Lansford, Tom. 2002. *All for One: Terrorism, NATO, and the United States*. Aldershot: Ashgate.

Larson, Deborah Welch. 1985. *Origins of Containment: A Psychological Explanation*. Princeton: Princeton University Press.

Lauren, Paul Gordon. 1988. *Power and Prejudice: The Politics of Diplomacy and Racial Discrimination*. Boulder: Westview.

Lawrence, Robert Z. 1996. *Regionalism, Multilateralism, and Deeper Integration*. Washington, D.C.: Brookings Institution.

LeDonne, John P. 1997. *The Russian Empire and the World, 1700–1917: The Geopolitics of Expansion and Containment*. New York: Oxford University Press.

Lee, Chung Hee. 1988. *Foreign Lobbying in American Politics*. Seoul: Seoul National University.

Lee, Jennifer. 2001. "U.S. May Help Chinese Evade Net Censorship." *New York Times* (August 30): A1, A10.

Leheny, David. 2001–2. "Tokyo Confronts Terror." *Policy Review* 110 (December–January): 37–47.

——. Forthcoming. "A Narrow Place to Cross Swords: 'Soft Power' and the Politics of Japanese Popular Culture in Asia." In Peter J. Katzenstein and Takashi Shiraishi, eds., *Beyond Japan: The Dynamics of East Asian Regionalism*. Ithaca: Cornell University Press.

Lehmbruch, Gerhard. 2001. "The Rise and Change of Discourses on 'Embedded Capitalism' in Germany and Japan and Their Institutional Settings." In W. Streeck and K. Yamamura, eds., *The Origins of Nonliberal Capitalism: Germany and Japan in Comparison*, pp. 39–93. Ithaca: Cornell University Press.

Lemke, Douglas. 2002. *Regions of War and Peace*. Cambridge: Cambridge University Press.

Lemoine, Françoise. 1998. "Integrating Central and Eastern Europe in the European Trade and Production Network." In J. Zysman and A. Schwartz, eds., *Enlarging Europe: The Industrial Foundations of a New Political Reality*, pp. 157–68. Berkeley: University of California, International and Area Studies, a BRIE/Kreisky Forum Project.

Lepenies, Wolf. 1999a. "The End of 'German Culture': (I) Exile and Emigration: The Survival of 'German Culture.'" Delivered as the Tanner Lecture on Human Values, Harvard University.

——. 1999b. "The End of 'German Culture': (II) Unification and European Integration: The End of 'German Culture.'" Delivered as the Tanner Lecture on Human Values, Harvard University.

Lincoln, Edward J. 1992. *Japan's Rapidly Emerging Strategy toward Asia*. Paris: OECD, Research Program on Globalisation and Regionalization.

———. 1993. *Japan's New Global Role.* Washington, D.C.: Brookings Institution.

Linden, Greg. 2000. "Japan and the United States in the Malaysian Electronics Sector." In M. Borrus, D. Ernst, and S. Haggard, eds., *International Production Networks in Asia: Rivalry or Riches?* pp. 198–225. London: Routledge.

Link, Werner. 1977. *The Socio-Political Culture of Germany and the United States: Distinctions, Linkages, and Transfers.* Bloomington: Indiana University, Institute for German Studies.

———. 1978. *The Contribution of Trade Unions and Businessmen to German-American Relations, 1945–1975.* Bloomington: Indiana University, Institute of German Studies.

Lippert, Barbara. 1996. *Auswärtige Kulturpolitik im Zeichen der Ostpolitik: Verhandlungen mit Moskau, 1969–1980.* Münster: Lit.

Lipset, Seymour Martin. 1990. *Continental Divide: The Values and Institutions of the United States and Canada.* New York: Routledge.

Liu, Hong. 2000. *Sino-Southeast Asian Studies: Toward a New Analytical Paradigm.* Singapore: National University, Department of Chinese Studies.

Locke, Richard M. 1995. *Remaking the Italian Economy.* Ithaca: Cornell University Press.

Luce, Henry R. 1941. *The American Century.* New York: Farrar and Reinhart.

Lundestad, Geir. 1986. "Empire by Invitation? The United States and Western Europe, 1945–1952." *Journal of Peace Research* 23, no. 3 (September): 263–77.

———. 1990. *The American "Empire": And Other Studies of Foreign Policy in a Comparative Perspective.* Oxford and Oslo: Oxford University Press and Norwegian University Press.

———. 1998. *"Empire" by Integration.* Oxford: Oxford University Press.

———. 1999. "'Empire by Invitation' in the American Century." *Diplomatic History* 23, no. 2: 189–217.

Lyman, Rick. 2000. "That'll Be 2 Adults and 50 Million Children." *New York Times* (March 7): E1, E3.

Maase, Kaspar. 1997. "'Amerikanisierung der Gesellschaft': Nationalisierende Deutung von Globalisierungsprozessen." In Konrad Jarausch and Hannes Siegrist, eds., *Amerikanisierung und Sowjetisierung in Deutschland 1945–1970,* pp. 219–41. Frankfurt: Campus.

Maeda, Toshi. 1999. "SDF Aid Flights Fly Legalistic Tightrope." *Japan Times* (November 24).

Mahoney, James. 2001. *The Legacies of Liberalism: Path Dependence and Political Regimes in Central America.* Baltimore: Johns Hopkins University Press.

Maier, Charles S. 1978. "The Politics of Productivity: Foundations of American International Economic Policy after World War II." In P. J. Katzenstein, ed., *Between Power and Plenty: Foreign Economic Policies of Advanced Industrial States,* pp. 23–49. Madison: University of Wisconsin Press.

———. 1989. "Alliance and Autonomy: European Identity and U.S. Foreign Policy Objectives in the Truman Years." In Michael J. Lacey, ed., *The Truman Presidency,* pp. 273–98. Cambridge: Cambridge University Press.

———. 2002. "The Culture of Culture: Toward a German Variant of Performative Democracy." *German Politics and Society* 20, no. 2 (Summer): 14–25.

Makihara, Minoru. 1998. "The Path Transformed: Redefining Japan's Role in the Information Economy." *Journal of International Affairs* 51, no. 2 (Spring): 555–64.

Mann, Michael. 1986. *The Sources of Social Power: A History of Power from the Beginning to A.D. 1760.* Vol. 1. Cambridge: Cambridge University Press.

——. 1993. *The Sources of Social Power: The Rise of Classes and Nation-States, 1760–1914.* Vol. 2. Cambridge: Cambridge University Press.

——. 2003. *Incoherent Empire.* London: Verso.

Mansfield, Edward D., and Helen V. Milner. 1997. "The Political Economy of Regionalism: An Overview." In Edward D. Mansfield and Helen V. Milner, eds., *The Political Economy of Regionalism,* pp. 1–19. New York: Columbia University Press.

——. 1999. "The New Wave of Regionalism." *International Organization* 53, no. 3 (Summer): 589–627.

Markovits, Andrei S. 2004. *European Anti-Americanism (and Anti-Semitism): Ever Present though Always Denied.* Working Paper No. 108. Cambridge: Harvard University, Center for European Studies.

Markovits, Andrei S., and Simon Reich. 1997. *The German Predicament: Memory and Power in the New Europe.* Ithaca: Cornell University.

Marks, Gary, Richard Haesly, and Heather A. D. Mbaye. 2002. "What Do Subnational Offices Think They Are Doing in Brussels?" *Regional and Federal Studies* 12, no. 3 (Autumn): 1–23.

Marte, Fred. 1994. *Political Cycles in International Relations: The Cold War and Africa, 1945–1990.* Amsterdam: VU University Press.

Mathews, Jessica. 1997. "Power Shift." *Foreign Affairs* 76, no. 1 (January–February): 50–66.

Mattli, Walter. 1999. *The Logic of Regional Integration: Europe and Beyond.* Cambridge: Cambridge University Press.

Mattli, Walter, and Anne-Marie Slaughter. 1998. "The Role of National Courts in the Process of European Integration: Accounting for Judicial Preferences and Constraints." In Anne-Marie Slaughter, Alec Stone Sweet, and J. H. H. Weiler, eds., *The European Court and National Courts—Doctrine and Jurisprudence,* pp. 253–76. Oxford: Oxford University Press.

McAllister, James. 2002. *No Exit: America and the German Problem, 1943–1954.* Ithaca: Cornell University Press.

McCormack, Gavan. 1996. *The Emptiness of Japanese Affluence.* Armonk, N.Y.: M. E. Sharpe.

McFarlane, John. 1999. "Containing Transnational Crime in the Asia-Pacific: Defining the Issues." In M. J. Hassan and M. C. Anthony, eds., *Taming Turmoil in the Pacific: Papers Presented at the 12th Asia-Pacific Roundtable,* pp. 167–92. Kuala Lumpur: ISIS Malaysia.

McGray, Douglas. 2002. "Japan's Gross National Cool." *Foreign Policy* 130 (May–June): 44–54.

McKendrick, David G., Richard F. Doner, and Stephan Haggard. 2000. *From Silicon Valley to Singapore: Location and Competitive Advantage in the Hard Disk Drive Industry.* Stanford: Stanford University Press.

McMichael, Philip. 1990. "Incorporating Comparison within a World-Historical Perspective: An Alternative Comparative Method." *American Sociological Review* 55 (June): 385–97.

——. 1992. "Rethinking Comparative Analysis in a Post-Developmentalist Context." *International Social Science Journal* 133: 351–65.

——. 2000a. "World Systems Analysis, Globalization, and Incorporated Comparison." *Journal of World Systems Research* 6, no. 3 (Fall/Winter): 68–99.

McMichael, Philip, and Chul-Kyoo Kim. 1994. "Japanese and South Korean Agricultural

Restructuring in Comparative and Global Perspective." In Philip McMichael, ed., *The Global Restructuring of Agro-Food Systems,* pp. 21–52. Ithaca: Cornell University Press.

——. 2000b. "A Global Interpretation of the Rise of the East Asian Food Import Complex." *World Development* 28, no. 3: 409–24.

McMurry, Ruth Emily, and Muna Lee. 1947. *The Cultural Approach: Another Way in International Relations.* Chapel Hill: University of North Carolina Press.

McNicoll, Geoffrey. 2005. "Demographic Future of East Asian Regional Integration." In T. J. Pempel, ed., *Remapping East Asia: The Construction of a Region,* pp. 54–74. Ithaca: Cornell University Press.

McVeigh, Brian J. 1998. *The Nature of the Japanese State: Rationality and Rituality.* London: Routledge.

Mead, Walter Russell. 2001. *Special Providence: American Foreign Policy and How It Changed the World.* New York: Knopf.

Mearsheimer, John J. 2001. *The Tragedy of Great Power Politics.* New York: W. W. Norton.

Medrano, Juan Díez. 2003. *Framing Europe: Attitudes to European Integration in Germany, Spain, and the United Kingdom.* Princeton: Princeton University Press.

Menju, Toshihiro, and Takao Aoki. 1995. "The Evolution of Japanese NGOs in the Asia Pacific Context." In Tadashi Yamamoto, ed., *Emerging Civil Society in the Asia Pacific Community,* pp. 143–59. Tokyo and Singapore: Japan Center for International Exchange and the Institute of Southeast Asian Studies.

Meyer-Larsen, Werner. 2000. *Germany Inc.: The New German Juggernaut and Its Challenge to World Business.* New York: John Wiley.

Miller, Karen Lowry, and John Templeman. 1997. "Germany's New East Bloc." *Business Week* (February 3).

Milner, Helen V., and Robert O. Keohane. 1996. "Internationalization and Domestic Politics: An Introduction." In R. O. Keohane and H. V. Milner, eds., *Internationalization and Domestic Politics,* pp. 3–24. Cambridge: Cambridge University Press.

Mitchell, J. M. 1986. *International Cultural Relations.* London: Allen and Unwin.

Mitrovich, Gregory. 2000. *Undermining the Kremlin: America's Strategy to Subvert the Soviet Bloc, 1947–1956.* Ithaca: Cornell University Press.

Mittelman, James H., and Richard Falk. 2000. "Global Hegemony and Regionalism." In Stephen C. Calleya, eds., *Regionalism in the Post–Cold War World,* pp. 9 99. Aldershot: Ashgate.

Mjøset, Lars, and Kristen Nordhaug. 1999. "Atlantic and Pacific Integration—A Comparative Study of Postwar Western Europe and East Asia." Paper presented at the International Studies Association annual convention, Washington, D.C., February 16–20.

Modelski, George. 1962. "SEATO: Its Functions and Organization." In G. Modelski, ed., *SEATO: Six Studies,* pp. 3–45. Melbourne: F. W. Chesire.

Montgomery, John. 1957. *Forced to Be Free: The Artificial Revolution in Germany and Japan.* Chicago: University of Chicago Press.

Moravcsik, Andrew. 2002. "How Europe Can Win without an Army." *Financial Times* (April 3): 13.

Morgan, Patrick M. 1997. "Regional Security Complexes and Regional Orders." In David A. Lake and Patrick M. Morgan, eds., *Regional Orders: Building Security in a New World,* pp. 20–42. University Park: Pennsylvania State University Press.

Morse, Ronald A. 1989. "Japanese Lobbynomics: Shaping America's Political Agenda." *Venture Japan* 1, no. 4: 29–35.

Moulton, Harold G. 1944. *The Control of Germany and Japan.* Washington, D.C.: Brookings Institution.

Mullen, Ruth. 1997. "Manga Magic." *Indianapolis Star* (August 2).

Munakata, Naoko. 2002. *Evolution of Japan's Policy toward Economic Integration.* Washington, D. C.: Brookings Institution.

Muñoz, Juan, Santiago Roldán, and Angel Serrano. 1979. "The Growing Dependence of Spanish Industrialization on Foreign Investment." In D. Seers, B. Schaffner, and M.-L. Kiljunen, eds., *Underdeveloped Europe: Studies in Core-Periphery Relations*, pp. 161–77. Atlantic Highlands, N.J.: Humanities Press.

Murakami, Yasusuke. 1990. "Two Types of Civilization: Transcendental and Hermeneutic." *Japan Review* 1: 1–34.

——. 1996. *An Anti-Classical Political-Economic Analysis.* Stanford: Stanford University Press.

Myers, Willard H., III. 1995. "Orb Weavers–The Global Webs: The Structure and Activities of Transnational Ethnic Chinese Criminal Groups." *Transnational Organized Crime* 1, no. 4 (Winter): 1–36.

Nadelmann, Ethan A. 1993. *Cops across Borders: The Internationalization of U.S. Criminal Law Enforcement.* University Park: Pennsylvania State University Press.

——. 1995. "The DEA in Europe." In C. Fijnaut and G. T. Marx, eds., *Undercover: Police Surveillance in Comparative Perspective*, pp. 269–89. The Hague: Kluwer.

Natsume, Fusanosuke. 2000. "Japan's Manga Culture." *Japan Foundation Newsletter* 27, no. 3 (March): 1–6.

Nau, Henry R. 2002. *At Home Abroad: Identity Power in American Foreign Policy.* Ithaca: Cornell University Press.

Naughton, Barry, ed. 1997. *The China Circle: Economics and Technology in the PRC, Taiwan, and Hong Kong.* Washington, D.C.: Brookings Institution.

Nelson, Richard R. 1990. "What Has Happened to U.S. Technological Leadership?" In G. Heiduk and K. Yamamura, eds., *Technological Competition and Interdependence: The Search for Policy in the United States, West Germany, and Japan*, pp. 3–24. Seattle: University of Washington Press.

Neumann, Iver B. 1999. *Uses of the Other: 'The East' in European Identity Formation.* Minneapolis: University of Minnesota Press.

Newhouse, John. 1997. "Europe's Rising Regionalism." *Foreign Affairs* 76, no. 1 (January–February): 67–84.

Niebuhr, Reinhold. 1954. *The Irony of American History.* New York: Charles Scribner's Sons.

Nisbett, Richard E. 2003. *The Geography of Thought: How Asians and Westerners Think Differently . . . And Why.* New York: Free Press.

Nolan, Mary. 1994. *Visions of Modernity: American Business and the Modernization of Germany.* New York: Oxford University Press.

Nonini, Donald M. 1993. "On the Outs on the Rim: An Ethnographic Grounding of the 'Asia-Pacific' Imagery." In A. Dirlik, ed., *What Is in a Rim? Critical Perspectives on the Pacific Region Idea*, pp. 161–82. Boulder: Westview.

Nossel, Suzanne. 2004. "Smart Power." *Foreign Affairs* 83, no. 2 (March–April): 131–42.

Nye, Joseph S., Jr. 1990. *Bound to Lead: The Changing Nature of American Power.* New York: Basic Books.

O'Brien, Richard. 1992. *Global Financial Integration: The End of Geography.* New York: Council on Foreign Relations.

Ogura, Kazuo. 1993. "A Call for a New Concept of Asia." *Japan Echo* 20, no. 3 (Autumn): 37–44.

Ohmae, Kenichi. 1985. *Triad Power: The Coming Shape of Global Competition*. New York: Free Press.

——. 1990. *The Borderless World*. London: Collins.

——. 1993. "The Rise of the Region State." *Foreign Affairs* 72, no. 2 (Spring): 78–87.

——. 1995. *The End of the Nation State: The Rise of Regional Economies*. New York: Free Press.

——. 1999. *The Invisible Continent: Four Strategic Imperatives of the New Economy*. New York: HarperCollins.

Okawara, Nobuo, and Peter J. Katzenstein. 2001. "Japan and Asia-Pacific Security: Regionalization, Entrenched Bilateralism, and Incipient Multilateralism." *Pacific Review* 14, no. 2: 165–94.

Oksenberg, Michel. 2001. "The Issue of Sovereignty in the Asian Historical Context." In Stephen D. Krasner, ed., *Problematic Sovereignty: Contested Rules and Political Possibilities*, pp. 83–104. New York: Columbia University Press.

O'Loughlin, John, and Luc Anselin. 1996. "Geo-Economic Competition and Trade Bloc Formation: United States, German, and Japanese Exports, 1968–1992." *Economic Geography* 72, no. 2 (April): 131–60.

Olsen, Johan P. 2002. "The Many Faces of Europeanization." *Journal of Common Market Studies* 40, no. 5: 921–52.

Oman, Charles. 1994. *Globalisation and Regionalisation: The Challenge for Developing Countries*. Paris: OECD.

——. 1999. "Globalization, Regionalization, and Inequality." In A. Hurrell and N. Woods, eds., *Inequality, Globalization, and World Politics*, pp. 36–65. Oxford: Oxford University Press.

Onishi, Norimitsu. 2004. "Long Indifferent, Japanese Are Drawn to South Korea." *New York Times* (February 22): 12.

Organisation for Economic Co-operation and Development. 1991. *Change in Focus in Information Technology Policies during the 1980s: A Comparison of Changing Public Policies in Austria, Germany, and Japan*. OECD/GD (91) 62. Paris: OECD.

Orrù, Marco, Gary G. Hamilton, and Mariko Suzuki. 1997. "Patterns of Interfirm Control in Japanese Business." In Marco Orrù, Nicole Woolsey Biggart, and Gary G. Hamilton, eds., *The Economic Organization of East Asian Capitalism*, pp. 188–214. Thousand Oaks, Calif.: Sage.

Orwall, Bruce. 2001. "Latin Translation: Colombian Pop Star Taps American Taste in Repackaged Imports." *Wall Street Journal* (February 13): A1, A6.

Osiander, Andreas. 1994. *The States System of Europe, 1640–1990: Peacemaking and the Conditions of International Stability*. Oxford: Clarendon Press.

——. 2001. "Sovereignty, International Relations, and the Westphalian Myth." *International Organization* 55, no. 2 (Spring): 251–87.

Ozawa, Terutomo. 1979. *Multinationalism Japanese Style: The Political Economy of Outward Dependency*. Princeton: Princeton University Press.

Paarlberg, Robert L. 1995. *Leadership Abroad: U.S. Foreign Economic Policy after the Cold War*. Washington, D.C.: Brookings Institution.

Pantel, Melissa. 1999. "Unity-in-Diversity: Cultural Policy and EU Legitimacy." In Thomas Banchoff and Mitchell P. Smith, eds., *Legitimacy and the European Union: The Contested Polity*, pp. 46–65. New York: Routledge.

Parsons, Craig. 2003. *A Certain Idea of Europe*. Ithaca: Cornell University Press.

Pastor, Manuel, and Carol Wise. 2003. "A Long View of Mexico's Political Economy: What's Changed? What Are the Challenges?" In J. S. Tulchin and A. D. Selee, eds., *Mexico's Politics and Society in Transition*, pp. 179–213. Boulder: Lynne Rienner.

Paul, T. V. 1996. "Great Powers without Nuclear Weapons? Explaining the Non-Nuclear Policies of Germany and Japan." Paper presented at the 1996 annual meeting of the American Political Science Association, San Francisco, August 29–September 1.

Pauly, Christoph. 2001. "Hollywood statt Babelsberg." *Der Spiegel* (October 15): 144–46.

Pauly, Louis W., and Simon Reich. 1997. "National Structures and Multinational Corporate Behavior: Enduring Differences in a Globalizing World." *International Organization* 51, no. 1 (Winter): 1–30.

Payne, Anthony, and Gamble, Andrew. 1996. "Introduction: The Political Economy of Regionalism and World Order." In A. Gamble and A. Payne, eds., *Regionalism and World Order*, pp. 1–20. New York: St Martin's.

Pellegrin, Julie. 2000. "The Political Economy of Competitiveness in an Enlarged Europe: Who Is in Charge?" Unpublished paper (March).

Pells, Richard. 1997. *Not Like US: How Europeans Have Loved, Hated, and Transformed American Culture since World War II*. New York: Basic Books.

Pempel, Aaron. 1991. "From the Bottom Up: Understanding Business-Government Relations from a Corporate Perspective." Undergraduate honors thesis, Government Department, Cornell University.

Pempel, T. J. 1982. *Policy and Politics in Japan: Creative Conservatism*. Philadelphia: Temple University Press.

Pempel, T. J., and Keiichi Tsunekawa. 1979. "Corporatism without Labor?" In P. C. Schmitter and G. Lehmbruch, eds., *Trends toward Corporatist Intermediation*, pp. 231–70. Beverly Hills, Calif.: Sage.

Perroux, François. 1950. "Economic Space: Theory and Applications." *Quarterly Journal of Economics* 64, no. 1 (February): 21–36.

Pilling, David. 2002. "Japan's Cartoon Hero." *Financial Times* (February 23–4): 7.

Pilling, David, and Richard McGregor. 2004. "Crossing the Divide: How Booming Business and Closer Cultural Ties Are Bringing Two Asian Giants Together." *Financial Times* (March 30): 13.

Piore, Michael, and Charles F. Sabel. 1984. *The Second Industrial Divide: Possibilities for Prosperity*. New York: Basic Books.

Pocock, J. G. A. 1997. "What Do We Mean by Europe?" *Wilson Quarterly* 21, no. 1 (Winter): 12–29.

Podhoretz, Norman. 1999. "Strange Bedfellows: A Guide to the New Foreign-Policy Debates." *Commentary* 108, no. 5 (December): 19–31.

Polelle, Mark. 1999. *Raising Cartographic Consciousness: The Social and Foreign Policy Vision of Geopolitics in the Twentieth Century*. Lanham, Md.: Lexington Books.

Pollak, Andrew. 1992. "Technology without Borders Raises Big Questions for U.S." *New York Times* (January 1): sec. 1, pp. 48–49.

Prakash, Aseem. 1997. "Book Review." *Indiana Journal of Global Legal Studies* 4: 575–91.

Press-Barnathan, Galia. 2003. *Organizing the World: The United States and Regional Cooperation in Asia and Europe*. New York: Routledge.

Prewitt, Kenneth. 1996a. "Presidential Items." *Items* (March): 15–18.

——. 1996b. "Presidential Items." *Items* (June–September): 31–40.

———. 2002. "The Social Science Project: Then, Now, and Next." *Items* 3, nos. 1–2 (Spring): 1, 5–9.

Purifoy, Lewis McCarroll. 1976. *Harry Truman's China Policy: McCarthyism and the Diplomacy of Hysteria, 1947–1951.* New York: Franklin Watts.

Pyle, Kenneth B. 1997. "New Orders and the Future of Japan and the United States in Asia." In *The 1997 Edwin O. Reischauer Memorial Lecture.* Tokyo: International House of Japan.

Rafael, Vicente L. 1994. "The Cultures of Area Studies in the United States." *Social Text* 41 (Winter): 91–111.

Ravenhill, John. 2003. "The Move to Preferential Trade in the Western Pacific Rim." *Asia Pacific Issues* 69 (June): 1–8.

Reger, Guido, and Stefan Kuhlmann. 1995. *European Technology Policy in Germany: The Impact of European Community Policies upon Science and Technology in Germany.* Heidelberg: Physica.

Reinicke, Wolfgang. 1998. *Global Public Policy: Governing without Government?* Washington, D.C.: Brookings Institution.

Reuber, Paul, and Günter Wolkersdorfer, eds. 2001. *Politische Geographie: Handlungsorientierte Ansätze und Critical Geopolitics.* Heidelberg: Selbstverlag des Geographischen Instituts der Universität Heidelberg.

Richardson, Michael. 1996. "Regional Pacts Seen as Threat: Target Dates Urged to Achieve Global Free Trade." *Financial Times* (April 26): 17.

Richtel, Matt. 2002. "Brain Drain in Technology Found Useful for Both Sides." *New York Times* (19 April): C1, C6.

Ridding, John, and James Kynge. 1997. "Empires Can Strike Back." *Financial Times* (November 5): 13.

Riding, Alan. 2004. "A Common Culture (From the U.S.A.) Binds Europeans Ever Closer." *New York Times* (April 26): E1, E5.

Risse, Thomas. 2001. "A Europeanization of Nation-State Identities?" In Maria Green Cowles, James Caporaso, and Thomas Risse, eds., *Europeanization and Domestic Change,* pp. 198–216. Ithaca: Cornell University Press.

Risse-Kappen, Thomas. 1995. *Cooperation among Democracies: The European Influence on U.S. Foreign Policy.* Princeton: Princeton University Press.

Rodgers, Daniel T. 1998. *Atlantic Crossings: Social Politics in a Progressive Age.* Cambridge: Belknap Press of Harvard University Press.

Rohlen, Thomas P. 1989. "Order in Japanese Society: Attachment, Authority, and Routine." *Journal of Japanese Studies* 15, no. 1: 5–40.

———. 1995. *A 'Mediterranean' Model for Asian Regionalism: Cosmopolitan Cities and Nation-States in Asia.* Stanford: Stanford University, Asia/Pacific Center.

———. 2002. *Cosmopolitan Cities and Nation States: Open Economics, Urban Dynamics, and Government in East Asia.* Stanford: Stanford University, Asia/Pacific Center.

Roobeek, Annemieke J. M. 1990. *Beyond the Technology Race: An Analysis of Technology Policy in Seven Industrial Countries.* Amsterdam: Elsevier.

Rosenbach, Marcel. 2001. "Frische Ware aus Fernost." *Der Spiegel* 10: 77–78.

Roseperry, William. 1989. *Anthropologies and Histories: Essays in Culture, History, and Political Economy.* New Brunswick, N.J.: Rutgers University Press.

Rothchild, Donald. 2000. "The Impact of US Disengagement on African Intrastate Conflict Resolution." In J. Harbeson and D. Rothchild, eds., *Africa in World Politics: The African State System in Flux,* pp. 160–87. Boulder: Westview.

Rotter, Andrew J. 1987. *The Path To Vietnam: Origins of the American Commitment to Southeast Asia*. Ithaca: Cornell University Press.

"Roundtable on Rethinking International Studies in a Changing Global Context." 2002. Special issue, *Items* 3, nos. 3–4 (Summer/Fall).

Rozman, Gilbert. 2004. *Northeast Asia's Stunted Regionalism: Bilateral Distrust in the Shadow of Globalization*. Cambridge: Cambridge University Press.

Rudolph, Suzanne H. 1987. "Presidential Address: State Formation in Asia—Prolegomenon to a Comparative Study." *Journal of Asian Studies* 46, no. 4 (November): 731–46.

———. Forthcoming. "Presidential Address: The Imperialism of Categories." *Perspectives on Politics*.

Ruggie, John G. 1982. "International Regimes, Transactions, and Change: Embedded Liberalism in the Postwar Economic Order." *International Organization* 36, no. 2 (Spring): 379–415.

———. 1991. "Embedded Liberalism Revisited: Institutions and Progress in International Economic Relations." In E. Adler and B. Crawford, eds., *Progress in Postwar International Relations*, pp. 201–34. New York: Columbia University Press.

———. 1993. "Multilateralism: The Anatomy of an Institution." In J. G. Ruggie, ed., *Multilateralism Matters: The Theory and Praxis of an Institutional Form*, pp. 3–47. New York: Columbia University Press.

———. 1996. *Winning the Peace: America and World Order in the New Era*. New York: Columbia University Press.

———. 1997. "The Past as Prologue: Interests, Identity and American Foreign Policy." *International Security* 21, no. 4 (Spring): 89–125.

———. 1999. "What Makes the World Hang Together? Neo-Utilitarianism and the Social Constructivist Challenge." In Peter J. Katzenstein, Robert O. Keohane, and Stephen D. Krasner, eds., *Exploration and Contestation in the Study of World Politics*, pp. 215–45. Cambridge: MIT Press.

Ruigrok, Winfried, and Rob Van Tulder. 1995. *The Logic of International Restructuring*. London: Routledge.

Rusk, Dean, and Thanat Khomen. 1962. "Joint Statement." *Department of State Bulletin* 46, 1187 (March 6): 498–99.

Rutenberg, Jim. 2001. "Violence Finds a Niche in Children's Cartoons." *New York Times* (January 28): A1, A19.

Said, Edward W. 2001. "The Clash of Ignorance." *The Nation* 273, no. 12 (October): 11–13.

Santa-Cruz, Arturo. 2003. "International Election Monitoring as an Emergent Norm: The Latin American Experience." PhD diss., Cornell University.

Sassen, Saskia. 1996. *Losing Control? Sovereignty in an Age of Globalization*. New York: Columbia University Press.

Sato, Kenji. 1997. "More Animated Than Life: A Critical Overview of Japanese Animated Films." *Japan Echo* 24, no. 5 (December): 50–53.

Saxenian, AnnaLee, and Jinn-Juh Hsu. 2001. "The Silicon Valley–Hsinchu Connection: Technical Communities and Industrial Upgrading." *Industrial and Corporate Change* 10, no. 4: 893–920.

Saxenian, AnnaLee, and Chuen-Yueh Li. 2002. "Bay-to-Bay Strategic Alliances: The Network Linkages between Taiwan and the U.S. Venture Capital Industries." *International Journal of Networking and Virtual Organisations* 1, no. 1: 17–31.

Schaede, Ulrike, and William W. Grimes. 2003. "Introduction: The Emergence of Permeable Insulation." In U. Schaede and W. Grimes, eds., *Japan's Managed Globalization: Adapting to the Twenty-first Century*, pp. 3–16. Armonk, N.Y.: M. E. Sharpe.

Scheingold, Stuart. 1971. *The Law in Political Integration: The Evolution and Integrative Implications of Regional Legal Processes in the European Community.* Occasional Papers in International Affairs, No. 21 (June). Cambridge: Harvard University, Center for International Affairs.

Scheller, Susanne. 2002. "Migration: Kulturelle und normative Determinanten divergierender Risikoperzeption in Deutschland und den USA." In Christopher Daase, Susanne Feske, and Ingo Peters, eds., *Internationale Risikopolitik: Der Umgang mit neuen Gefahren in den internationalen Beziehungen*, pp. 65–85. Baden-Baden: Nomos.

Scherfenberg, Ulrich. 1984. *Die Auswärtige Kulturpolitik der Bundesrepublik Deutschland in der Peripheren Region Lateinamerika: Rahmenbedingungen, Formen, Inhalte, Ziele und Auswirkungen.* Munich: Fink.

Schilling, Mark. 2003. "Comic Culture Is Serious Business." *Japan Times* (March 23).

Schlesinger, Arthur. 1989. "Our Problem Is Not Japan or Germany." *Wall Street Journal* (December 22): A6.

Schmidt, Gustav, and Charles F. Doran. 1996. *Amerika's Option für Deutschland und Japan: Die Position und Rolle Deutschland's und Japan's in regionalen und internationalen Strukturen—die 1950er und 1990er Jahre im Vergleich.* Bochum: Universitätsverlag Dr. N. Brockmeyer.

Schmidt, Klaus-Dieter, and Petra Naujoks. 1993. *Western Enterprises on Eastern Markets: The German Perspective.* Kiel Working Paper No. 607 (December). Kiel: Institut für Welt-Wirtschaft.

Schmidt, William E. 1993. "In Europe, America's Grip on Pop Culture Is Fading." *New York Times* (March 28): A3.

Schodt, Frederik L. 1996. *Dreamland Japan: Writings on Modern Japan.* Berkeley, Calif.: Stone Bridge Press.

Scholte, Jan Aart. 2000. *Globalization: A Critical Introduction.* New York: St. Martin's.

Schoppa, Leonard J. 1997. *Bargaining with Japan: What American Pressure Can and Cannot Do.* New York: Columbia University Press.

——. 1999. "The Social Context in Coercive International Bargaining." *International Organization* 53, no. 2 (Spring): 307–43.

Schreurs, Miranda A. 2002. *Environmental Politics in Japan, Germany, and the United States.* New York: Cambridge University Press.

Schroeder, Paul W. 1994. *The Transformation of European Politics, 1763–1848.* Oxford: Clarendon.

Schurmann, Franz. 1974. *The Logic of World Power: An Inquiry into the Origins, Currents, and Contradictions of World Politics.* New York: Random House.

Schwarz, Jürgen. 1982. *Structural Development of the North Atlantic Treaty Organization.* Munich: Hochschule der Bundeswehr.

Schweigler, Gebhard. 1991. "The United States and the New World Order." Paper presented at the 13th European-Japanese Conference (Hakone XIII) of the Japanese Center for International Exchange, April 16–18.

Scott, Allen J. 1998. *Regions and the World Economy: The Coming Shape of Global Production, Competition, and Political Order.* Oxford: Oxford University Press.

Sedgwick, Mitchell W. 1994. "Does the Japanese Management Miracle Travel in Asia?

Managerial Technology Transfer at Japanese Multinationals in Thailand." Paper presented at the Workshop on Multinationals and East Asian Integration, at MIT Japan Program, Cambridge, November 18–19.

Seki, Mitsuhiro. 1994. *Beyond the Full-Set Industrial Structure: Japanese Industry in the New Age of East Asia.* Tokyo: LTCB International Library Foundation.

Sender, Henny. 1991. "Inside the Overseas Chinese Networks." *Institutional Investor* 25, no. 10 (September): 29–43.

Servan-Schreiber, Jean-Jacques. 1968. *The American Challenge.* New York: Atheneum.

Shafer, D. Michael. 1994. *Winners and Losers: How Sectors Shape the Developmental Prospects of States.* Ithaca: Cornell University Press.

Shibasaki, Atsushi. 1997. *International Cultural Relations and Modern Japan: History of Kokusai Bunka Shinkokai, 1934–1945* [Kindai Nihon to Kokusai Bunka Koryu: Kokusai Bunka Shinkokai no Sousetsu to Tenkai]. Tokyo: Yushindo.

———. 1999. "The Founding of KBS—Historical Characteristics of the Foreign Cultural Policy of Prewar Japan [Kokusai Bunka Shinkokai no Sosetsu: Senzen Nihon no Taigai Bunka Seisaku no Rekishiteki Tokushitsu]." *Research in International Relations [Kokusai Kankeiron Kenkyu]* 11: 39–64.

Shillony, Ben-Ami. 1981. *Politics and Culture in Wartime Japan.* Oxford: Clarendon.

Shin, Michael D. 2004. "The Cultural Policies of the So-Called 'Cultural Policy' (*Bunka Seiji*), 1919–1925." Unpublished paper, Cornell University.

Shinn, James. 1998. "Introduction." In J. Shinn, ed., *Fires across the Water: Transnational Problems in Asia,* pp. 158–74. New York: Council on Foreign Relations.

Shiraishi, Saya. 1997. "Japan's Soft Power: Doraemon Goes Overseas." In Peter J. Katzenstein and Takashi Shiraishi, eds., *Network Power: Japan and Asia,* pp. 234–72. Ithaca: Cornell University Press.

Shiraishi, Saya, and Takashi Shiraishi. 1993. "The Japanese in Colonial Southeast Asia: An Overview." In Shiraishi and Shiraishi, eds., *The Japanese in Colonial Southeast Asia,* pp. 5–20. Ithaca: Cornell University, Southeast Asia Program.

Shiraishi, Takashi. Forthcoming. "The Third Wave: Southeast Asia and Middle-Class Formation in the Making of a Region." In Peter J. Katzenstein and Takashi Shiraishi, eds., *Beyond Japan: The Dynamics of East Asian Regionalism.* Ithaca: Cornell University Press.

Shore, Chris. 1996. "Transcending the Nation-State? The European Commission and the (Re)-Discovery of Europe." *Journal of Historical Sociology* 9, no. 4 (December): 473–96.

Siaroff, Alan. 1994. "Interdependence versus Asymmetry? A Comparison of the European and Asia-Pacific Economic Regions." Paper presented at the International Studies Association-West Meetings, Seattle, October 14–15.

Simões, Vitor Corado. 1992. "European Integration and the Pattern of FDI Inflow in Portugal." In J. Cantwell, ed., *Multinational Investment in Modern Europe: Strategic Interaction in the Integrated Community,* pp. 256–97. Brookfield, Vt.: Edward Elgar.

Simon, Sheldon W. 1998. "Security Prospects in Southeast Asia: Collaborative Efforts and the ASEAN Regional Forum." *Pacific Review* 11, no. 2: 195–212.

Simons, Marlise. 1999. "In New Europe, a Lingual Hodgepodge." *New York Times* (October 17): 8.

Sittner, Gernot, and Thomas Steinfeld. 2001. "Ein Dialog Muss Auch Praktisch Sein." *Süddeutsche Zeitung* (November 26): 16.

Smith, David A. 1997. "Technology, Commodity Chains, and Global Inequality: South

Korea in the 1990s." *Review of International Political Economy* 4, no. 4 (Winter): 734–62.

Smith, Michael E. 1996. *The 'Europeanization' of European Political Cooperation: Trust, Transgovernmental Relations, and the Power of Informal Norms.* Berkeley: University of California, Center for German and European Studies.

Smith, Peter. 2001. "Strategic Options for Latin America." In Joseph S. Tulchin and Ralph H. Espach, eds., *Latin America in the New International System,* pp. 35–72. Boulder: Lynne Rienner.

Smith, Shannon L. D. 1997. "The Indonesia-Malaysia-Singapore Growth Triangle: A Political and Economic Equation." *Australian Journal of International Affairs* 51, no. 3: 369–82.

Soares de Lima, Maria Regina. 1999. "Brazil's Alternative Vision." In Gordon Mace, Louis Bélanger, et al., *The Americas in Transition: The Contours of Regionalism,* pp. 133–51. Boulder: Lynne Rienner.

Sobieck, Stephen M. 1994. "Democratic Responses to International Terrorism in Germany." In D. A. Charters, eds., *The Deadly Sin of Terrorism: Its Effect on Democracy in Six Countries,* pp. 43–72. Westport, Conn.: Greenwood.

Solingen, Etel. 1998. *Regional Orders at Century's Dawn: Global and Domestic Influences on Grand Strategy.* Princeton: Princeton University Press.

———. 2001. "Mapping Internationalization: Domestic and Regional Impacts." *International Studies Quarterly* 45, no. 4: 517–55.

———. 2005. "East Asian Regional Institutions: Characteristics, Sources, Distinctiveness." In T. J. Pempel, ed., *Remapping East Asia: The Construction of a Region,* pp. 31–53. Ithaca: Cornell University Press.

Soskice, David. 1994. "Germany and Japan: Industry-Coordinated versus Group-Coordinated Market Economy." Paper presented at the conference "Political Economy of the New Germany: Coordinated Economy," Cornell University, Ithaca, October 14–16.

Spiegel, Steven L. 1985. *The Other Arab-Israeli Conflict: Making America's Middle East Policy from Truman to Reagan.* Chicago: University of Chicago Press.

Spiro, David E. 1997. "Where Does the Buck Stop? The National Bases of Internationalized Money." Paper presented at the annual meeting of the American Political Science Association, Washington, D.C., August 27–31.

———. 1999. *The Hidden Hand of American Hegemony: Petrodollar Recycling and International Markets.* Ithaca: Cornell University Press.

Stallings, Barbara, and Wolfgang Streeck. 1995. "Capitalisms in Conflict? The United States, Europe, and Japan in the Post-Cold War World." In B. Stallings, ed., *Global Change, Regional Response: The New International Context of Development,* pp. 67–99. New York: Cambridge University Press.

Stanciewicz, Michael. 1998. "Preface: The Bilateral-Multilateral Context in Northeast Asian Security." In Byung-Joon Ahn and Konstantin Sarkisov, *Korean Peninsula Security and the U.S.-Japan Defense Guidelines: An IGCC Study Commissioned for the Northeast Asia Cooperation Dialogue VII, Tokyo, Japan, 3–4 December 1997.* IGCC Policy Paper 45. San Diego: University of California Institute on Global Conflict and Cooperation.

Steinberg, Philip E. 2001. *The Social Construction of the Ocean.* Cambridge: Cambridge University Press.

Stern, Eric, and Bengt Sundelius. 1997. "Sweden's Twin Monetary Crises of 1992: Rigidity and Learning in Crisis Decision Making." *Journal of Contingencies and Crisis Management* 5, no. 1 (March): 32–48.

Stone, Diane. 1997. "Networks, Second Track Diplomacy, and Regional Cooperation: The Role of Southeast Asian Think Tanks." Paper presented at the thirty-eighth annual International Studies Association convention, Toronto, Canada, March 22–26.

Stone Sweet, Alec. 1998. "Constitutional Dialogues in the European Community." In Anne-Marie Slaughter, Alec Stone Sweet, and J. H. H. Weiler, eds., *The European Court and National Courts—Doctrine and Jurisprudence*, pp. 305–30. Oxford: Oxford University Press.

———. 2000. *Governing with Judges: Constitutional Politics in Europe*. Oxford: Oxford University Press.

Stone Sweet, Alec, and Thomas L. Brunell. 1998. "The European Court and the National Courts: A Statistical Analysis of Preliminary References, 1961–95." *Journal of European Public Policy* 5, no. 1 (March): 66–97.

Storper, Michael. 1995. "The Resurgence of Regional Economies, Ten Years Later: The Region as a Nexus of Untraded Interdependencies." *European Urban and Regional Studies* 2, no. 3: 191–221.

———. 1997. *The Regional World: Territorial Development in a Global Economy*. New York: Guilford Press.

Stubbs, Richard. 1999. "War and Economic Development: Export-Oriented Industrialization in East and Southeast Asia." *Comparative Politics* 31, no. 3 (April): 337–55.

———. 2005. *Cold War Economies: Rethinking the Political Economy of the Asian 'Miracle'*. Basingstoke: Palgrave.

Szanton, David L., ed. 2003. *The Politics of Knowledge: Area Studies and the Disciplines*. Berkeley: University of California Press/University of California International and Area Studies Digital Collection, vol. 3. http://repositories.cdlib.org/uciaspubs/editedvolumes/3.

Tachiki, Dennis S. 2001. "Japanese FDI after the Asian Crisis: The Role of Production Networks in Regional Integration." Paper presented at the Fifty-third Annual Meeting of the Association of Asian Studies, Chicago, March 23.

Tadokoro, Masayuki. 2000–2001. "Japan's Pop Culture Spreads through Asia." *Correspondence* 7 (Winter): 24.

Takahashi, Rikimaru. 1998. "International Cultural Relations as Ideological Warfare: The Prewar Activities of the KBS [Shisosen to shite no Kokusai Bunka Koryu: Senzen no Kokusai Bunka Shinkokai no Katsudo o Megutte]." *Bulletin of Graduate Research in the Social Sciences [Shakai Kagaku Kenkyuka Kiyo Bessatsu]* 2 (March): 95–115.

Tang, Ming, and Myo Thant. 1994. "Growth Triangles: Conceptual and Operational Considerations." In M. Thant, M. Tang, and H. Kakazu, eds., *Growth Triangles in Asia: A New Approach to Regional Economic Cooperation*, pp. 1–28. New York: Oxford University Press.

Tarrow, Sidney. 2005. *The New Transnational Activism*. New York: Cambridge University Press.

Taylor, Paul. 1993. *International Organization in the Modern World: The Regional and the Global Process*. London: Francis Pinter.

Taylor, Peter J. 1988. "World-Systems Analysis and Regional Geography." *Professional Geographer* 40, no. 3: 259–65.

——. 1990. *Britain and the Cold War: 1945 as a Geopolitical Transition.* London: Francis Pinter.

——. 1991. "A Theory and Practice of Regions: The Case of Europe." *Environment and Planning D: Society and Space* 9: 183–95.

——. 1992. "Nationalism, Internationalism, and a 'Socialist Geopolitics': A Review Essay." *Antipode* 24, no. 4: 327–36.

——. 1995. "Beyond Containers: Internationality, Interstateness, Interterritoriality." *Progress in Human Geography* 19, no. 1: 1–15.

Theiler, Tobias. 1999. "The 'Identity Politics' of the European Union." D. Phil., Oxford University.

Thomas, Daniel C. 2001. *The Helsinki Effect: International Norms, Human Rights, and the Demise of Communism.* Princeton: Princeton University Press.

Thomas, Kenneth P., and Mary Ann Tétrault, eds. 1999. *Racing to Regionalize: Democracy, Capitalism, and Regional Political Economy.* Boulder: Lynne Rienner.

Thornton, William H. 2002. *Fire on the Rim: The Cultural Dynamics of East/West Power Politics.* Lanham, Md.: Rowman and Littlefield.

Thurow, Lester C. 1992. *Head to Head: The Coming Economic Battle between Japan, Europe, and America.* New York: William Morrow.

Tilly, Charles. 1984. *Big Structures, Large Processes, Huge Comparisons.* New York: Russell Sage Foundation.

Tilton, Mark, and Patricia Boling. 2000. "Changing Institutions to Promote Stable Growth in Japan and German." Paper presented at the conference "Japan and Germany in a Globalizing Economic Environment: Saving Institutional Strengths or Radically Converging on International Standards?" Duisburg University, Germany, April 13–14.

Trachtenberg, Mark. 1999. *A Constructed Peace: The Making of the European Settlement, 1945–1963.* Princeton: Princeton University Press.

Trubowitz, Peter. 1998. *Defining the National Interest: Conflict and Change in American Foreign Policy.* Chicago: University of Chicago Press.

Tucker, Robert W., and David C. Hendrickson. 1990. *Empire of Liberty: The Statecraft of Thomas Jefferson.* New York: Oxford University Press.

Tulchin, Joseph S., and Andrew D. Selee. 2003. "Introduction." In J. S. Tulchin and A. D. Selee, eds., *Mexico's Politics and Society in Transition*, pp. 5–25. Boulder: Lynne Rienner.

Tuschhoff, Christian. 2002. "The Ties That Bind: Allied Commitment and NATO before and after September 11." *German Issues* 27: 71–95.

——. 2003. "Why NATO Is Still Relevant." *International Politics* 40, no. 1 (March): 101–20.

Tyrrell, Ian. 1999. *True Gardens of the Gods: Californian-Australian Environmental Reform, 1860–1930.* Berkeley: University of California Press.

Uchitelle, Louis. 1998a. "Global Tug, National Tether: As Companies Look Overseas, Governments Hold the String." *New York Times* (April 30): D1, D6.

——. 1998b. "Some Economic Interplay Comes Nearly Full Circle." *New York Times* (April 30): D6.

United Nations Conference on Trade and Development. 1998. *World Investment Report 1998: Trends and Determinants.* New York: United Nations, UNCTAD.

United States Census Bureau. 2004. *Foreign Trade Statistics.* www.census.gov/foreign-trade/balance (accessed July 31, 2004).

University of Tokyo Study Group on International Cultural Relations. 1997. "International Cultural Exchange and Cultural Cooperation between ASEAN and Japan: Historical Development and Present Situation: Interim Report. Commissioned by The Japan Foundation Asia Center." October.

———. 1998. "International Cultural Exchange and Cultural Cooperation between ASEAN and Japan: Historical Development and Present Situation: Final Report. Commissioned by The Japan Foundation Asia Center." April.

U.S. Senate. 1949. *North Atlantic Treaty: Hearings before the Committee on Foreign Relations,* 81st Cong., 1st sess. Washington, D.C.: Government Printing Office.

Vaitsos, Constantine. 1982. "Transnational Corporate Behaviour and the Enlargement." In Dudley Seers and Constantine Vaitsos, with the assistance of Marja-Liisa Kiljunen, eds., *The Second Enlargement of the EEC: The Integration of Unequal Partners,* pp. 136–62, New York: St. Martin's.

Värynen, Raimo. 2003. "Regionalism: Old and New," *International Studies Review* 5, no. 1 (March): 25–52.

Van Tulder, Rob, and Gerd Junne. 1988. *European Multinationals in Core Technologies.* New York: John Wiley.

Verniere, James. 1999. "Un-American Dream: Raft of Films Made in Hollywood by Foreigners." *Chicago Tribune* (November 27).

Vernon, Raymond. 1971. *Sovereignty at Bay.* New York: Basic Books.

———. 1977. *Storm over the Multinationals: The Real Issues.* Cambridge: Harvard University Press.

Veseth, Michael. 1998. *Selling Globalization: The Myth of the Global Economy.* Boulder: Lynne Rienner.

Vogel, Steven K. 1996. *Freer Markets, More Rules: Regulatory Reform in Advanced Industrial Countries.* Ithaca: Cornell University Press.

Wade, Robert. 1996. "Globalization and Its Limits: Reports of the Death of the National Economy Are Greatly Exaggerated." In Suzanne Berger and Ronald Dore, eds., *National Diversity and Global Capitalism,* pp. 60–88. Ithaca: Cornell University Press.

Wagnleitner, Reinhold. 1994. *Coca-Colonization and the Cold War: The Cultural Mission of the United States in Austria after the Second World War.* Chapel Hill: University of North Carolina Press.

Wallander, Celeste M. 1999. *Mortal Friends, Best Enemies: German-Russian Cooperation after the Cold War.* Ithaca: Cornell University Press.

Waltz, Kenneth N. 1967. *Foreign Policy and Democratic Politics: The American and British Experience.* Boston: Little, Brown.

———. 1979. *Theory of International Politics.* Reading, Mass.: Addison-Wesley.

Wan, Ming. 1995. "Spending Strategies in World Politics: How Japan Has Used Its Economic Power in the Past Decade." *International Studies Quarterly* 39, no. 1 (March): 85–108.

Warshaw, Steven. 1975. *Southeast Asia Emerges: A Concise History of Southeast Asia from Its Origins to the Present.* Berkeley: Diablo Press.

Washington, George. 1896. *The Farewell Address of George Washington to the People of the United States of America.* [Savannah, Ga.]: General Society, Sons of the Revolution.

Way, Christopher. Forthcoming. *Manchester Revisited: Economic Interdependence and Conflict* (working title). Ithaca: Cornell University Press.

Webb, Leicester C. 1962. "Australia and SEATO." In G. Modelski, ed., *SEATO: Six Studies,* pp. 49–83. Melbourne: F. W. Chesire.

Weidenbaum, Murray, and Samuel Hughes. 1996. *The Bamboo Network: How Expatriate Chinese Entrepreneurs Are Creating a New Economic Superpower in Asia.* New York: Free Press.

Weidenfeld, Werner. 1996. *The Transatlantic Challenge: German Contributions to the German-American Partnership in the Cultural and Public Relations Spheres.* New York: German Information Center.

Weiler, John H. H. 2000. "Federalism and Constitutionalism: Europe's Sonderweg." *Jean Monnet Working Paper No. 10.* New York: New York University Law School, Jean Monnet Center for International and Regional Economic Law and Justice.

Weiner, Tim. 2003. "Free Trade Accord at Age 10: The Growing Pains Are Clear." *New York Times* (December 27): A1, A8.

Weiss, Linda. 1999. "Globalization and National Governance: Antinomy or Interdependence?" *Review of International Studies* 25, no. 5 (December): 59–88.

Werz, Nikolaus. 1992. "External Cultural Policy: Continuity or Change." *Aussenpolitik* 92, no. 3: 246–55.

Westerfield, H. Bradford. 1955. *Foreign Policy and Party Politics: Pearl Harbor to Korea.* New Haven: Yale University Press.

Westney, D. Eleanor. 1999. "Organization Theory Perspectives on the Cross-Border Transfer of Organizational Patterns." In Paul Adler, Mark Fruin, and Jeffrey Liker, eds., *Re-Made in America,* pp. 385–408. New York: Oxford University Press.

Whitaker, Arthur P. 1954. *The Western Hemisphere Idea: Its Rise and Decline.* Ithaca: Cornell University Press.

White, David. 1997. "Spain Prepares to Fight for EU Grants." *Financial Times* (November 18): 4.

White, George W. 2000. *Nationalism and Territory: Constructing Group Identity in Southeastern Europe.* Lanham, Md.: Rowman and Littlefield.

Williams, Frances. 2002. "Foreign Investment Dives in US and UK." *Financial Times* (25 October): 7.

Williams, Lee E. 1976. *Southeast Asia: A Short History.* New York: Oxford University Press.

Winner, Langdon. 1977. *Autonomous Technology: Technics-out-of-Control as a Theme in Political Thought.* Cambridge: MIT Press

Witte, Bruno de. 1998. "Sovereignty and European Integration: The Weight of Legal Tradition." In Anne-Marie Slaughter, Alec Stone Sweet, and J. H. H. Weiler, eds., *The European Court and National Courts—Doctrine and Jurisprudence,* pp. 277–304. Oxford: Oxford University Press.

Wolfers, Arnold. 1962. *Discord and Collaboration: Essays on International Politics.* Baltimore: Johns Hopkins University Press.

Wolters, O. W. 1982. *History, Culture, and Region in Southeast Asian Perspectives.* Singapore: Institute of Southeast Asian Studies.

Wong, Anny. 1991. "Japan's National Security and Cultivation of ASEAN Elites." *Contemporary Southeast Asia* 12, no. 4 (March): 306–30.

World Bank. 2004. *World Development Indicators.* Washington, D.C.: World Bank.

Wortmann, Michael. 1991. *German Direct Investment in the Spanish Economy following Spain's Entry to the EEC: Summary of the Main Findings of the German Team.* Berlin: FAST.

Yamamura, Kozo, and Wolfgang Streeck, eds. 2003. *The End of Diversity? Prospects for German and Japanese Capitalism.* Ithaca: Cornell University Press.

Yamazaki, Masakazu. 1996. "Asia, a Civilization in the Making." *Foreign Affairs* 75, no. 4 (July–August): 106–18.

Yergin, Daniel. 1991. *The Prize: The Epic Quest for Oil, Money, and Power.* New York: Simon and Schuster.

Yeung, Henry Wai-chung. 2003. "Financing Chinese Capitalism: Principal Banks, Economic Crisis, and Chinese Family Firms in Singapore." Paper presented at the conference "Cultural Approaches to Asian Financial Markets," Cornell Law School, Ithaca, April 26.

Yu, Kie-Un. 1999. "Global Division of Cultural Labor and the Korean Animation Industry." In John A. Lent, ed., *Themes and Issues in Asian Cartooning: Cute, Cheap, Mad, and Sexy,* pp. 37–60. Bowling Green, Ohio: Bowling Green State University Popular Press.

Yuan, Jing-dong, and Lorraine Eden. 1992. "Export Processing Zones in Asia: A Comparative Study." *Asian Survey* 32, no. 11 (November): 1026–45.

Yue, Chia Siow, and Wendy Dobson. 1997. "Harnessing Diversity." In W. Dobson and C. S. Yue, eds., *Multinationals and East Asian Integration,* pp. 249–65. Ottawa and Singapore: International Development Centre and Institute of Southeast Asian Studies.

Zakaria, Fareed. 1998. *From Wealth to Power: The Unusual Origins of America's World Role.* Princeton: Princeton University Press.

Zeitlin, Jonathan. 2000. "Introduction: Americanization and Its Limits: Reworking US Technology and Management in Postwar Europe and Japan." In Jonathan Zeitlin and Gary Herrigel, eds., *Americanization and Its Limits: Reworking US Technology and Management in Post-War Europe and Japan,* pp. 1–50. Oxford: Oxford University Press.

Zemans, Joyce. 1999. "A Comparative Overview." In Joyce Zemans and Archie Kleingartner, eds., *Comparing Cultural Policy: A Study of Japan and the United States,* pp. 19–60. Walnut Creek, Calif.: Sage/Alta Mira.

Zhu, Tianbiao. 2000. "Consistent Threat, Political-Economic Institutions, and Northeast Asian Developmentalism." PhD diss., Cornell University.

——. 2002. "Developmental States and Threat Perceptions in Northeast Asia." *Journal of Conflict, Security and Development* 2, no. 1 (April): 6–29.

Znined-Brand, Victoria. 1997. *Deutsche und Französische Auswärtige Kulturpolitik: Eine Vergleichende Analyse. Das Beispiel der Goethe-Institute in Frankreich Sowie der Instituts und Centres Culturels Français in Deutschland seit 1945.* Frankfurt: Peter Lang.

Zysman, John, Ellen Doherty, and Andrew Schwartz. 1996. "Tales from the 'Global' Economy: Cross-National Production Networks and the Re-organization of the European Economy." *Working Paper No. 83.* Berkeley: University of California, Berkeley Roundtable on the International Economy.

Zysman, John, and Andrew Schwartz. 1998. "Reunifying Europe in an Emerging World Economy: Economic Heterogeneity, New Industrial Options, and Political Choices." *Journal of Common Market Studies* 36, no. 3: 405–29.

INDEX

CORNELL STUDIES IN POLITICAL ECONOMY

A series edited by Peter J. Katzenstein

Fair Shares: Unions, Pay, and Politics in Sweden and West Germany
by Peter Swenson

Union of Parts: Labor Politics in Postwar Germany
by Kathleen Thelen

Democracy at Work: Changing World Markets and the Future of Labor Unions
by Lowell Turner

Fighting for Partnership: Labor and Politics in Unified Germany
by Lowell Turner

Troubled Industries: Confronting Economic Change in Japan
by Robert M. Uriu

National Styles of Regulation: Environmental Policy in Great Britain and the United States
by David Vogel

Freer Markets, More Rules: Regulatory Reform in Advanced Industrial Countries
by Steven K. Vogel

The Political Economy of Policy Coordination: International Adjustment since 1945
by Michael C. Webb

The Myth of the Powerless State
by Linda Weiss

The Developmental State
edited by Meredith Woo-Cumings

The End of Diversity? Prospects for German and Japanese Capitalism
edited by Kozo Yamamura and Wolfgang Streeck

International Cooperation: Building Regimes for Natural Resources and the Environment
by Oran R. Young

International Governance: Protecting the Environment in a Stateless Society
by Oran R. Young

Polar Politics: Creating International Environmental Regimes
edited by Oran R. Young and Gail Osherenko

Governing Ideas: Strategies for Innovation in France and Germany
by J. Nicholas Ziegler

Internationalizing China: Domestic Interests and Global Linkages
by David Zweig

Governments, Markets, and Growth: Financial Systems and the Politics of Industrial Change
by John Zysman

*American Industry in International Competition: Government Policies
and Corporate Strategies*
edited by John Zysman and Laura Tyson